FIRST AMONG CHAMPIONS

Other books by this author:

NAPIER
The First to Wear the Green

The Racing 1500s

FIRST AMONG CHAMPIONS

THE ALFA ROMEO GRAND PRIX CARS

DAVID VENABLES

Haynes Publishing

First published in May 2000

British Library Cataloguing in Publication Data:
A catalogue record for this book is available from the British Library.

ISBN 1 85960 631 8

Library of Congress catalog card number 99-80190

Haynes Publishing, Sparkford, Nr Yeovil, Somerset, BA22 7JJ.
Tel: 01963 442030 Fax: 01963 440001
Int. tel: +44 1963 442030 Fax: +44 1963 440001
E-mail: sales@haynes-manuals.co.uk
Web site: www.haynes.co.uk

Haynes North America, Inc.
861 Lawrence Drive, Newbury Park,
California 91320 USA

Designed & typeset by
G&M, Raunds, Northamptonshire
Printed and bound in Great Britain by
J.H.Haynes & Co. Ltd., Sparkford

All photographs not otherwise credited are from the
Centro Documentazione Storica, Fiat Auto, Arese.

Contents

Preface

WHEN I BEGAN WRITING this book it was on another subject; it was intended to be a history of the Tipo 158 Alfa Romeo. To set the scene I had to give an outline of Alfa Romeo racing history, and as I did this, first it grew rapidly, and second I realised that amid the numerous books written about Alfa Romeo, no one had concentrated purely on the history of the company's racing cars. With the agreement and encouragement of Darryl Reach of Haynes, I changed direction and this is the result.

There have been many superb books on Alfa Romeo and I freely admit that I have trodden the ground already covered by Peter Hull and Roy Slater with their history, by Angela Cherrett with her books on the 6C and 8C, by Simon Moore on the 2.9, and in Luigi Fusi's three masterpieces. However, while much of the story has been told before, I have been able to draw on some new sources of material and I have tried to gather together the various aspects of this part of Alfa Romeo history for the first time. The sports cars have been deliberately omitted except where they form a part of my story; I felt that the specialist books on the subject had already covered the subject, and that to include the sports car racing history would have made a book that would have been too long and impracticable.

I would have been happier to have stopped the story on a triumphant note at the end of 1951; the events of the 1970s and 1980s are dismal, but I felt that they had to be recounted to make the story complete. It is sad, but I fear that the story is complete, as it seems unlikely that Alfa Romeo will ever appear again in grand prix racing. For the last 50 years red grand prix cars have been associated with Ferrari, and few followers of modern racing will appreciate that for nearly 40 years red cars were synonymous with Alfa Romeo. I hope this story will go some of the way to redressing the balance and may revive memories of the racing cars that carried the *quadrifolio*.

Fellow members of the Vintage Sports Car Club have given me great help in the task of writing this book, and some deserve a special mention for their kindness and support. Guy Griffiths has been a constant source of strength and advice from the very beginning – it was he who suggested the original 158 project, and he has also found many photographs of his own, or from his collection. Angela Cherrett, who apart from her writings on the marque, is the secretary and guiding force of the Alfa Romeo Section of the VSCC, has been unstinting of her time, with advice and information and also by reading the first drafts of the early chapters. Carol Spagg loaned me the invaluable tapes of her interviews with Gianbattista Guidotti and also gave me access to the papers she collected when she had the only Tipo 158 in private ownership. David Thirlby, whom I assist in the editing of the VSCC Bulletin, has given constant encouragement, reading and re-reading the manuscript, pointing out errors and solecisms, and persuading me to delete some of the more purple prose when I became carried away with the story! I am also very grateful to David's secretary Paula Wright for her diligent proof-reading. John Maitland has given me unfettered access to his remarkable motoring library, has spent many hours researching obscure points on my behalf, and has also let me have many rare photographs. Graeme Simpson of Motor Racing Tradition has let me have some unusual photographs of high quality.

I am particularly grateful to Elvira Ruocco, the archivist of Centro Documentazione Storica at Arese, to whom I was introduced by Angela Cherrett. Elvira permitted me to have full access to the Alfa Romeo archives, answered my obscure questions and took much time and care to find many of the photographs.

There are many others who have helped, including Alan Cox, Paul Clements, Donald Davidson of the Indianapolis Hall of Fame Museum, Neil Eason-Gibson, David McKinney, Julian Majzub, Paul Parker of the Karl Ludvigsen Library, John Loveridge of Ricardo Consulting Engineers plc, Gerald Roush, John Watson, Geoff Willoughby, and Keith Woodcock. I know that there have been many others, and I apologise if I have overlooked anyone – the omission was not intentional.

David Venables
April 2000

Chapter 1

The beginning of the tale

THIS STORY MIGHT NEVER have happened but for the meanness of the French motor manufacturer, Alexandre Darracq. As the 19th century came to an end, Darracq, who was born in Bordeaux in 1855, had decided like many others that there was money to be made from the manufacture of bicycles, motor cycles and motor cars, particularly if he could make them very cheaply. He began in 1891 with the Gladiator cycle, then realised that there was much more money to be made by producing motor cars in large quantities. After an unsuccessful attempt with electric cars in 1898, Darracq bought the patents of a belt-driven 5hp car, with a single-cylinder horizontal engine, from a rival manufacturer, Léon Bollée, for 250,000FF, or about £500,000 at today's values. This turned out to be a better deal for Bollée than for Darracq, as Louis Renault had just produced his De Dion-engined voiturette with its revolutionary shaft drive to the rear axle, and the motoring public quickly realised that this was a better method of propulsion than the belts offered by the Bollée design.

Poorer but wiser, Darracq now built a new car with a tubular frame, a 785cc front-mounted vertical single-cylinder engine and, copying Renault, a shaft drive. This car appeared in 1900 and was a success, so Darracq followed it with a 1.9-litre twin. Like all ambitious manufacturers at that time, Darracq realised that the burgeoning sport of motor racing offered unequalled publicity for successful competitors. One of the Darracq twin-cylinder cars, driven by Henri Farman, ran in the touring car race from Pau to Peyrehorade on 17 February 1901, an open road event of 206 miles (331km) and won the class for light cars (400 to 650kg). Five weeks later Farman repeated the victory in the Nice–Salon–Nice race, over 243 miles (390km), leading home three more Darracqs in the light car class. The marque was now properly established, larger four-cylinder cars followed and the firm continued to expand its racing activities. The capital to assist the expansion of Darracq came from England; in 1905 there was a reorganisation, and the company A. Darracq (1905) Ltd was registered in London.

The four-cylinder cars can be ignored, as only the single-cylinder and twin-cylinder Darracqs have a place in Alfa Romeo history. In 1903 the 9hp single-cylinder had been reduced to 8hp and was joined by 9hp and 12hp twins with armoured wood frames. In 1904 the 9hp twin was dropped, and now the 8hp single and 12hp twin continued with pressed steel frames. Their design stemmed from that of the cars that had raced, and the famous veteran 'Genevieve' was an example of the 12hp twin. By 1906 Darracq had discovered that essential fact of a car manufacturer's life: if a model is improved in stages, the price goes up with the quality. He was no longer making the cheap cars he had intended, but still believed that his fortune lay with cheap mass-produced vehicles, and in 1907 a new bottom-of-the-range series of cars was introduced. These had a pressed steel frame, and the smaller model was a single with a capacity of 1039cc, the larger being a 1527cc twin. A new factory was built at Suresnes, in the suburbs of Paris, to produce the new range.

Darracq cars were already well-known in Italy due to the efforts of Ernesto Werheim, who held the agency for Turin, and Agostinelli, the company's agent in Rome. At a shareholders' meeting in London on 2 February 1906 the Chairman, John Smith-Winby, announced that the company had further plans for expansion and would be forming an Italian associated company, Società Italiana Automobili Darracq, to assemble the economy Darracq single and twins in a factory at Naples, using parts made at Suresnes. The finance for this venture came largely from Italian sources, and it was soon realised that Naples was the wrong choice. It was too far to transport the Darracq parts, the main market for the cars being in the industrial north, and, probably just as important, the workforce in the north had an engineering ethos lacking in the south.

Alexandre Darracq therefore intervened, and at the beginning of 1907 he seems to have been influential in the choice of a new site on the north-western outskirts of Milan. The 4.6-acre (1.86-hectare) site was known as Il Portello and took its name from the nearby Trattoria del Portello, which had formerly been an old coaching inn. A modern single-storey factory was built covering 8000 square metres. Sadly, today there is no longer an Alfa Romeo factory on this site, which now contains huge buildings for the Fiera complex. For many years 33 Via M. U. Traiano was the firm's office address, the street being named after Marcus Ulpius Traianus, Emperor of Rome from AD98 until AD117 and better known to the English-speaking nations as the Emperor Trajan.

The new venture was in trouble almost immediately. At the end of 1907 there was a slump in the European motor industry and there was little demand for the Italian Darracqs. Demand was further diminished by the evident unsuitability of the cars for the hilly and mountainous conditions that existed in a lot of northern Italy – the cars did not have enough power. There were also production delays, and those who had ordered the cars did not get them; the first deliveries did not begin until September 1908. To compound all these problems, Alexandre Darracq, no doubt with an eye to saving money and increasing the Parisian profits, was unloading sub-standard parts on the Italian subsidiary.

By the early months of 1909 the Portello venture was facing bankruptcy, and the Italian backers took drastic steps. The managing director, Henry Elliott, an English appointee, was dismissed and replaced by Ugo Stella, who took some decisive steps to save the ailing concern. With the approval of the board, the Darracq ties were broken and a new company was formed, supported by a loan of 500,000 lira from Banca Agricola Milanese. This was called (Società) Anonima Lombarda Fabbrica Automobili, or ALFA for short. The reconstruction of the company was approved at an Extraordinary General Meeting on 24 June 1910, when Celestino Biglia became President, with Alexandre Darracq and John Smith-Winby remaining as directors. As Smith-Winby was still on the board, there must have been some English capital remaining in the new company.

In an inspired move, Giuseppe Merosi was appointed as chief designer. Merosi had been born at Piacenza in 1872 and had qualified as a surveyor or *geometra* at the Piacenza Istituto Tecnico. In 1893 he had joined Vittorio Bassi in a small venture to make bicycles. Bassi had already gained experience with bicycles at the Gladiator factory in Paris. Bassi e Merosi built the 'Endless' bicycle, which soon gained an excellent reputation, but after four years, in 1898, the partnership was dissolved and Merosi joined the established bicycle and sewing-machine manufacturer, Orio e Marchand, which had moved its factory from Milan to Piacenza. The Marchand brothers had come from Paris, where their father had been involved with the Peugeot bicycle, but Orio e Marchand now wanted to make motor cycles and cars. Merosi designed a 1½hp motor cycle, which received favourable press reports, and he began riding motor cycles in competition as a 'works' rider for Orio e Marchand.

Orio left the firm in 1900 and the Marchand brothers encouraged Merosi to start designing cars. He produced a 5hp twin-cylinder design in 1900–01, followed by a four-cylinder 10hp in 1902. Merosi had now become a key figure with Marchand, and it was a disaster for the firm when he left in 1904 to join Fiat in Turin. He did not stay there long, as in the

1910: An artist's impression of the ALFA factory at Portello.

autumn of 1906 he moved to FAV Edoardo Bianchi, which had opened a new factory at Via Paolo Frisi in Milan. There he was appointed chief designer, which gave him the opportunity to design larger and more sporting cars.

One of the first designs was a 7.4-litre car that was to run in the Kaiserpreis races at Homburg in Germany in June 1907. These races were intended for what would now be called sports-racing cars, and two Merosi-designed Bianchis competed, one driven by Tomaselli and the other by Carlo Maserati, the eldest of a family of engineering brothers whose products will feature again in this story. Both cars qualified in the eliminating heat on 13 June; in the final, the following day, Tomaselli finished the course, albeit at the back of the field.

Merosi's talents were now in full flight and his next design was the 11.4-litre 70hp E-type Bianchi. In 1908 he abandoned the T-head side-valve layout of the earlier Bianchis and adopted the then advanced L-head side-valve monobloc for his G-type design.

When he joined ALFA at Portello during the summer of 1909, Merosi began work on the designs of two cars; these were approved by Stella at a meeting on 1 September 1909, and work on the new cars began at Portello on 1 January 1910. The larger car was the 24hp model, and for this Merosi had evolved a straightforward design with a 100mm x 130mm 4084cc side-valve engine developing 42hp, and a four-speed gearbox mounted in a channel-section frame with quarter elliptic suspension at the front and rear. The wheelbase of the standard touring model was 10ft 6in (320cm), but perhaps Merosi's earlier initiation into motor sport was influential, as there was also to be a short-chassis Corsa model with a wheelbase of 9ft 6in (290cm). The 12/15hp model had an 80mm x 120mm 2114cc side-valve engine with a three-speed gearbox. Both designs had little in the way of advanced features or showed much original thought, but were well laid out with

good detail work. According to Luigi Fusi, the first 50 cars were marketed as Darracqs, but other published records state that only 20 cars in all were built in 1910.

It seems certain that as soon as ALFA came into being in June 1910, the cars bore a radiator badge designed for the new ALFA concern. In his book *Le Alfa di Merosi et di Romeo*, Luigi Fusi describes how this badge evolved. Ugo Stella asked Merosi to design a new badge, and when a young member of Merosi's team, Romano Cattaneo, was waiting for a No 14 tram in Piazza Castello, in the centre of Milan, he happened to glance at the heraldic devices of the Visconti family, who became the Dukes of Milan in medieval times, displayed on the Castello Sforzesco. One of these was a crowned serpent, and Cattaneo suggested that this should be incorporated in the new badge, Merosi agreed, but decided that the serpent should be accompanied by the cross of St George, the emblem of the City of Milan. The two emblems were surrounded by a border containing the words 'ALFA' and 'Milano'. The plate attached to each car, with the chassis and engine number stamped on it, also bore a *quadrifolio*, or four-leafed clover, an international symbol of good luck later to be carried on the bonnets of all Alfa Romeo grand prix cars.

In 1911 the 12hp was uprated and renamed as the 15/20hp. The building of a car called the Corsa 24hp was an indication that the new firm had ambitions to try its hand in the competition field, and on 23 April 1911 an Alfa took part in its first competitive event. Nino Franchini, the factory tester, drove a 12/15hp, with the 15/20hp modifications, in the Criterium di Regolarità at Modena. Franchini had previously been a regular competitor with a Bianchi and was probably the factory tester for that firm, so it seems likely that he moved to ALFA with Merosi.

The Criterium was a road trial in five stages over 1500km, and finished on 29 April. An official observer was carried in each competing car to ensure that any work on the car during the stages was penalised, and the cars were impounded at the end of each stage. One report states that Franchini

23 April 1911: Nino Franchini with an ALFA 12/15 in the Criterium di Regolarità at Modena, the marque's first competitive event. Giuseppe Campari sits beside the driver.

came equal first with five other competitors, having completed the course without penalty, but another report says that he incurred a penalty that put him one place behind the victorious five. This seems to have been the only significant competition in which the 12/15hp took part.

A date of great significance in Alfa Romeo history was 14 May 1911, when an Alfa appeared in its first racing event, the Targa Florio on the Madonie circuit in Sicily. The Targa Florio had been established in 1906 by Count Vincenzo Florio, and by 1911 had already become a legendary event thanks to the heroic feats that drivers performed during the 90-mile (148km) laps of the race through the Sicilian mountains. The course, over unmade roads, began at the village of Cerda, 30 miles (45km) east of Palermo on the north coast of the island. In his book *Targa Florio*, W. F. Bradley described the course:

'More than 90 miles of the most crazy highway it was possible to imagine, with the road struggling painfully to attain altitude, twisting, doubling back on itself as if giving up in despair, then resolutely attacking the vertical mass in a rage of determination to reach the fortified village towering above it.'

It climbed into the mountains to a height of 3670 feet (1120 metres) before returning to the coast and the start, and to the only appreciable straight of 5 miles (8km). For its racing début, ALFA was tackling the toughest competition of all. The 1911 event, over three laps of the circuit, was limited to four-cylinder cars with a bore of less than 100mm; two stripped and tuned Corsa 24s were entered for Franchini and for Ronzoni, an enthusiastic customer.

The race was run in appalling conditions. There was heavy rain and the road turned into deep mud. At the end of the first lap Franchini was in second place, 5 minutes behind the Lancia of Mario Cortese, but at the end of lap two Franchini led by 6 minutes, pursued by Ernesto Ceirano's Scat. During the third lap, possibly momentarily blinded by a splash of mud, Franchini ran wide on a corner in the village of Caltavuturo and damaged a front wheel, so the Alfa was forced to retire. Ronzoni also fell foul of the conditions with the second car and stopped. In its report of the race

Motori, Aero, Cicli e Sports commented that Franchini's driving was 'a little agitated', while Ceirano was 'more calm', which may have had something to do with the outcome.

Working with Merosi on the design of the new range of Alfas was Antonio Santoni, an engineer who may have been with him at Bianchi. Santoni was keen to build an aircraft, with the aim of being the first to fly over the Alps. Aided by Nino Franchini, he completed a design that was approved by Ugo Stella, who authorised its construction. The power unit for this early flying machine was a 4084cc 24hp engine, and to gain more power it was fitted with a centrifugal supercharger designed and patented by Santoni. With this extra boost, the engine developed 36bhp at 1680rpm, and the aircraft made its first flight on 17 September 1910, piloted by Franchini; it thus seems likely that ALFA was one of the initial pioneers of supercharging. However, the aim of the Alpine record was frustrated by a Bleriot, which made the flight on 29 September, although it ended tragically when the pilot, Georges Chavez, a Peruvian, was killed landing at Domodossola. The Alfa-powered aircraft was subsequently used by a flying school in Milan.

In 1912 there were nearly 200 men working at Portello and the rising sales indicated the need for a wider range of cars. Merosi set to work on the designs of a new car that would have much greater sporting potential. This was the 40-60hp, on which he started in the latter part of the year; the 40 indicating the taxable size of the engine and the 60 the anticipated output. The car had a four-cylinder 6082cc engine with dimensions of 110mm x 160mm and overhead valves operated by push rods. With separate inlet and exhaust camshafts, it developed 70bhp, so the '60' part of the car's title indicated commendable modesty on the part of ALFA, unlike some manufacturers. The chassis used many components from the 24hp and had the same wheelbase, but the track was widened to 4ft 9in

26 May 1912: Giuseppe Baldoni with a 24hp on his way to the Targa Florio.

(145cm). Twenty-seven 40-60hp cars were built before the War stopped production.

There was very little sporting participation in 1912, though this was not entirely due to a lack of inclination on the part of ALFA, as there was very little sporting activity in Italy that year. The only action came from a customer, Giuseppe Baldoni, who ran a 24hp in the Targa Florio, which had the extra title that year of the Giro di Sicilia, and was one lap of the island, a distance of 605 miles (975km). The winner was an Englishman, Cyril Snipe, who drove a Scat with his co-driver Pedrini; they were on the road for 24hr 37min, while the last car, a Primavesi, took 39hr 24min to finish. Baldoni had no success and retired.

It is interesting that in 1912, while Italy had virtually no motoring sport at all, in England there were regular race meetings at Brooklands throughout the summer and numerous sprints and hill climbs. Twenty years later, Italy would be regarded as the home of European motor racing, while the sport in England would be sparse and struggling.

Although the 1913 Italian sporting calendar was more lively, ALFA ignored the Targa Florio cum Giro in May, and there was no ALFA competition activity until the end of the season, but the spirit was willing and a competition version of the 40-60 was built. This had the short Corsa chassis and the engine was fitted with two carburettors. The compression ratio was raised from the 4.35:1 of the touring car to 5.5:1, and the output went up from 70bhp at 2200rpm to 80bhp at 2400rpm. On 28 September the Corsa 40-60 made its competition début at the Parma–Poggio di Berceto hill climb, held in honour of the centenary of the birth of the composer Giuseppe Verdi.

It was quite a formidable event. The course was 33 miles (53km) long and ran south-west from Parma, along the road to La Spezia. It rose 2400 feet (740 metres) before it reached Poggio di Berceto. Nino Franchini made second fastest time (44min 29.6sec) with his 40-60 and won the

28 September 1913: Two views of Nino Franchini with a 24hp, accompanied by Antonio Santoni, on the way to the Parma–Poggio di Berceto hill climb. Giuseppe Merosi drove the car and was seventh in his class.

unlimited class, while in second place in this class, driving another 40-60 and setting a time of 46min 25sec, was a 21-year-old factory test driver, Giuseppe Campari, beginning a legendary career. With a fine tenor voice of professional standards, Campari was torn between the world of grand opera and motor racing, so it was wholly fitting that he should begin racing in an event dedicated to Verdi. Merosi himself drove a 24 and took seventh place in the 4-litre class.

Perhaps the Parma success was the spur, but ambitions of racing glory now began to flourish at Portello, and Merosi commenced a much more challenging project. In October 1913 he started work on the designs for a full grand prix car that was intended to run in the 1914 Grand Prix de l'Automobile Club de France (the French

Grand Prix), which was to be held at Lyon on 4 July. This was then the premier motor racing event and victory was the aim of all European manufacturers with any sporting pretensions. The Grand Prix Alfa had a 4490cc engine with dimensions of 100mm x 143mm. Merosi must have been keeping in touch with the latest racing trends north of the Alps, and particularly the work of Ernest Henri, for his design was right up-to-date, with twin overhead camshafts, and also innovative, the camshafts being driven by a combination of chains, spur gears and vertical shafts from the front of the engine. There were four valves per cylinder at a 90-degree angle.

There was one snag, however: it only developed 88bhp at 2950rpm, which was rather feeble compared with the opposition. Despite the advanced specification there must have been something wrong in the design, which lacked the magic and, more important, the power of the Henri devices. Henri's 1914 GP Peugeot developed 112bhp, and the GP Mercedes, which won the 1914 Grand Prix, developed 115bhp.

The GP Alfa chassis was very similar to the 40-60 and shared some common parts. The engine was bench-tested in February 1914, and the only car to be built was finished and road-tested in May. For reasons that have never been discovered, the car did not run in the GP de l'ACF in July. Luigi Fusi, in *Le Alfa di Merosi e di Romeo*, says that the car was not considered ready until the end of July, so had missed the race. It is possible that the financial pressures that were beginning to affect the ALFA concern may have been a cause, but it is probably more likely that it was realised that the car was not fast enough to be competitive; its maximum speed was about 90mph (145kmh), which was mediocre compared with the 115mph (185kmh) of the Mercedes and Peugeot. With Sankey artillery wheels, the GP Alfa had a very old-fashioned and dated look compared with the cars that competed in the 1914 Grand Prix.

Although the GP car did not race, Portello was busy with a competition season in 1914 using the Corsa 40-60s. In May there was a week of events in Sicily. Once again, the Targa Florio was a two-day event, combined with the Giro di Sicilia; running round the island over a total distance of 605 miles (975km), it was run on 24 and 25 May, and three 40-60s were entered. Franchini retired during the first 267-mile (430km) stage of the Giro, from Palermo to Siracusa. Eraldo Frascassi, another factory test driver who had driven a Ford, presumably a Model T, in the 1912 and 1913 Targa/Giro marathons, was placed tenth, though he was an hour behind the leading Scat of Ceirano, while Campari trailed home in 16th place a further 40 minutes in arrears.

Next day, on the 338-mile (545km) run back to Palermo, both the 40-60s dropped out. The problems cannot have been serious as Franchini and Campari were out again on Sunday 31 May, running in the Coppa Florio over three laps of the Madonie circuit. This time the results were

Summer 1914: Merosi sits at the wheel of the Grand Prix Alfa.

Summer 1914: The engine of the Grand Prix Alfa.

more satisfying; the two cars finished in third and fourth places. Franchini was only 14 minutes behind the winner, Felice Nazzaro, after over 8 hours of racing, with Campari another 6 minutes behind. After Franchini's mud-in-the-eye experience in the 1911 Targa Florio, the cars were fitted with an off-side front mudguard. On 25 June, three days before the assassination of Archduke Ferdinand at Sarajevo, Campari came second in the Parma–Poggio di Berceto hill climb with a 40-60, while Franchini was ninth with a 24hp.

When the rest of Europe went to War in August 1914, Italy stood on the touchline. There had been considerable unrest in the country since the beginning of the year; the government feared a left-wing revolution while the powerful Socialist Party opposed the War, so a neutral stance was the outcome. The Italian economy was depressed, so on 1 August, as Germany mobilised and declared War on Russia, the Italian Government imposed a ban on strategic exports. ALFA was already in financial trouble, and this ban, which included motor cars, was almost the last straw. A few days later the Government passed a temporary Postponement of Payments Act, which prevented the payment of bills and suspended all credit. This brought ALFA to an insoluble crisis; the works closed and the workforce was dismissed. Bowing to trade union pressure, Ugo Stella revoked the notices and it was declared that the workers were laid off instead, but as far as they were concerned it was the same thing – no work.

On 24 May 1915 Italy joined the conflict, with a declaration of War on the Austro-Hungarian Empire, a decision taken in part with the hope of securing the disputed areas of Trentino and Trieste from Austria. ALFA's chief creditor was Società Italiana di Credito Provinciale (SICP), which now held almost all the shares, having bought them from Alexandre Darracq and the other foreign shareholders, who were probably glad to salvage what they could from the wreck. On 4 August 1915 SICP appointed Nicola Romeo as Public Administrator of ALFA.

Nicola Romeo, a native of Naples, was

31 May 1914: Franchini with the 40-60, which was third in the Coppa Florio.

then 39 years old. The son of an elementary schoolmaster, he had risen from a poor background to train as an engineer, first in Naples, where he received his diploma, then for a year at Liege University in Belgium. His first venture was to become the Italian agent for Robert Blackwell & Co, an English firm that made railway equipment. Romeo, who was now established in Milan, prospered and in 1907, with the financial backing of Eduardo Fucito, a boyhood friend and fellow engineer, he founded Società Accomandita Ing Nicola Romeo & C, with the primary purpose of taking on the Italian agency for Ingersoll-Rand, the American manufacturer of industrial compressors and drilling equipment. Romeo found that the imported machinery had a ready market in the many civil engineering projects that were being started at that time, so to increase sales and profits he began to import the American products in knocked-down form and assembled them in a factory in the Via Ruggero di Lauria, within walking distance of the ALFA factory at Portello. There was a great demand for the products of Romeo's new factory and he soon became a rich man. In 1911

Società Romeo expanded and more finance was provided by Angelo Pogliano, the director of SICP.

In December 1914 Pogliano became managing director of the Banca Italiana di Sconto (BIS), which had been founded for the purpose of financing industrial activity relating to the War. Pogliano was offered a contract by the Ministry of War to supply 10,000 75mm shells a day, worth 23 million lire, about £750,000, or £40m at today's values. This contract was well beyond the capacity of the small Romeo assembly factory, but ALFA had the facilities at Portello.

Under Pogliano's aegis, SICP, as the principal shareholder and creditor of ALFA, now began the liquidation of the company, and after the appointment of Romeo as administrator, an Extraordinary General Meeting sanctioned the transfer of control of ALFA to BIS. Zefferino Pogliano, Angelo's younger brother, was appointed as liquidator and at once the ALFA assets were vested in Società Romeo. Now he had control of Portello, Romeo was able to take on the munitions contract.

A solitary voice protested at the take-over,

that of Giuseppe Merosi, but his objections were probably based more on sentiment than realism. The arms contract meant that work started at Portello again, and Romeo now bought land next to the original site on which three new workshops, including a foundry, a forging shop and test department, were built. With nationalistic fervour Romeo called these new workshops 'Trento, Trieste and Gorizia'. So quickly did the factory grow that within seven months of the take-over the workforce had expanded from 50 to over 4000. The production also embraced grenades and fuses, while the Italian war effort stimulated the demand for air compressors, a version called the 'Piccolo Italiano' being used for digging trenches. All car production had ceased, but the 15-20 engine was now used to drive compressors and the 20-30 chassis was used for ambulances and light trucks. The company also now began making Isotta Fraschini aero engines under licence.

In February 1918 the renamed Società Anonima Italiana Nicola Romeo & C became a public company, and in May the new company bought the German-owned Costruzione di Meccaniche di Saronno, which had a large factory outside Milan, with a view to making railway equipment at the end of the War. Railway rolling-stock seemed to offer an attractive future, so later in 1918 the Officine Meccaniche di Roma and the Officine Ferroviarie Meridionali of Naples were also bought up. At the behest of the Italian Government, the company started to make American Titan tractors under licence. At the end of the War in November 1918, SA Romeo was a large and prosperous concern with interests in many industrial areas, and Nicola Romeo was an even richer man. It seems initially that there was no desire to return to car production, but in the months after the end of the War, business had not boomed for the company as expected, and probably with industrial capacity being under-used, the decision was taken early in 1919 that cars should be made again.

Chapter 2

A legend begins

Giuseppe Merosi, despite his objections, stayed with the company during the War and, perhaps as retribution, was 'exiled' to Naples where he supervised production at the rail-wagon factory. He contended that the old ALFA company owed him money, so he left the company in May 1918 and brought proceedings against SA Romeo for payment. However, his talents were needed now the company was to build cars again, so the breach was healed and he returned to Portello as technical consultant in August 1919 with a five-year contract.

It took a long time to reorganise the Portello factory and prepare it once more for car manufacture. To tide over the company until a completely new range of cars could be designed, Merosi took out the designs for the old 24hp model and re-worked them to evolve the 20-30 ES Sport. The main change was a larger bore, from 100mm to 102mm, which increased the capacity to 4250cc; with other modifications the power went up from 49bhp at 2400rpm to 67bhp at 2600rpm, and the chassis was shortened. In many other respects the car still showed its Edwardian antecedents.

The return to production went painfully slowly and in 1920 only three 20-30 ES models were built. The cars now bore a badge declaring them to be products of 'Alfa-Romeo, Milano'. It seems that car production was only intended to provide an image for the industrial products and was not expected to make a major contribution to the company.

Italy was in turmoil throughout 1920. The country was experiencing a severe post-war depression and the Christian Democrat Government under Francesco Nitti was struggling to control and contain continuous Communist-instigated strikes and riots. The Government fell in June and the new administration under Giovanni Giolitti managed little better. At the end of August 1920 he permitted the opposition Socialist Party to organise the workers' occupation of the major factories in the country. Italy was paralysed and the lire fell from 30 to the pound sterling to 105. Unemployment soared and there was rapid inflation; there was hunger in the cities, public buildings were attacked, and in many areas the flourishing Communist Party declared the establishment of local soviets. Into this chaos, with a Communist revolution seemingly imminent, stepped Benito Mussolini and his emerging Fascist Party, which offered immediate and often brutal opposition to the Communists. While many did not like Mussolini and the methods of his supporters, they seemed to offer a better solution than a Communist state. Support for the Fascists grew, even among some industrialists and financiers.

Portello was not immune from the troubles and was occupied on 30 August. However, the protests of the workers seem to have abated quite quickly and the factory was working normally in the late autumn. Production began in earnest in 1921, and during that year 119 20-30 ES cars were built, together with 50 examples of the 35-50hp G1 model, the first of Merosi's post-war designs. This was a luxury touring car with a side valve 6597cc six-cylinder engine; a design Edwardian in concept and showing little imagination, it failed to find buyers, and only 52 were built.

With the post-war chaos there was virtually no motor racing in Europe in 1919, but with the sporting enthusiasm for which Italy was to be renowned for the next 20 years, two events were organised in that autumn. The Auto Club Parma had the distinction of staging the first post-war speed event in Italy when it ran the Parma–Poggio di Berceto climb on 5 October. For this event the 1914 GP car was dusted down and given its first competitive run. Nino Franchini drove it, accompanied by a young factory mechanic, Attilio Marinoni, who had ambitions to race himself. The lack of power of the GP engine was evident, and the best that Franchini could do was fifth place overall and third place in the 4500cc class. Three 40-60s were also entered, but it was not Alfa's day and all three failed to reach the finish. The event was won by a 32-year-old agricultural machinery engineer from Mantua, Antonio Ascari, driving a 1914 GP Fiat. Ascari had just been given the sole Alfa Romeo agency for Lombardy and had opened a showroom at 4 Via Castelvetro, Milan, which at that time must have been a venture more of faith than profit.

Sicily had been less affected by the War

5 October 1919: Contrer and Baldoni with a 40-60 at the start of the Poggio–Parma di Berceto hill climb.

than most places and Count Florio managed to organise the first post-war Targa Florio on 23 November. The race was run on a shortened Madonie course, known as the Polizzi circuit, which cut out some of the mountains and had a lap of 67 miles (108km). The Sicilian weather is usually still mild in November, but it rained the day before the race, and during the night there was rain, hail and snow. On the morning of the race the mountains were capped with snow and rain clouds hung over the higher parts of the course. The conditions in the mountains were as bad as could be, the road reduced to a sea of mud.

Three Alfa Romeos were entered under the name of Alfa Corse, the first time this legendary title appeared in an entry list. Campari and Fracassi drove 1914 40-60 models uprated with a slight power increase and, since the Parma meeting, fitted with centre-lock wire wheels, replacing the artillery wheels of 1914, probably to anticipate the likelihood of frequent wheel changes. Franchini had the GP car again. No glory was gained in the mud as all three dropped out; Campari had punctures on

the second lap while Franchini had set off at a good pace, but struck a wall in Polizzi and buckled a wheel. Fracassi's problems are not recorded, but it is likely that the drivers were not too remorseful when they looked at the grim conditions. Ascari had driven his GP Fiat and had battled for the lead with the eventual winner, André Boillot (Peugeot), until he went off the road.

The world was returning to normality at the beginning of 1920 and a fuller motor racing calendar was planned. The Parma club had moved the date of its Parma–Poggio di Berceto hill climb to 30 May. Campari, who must have known his way up the hill by now, was entered with a 40-60, now looking much more sporting with an outside exhaust. Marinoni was the riding mechanic and the pair gained the very first outright win for Alfa Romeo with a time of 38min 25.4sec, just edging out Guilio Masetti's 1914 GP Fiat by the narrow margin of 3 seconds.

Two weeks later, on Sunday 13 June, Campari was at the village of St Piero, in the Apennines, north of Florence, for the first Circuito del Mugello. This was a six-lap race

of 242 miles (389km). The 40-mile (65km) lap ran through the mountains, and one leg was over the Futa Pass on the main road from Florence to Bologna. Campari was again driving a 40-60 and was accompanied by Marinoni. Alfa Corse, doubtless impressed with his Targa Florio drive, had also entered Antonio Ascari with another 40-60, but he did not start. There were 30 entries for the race and it seemed likely that the winner would be one of the Masetti brothers, Carlo and Giulio, who were both driving 1914 GP Fiats. The 40-60 did not have the speed to match the Fiats, and at half distance, after 3 hours of racing, the Fiats led, pursued by Campari. On the fourth lap, Giulio Masetti stopped with a broken oil pipe, and on the next lap, when his win seemed almost certain, brother Carlo went off the course and his Fiat overturned. This left Campari with a lead that he could not have anticipated, but he pressed on to win the first circuit victory for Alfa Romeo; countless more were to come. It had been a tough race and only three other cars finished. Augusto Tarabusi with a Diatto was second, 1hr 16min behind. It was an indication of the toughness of the course that Campari's average speed had only been 37.80mph (60.82kmh).

The ebullient Campari was out again a week later with a 40-60, at Pontassieve outside Florence, for the 9.4-mile (15.1km) Coppa delle Consuma hill climb, where he was third fastest behind one of the Masetti brothers, who had mended his GP Fiat.

A slightly shadowy but influential figure at Alfa Romeo during this period was Giorgio Rimini. Rimini had worked with Nicola Romeo as early as 1915 and was described by Luigi Fusi as Romeo's secretary, but he also seems to have been commercial director of the company and was responsible for the development of car sales. As racing was an effective way of getting publicity, Rimini was responsible for Alfa Romeo's competition programme. He was at Parma–Berceto and Mugello in 1920, and was impressed by the driving and also the technical ability of a 22-year-old competitor, Enzo Ferrari. Ferrari was driving a 1913 8-litre IM model Isotta-Fraschini, which had first raced at Indianapolis; he was third at Parma, although he retired at Mugello.

Ferrari was born on 18 February 1898 in Modena, where his father owned a small engineering workshop. When he left the Italian Army in 1918 he got a job as a test and delivery driver for a small firm renovating army vehicles in Turin, and was befriended by Ugo Sivocci. Sivocci was already a recognised competition driver and worked for CMN (Costruzini Mecchaniche Nazionale) in Milan as a test driver. Encouraged by Sivocci, Ferrari joined CMN as a test driver and drove a factory-entered 2.3-litre 15-20 model at the Parma hill climb in 1919, where he came fifth in his class and 11th overall.

Ferrari's first race was the 1919 Targa Florio, where his 15-20 CMN completed the course outside the time limit. There is a suggestion that after Mugello, in June 1920, Rimini persuaded Ferrari to buy a sporting-bodied G1, and it is mentioned in his memoirs, though a G1 would have been an expensive buy and would have been a pointless acquisition for an ambitious young competition driver. Business deals apart, Rimini appreciated Ferrari's talent, and by October the latter had signed up with Alfa Romeo to drive as a member of the Alfa Corse team in the Targa Florio. The race was held on 20 October.

The entry was smaller than in previous years. Alfa Corse entered two cars: Campari had the 1914 GP and Ferrari was driving a 40-60. As seemed almost inevitable, the race was run in appalling conditions. It had rained for several days beforehand and was still doing so on race day. The Madonie circuit was a sea of mud and obstructed with rocks and fallen trees. Campari led for two laps then stopped when his magneto was drowned in water and mud. Ferrari started at a steady pace, but Campari's retirement left him in second place behind Meregalli's Nazzaro; he chased the leader and set fastest lap, but was unable to close the gap and finished second, but the drive had cemented his place with Alfa Romeo. Alfa Romeo now must have had a contract, or at least an understanding, that the Alfa Corse cars would run on Pirelli tyres, and at the end of the season the results at Parma, Mugello and in the Targa Florio were publicised in a combined advertisement by Antonio Ascari and Pirelli.

In a final fling at the end of the season, the Alfa Corse team ran at the Gallarate sprint on the 14 November. This was a course over a flying kilometre on the road between Milan and Lake Maggiore. In the 'Macchine di Serie' class, Ferrari was first, timed at 74mph (120kmh) in a 40-60, ahead of Ascari's 20-30 ES (67mph/108kmh), while in the 4½-litre class Campari ran the GP and was timed at

20 October 1920: A Pirelli publicity photo after the Targa Florio showing, on the left, Campari, accompanied by Giulio Ramponi with the GP, while in the centre is Enzo Ferrari with the 40-60 in which he took second place. The car on the right is a GP Nazzaro driven by Baldoni.

78.7mph (126.76kmh); he won the class but it showed once more that speed was not one of the GP's stronger qualities.

Presumably the terms of employment were better with Alfa Romeo than CMN, as during the winter of 1920/21 Ugo Sivocci followed Enzo Ferrari and began work at Portello as a test driver and member of the Alfa Corse team. Giorgio Rimini quickly appreciated his value and soon after his arrival Sivocci was made head of the testing department. Once again, the Parma hill climb began the season on 8 May 1921, and a full Alfa team turned up. Campari had a 40-60, Ascari was driving the GP, while new boy Sivocci was given a 20-30 ES. Campari came second overall with a

time of 36min 46.2sec, but was still unable to get the better of the 1914 GP Fiats, this time one being driven by Carlo Niccolini. Ascari and Sivocci were running in the 4½-litre class and came first and second. Giorgio Rimini, keeping an active and participating interest in his competition responsibilities, went along as Ascari's riding mechanic, and his time gave him fourth place overall.

The engine of the GP had been rebuilt during the winter, with the porting and valve gear modified and light alloy pistons fitted. This work had increased the power to 102bhp at 3000rpm, which was better, but still a lot less than the output achieved by the potential rivals in 1914. The engine's

relative lack of power during its life must have been a consequence of the design of the ports and combustion chamber; valve timing may also have been a factor. Little was known at that time about the relationship between port design and gas velocity.

Hoping for better weather, and probably to the great relief of the competitors, Count Florio moved the date of the 1921 Targa Florio to Sunday 29 May. There was an all-out effort at Portello and five cars were prepared for the race. Campari had his usual 40-60 and Ascari was driving the GP, both entered by Alfa Corse. There were also three 20-30 ESs for Ferrari, Sivocci and Baldoni, but surprisingly these had been entered by the drivers concerned. In practice Ascari recorded the best time, which showed that not only was he becoming a driver to be reckoned with, but also that the GP, with its winter modifications, was now

8 May 1921: The team lines up outside the Portello factory before going to the Parma–Poggio di Berceto hill climb. From left to right: Merosi and Sozzi with a G1; Ferrari and Conti with a 20-30; Ascari and Rimini with the GP; Sivocci and Marinoni with a 20-30; and Campari and Fugazza with a 40-60.

8 May 1921: Ascari and Rimini with the GP at the Parma–Poggio di Berceto hill climb.

an improved car. The race attracted 38 entries, including a 7¼-litre 28/95 Mercedes, entered by the Stuttgart factory, the first time that a factory-entered German car had been allowed to race since the end of the War.

Any hopes that the GP Alfa would be able to match its new-found pace against the Mercedes were soon dashed, as it fell out when one of the new alloy pistons seized during the first lap. Although it rained in the early stages, the weather was better than in previous years, which encouraged a tremendous battle for the lead. The principal contenders were Giulio Masetti with his GP Fiat and Max Sailer with the 28/95 Mercedes, and they fought for the lead throughout the race. Sailer led by 21 seconds at the end of the first lap, but then Masetti went ahead and stayed there, winning by just over 2 minutes. Campari was not left out of it and was still in with a

chance at the start of the last lap. He finished third, but only 5 minutes behind Masetti after 7½ hours of racing. The 20-30 ESs were not outclassed, and Sivocci was fourth, 90 seconds behind Campari, being chased home by Ferrari in fifth, another 2 minutes behind.

Although Alfa Romeo had not won, the result must have been satisfying to Nicola Romeo, but he must have known, as Brock Yates pointed out in his book *Enzo Ferrari*, that 'the modest firm of Alfa Romeo was still operating in the minor leagues of the automobile business', and it was also operating in the minor leagues of motor racing. The Targa Florio was an heroic event but it attracted very few non-Italian entries and the other events in which the Alfa Corse cars were running were only minor club meetings. In 1921 grand prix racing was

revived with the GP de l'ACF at Le Mans in July and the first Gran Premio d'Italia at Brescia in September, but it was an indication of the company's lowly status that it had no car eligible or suitable for this class of racing.

Wanting to repeat the 1920 victory, a full Alfa team went to Mugello on 24 July. The Circuit of Mugello had already gained a reputation and was being called the 'Targa Florio of the North', and this brought in 31 entrants. Campari was the official Alfa Corse entry with a 40-60, Ascari drove the GP and the 20-30 ESs of Sivocci and Ferrari were private entries. The race was over six laps of the mountainous circuit, and the cars were started at 2-minute intervals.

During the first lap Campari caught up with the Isotta Fraschini of Alfieri Maserati. He tried to pass and, in the cloud of dust,

May 1921: A team line-up at Portello before the Targa Florio. No 21 is Sivocci (20-30), No 20 Ferrari (20-30), and No 34 Campari (40-60).

29 May 1921: Campari, with Fugazza as the riding mechanic, takes third place at the Targa Florio with his 40-60.

the cars collided, and Campari had to make a long stop to repair the damage. This left Niccolini with a 1914 GP Fiat in the lead. The race was sub-divided into capacity classes and Ascari led the 4½-litre class from Ferrari and Sivocci. At the start of the fifth lap Ascari went off the road when blinded by dust from another car. The GP overturned and Ascari injured his leg. Ferrari now led the class, but only by a narrow margin, as Sivocci had put up fastest lap and was closing on him. Meanwhile Campari had been driving heroically to make up for lost time, but at the start of the last lap he was 9 minutes behind Niccolini's Fiat. Halfway round the lap the Fiat stopped as the exhaust pipe had broken and set the body alight. Campari swept into the lead and went on to win, Ferrari was second overall and won his class, while completing the Alfa Romeo triumph was Sivocci, who finished third.

Ascari was made of tough stuff. His leg had mended sufficiently by 7 August for him to be a member of the Alfa Romeo team in the first Alpine Cup, a successor to the 1913 event and the precursor of the later Alpine Trials. Three 20-30 ESs were entered with touring bodies, and the other members of the team were Sivocci and Ferrari. The event was in five stages, covered a distance of 1450 miles (2300km) and ended on 15 August. On the last day Ascari was leading the event outright when he swerved off the road during the descent of the Madonna di Campiglio to avoid a collision with a cart and ended in a stream, but fortunately without injury. Sivocci came fourth overall and Ferrari was fifth; the 20-30s won their class.

The motor car and motor racing had already captured the Italian imagination, and evidence of this came in September when there was a speed week at Brescia, which encompassed the Gran Premio d'Italia, a formula libre race, and speed trials. The first event was the Gran Premio and the race was a straight fight between three Ballots and three Fiats. Ugo Sivocci

had been released by Alfa Romeo to drive one of the Fiats; by securing his services Fiat must probably have felt that he was the best bet among the Alfa Corse drivers. During the race the Fiats had tyre troubles and the Ballots ran away with the race. Sivocci lasted for 18 of the 30 laps, then retired with a sick engine.

The speed week ended with the formula libre race for amateur drivers called the Gran Premio Gentlemen, which in the circumstances should perhaps have been called the GP Lady & Gentlemen. The amateur status of some of the drivers must have been doubtful, as Campari was entered by Alfa Corse with the GP, and in addition 20-30 ESs were privately entered by Franco Caiselli and the Baronessa Antonietta d'Avanzo. The latter has a small place in motor racing history, being the first woman to drive an Alfa Romeo in a speed event; she may also have been instrumental in showing Enzo Ferrari the possibilities of

a 12-cylinder engine. In 1921 she competed at the Fano speed week in Denmark driving a 12-cylinder Packard, and when she took the car back to Milan she visited Ascari's showroom and part-exchanged it for a Fiat 501; while Ascari had the Packard, Ferrari spent a long time looking at it.

The Gentlemen's race was 25 laps of the 10.7-mile (17.2km) circuit, a distance of 268 miles (432km). Alfa Corse also entered a 40-60 for Ferrari, but this took itself out of the entry list somewhat abruptly when Ferrari went off the road during practice, swerving to avoid some stray cattle on the course and wrecking his car, though he escaped unhurt. Campari set off steadily and when Niccolini's Indianapolis Fiat dropped out on lap 10, he took the lead, chased by Masetti's 1914 GP Mercedes. It seemed that the GP was finally to win a race, but on lap 21 Campari spun, letting Masetti into the lead. Campari then came

11 September 1921: Ferrari and Merosi stand beside the wreck of Ferrari's 40-60 after his practice accident at the GP Gentlemen at Brescia. Rimini proposes a toast.

11 September 1921: Baronessa Avanzo in her 20-30 after taking third place in the GP 'Gentlemen'. Ramponi sits in the car and Merosi stands on the right.

into his pit with a misfire. A plug change and the addition of much water were expected to effect a cure, but during the stop the radiator cap was damaged. On the penultimate lap the water ran away and the engine seized. Meanwhile the Baronessa kept going steadily and brought her 20-30 ES into third place, which was probably worth more to Alfa Romeo in terms of publicity than an outright win by Campari.

Away from the racing world, things were still not going well for Alfa Romeo. The inflation of the lira was leaving the company seriously under-capitalised, and on 30 December 1921 BIS collapsed. This caused a major financial crisis in Italy, and the effect on Alfa Romeo, the bank's second largest debtor, was immediate. The Italian Government established the Banca Nazionale di Credito (BNC) to salvage the assets of the debtor companies vested in BIS.

In 1922 Italy was once again in political turmoil. In August there was a general strike, and daily street fighting broke out between the Fascists and their Socialist opponents. Mussolini declared that if the Government would not stop the strike, the Fascists would. The *squadristi*, the uniformed activist arm of the Fascist Party commanded by Italo Balbo (later Marshal Balbo), burned the buildings of the Socialist Party and broke up the presses of *Avanti*, the Socialist newspaper in Milan. At a party congress in Naples in October, urged on by his supporters, Mussolini said, 'Either the Government will be given to us or we shall seize it by marching on Rome.' On 27 October 1922 several columns of Fascists began the celebrated March on Rome, and the next day Mussolini received an invitation from King Victor Emmanuel to form a government. Mussolini did not march himself, but, rather more prosaically, went

from Milan to Rome by train, wearing the uniform black shirt of the Fascists and, to add dignity, a bowler hat and spats! As the assets of Alfa Romeo were now in the hands of the Government-controlled BNC, so the company came under the control of the new Fascist Government.

The economic and political problems in Italy had a drastic effect on the production and sales of Alfa Romeo in 1922, and only six cars were built during the year; if the firm had not been state-controlled it would surely have gone into liquidation. However, if there was no activity on the factory floor, Giuseppe Merosi was hard at work in the drawing office on a new design that at last broke away from the Edwardian heritage. Late in 1920 he began work on the RL, which was intended to be a 3-litre general-purpose design that could be the basis for both touring and racing cars, with the possibility of also becoming a grand prix car. The grand prix formula was changed in 1922 to a 2-litre limit, which put paid to the highest racing aspirations, but the design fulfilled all the other hopes for it.

The engine was a conventional push rod overhead-valve six-cylinder, and was made in two sizes. The single-carburettor RL Normale, or RLN, had dimensions of 75mm x 110mm (2916cc) and developed 56bhp at 3200rpm. The twin-carburettor RL Sport, or RLS, was 76mm x 110mm (2996cc) and gave 71bhp at 3500rpm. The four-speed gearbox in unit with the engine, and the chassis was entirely conventional and typical of the vintage era. The proto-type was first shown to the world in the Alfa Romeo showroom at 18 Via Dante, Milan, on 13 and 14 October 1921, but with all the problems besetting Alfa Romeo it took nearly a year before production started, hence only the six cars appearing in 1922. Presumably a prospective customer could look at the Alfa Romeo range in the Via Dante, but if he wanted to buy one he had to go to Antonio Ascari at Via Castelvetro.

The 1922 Targa Florio was bigger and

2 April 1922: Augusto Tarabusi in an experimental RL before the start of the Targa Florio; he retired on the opening lap.

2 April 1922: Enzo Ferrari finished in 16th place in the Targa Florio with this 20-30.

better than ever; there were 46 entries, and in addition to the Italian entries there were works teams from Mercedes, Austro-Daimler, Steyr, Wanderer and Ballot, so it was truly an international event. Although probably not realised by the other entrants, Mercedes had opened a new chapter of racing design; two of the seven Mercedes entries were 10/40/65PS models, which were supercharged. This was the first time that forced-induction engines had appeared in a race – the reign of the supercharger was about to begin and would last for the next 30 years. One of the drivers in the Austro-Daimler team was a young newcomer, Alfred Neubauer, who would have a considerable, and not wholly beneficial, influence on the fortunes of Alfa Romeo racing in the years to come.

The race was held on 2 April and Alfa Romeo made a big effort. Alfa Corse entered the prototype RL to be driven by Augusto Tarabusi. There were also three ES models for Ascari, Sivocci and Ferrari, and a 40-60 for Campari. Two more ESs were entered by private owners, one being Baronessa Avanzo. The race was not a notable success for Alfa Romeo. Tarabusi went off the road on the opening lap and while the other members of the team finished, they were not fast enough to keep up with Mercedes and Ballot; Ascari's ES was the highest placed, finishing fourth.

It was probably hoped that a return to the happy hunting ground of Mugello on 18 June would revive the good fortunes of Portello, but once again it was disaster. Campari had a 40-60 and was supported by Ascari and Ferrari with ESs. The cars were started at 1-minute intervals. Masetti took the lead with his 1914 GP Mercedes and caught up with Campari, who had started a minute before him. On lap three Campari fought back, closed on Masetti and tried to pass him, but the cars collided. Masetti went off the road and Campari managed to limp back to the pits but had to retire. Ascari had crashed on the opening lap and Ferrari stopped a lap later. During that summer of 1922 Ferrari had loosened his links with Alfa Romeo slightly, returning to

Modena to open a coachbuilding and body repair shop business, Carrozzeria Emilia: Enzo Ferrari & C, in the Via Jacopo Barozzi on the outskirts of the city.

In the autumn of 1922 the Monza race track was opened. This combined road and banked track circuit was only 10 miles (15km) from Milan, so it became the ideal local test track for Alfa Romeo. At that time the bankings were very shallow and probably as much of a danger as a help to a driver at speed – the steeply banked Monza speed bowl was many years in the future. The track was inaugurated by the Gran Premio d'Italia on 3 September. No Alfa Romeos ran in this race, but seven weeks later, on 22 October, Alfa Corse was out in force for the 249-mile (400km) formula libre Gran Premio d'Autunno, which used the same combined Monza road and track circuit.

The race was divided into two classes, for cars over and under 3 litres. Campari, with a 40-60, ran in the large-capacity class, while Sivocci and Ascari drove RLs among the 3-litres. It was a wet day and the race was run in a continuous downpour.

1923: An RL Targa engine.

Campari was not in the running, as he stopped for a wheel change after eight laps then retired with a faulty gearbox on lap 18. It was a different story for Sivocci. At the start Alfieri Maserati, driving a GP Diatto, led with Sivocci back in fifth place, but the RL began to move up the field, and when Maserati stopped to refuel and change a wheel, Sivocci led the class. Two laps later Sivocci spun on one of the banked turns and ended up in the mud at the side of the track, but he pushed the car back onto the track and was able to get going again. Sivocci now chased Maserati and on lap 30 he took the class lead. On lap 32 Maserati was in front again, but he stopped for more fuel and the RL was back into the lead. With four laps to go, Maserati pursued Sivocci and regained the lead, but then he eased off and Sivocci just failed to catch him on the run to the flag, losing by 10 seconds after over 3 hours of racing.

The following year production was well under way, and for Alfa Romeo a new annual record was established, with 610 RLNs and 215 RLSs built. Merosi had now developed a more sporting version of the RLS intended for racing. This had increased compression and improvements such as lightened valve gear; two sizes of this improved engine were built, one with the standard dimensions and capacity, which developed 88bhp at 3600rpm, the other with a bore of 78mm, which increased the capacity to 3154cc and the output to 95bhp. These cars became known as the Targa Florio models and had racing bodies with bolster fuel tanks. The wheelbase was reduced from the 10ft 3in (314cm) of the RLS to 9ft 3in (288cm). Peter Hull and Roy Slater suggest in *Alfa Romeo – a History* that Sivocci's car that ran so well at Monza in October 1922 was a Targa prototype, being much too nimble to have been an ordinary RLS.

After the impressive entry of the previous year, the list for the 1923 Targa Florio was thin. There were only 19 entries and of these the only foreign runners were a team of three 4-litre Steyrs and a Peugeot driven by André Boillot. Alfa Corse entered four of the new RL Targas for Campari, Ascari, Sivocci and Giulio Masetti; the latter must have been signed up on the assumption that, as the winner in the two previous years, it was better to have him on their side. Enzo Ferrari had also entered an ES.

On race day, 15 April, the Madonie circuit was in poor condition as, with a dreary inevitability, heavy rain had fallen the previous night. At the end of the first lap Rutzler (Steyr) was in front, 1 minute ahead of Campari; next were Maserati with a new supercharged Diatto and Sivocci. Campari dropped back, was passed by Maserati then fell out, but Ascari started to motor fiercely and by the end of the second lap was only 5 seconds behind the Diatto. On lap three Rutzler retired, but Ascari went off the road and burst a tyre, while Maserati also had his problems and fell back. This left Sivocci in the lead, but Ascari had replaced the wheel, got the car back on the road and was going again, driving with astonishing elan. On the last lap he took the lead once more and a win seemed certain, but he stopped within sight of the finish and began working furiously on his car. He got it going, restarted and crossed the line before Sivocci appeared, but gave a lift to two helpers whom he carried the short distance to the line, as well as his riding mechanic.

The outraged race officials demanded that he should return to the place where he had stopped and cover the remaining distance again, this time without the helpers. History does not relate if he reversed over the distance or drove against the oncoming racers. As he was doing this, Sivocci swept past to win and Ascari had to settle for second place. Meanwhile Masetti had worked up to fourth place behind Minoia's Steyr, so the RL Targa Alfa Romeos took first, second and fourth places and the marque had gained its first international victory.

Three weeks later Ascari had his reward

15 April 1923: Ascari's RLTF on the way to the finish of the Targa Florio with Ramponi hanging on to the radiator and the two helpers enjoying an unlawful ride.

when his RL Targa won the 117-mile (188km) Circuito di Cremona. The principal opposition in a small field was Maserati's Diatto, but Ascari led all the way and won by 17 minutes. A piece of motor racing history was made at Ravenna on 17 June when Enzo Ferrari won the 166-mile (267km) Circuito di Savio in his privately entered RL. It rained throughout the night before the race and the event was nearly cancelled as the roads were flooded, but sun and wind dried out the course in time. Ferrari led all the way, but was closely pursued throughout the race by the Fiat 501 of Eduardo Weber, who was soon to become much better known as a manufacturer of carburettors. Ferrari's victory was watched by the parents of Francesco Baracca, the leading Italian fighter ace of the First World War. It is said that they were so impressed with Ferrari's driving, which presumably reminded them of the daring of their deceased son, that after the race they presented Ferrari with the badge of a prancing horse on a yellow background, which their son had carried on his fighter; thenceforth this badge became Ferrari's personal

'symbol' and was in due course to be a symbol of much greater significance. In his biography of Enzo Ferrari, Brock Yates suggests that this badge was not that of Baracca personally, but was that of his squadron No 91a, and originally had been on a German Albatros B11 shot down by Baracca in 1916, actually representing the city shield of Stuttgart! It did not appear on a racing car until 1932.

While the improved RL Targas had been showing their paces, Giuseppe Merosi was busy on two more advanced projects. The first was the redesign of the RL engine to obtain more power for competitions. To achieve this the racing engines were given seven main bearings instead of the four that Merosi had previously deemed adequate. This new engine again came in two sizes, one with the original capacity of 2994cc, and an enlarged version with dimensions of 80mm x 120mm, which gave a capacity of 3620cc. This bigger engine developed 125bhp at 3800rpm.

The second project was more fundamental. Since the autumn of 1922 Merosi had been designing a full grand prix car, which

was intended to be ready for the Gran Premio d'Italia at Monza on 9 September 1923. The engine was a twin overhead cam six-cylinder unit with a capacity of 1990cc. It had built-up steel cylinder blocks and roller main and big-end bearings. It was unsupercharged, but the intention was that it would eventually be supercharged, with a Roots-type unit driven from the front of the crankshaft. The chassis was conventional and the car had the regulation two-seat body. The car was known as the GPR model, or P1, and the first to be completed was tested at Monza by Ascari, Campari and Sivocci on 16 August 1923, running with an unpainted body. It was reported that during this preliminary test Ascari was timed at 112mph (180kmh).

10 June 1923: Ascari's RLTF makes a refuelling stop during the Circuito di Mugello. He finished in third place.

Three cars, now resplendent in red, were entered for the Gran Premio, and the day before the race Sivocci went off the road at Vialone Curve during the final practice session. Some reports state that he hit a tree

16 August 1923: Sivocci testing the newly completed P1 at Monza.

and others that the car overturned. He was killed instantly, although the riding mechanic escaped with a shaking. The decision was made to withdraw the remaining two cars from the race.

History has always regarded the P1 as a complete failure, and it has been described as underpowered and ill-handling. The power output has been variously quoted at 'about 80', 93 and 95bhp. When the P2 was being built some months later, the P2 supercharger was given a first test by fitting it to the P1 engine. To ascertain the benefits of forced induction, the P1 was bench-tested beforehand and was found to develop 93bhp, so it may be assumed that this is a reliable figure. The 1922 GP Fiat developed 92bhp, the unsupercharged T35 Bugatti, which appeared at Lyon in 1924, developed 90bhp, and the Sunbeam that won the 1923 GP de l'ACF gave a reported 103bhp, so while the 93bhp of Merosi's design may not have been at the top of the class, it was certainly comparable with the opposition. The reported 112mph also indicates a reasonable power output. If the car had been as difficult to drive as suggested, this would have been evident in the August testing, and it seems unlikely that three cars would have been built and entered for the Monza race. It may be surmised that Merosi's P1 design could have suffered from the 'rubbishing' of those who followed him.

Probably spurred on by the shock of Sivocci's death, it seems that a 'Merosi must go' faction was gaining strength within Alfa Romeo. While he was accepted as a competent designer of touring and sports cars, his failure, or apparent failure, to produce a design of racing car capable of success at the highest level meant that his days as the chief designer were numbered.

One of the design team that had produced the 1923 Grand Prix Fiat, the Tipo 805, was Luigi Bazzi. At Tours, during the 1923 Grand Prix de l'ACF, Bazzi had a row with Carlo Fornaca, Fiat's chief designer, perhaps prompted by the failure of the 805 to pull off the win expected of it. When he returned to Turin after the race, Bazzi told his friend Enzo Ferrari that he was unhappy about remaining with Fiat. Ferrari suggested that he should join Merosi's design team at Portello, where they were putting the final touches to the P1, so Bazzi moved to Alfa Romeo forthwith.

According to Enzo Ferrari, probably just after Sivocci's death at Monza, he was asked by Giorgio Rimini if he knew of a designer who had the necessary talent to take over Merosi's job. Ferrari put the problem to Bazzi who suggested that Rimini should

8 September 1923: The P1 at the paddock gate at Monza during practice for the GP d'Italia. On the right are Ascari, Rimini, Ramponi and Sozzi.

8 September 1923: The P1 team during practice for the GP d'Italia: No 6 is Ascari, No 17 is Sivocci and No 12 is Campari. Ferrari and Rimini stand behind No 6, and Merosi is behind No 17.

seek out Vittorio Jano, who was then with Fiat and had played a major part in the design of the Tipo 805 that had redeemed itself a few days earlier by winning the Gran Premio; he had also assisted Severino Rossi, who managed the Fiat racing team. Rimini decided that Jano was his man, so sent Ferrari as an emissary to Turin, where he first put the proposition to Jano's wife, Rosina. She said that Jano would not move, but then Ferrari spoke to Jano himself, who said he would consider the proposal if it was put to him by someone from Alfa Romeo with full authority; he would 'speak to the organ grinder, not the monkey'. This must have rankled with the proud Ferrari, but he reported the position to Rimini and Jano then received a visit from Eduardo Fucito, who offered double the salary he was receiving with Fiat and also offered him living expenses and a bonus. The wooing was successful and Jano began work at Portello at the beginning of October 1923. Merosi was moved on to less demanding projects; he accepted this humiliation with good grace and stayed on with Alfa Romeo until 1926.

Chapter 3

The Golden Age

Vittorio Jano was born in 1891. His father was the technical head of the Turin arsenal and after studying at the Istituto Professionale Operaio at Turin he worked first for the Rapid company, then joined Fiat in 1911. Despite the setback with the P1, Nicola Romeo still wanted to go grand prix racing, so the first task set for Vittorio Jano was to design a new grand prix car. He had a team of ten with him, and they must have worked with astonishing rapidity, because according to Luigi Fusi, who was one of the team, much of the engine design was completed by the end of October and the first engine was being bench-tested at the end of March 1924.

Jano's design was a landmark in Alfa Romeo history and established the pattern of engine design at Portello for the next 14 years. Jano readily admitted that he had learned a lot at Fiat, and the engine of the P2, as it became known, showed its relationship to the Tipo 805 Fiat of 1923. It was a twin overhead camshaft straight-eight with dimensions of 61mm x 85mm and a capacity of 1987cc. The cylinder blocks were fabricated in steel, in pairs with integral heads, having two valves per cylinder, and the camshafts were driven by spur gears from the rear of the crankshaft. The engine was supercharged with a Roots blower that ran at a high pressure for 1924, 10.5psi (0.7 bar). The supercharger drew air from two intakes and blew this along a pipe on the off-side to a single Memini carburettor at the rear of the engine. The power was initially 140bhp at 5500rpm. In later years Jano said that with modern fuels and valve springs the engine would have been capable of turning at 8/9000rpm without problems.

This impressive engine was installed in a conventional chassis, with semi-elliptic springing all round. The front springs passed through forged housings in the axle beam; this had been a feature of the GP Fiat and would later be more widely associated with Bugatti. The car was fitted with a typical two-seat racing body, and the complete car weighed approximately 1650lb (750kg).

1924: An aerial view of the Portello factory.

The first car was road tested before the end of May, and much of this was done by Ascari. It is curious that both camboxes had the name 'Romeo' cast into them, with no mention of 'Alfa'. The cars were built by SA Nicola Romeo, so strictly they could be called Romeo, but it also raises the interesting possibility that Nicola Romeo paid for the P2s from his own pocket and the cars were not funded from the resources of the company. This is only surmise and there is no surviving evidence on the matter, but in the circumstances of the company at that time, it remains a possibility. Nicola Romeo always seemed to have a particular interest in the P2s and was always present when they raced in 1924 and 1925.

The P2 was designed and built at Portello in conditions of the utmost secrecy and no one, apart from those immediately involved with the car, knew that it existed. While the P2 project burgeoned, a team of the uprated RL Targas was being prepared for the 1924 Targa Florio. Three cars were entered by SA Nicola Romeo, and a fourth car was entered privately by Giulio Masetti. The three works entries were driven by Ascari, Campari and the French veteran grand prix driver Louis Wagner. The race was held on 27 April, and after the poor entry of 1923 was back to its full glory with a field of 41 cars. The quality was also high: Fiat sent two Tipo 805s and Mercedes ran a team of three of its new 2-litre GP cars. In addition there were works-entered GP Ballots and also factory entries from Hispano-Suiza, Peugeot, Itala and Steyr. Unusually for the Targa Florio, race day was hot and dry, so instead of mud the drivers had to cope with dust.

At the end of the first lap Masetti, profiting from his experience, led from the exotic tulipwood-bodied Hispano-Suiza of André Dubonnet, the aperitif heir; Ascari was fourth. On lap two Werner, in the leading Mercedes, accelerated and went to the front, pursued by Ascari, while Masetti and Campari were fourth and fifth, so the chances for Alfa Romeo looked bright, as the supercharged Mercedes was not expected to last the distance. At three laps the order remained, and on the start of the fourth and last lap Werner had a lead of 2 minutes, but Ascari was making up time. Werner was ahead on the road, so finished first and then had to stand, watching the clock, wondering if Ascari could make up the deficit. As the RL reached the last corner, in sight of the finish, the engine seized and Ascari and his mechanic, Giulio Ramponi, jumped out and began to push the car towards the line, cheered on by the crowd. The clock ticked away the vital seconds while they pushed and the waiting Werner knew that he had won. Before Ascari and Ramponi, straining and sweating, could reach the line, Masetti had finished, so Ascari pushed home into third place and once again had lost the race within sight of the line. The RL Targas had finished second and third, while Campari brought his RL home in fifth place. Wagner lost a lot of time when he knocked down a soldier who had rushed into the path of his car, but finished tenth.

A month later, on 25 May, Enzo Ferrari ran an RL Targa that he had entered in the Circuito del Savio at Ravenna, run over 25 laps of the 8.9-mile (14.3km) circuit. The cars were started at intervals, but against the clock, and Ferrari led all the way. In second place, two laps behind, was a new driver, Tazio Nuvolari, with a 1500cc Chiribiri. Nuvolari was dividing his time between racing cars and motor cycles and was to become the Italian motor cycle champion for 1924. A week later Ferrari was out again in the Circuito del Polesine, a 15-lap, 185-mile (297km) race held on a circuit between Ferrara and Padua, and once again his RL Targa won easily, chased home as before by Nuvolari.

The new P2 was tested at Monza on 3 June, and with almost no publicity, still unpainted and in bare aluminium, it was entered for the Circuito di Cremona on 9 June, driven by Ascari with Luigi Bazzi as his riding mechanic. The Cremona race was unusual: a five-lap race, it was run over an imperial distance of 200 miles (321km). Campari, with an RL Targa, and Nuvolari, again with his Chiribiri, were Ascari's greatest rivals, but both dropped out and the P2 gained its first victory. It dominated the race, winning by a remarkable margin of two laps and finishing nearly 54 minutes ahead of the second-placed car. Ascari's average speed was 98.31mph (158.08kmh). Part of the 40-mile (64km) lap was a straight of 10km over which the cars were timed. Campari did 178kmh (110.5mph), but the P2 was timed at 195kmh (121.09mph).

Now it was Campari's turn to try the new car and on 13 July he was sent down to Pescara, on the Adriatic coast, where the Coppa Acerbo was being held, the first in a series of famous races on the long triangular circuit that ran through the mountains, and with the fast straight beside the sea. Unfortunately it did not turn out quite as intended. Reports differ as to what befell Campari and the P2. He was in the lead when one report states that the gearbox broke, another that he burst a tyre and, having no spare, carried on the rim but stopped at his pit and retired as he had lost too much time. Enzo Ferrari gained a win he probably did not expect, with his faithful RL Targa. The continuing successes of the RL cars, often against strong opposition, must have given some comfort to Merosi.

The scene was now set for the P2's début in racing at the highest level, with the Grand Prix de l'ACF (the French Grand Prix), held at Lyon on 3 August. Six P2s had been built and Alfa Corse entered four to be driven by Ascari, Campari, Louis Wagner and Ferrari; the latter's performances in recent races had undoubtedly secured his place as a front-line grand prix driver. The Lyon race was run over part of the circuit used for the 1914 Grand Prix some 12 miles (19km) south of Lyon; the circuit was 14.4 miles (23.12km), and the race was of 35 laps, a distance of 503.4 miles (809.5km).

The Alfa Corse team travelled from Milan to Lyon by train. Known in their brown overalls as 'The Brown Men', they soon became very popular with the other teams and were noted for their cheerful and friendly demeanour. The official practice was held from Friday 18 until Tuesday 22 July between 5.00am and 8.30am. After that, further practising on the circuit was forbidden, so the teams all frequented the same straight stretch of Route Nationale for testing and checking their cars. In addition to the P2s, the team had brought a P1, which was used on the circuit for establishing the correct gear ratios for the race. The Alfa Romeos were running on Pirelli 31-5 balloon tyres, all were painted a dark red, and had the *quadrifolio* on the bonnet. The cars of Campari and Wagner had pointed tails, but Ascari's had a cut-off tail with the spare wheel mounted on it.

Practice showed that it was a hard circuit and would need a tough car and driver to last the distance. Enzo Ferrari did a few practice laps with Bazzi as his riding mechanic, then decided that he did not feel equal to the demands of the race. He went home to Italy immediately by train, not waiting for the race, and his car was withdrawn from the entry list. The true reason for his defection has never been established, but it seems most likely that he was still badly affected by the death of Sivocci who, in some ways, had been a father figure. This left the Alfa Romeo team with three cars.

The Grand Prix on Sunday 3 August was the climax to a four-day meeting that included races for motor cycles, cycle cars, pedal cyclists and touring cars on the preceding days. The weather for the race day was superb as the cars lined up on a two-by-two grid for a mass start, and the drivers were lectured on their driving by Surcoeuf, the secretary of the meeting. This irritated some of the drivers, there were humorous interruptions and Dario Resta revved up his Sunbeam as the 'Marseillaise' was played. Then the field lined up and was led to the line by motor cyclists; as the cars crossed

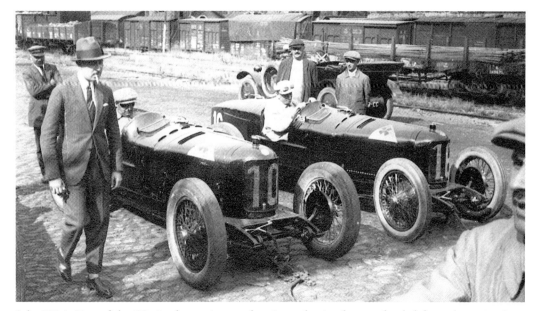

July 1924: Two of the P2s in the station yard at Lyon, having been unloaded from the train. Jano looks round on the right of the photo.

the flag was dropped for a rolling start.

Practice had shown that the Sunbeams were the fastest cars, and Segrave's own

Sunbeam went into the lead with Ascari a few lengths behind. Pietro Bordino now put on a spurt with his Fiat 805 and passed

July 1924: The P2s of Ascari and Wagner are towed out for practice at Lyon behind a crowded RL.

August 1924: Campari's P2 is checked over before the French Grand Prix. The driver stands behind his car.

Ascari. Segrave continued to lead but Bordino went in front as the Sunbeam stopped at the pits with a defective magneto at the end of the third lap. Ascari was keeping station with Bordino while Guinness's Sunbeam was battling with Campari for third place. During his duel with Guinness, Campari set a new lap record at 72.94mph (117.28km). Perhaps being pushed too hard by Ascari, Bordino's

3 August 1924: The P2 team lines up. No 10 is Campari, No 19 is Ferrari's car, though he is not sitting in it, No 16 is Wagner and No 3 is Ascari. (John Maitland Collection)

brakes now began to fade and he overshot a corner on lap nine, which let Ascari take the lead. He was not there for long, however, as Bordino, despite the brakes, came back at him and took the lead again. He held it for two laps but eventually had to stop as the brakes were beyond redemption. The Fiat challenge was broken and Ascari was in front, followed by Guinness, who had a 20-second advantage over Campari.

The direct wheel-to-wheel encounter on the road was something of a novelty to the Italian drivers, who had been brought up in a world where they usually raced against the clock, but they were showing that they were naturals in this new racing environment. Ascari now made his refuelling stop, and while in the pits was passed by Guinness, Campari and Divo's Delage, so close was the racing. Guinness then stopped for fuel, so Campari was the new leader. As Campari and Divo refuelled, Ascari resumed his lead on lap 20. A lap later, Guinness was out with bearing failure and the P2s were in first and second place, running together with Ascari in front, then for a while Campari took the lead on lap 27. Divo was chasing the Italian pair in his Delage, but not making much impression, and it seemed that the Alfa Romeos were going to gain a crushing victory.

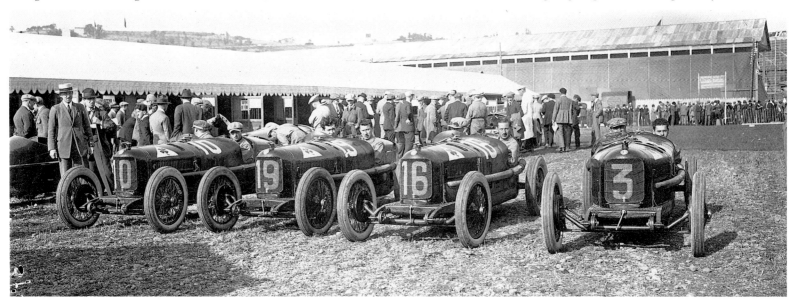

3 August 1924, Lyon: Ramponi pushes Ascari's P2 in vain – the cylinder head has cracked. (Guy Griffiths Collection)

3 August 1924, Lyon: On his way to victory, Campari sweeps through Le Virage des Esses. (John Maitland Collection)

However, the race was not yet over and all was not well with Ascari's P2, which was audibly losing its tune and slowing; on lap 32 he came into the pits with a very hot engine. Giulio Ramponi, his riding mechanic, changed all the plugs and much water was added to the radiator. Ominously, water was running from the exhaust pipe as Ramponi, and then Ascari himself, tried to restart the engine on the handle. Ramponi then tried to push-start the car, but it was no use, the cylinder head was cracked and Ascari's race was run, only two laps and 28 miles away from victory after 6½ hours of racing.

Campari was now in front, but still the outcome was not certain as Albert Divo had found more speed, no doubt realising that if one P2 could fail, so could the other. However, Campari held on and crossed the line 66 seconds in front of the Delage after over 7 hours of racing. Wagner had gone steadily in the third P2, never running lower than sixth, and he finished in fourth place behind Benoist's Delage.

3 August 1924: Campari has won the GP de l'ACF. A Lyon sausage is on the bonnet and Charles Faroux (with armband), the famous French journalist, offers congratulations: Rimini (in boater) is telling Campari how it was done. Marinoni, Campari's riding mechanic, is between Faroux and Rimini.

3 August 1924: Ascari and Campari feel the quality of the Coupe Hartford. Campari, the winner, looks less happy than Ascari, who has lost. Rimini (in boater) shows his delight.

The victorious Campari and his riding mechanic Marinoni were mobbed by a jubilant team. A huge sausage, an enormous specimen of the local speciality, was draped across the bonnet of the P2, champagne flowed liberally; and Campari received the Coupe Hartford, presented to the winner by the shock absorber manufacturer. From being a small provincial firm almost unknown outside Italy, in a few short hours Alfa Romeo had become the leading motor racing company in Europe; henceforth the name would command awe and respect in the motor racing world. A happy team loaded the P2s on to the train in Lyon for the journey back to Milan.

The Alfa Corse team did not send the P2s to the Gran Premio d'España at San Sebastian on 25 September, so Segrave gained the victory that had eluded him at Lyon; in second place was a T35 Bugatti, a team of which had run at Lyon but had been held back by tyre and wheel problems. With this car and its derivatives, Bugatti was about to start a climb to the pinnacles of grand prix racing and would soon be a formidable opponent to Alfa Romeo.

Alfa had shunned the Spanish race as it was reserving its energies for the Gran Premio d'Italia on home ground at Monza, which should have been run on Sunday 7 September. Practice began on 2 September and during the first morning Salamano, driving an 805 Fiat, had a slight accident and hurt his arm. His team mate Bordino must have indulged in some over-energetic driving, as he aggravated an old arm injury, so as the Fiat team found itself with a driver shortage it was withdrawn from the race before the end of the first day of practice. Mercedes had entered a team of four eight-cylinder cars designed by Ferdinand Porsche. The first arrived at Monza late in the afternoon of the first day, carried by a transporter converted from a large touring car. It was tested as soon as it arrived and came into the pits shrouded in steam as the bronze cylinder head castings were porous. Mercedes told the organisers, Reale Automobile-Club d'Italia (RACI), that the cars were unfit to race and they were going home. Therefore, by the end of the first day of practice the entry had been so diminished that the RACI decided that, to hold a race of any significance, it would have to postpone it until Sunday 19 October. Mercedes had indicated that the cars would have new welded steel cylinders and water jackets by then, and the Fiat drivers were also expected to be fit.

Mercedes produced four cars when the teams assembled for the race, but there was no sign of Fiat. No reason has ever been established for their defection but it is likely that they knew they were not fast enough to beat the P2s and a crushing defeat in front of the Italian crowd could not be contemplated. The field was therefore still thin for the 497-mile (799km) race. Four P2s were entered for Ascari, Campari, Wagner and Ferdinando Minoia. Minoia had driven 'works' Mercedes, Steyr and Benz in the two previous seasons and had raced an

The Lyon victory was soon advertised.

Isotta-Fraschini in the Targa Florio as early as 1907. He was known as a steady, rather than a fiery driver. As reserve driver, Alfa Corse nominated Cesare Pastore, who had driven a Fiat 805 at Lyon and was now

unemployed. There was no car for Enzo Ferrari, who seemed to have retired from the sport for the time being. The P2s were racing against three Roland-Pillains, four Mercedes and two Chiribiris; the other

October 1924: Ascari and Ramponi sit in their P2 at the scrutineering at Monza.

October 1924: The Monza paddock during practice for the GP d'Italia: No 9 is Wagner's P2, No 1 is Ascari's and No 5 Campari's. No 6 is Neubauer's Mercedes.

French teams had stayed away. They too knew that their chances of beating the Alfa Romeos were slim.

The postponement, and perhaps the lack of Fiats, must have been a discouragement, because despite the fine autumn day, it was only a small crowd that turned up at 10.00am to watch Ascari take the lead from the start and stay there for the full 80 laps. He was chased by Masetti's Mercedes for two laps, but then the other three P2s swept past and the Alfa Romeos moved into the first four places. While Ascari carried on serenely in front, the other Alfa Romeos swapped places, although at half distance they had settled down in the order Wagner, Campari and Minoia. At his refuelling stop, Campari handed his car over to Pastore. The Mercedes were fast but were unable to offer any challenge to the Alfa Romeos, the drivers finding that they handled treacherously. Just after half distance Count Zborowski crashed his Mercedes on the Lesmo bend and was killed, although his accident was subsequently attributed to a

19 October 1924: The P2 team wait for the parade before the start.

patch of oil on the track, rather than the handling. Max Sailer, the Mercedes director, flagged down the two surviving cars of Werner and Neubauer, which left the P2s to cruise home to a overwhelming 1–2–3–4 victory, with Ascari leading Wagner, Pastore and Minoia. The jubilation of the team was slightly subdued by the knowledge of Zborowski's death, but they knew that in one season they had become the acknowledged champions of the grand prix world and had humbled teams whose racing experience went back to the beginning of the century.

It was expected that in 1925 the opposition would seek its revenge, so the laurels were not sat upon at Portello. There was also a bigger prize to aim for, as a World Grand Prix Championship had been instituted. This would comprise the grand prix races at Spa, Montlhéry and Monza and the Indianapolis 500.

During the winter, at the suggestion of Ascari, Jano tested the P2 on 'Elcosina' fuel, an ethyl-alcohol mixture. The supercharger

19 October 1924: Ascari has won the GP d'Italia. From left to right: Ramponi; the infant Alberto Ascari; a delighted Antonio Ascari; and a capped and gloved Nicola Romeo. (Guy Griffiths Collection)

now blew into Memini carburettors, each one serving four cylinders, which produced very useful results, pushing the output from 142 to 154bhp. Armed with this extra power, the P2s went forth again in 1925, in other respects little changed, though the brakes were enlarged.

For the new season there was one fundamental change in the regulations of grand prix racing: in future riding mechanics would be banned. The riding mechanic was a relic of the days of open road races in the earliest days of the sport and the ban was wholly sensible, as all too often the mechanic came off worst in an accident. It had been the job of the mechanic to keep an eye on the following traffic, so now a rear view mirror became compulsory. As there was no longer a need for a mechanic's seat, Jano replaced this with the oil tank, which had previously been in the scuttle. The space in the scuttle was now filled with an extra 5-gallon (22.5-litre) fuel tank to give the car a greater range.

The first victory of the season was gained by Guido Ginaldi when he won the Coppa Acerbo at Pescara with an RL, after Materassi had retired from the race in his Itala with incurable tyre problems. That was a week before the first engagement for Alfa Corse and the P2s, on the new Spa-Francorchamps circuit in the Belgian Ardennes. The 1925 circuit bore little resemblance to the circuit used until the 1970s, parts of which are still used for the Grand Prix de Belgique. Although the outline of the road remained the same through the years, in 1925 it was narrow

1925: The P2 engine with the supercharger now blowing through the pair of Memini carburettors.

and poorly surfaced, and the line of most of the corners was much sharper. Here the first Grand Prix de Belgique was held on 28 June 1925, a race that was also granted the honorary title of 'Grand Prix d'Europe'.

Grand prix racing had dropped away sharply from the high point of Lyon the previous year. At Lyon six factory teams had entered and there had been 20 starters. Perhaps the opposition was becoming awed by the apparent invincibility of the Alfa Corse team. The Sunbeam and Bugatti teams were entered but did not turn up – no reason was given for the absence of the Sunbeams, but Ettore Bugatti said he could not afford to come! This reduced the field to seven runners, so it became a straight fight between the three P2s and the four works V-12 Delages over 54 laps of the 9.31-mile (14.97km) circuit, a total distance of 502.74 miles (808.42km).

In practice it was noticed that the Alfa

Romeo mechanics gave very little attention to their cars, unlike the Delage rivals who were working continuously and making many adjustments. The Belgian crowd showed a strong preference for the Delage team, which was cheered loudly when the cars formed up on the starting grid, while the P2s were greeted with silence. The Alfa Romeo drivers were Ascari, Campari and Gastone Brilli Perri. Brilli Perri, a 32-year-old Florentine nobleman, had raced regularly in Italian events since 1919 and had been a driver for the Steyr team as well as driving a Fiat. The three P2s had the bob-tailed body with the spare wheel behind.

Ascari took the lead immediately from Campari, while Benoist with the leading Delage was third in front of Brilli Perri, but a

lap later the first Delage was out, Benoist's fuel tank having split. Woe piled upon woe for Delage as Paul Torchy also went out on the next lap. Meanwhile Ascari was pulling away. After five laps he was 40 seconds in front of Campari and over 3 minutes ahead of Divo's Delage, which had passed Brilli Perri. Further misfortune now struck the Delage team as René Thomas's car caught fire. To wipe some of the smiles off the Alfa Corse faces and to dispel complacency, Brilli Perri had been forced to retire on lap 18 with a broken rear spring, possibly caused by the indifferent road surface.

The V-12 Delages had been improved during the winter with the fitting of twin superchargers. A number of authorities, including Laurence Pomeroy in *The Grand*

28 June 1925: Campari waits in his P2 before the start of the GP de Belgique at Spa-Francorchamps. Brilli Perri's car is behind, while Giorgio Rimini and Nicola Romeo are on the extreme right.

Prix Car, suggest that a fundamental error was made as no relief valve was included in the induction pipe. It was reported that back pressure held the inlet valves open and the pistons took a toll of the valves. It is difficult to argue with such an authority as Pomeroy, but this seems technically improbable. Whatever the reason, Divo kept going until half distance, then stopped. The two surviving P2s roared on faultlessly to win, with Ascari leading Campari home by 22 minutes, after 6hr 42min 57sec on the road.

As a gesture of confidence in the team, during the race Jano had a table laid on the track in front of the Alfa Romeo pit and ate his lunch in full view of the jeering and unappreciative crowd, who understandably found the demonstration of Alfa Romeo supremacy somewhat boring. During their refuelling stops Ascari and Campari were invited to join him for a hasty snack; presumably Nicola Romeo, who attended the race and had probably paid for the meal anyway, made up the party. When the team returned to Milan they had a triumphal procession through the city reminiscent of the triumphs of the Roman Emperors. Mussolini ordered aircraft of the Regia Aeronautica to fly over the procession, scattering flowers upon it.

Meanwhile the Delage team went home after Spa and worked very hard as they had four weeks to make the cars fit to uphold French honour in the Grand Prix de l'ACF. This was to be a complete breakaway from tradition, being held on the new combined artificial road and track course at Montlhéry about 20 miles (30km) south-west of Paris on 26 July. The race was over 80 laps of the artificial road circuit and also used half of the banked track, the distance being 621.37 miles, or virtually 1000km. This time the Sunbeams and Bugattis came to battle with the Delages and the P2 Alfa Romeos, which were being driven again by Ascari, Campari and Brilli Perri.

During practice Brilli Perri rolled his P2 but was unhurt and the car was repaired in time for the race. There was litigious drama the evening before the race. During practice the five T35 Bugattis ran with a cowl over the passenger's seat, something forbidden by the regulations. The Delage team had wanted to do the same thing, but had already checked with the ACF and been told that the cowls were illegal, so they lodged a protest. Ettore Bugatti said he would withdraw the cars if he was forced to remove the cowl. Eventually a compromise was reached and the offending cowls were partially cut back.

The race began at 8.00am with a rolling start led by a Peugeot and a Mathis saloon. De Vizcaya's Bugatti initially led the field of 14, but halfway round the first lap it was almost inevitable that Ascari was in front, and at the end of the lap he led from Divo's Delage and Masetti's Sunbeam. Campari was fifth behind Wagner's Delage and Brilli Perri was seventh. On the next lap, Campari and Brilli Perri had moved up to second and third, but then Brilli Perri lost his place to Wagner and came into the pits for a plug change, which dropped him right to the back of the field.

The two P2s were now firmly in the lead when, on the tenth lap, a light rain began to fall. Ascari signalled – by cutting his engine as he passed the pits – that he would come in on the next lap. He stopped for 2min 8sec while the rear wheels were changed, but restarted before Campari went by. Campari now made his stop, taking 2min 29sec and being kept at the pit longer than intended while an official insisted that the tools were cleared from the track before the Alfa Romeo restarted. This slight hold-up let Benoist's Delage up into second place, but Ascari continued to extend his lead.

Towards the end of lap 22 Ascari came round the long, fast left-hand bend at the end of the straight before the course rejoined the banked track. He skidded, probably caused by the wet road, and as he corrected the skid the left front hub cap of the P2 caught in the paling fence that lined the track. The car tore down over 100 metres of fence, dug into the soft earth at the side of the road and overturned. Ascari was thrown out and the car rolled over his

26 July 1925: Ascari's P2 after his fatal crash in the GP de l'ACF at Montlhéry. (Ludvigsen Library)

legs and ended upside down across the track. He was grievously hurt and was rushed to an army ambulance, which set off for Paris, but he died of his injuries during the journey.

Campari had passed Benoist, who was in his pit at the time of the accident, and he carried on in the lead, knowing that Ascari had crashed but not realising the gravity. On lap 41 Campari made another pit stop. When told of Ascari's death he climbed out of the car and went behind the pit to hide his grief. Brilli Perri now made a routine stop and Nicola Romeo decided that the team could not continue to race, so the cars were withdrawn. The engines of both cars were revved to peak revs and switched off; then the cars were pushed away. The tragic race ran its course and the

Delages took first and second places. When Benoist, the winner, received the victor's garlands, he drove his Delage round the course and laid them at the place where Ascari had crashed.

The team's homecoming to Milan was very different from the joyous celebration four weeks earlier. The whole city was in mourning when the funeral of Antonio Ascari was held on Thursday 30 July. The team formed part of the cortège that carried him to the Cimitero Monumentale, not far from Portello. Antonio Ascari was 37 years old, and his widow was accompanied to the cemetery by his seven-year-old son, Alberto, who would eventually achieve a

racing glory that would even eclipse that of his father.

Alfa Romeo grieved for Ascari but the world went on. The team was entered for the Gran Premio d'Italia at Monza on 6 September with cars for Campari and Brilli Perri. There was discussion about filling Ascari's place, and during practice for the Gran Premio several drivers were given a trial. One of these was Tazio Nuvolari, who set off in a P2 at a colossal pace, but after a few laps he lost control and overturned the car. He escaped with cracked ribs and his driving for Alfa Romeo was postponed for the time being. As none of the trialists matched up to the team's needs, Ascari's

6 September 1925: Campari waits for the start of the GP d'Italia at Monza in his P2. (John Maitland Collection)

place was taken by the American driver Peter de Paolo, who was of Sicilian origin and spoke a form of Brooklyn Italian. His P2 was looked after by Giulio Ramponi, Ascari's riding mechanic in 1924. The Delage team entered but then scratched, but there were two Diattos and, more unusual, two Duesenbergs from the United States.

Duesenberg was not unfamiliar with European racing as Jimmy Murphy's 3-litre car had won the 1921 French Grand Prix. The cars entered for Monza were 122s, one of which had already won the Indianapolis 500 in May 1925 driven by de Paolo, so Duesenberg was still in with an outside chance of winning the Championship. The Monza entries were driven by Tommy Milton and Peter Kries, and a third car was to have been driven by de Paolo, but as it was not ready he was available for the P2 drive. To comply with European regulations, dummy two-seat body shells were fitted over the cars' normal single-seat

bodies at the Isotta-Fraschini factory. In 1926 the grand prix formula was changed to a limit of 1½ litres, and in anticipation of this Ettore Bugatti had entered five T39s, which were T35s reduced to 1½ litres; two 1500cc Chiribiris kept the Bugattis company. Practice showed that the American challenge was significant as the Duesenbergs were fast and their centrifugal superchargers were suited to Monza's fast curves.

To the surprise of the crowd, and probably of the racing teams too, Kries made a superb start from the second row of the grid and took his Duesenberg into the lead. He stayed there for two laps, then slid off the road at Lesmo, which left Campari in front, probably much to the relief of the partisan crowd and the Alfa Corse team. Campari was followed by Brilli Perri and de Paolo, while Milton, who had lost all the gears but top at the start, managed to get his Duesenberg up to fourth place. Milton was not giving up and passed de Paolo on lap

10 to take third place. When the P2s came in to refuel on laps 33 and 34, Milton took the lead and stayed there until he stopped for fuel on lap 39; his stop was slow and his getaway was difficult with only one gear, so he dropped back to third behind de Paolo. Campari's stop had been prolonged as there were ignition bothers, so Brilli Perri, who had made a very rapid stop, now took the lead. Milton's chances now faded as he had to make another stop to replace a broken oil pipe, which took 20 minutes.

When Campari's car restarted it was taken over by Giovanni Minozzi who now started working very hard to make up lost ground. He drove so well that he had taken third place from Milton during the Duesenberg's protracted stop, so the P2s were now running 1–2–3. It looked set fair for an Alfa Romeo clean sweep, but on lap 73 de Paolo came into the pits for a long stop to replace a broken exhaust pipe and slipped back to fifth, being passed by Costantini, with one of the T39 Bugattis, and Milton. Brilli Perri was flagged off as the winner after 5hr 14min 33.3sec of racing; 20 minutes later the Campari/Minozzi P2

6 September 1925 GP d'Italia: The start, with Campari (P2), Albert Guyot (Rolland-Pilain) and Emilio Materassi (Diatto) on the front row. The white Duesenbergs can be seen behind.

finished in second place, with de Paolo fifth behind the Bugatti and the Duesenberg. The victory secured the World Grand Prix Championship for Alfa Romeo and the company received a splendid gold trophy to mark the triumph. Henceforth the marque's badge would be surrounded with a laurel wreath in honour of this feat. There was one more grand prix, the Spanish event at San Sebastian, but Alfa Corse had not entered, probably as it did not count for the Championship, and the Delage team took the first three places.

While Alfa Romeo had been triumphant on the race track, in the commercial world it had been a rather different story. In 1924 production of the RL variants, and the smaller four-cylinder version, the RM, was 690, and in 1925 this rose to 1109, but the company was still in financial difficulties. Even though Mussolini was now using Alfa Romeos as his official cars, BNC was losing confidence in Nicola Romeo's abilities to manage the industrial conglomerate, and

during 1924 the locomotive factory at Saronno and the rolling-stock plant in Rome and Naples were sold off. On 22 March 1925 BNC, as the controlling shareholder, removed Romeo from the post of general manager and appointed him to be one of a management committee of three, with Ambrogio Molteni and Carlo Fachini. Romeo was declared to be nominal president, but without any powers.

On 21 October the new management committee decided that the company would withdraw from motor racing and the funds saved would be invested in a development programme of new models. With the change in the grand prix formula this was a sound commercial decision, as the P2 was superseded and a team of new cars would have been necessary. On 31 December 1925 BNC decreed that the company would in future concentrate solely on car, lorry and aero engine manufacturing. Pasquale Gallo, a BNC nominee, was appointed managing director.

Gallo had already been used by BNC to put the Itala company back on its feet after a financial disaster. At Alfa Romeo he made his first task the removal of Romeo's team of supporters. Eduardo Fucito was the first to go, followed by Giorgio Rimini. Gallo was now in sole charge, but on 6 November 1926 the Government created the Istituto di Liquidazione, which was charged with taking over all the assets controlled by BNC. The progression towards full government control, which had begun when the Alfa Romeo assets had been controlled by BNC, was now completed and SA Ing Nicola Romeo & C was effectively nationalised. Gallo himself now fell foul of his Fascist masters, not being a Fascist Party member but a member of the Liberal Party. By the beginning of 1927 the eruptions within Alfa Romeo seem to have left the management in the hands of Molteni and Fachini as the government nominees; Nicola Romeo was still a shareholder, but no longer had any control over the company.

Chapter 4

Busy interlude

WHEN HE JOINED Alfa Romeo in the autumn of 1923, Jano had been given two directives. Apart from the P2, he had also been required to put in hand the design of a new series of road cars that would replace the Merosi productions, which were now rapidly becoming obsolete. His brief was to produce a touring car with sporting aspirations that would capitalise on the racing successes of the firm and would also be a practical commercial proposition. The outcome was one of the great designs of the inter-war years.

Jano designed a car that was a very happy halfway house between the small economy cars that were now coming on to the market in large numbers and the larger luxury and sporting cars. He produced a six-cylinder 62mm x 82mm 1487cc engine with a single overhead camshaft driven from the rear of the engine, the crankshaft being carried in five main bearings. The chassis was conventional but well balanced with rod-operated four-wheel brakes. The prototype chassis was shown at the Milan Salon in April 1925, but production was slow to

start, perhaps delayed by the managerial problems, and only six more prototypes were produced in 1926. In 1927 production began properly and 356 cars were made. The next development of the 6C-1500, during 1928, was the introduction of a sporting version that had a detachable cylinder head with twin overhead camshafts. This sports engine developed 54bhp.

Although the company had turned its back on grand prix racing, this had not killed off the passion for motor racing. To satisfy the political masters, the P2s had allegedly been sold and were now nominally in private hands. On 28 March 1926 two cars driven by Gastone Brilli Perri and Giovanni Bonmartini came second and third in the 40-lap 186-mile (300km) Premio Reale di Roma behind the T35 Bugatti of Count Maggi. The field was full of T35 Bugattis, and at half distance Brilli Perri took the lead, but with two laps to go he stopped with a puncture. As an indication that the factory still had an especially close interest in the cars, the wheel was changed by Ramponi, who was managing the pit; unfortunately the stop lost time and the P2 was passed on the last lap by Maggi's Bugatti. At half distance Bonmartini handed over his P2 to Attilio Marinoni, Campari's former riding mechanic, another pointer to the factory's interest.

Once in production, the 6C-1500 entered competition and in its first race on 5 June 1927, the Circuit of Modena sports

1925: This scene at the start of the 1925 Targa Florio captures the atmosphere of the race at that time.

car event, it won the 1500cc class driven by Enzo Ferrari, who had taken up competition driving again. His relationship with Portello must have been as good as ever, for it was rumoured that his car used the prototype twin-cam engine for this event.

The P2s were given some outings again in 1927. The changes of driver and the infrequent appearances all seem to point to the cars still being factory owned, though when the Fascist masters enquired about it, probably much ado was made of the cars being privately owned and being prepared at Portello by the factory mechanics 'at the customer's expense'. Count Maggi abandoned his usual Bugatti and shipped a P2 from Genoa to Tripoli for the Gran Premio di Tripoli at the beginning of the season, on 6 March. The effort was not rewarded as he stopped after two laps with a broken throttle linkage while lying second. It was reported that he had bought the car from Portello, but Tripoli was his only outing with it and it seems possible he may have hired it for the race. It was more like old times on 6 August when Campari turned up with a P2 at the Coppa Acerbo on the very fast Pescara circuit. It was a very hot day but this did not affect the car or the driver, who won the 20-lap 316-mile (509km) race by an enormous margin, finishing over a lap in front of his nearest opponent.

The 1500cc grand prix formula had not been a great success, getting very little support from manufacturers. Delage swept the board and the only opposition came from Bugatti and the Talbots of the Sunbeam Talbot Darracq combine. The fields had been pitifully small and the 370-mile (594km) Grand Prix d'Europe at Monza on 4 September had only six starters. The RACI, realising that the Grand Prix would not attract many paying customers with such a paltry entry, ran the Gran Premio di Milano on the same day. This was run in many five-lap heats (31 miles/50km) and a five-lap final. The heats were run before the GP d'Europe and the final was the finale of the day.

Unfortunately it was a very wet day so the crowds stayed away anyway. Campari ran a P2 in the 2-litre heat and came second, 2 seconds behind Maggi, who seemed to have abandoned the P2 and gone back to his T35C Bugatti. The 1500cc heat was won by a remarkable car, a new Tipo 806 Fiat, which had a V-12 (or more accurately a double-six) engine. This was intended to be Fiat's contender for the 1½-litre formula, though it seemed rather pointless as the formula was to change only four months later, and the Monza race was its only outing. In the final, Maggi led from Campari, but then the Fiat, driven by Bordino, went past both of them and won easily, while Campari pulled away from Maggi to take second place.

In 1928 production of the old RL series finished, but the 6C-1500s were leaving Portello steadily and in that year 527 were produced. By now the competition successes were almost commonplace and the 6C-1500 Sport was the essential equipment for the well-to-do young Italian with motor sporting aspirations. Jano now introduced another development, and in the Mille Miglia on 31 March 1928 Campari, with Ramponi as his co-driver, ran a supercharged 6C. The engine was moved back in the frame to make room for the Roots supercharger, and the engine developed 76bhp at 4800rpm. The car, which became known as the MMS (Mille Miglia Speciàle) model, won the race outright, while the first seven places were taken by the 6C in the 1500cc class.

The 1500cc grand prix formula finished at the end of 1927. It had been dominated by the eight-cylinder Delage, one of the greatest racing cars of all time, but grand prix racing was almost dying on its feet by the end of the 1927 season, and if the formula had been extended there would have been no fields at all. The Commission Sportive International (CSI) now made an inspired move by introducing a new formula with maximum and minimum weight limits. This was almost universally ignored, but in reality it was an open invitation from the CSI to race organisers to run grands prix as formula libre races where there was no restriction on what could race. The effect was that cars from the 1922–24 2-litre formula could run in grands prix again, so the P2 was promoted to become a front-line racing car once more.

When the entry list for the 1928 Targa Florio was published there was a surprise, for in the list there were two cars entered by Alfa Corse. There had been official entries of the 6C-1500 in sports car events, and particularly the Mille Miglia, but an entry in a pure racing car event indicated a change of policy. The other surprise was the choice of car. Instead of the P2, the 6C-1500 MMS was selected, though there was wisdom in this decision as a lighter, more nimble car would probably be better suited to the unusual conditions of the Madonie circuit. The drivers were Campari and Marinoni, who was now being promoted from the left-hand mechanic's seat to the right-hand driver's seat.

The two MMSs faced a tough task as the bulk of the field was made up of T35C and T35B Bugattis, the power output of the latter being probably double that of the MMS. The race was run on 6 May, which was fine and dry, so dust rather than mud was the hazard. The MMSs ran in the 1500cc class, which was flagged away first at 2-minute intervals. At the end of the first lap Divo, now with a T35B Bugatti, led, but in second place, also driving a T35B, was Elizabeth Junek, still regarded by many as the greatest woman racing driver of all. Campari was third behind Mme Junek. On the next lap the formidable Czech lady took the lead from Divo. Campari also passed Divo and was about 20 seconds behind Mme Junek. Campari then forged on and pulled out a minute lead over Divo and Junek by the end of lap three. He was still leading at the beginning of the fifth and final lap, but then he punctured a tyre and had to drive about 12 miles (20km) on the rim before he could change it. With a full complement of tyres he now drove all out to finish the lap and make up lost time, but it was too late and Divo beat him by just 97 seconds. Mme Junek also had mechanical troubles and was fifth. Marinoni's MMS had dropped out on the fourth lap, but the result justified the choice of the MMS, and for Jano it must have been particularly gratifying as it showed that even against pure racing cars his improved sports car was more than competitive.

The decision to let Alfa Corse enter racing cars again must have had a political origin. As another factor, the economic stringencies that had partly brought about the previous curtailment were easing. Campari was entered by Alfa Corse in the Circuito di Mugello with a P2 on 6 June. He set fastest lap but then fell out with fuel feed problems. Alfa Romeo honour was upheld by Enzo Ferrari with an MMS; he came second and was now getting back into the form he had shown five years before. Just to confuse the issue, Campari now entered a P2 in the Circuito di Cremona under his own name. He finished sixth and last, badly delayed by punctures, but received a special award for setting the fastest speed over the measured 10km speed trap on the long straight. He was timed at over 135mph (217kmh), so the P2 was as fast as ever. On 4 August it all came right for Campari in the Coppa Acerbo at Pescara. Driving the P2, again entered in his name, he walked away from the rest of the field, winning by 8 minutes. During the 20-lap race he made four pit stops, but only one was to refuel – the other three were 'to make himself comfortable and refresh himself', according to an elegantly euphemistic report!

It was reported that after the Pescara race Campari sold the P2 for 75,000 lire, the equivalent of £800 (say £26,000 at today's prices), which again confuses the question of ownership. The buyer was Achille Varzi. Then 24 years old, Varzi had started racing motor cycles in 1923, riding a Garelli, and immediately showed his class, becoming Italian 350cc champion that year. In 1926 he was the national 500cc champion with a Sunbeam, but switched to cars in 1928, starting with a T35C Bugatti. W. F. Bradley described him as 'cold-blooded, methodi-

6 May 1928: Attilio Marinoni makes a pit stop in his 6C-1500 MMS during the Targa Florio. He retired on the fourth lap, but Campari was second in a similar car.

cal, precise'. Varzi's Bugatti was part of the Scuderia Nuvolari, which had been started by Nuvolari for the 1928 season, the third member of the team being Caesare Pastore, who had done a brief stint with a P2 at Monza in 1924. Nuvolari arranged finance for the team and may have owned Varzi's car, though Varzi must have had money in it. Nuvolari was responsible for the preparation of the team cars, but he had more skill as a driver than as a mechanic or mechanical supervisor, and the new team had a poor record of reliability. Varzi broke with Nuvolari, perhaps suspecting that the principal aim of the team was to provide a means of subsidising Nuvolari's racing, and decided to go it alone by buying the P2. Tazio Nuvolari was a proud man and his rejection by Varzi must have wounded him and may have been the reason for their mutual antipathy, which lasted for the rest of their lives. It is an indication of the potential of the four-year-old P2 that Varzi chose it, rather than getting his own Bugatti or one of the new, and increasingly successful, Maseratis.

Apparently without the P2, Campari appeared at the Circuito di Montenero, outside Livorno, on 19 August with an MMS; according to *L'Auto Italiana* it was fitted with a prototype 1700cc engine. In this 10-lap 139-mile (224km) race he started off lying second to Emilio Materassi's 1500cc GP Talbot and was followed by Nuvolari's T35C Bugatti, but eventually the extra power of the Bugatti prevailed and the MMS finished third, though again it had shown that it was quite capable of keeping up with much larger and potentially faster cars.

The major race of the year was the Grand Prix d'Europe at Monza on 9 September. This was the only grand prix in 1928 to be run to the strict terms of the new grand prix formula, with the weight limits imposed, though this probably made no difference to the cars involved. The P2 was entered by Campari, with Varzi as the driver and Campari himself nominated as the second

driver. The race was over 60 laps of the full road and banked circuit, a distance of 373 miles (600km). From the balloted starting grid, 'Williams', the Anglo-French driver with his factory T35B Bugatti, took the lead, followed by Nuvolari's Bugatti and Materassi's Talbot. 'Williams' was out after four laps, and Nuvolari now headed a slip-streaming bunch with Brilli Perri, also driving a GP Talbot, Varzi, and Baconin Borzacchini with a factory 2-litre 8C Maserati. Materassi made a short stop to tighten a loose wheel and was working hard to catch up the leaders again when Brilli Perri dropped back, making the duel three-cornered, but Materassi was up to fifth. On lap 17 Materassi came up to lap some back-markers on the main grandstand straight when he swerved off the course and the Talbot jumped the safety ditch, ploughing into the crowd. Materassi was thrown out and killed, as were 22 spectators.

Despite the horror of the crash, the organisers decided that the race should go on. Nuvolari had slowed with problems, which left Varzi in front, but he was caught by Louis Chiron's T35B blue Bugatti, which started to pull away from the red P2. Chiron stopped for fuel but was away again before Varzi caught up. Varzi now also stopped and handed the car over to Campari, but he had been helping at the scene of the crash and after the horrors he had witnessed had no heart for racing. Campari did five slow laps then came in and handed the car back to Varzi. The race ran out with Chiron as the winner, Varzi second and Nuvolari, who had speeded up again, third. This tragic race was the last major event of the season, and showed that the P2 was still the equal of any car racing, and also that there was now a new star in Varzi.

At a board meeting on 28 May 1928 Nicola Romeo was persuaded to hand over his remaining shares in SA Nicola Romeo to the Istituto di Liquidazione in return for the cancellation or settlement of his debts in other ventures. There is a story, perhaps apocryphal, that he was so bitter at his

treatment that he never rode in an Alfa Romeo again.

Following Romeo's departure at the beginning of 1929, Prospero Gianferrari was appointed managing director of the company. The Fascist Government had militaristic ambitions, and in 1927 the company was given a contract to manufacture Bristol Jupiter aero engines under licence. The nine-cylinder Jupiter developed 400bhp, and in the mid-1920s was one of the main powerplants in service with the RAF, being used in the main British front-line fighters. This engine would offer a similar facility to the growing Regia Aeronautica. Soon Jano received directions to design an original Alfa Romeo aero engine, and within a short time, having taken a close look at the Bristol Jupiter, he produced the nine-cylinder D1 radial design.

Jano also developed the 6C, and the 1700cc engine that had been given a preliminary canter at Livorno went into production in the autumn of 1928. Jano had enlarged the 1500 engine by increasing the bore to 88mm, making the capacity 1752cc. The new car was known as the 6C-1750, with twin camshafts, as the Sport model when unsupercharged, and as the Super Sport when a supercharger was fitted. The chassis was similar to that of the 6C-1500. The production 1750 had a victorious competition début in the 1929 Mille Miglia, driven by Campari and Ramponi, and went on to gain many successes in sports car events during the 1929 season.

Varzi's results in 1928 showed that he was now quite as good as Campari and Nuvolari, then acknowledged as Italy's best drivers, so it was not unexpected when he was signed up by Alfa Corse and entered in the first grand prix of the season, the Gran Premio di Tripoli on 24 March. It was surprising that the race was held. Race day was the tenth anniversary of the founding of the Fasci di Combattimento, the first nucleus of the Fascist Party. To celebrate this Mussolini directed that there should be a plebiscite for the Italian people to sanc-

13 May 1928: *The old RL Targas were still being raced. Here Amedeo Silletti leads a Salmson in the Coppa di Messina at Messina. He finished seventh.*

24 April 1929: *Enzo Ferrari looks cheerful before the start of the Circuito d'Alessandria in his 1750SS, but he retired on lap seven. The stains on the tail indicate that methanol fuel is being used.* (Guy Griffiths Collection)

tion the 'dispersal', or more accurately the ejection, of the last non-Fascist elements from the Italian Parliament chamber. All sporting events were cancelled so that the populace could vote 'Yes' – there was probably no provision for an alternative on the ballot paper – but the Tripoli race was spared as Tripoli was a colony and the population did not have a vote. The drivers must have been allowed, or directed, to cast a postal or proxy vote before joining the Tripoli ferry.

For the first half of the race there was a fierce four-cornered battle between Varzi, the Maserati of Borzacchini, Nuvolari's Bugatti, and Brilli Perri's Talbot, then Varzi had tyre problems, though one report says he was stopped by a split fuel tank.

Varzi had a change of fortune in the Circuito d'Alessandria a month later. It was a fine, dry day and he was never headed, winning the eight-lap 159-mile (255km) race in an impressive manner and coming home nearly 5 minutes in front of Borzacchini's Maserati. Initially, Brilli Perri's Talbot gave the P2 a stern chase, but then it ran out of oil.

For the Targa Florio on 5 May Alfa Corse brought Brilli Perri back into the fold. He was entered, with Varzi and Campari as his team-mates, in a trio of the new 1750 SSs. Campari had an off day; being not as fast as his team-mates and offering no real challenge, while Brilli Perri was the fastest of the trio but never ran higher than fourth until the end of the last lap, when he moved up to third after Borzacchini's Maserati blew up just before the finish. Varzi's engine had broken on the third lap. The relative failure of the Alfa Corse cars in the Targa Florio caused concern at Portello and it may have led to discussions on how the racing programme could be improved.

If the 1750 SS had let the side down in Sicily, the old faithful P2 could still be relied upon to do its stuff. Alfa Corse entered Varzi's car for the Premio Reale di Roma on 26 May; accompanied by a second P2 entered for Gastone Brilli Perri, who found himself back behind the wheel of a P2 after a gap of four years. The race had classes up to and over 2 litres, and Brilli Perri's car had been bored out to 61.5mm, increasing the capacity to 2006cc, taking it into the larger class. Hans Stuck, who was European hill climb champion had entered his Austro-Daimler.

As a specialist in smart getaways, Stuck beat the field as the flag fell and led for two laps, but then Brilli Perri and Varzi swept past and proceeded to run away with the race. Divo and Nuvolari gave chase with their Bugattis, but gradually fell back. It was a 30-lap race, and on lap 21 Varzi came in for fuel. Brilli Perri had hoped to go through without stopping, but with two laps to go he realised that his plan was not going to work and came in to refuel. While he was still in the pit, Varzi took the lead and went on to win by 47 seconds; Divo, who was third, finished nearly 10 minutes behind Brilli Perri. The entry list for this race would have flattered some grandes épreuves and it must have been a bit galling for drivers, who had spent a lot of money buying the latest Bugattis and Maseratis, to have been so soundly beaten by two five-year-old cars.

Two weeks later the Italian circus was at Mugello; this race was still being run on the 38.4-mile (61.7km) circuit with a rough unmade surface for much of the course; with the Targa Florio, it was a throwback to the open road races of the past. Eight 1750 SSs and two MMSs were included in the entry of 32 cars. Campari and Varzi were in SSs, as was Ferrari, and they were joined by Nuvolari, who had abandoned his Bugatti for this race. Gastone Brilli Perri showed his ability by leading the race all the way with his 1500cc GP Talbot. The usual Alfa Romeo stars had a poor day: Varzi hit a wall and had to change a wheel, while Nuvolari and Ferrari both had mechanical bothers that dropped them down the field, and Campari was off form again. The best Alfa Romeo was the SS of Ernesto Benini, who was third, while a new driver, Carlo Pintacuda, was fourth with an MMS, ahead of Varzi. Pintacuda would appear again.

The SSs and MMSs were now a regular feature in the entry lists, and there was a strong contingent at Montenero on 21 July. The race was now called the Coppa Ciano in honour of the Italian foreign minister Count Ciano, who was Mussolini's son-in-law. Among the profusion of amateur drivers Varzi's P2 stood out.

The cars were flagged away individually, and at the end of the first lap Varzi and Brilli Perri had done an identical time and shared the lead. Brilli Perri's Talbot then led for three laps, but he made a long pit stop that put him down to fifth place, so Varzi ran on unchallenged and won the 10-lap race by nearly 2 minutes. Nuvolari had found the 1750 SS to his liking; L'Auto Italiana reported that he '… was running a steady race thanks to his magnificent gifts as a

5 May 1929: Gastone Brilli Perri waits for the start of the Targa Florio in his 1750 SS. He finished third.

9 June 1929: Ernesto Benini sits in his 1750 SS after finishing the Circuito di Mugello in third place. (John Maitland Collection)

daring driver', which seems a slight contradiction in terms, but he was second in front of Campari, who seemed to be getting his form back.

The Gran Premio di Monza on 15 September was a race with a difference. The RACI asked Vincenzo Florio to organise it and he decided to abandon the Grand Premio d'Italia and run a formula libre race instead, using only the banked track. The event would have three eliminating heats of 22 laps and a 22-lap final, so each race was 61 miles (98km). The entry justified the break with tradition. The Maserati brothers, realising that they needed something dramatically different to beat the P2, devised a fierce new motor car, the V4, which used two 2-litre Tipo 26 engines in parallel, with a common crankcase, mounted in a widened Tipo 26 frame; Alfieri Maserati himself was the driver. The American 'Leon Duray' brought two Miller 91 track racers, which should have been ideally suited to the Monza track. There were also three Mercedes-Benz entries: Caflisch had a stripped SS sports car, but Rosenberger and Momberger were virtually works entries and had the much faster SSKs that the company was using for formula libre grands prix as well as sports car races. As an indication that it was a serious race, the P2s were entered by Alfa Corse, with drivers Varzi and Brilli Perri.

Both the P2s ran in the second heat. Brilli Perri won after a battle with Borzacchini's Maserati, and Varzi lost time when he stopped to tighten a loose filler cap, but once going again he ran through the field and finished third. The Millers did not put up the show that had been forecast as they were very fast but brittle. There were eight runners in the final and at some time seven of them led the race. Varzi led at first, then swapped places with the V4 Maserati. Brilli Perri stopped for a wheel change after throwing a tread, and the pressure that Varzi was maintaining gradually wore down the opposition, allowing him to come home to win at an average speed of 116.68mph (187.62kmh). Nuvolari, who was driving the Talbot usually driven by Brilli Perri, was second, 1min 37sec behind, but a minute in front of Momberger's Mercedes, which beat Brilli Perri's P2 by only 1.2 seconds. Varzi shared the fastest lap with Alfieri Maserati's V4 at 124.27mph (199.82kmh).

A week after the Monza race Varzi was back at the track again having a 'busman's holiday' racing a 500cc Sunbeam in the Gran Premio delle Nazione. This was to be his last motor cycle race and he went out in style. He set such a pace that 13 other riders in his class dropped out and he came home to win, having ridden the last four laps by himself. It probably added the final touch of pleasure, and made the day even better for Varzi, that Nuvolari, who was riding a 350cc Bianchi, dropped out.

The following Sunday, 29 September, Varzi was with Brilli Perri taking the P2s to Cremona for the five-lap 200-mile race. It was a two-day meeting and in addition to the race there were speed record attempts on the 10km straight. Borzacchini brought out the Maserati V4 and set a new International Class C record of 152.9mph (246.86kmh) for the 10km distance. In the race the cars ran against the clock and at the end of the first lap Brilli Perri led Varzi by 30 seconds. At half distance the gap had opened to 3 minutes, but Varzi then speeded up and by the finish had cut Brilli Perri's lead down to 12 seconds. During the race Varzi's P2 was timed through the 10km speed trap at 138.77mph (223.14kph). Peter Hull comments in *Alfa Romeo* that this was the fastest speed at which a grand prix car was officially timed before the start of the 750kg formula in 1934.

It had been a long season and the last race was the Grand Prix de Tunisie in Tunis on 17 November, for which most of the leading drivers travelled across the Mediterranean, Varzi and Brilli Perri taking the Alfa Corse-entered P2s. The grid was by ballot and Varzi was on the fifth row, but at the start he cut through the rows in front of him to take the lead; this must have been an impressive and difficult feat, as it was narrow at the start line and the two-by-two grid took up all the road. At the end of the first lap Borzacchini led with the V4 Maserati, but Varzi and Brilli Perri were only inches behind. On the next lap Varzi dropped out, lacking fuel pressure, and Borzacchini fell out as well, so Brilli Perri stayed in front, staving off attacks from a pack of following Bugattis. He finished the 40-lap race 21 seconds in front of Marcel Lehoux's T35B Bugatti.

It is an article of faith among historical commentators that the grand prix races of 1928 and 1929 were dominated by Bugatti, with the other marques very much also-rans, but a study of the results shows that the pre-eminent machine was the P2 Alfa Romeo. It was probably fortunate for the Bugatti drivers, and for the maintenance of the legend of Bugatti domination, that the P2s stayed south of the Alps and did not make forays into France.

Mussolini liked motor racing and held the view that successful racing cars and drivers were a measure of the virility and modern outlook of his Fascist society. This was an attitude that would also be held in a much more grandiose manner north of the Alps in a few short years. It is not known how much autonomy Gianferrari and Jano had in the design and construction of cars in the late 1920s, but they must have realised that the P2 would soon be outclassed, either by Bugatti or Maserati. The need was coming for a new Alfa Romeo racing design, and it is likely that if there was not a governmental direction on the matter, there would certainly have been enthusiastic encouragement.

It seems that Jano began work on a new design early in 1929. This was to be a straight-eight and would be intended primarily as a competition car, but with the

'Il Duce': Benito Mussolini in a characteristic pose. (Guy Griffiths Collection)

possibility of limited production as a high-performance touring car. In *Alfa Romeo 8C*, Angela Cherrett mentions a letter dated 3 September 1929 from Jano to F. W. Stiles, the British concessionaire for Alfa Romeo, in which Jano says, 'Regarding the "Eight Cylinder", I am not yet able to guarantee that these cars will be ready for next year; in fact it is a very difficult undertaking. Let's talk about it when we next meet.' Clearly, by the autumn of 1929, the 8C was under way.

Chapter 5

The Scuderia Ferrari is born

During the winter of 1929/30 it was evident that the 8C would not be ready to race during the 1930 season, so three of the P2s were given a substantial face-lift in the hope that this would give them an extra lease of life for one final season of racing. One seems to have been the Varzi car and the other two were those still kept at Portello. New and lower frames were made and fitted with new front and rear axles, the springs were mounted outside the chassis and at the front, were now bolted down on to conventional axle pads. Much larger brakes were used and the cars now had radiators akin to those of the 1750. A spare wheel was mounted vertically and partially exposed in the tail. A reworking of the carburation and manifolding raised the power to 175bhp. These nearly new cars were known as P2 Modificatos.

It had been intended to send two P2 Modificatos to Tripoli for the Gran Premio on 23 March with Varzi and Brilli Perri as the drivers, but the entries were scratched as the cars were not ready. Brilli Perri went to the race with one of the Scuderia Materassi 1500cc Talbots, and while practising on the eve of the race he went off the road and was killed when he was thrown out of the Talbot. Gastone Brilli Perri had been a wholly reliable third-string driver of the P2 team in 1925 and his drives with a P2 in 1929 showed that he was then probably driving even better and was capable of tackling Varzi and Nuvolari on equal terms. It was an indication of the regard for his ability at Portello that he seemed to be given the P2 drives in preference to Campari, and was already picked as a team member for the 1930 season. Apart from his ability, he was much liked by the Alfa Corse team as a cheerful, extrovert character who got on with the job without fuss or histrionics.

A P2 Modificato was also entered for Enzo Ferrari in the first grande épreuve of the season at Monaco, but it was a non-starter. The relationship between Ferrari and Portello had changed. After his virtual retirement from racing following his retreat from the 1924 French Grand Prix, Ferrari had concentrated on building up an Alfa Romeo dealership for the regions of Emilia, Romagna and Marche, based in Modena. Baconin Borzacchini's successful attempt on the Class C record at Cremona was the first time that an international class record had been broken on Italian soil. To celebrate the feat the AC di Bologna held a dinner in Borzacchini's honour, and at the

Late 1920s: The exterior of the Portello factory.

dinner Ferrari had a discussion with Alfredo Caniato, a hemp merchant from Ferrara, and Mario Tadini, a local resident. Both Caniato and Tadini had been racing 6Cs during 1929 and wanted to improve their chances of success. Ferrari suggested that this could be done by forming a racing team and pooling their resources.

This suggestion quickly bore fruit: on 15 November an agreement was drawn up, and on 1 December 1929 Società Anonima Scuderia Ferrari was formed, with a capital of 200,000 lire. Alfredo Caniato was joined by his brother Augusto and, with Tadini, they subscribed 130,000 lire; Ferrari himself contributed 50,000 lire, while Alfa Romeo contributed 10,000 lire and Feruccio Testi and Pirelli provided 5000 lire each.

The intention was to attract rich drivers who would have their cars prepared and entered by the Scuderia; Alfa Romeo would supply the cars at very favourable terms. This arrangement was clearly to the benefit of Alfa Romeo; the Scuderia would be a semi-official team and would represent the factory at the lesser events, mainly for sports cars, leaving Alfa Corse to devote itself to the major events, particularly grand prix racing. To ensure that a leading driver was part of the team, terms were agreed with Giuseppe Campari. The Scuderia established a temporary headquarters with a workshop in the Carlo Gatti machine tool company in the Via Emilia at Modena.

The Scuderia Ferrari entered three 6Cs for the 1930 Mille Miglia, but all retired. The race was a bitter duel between the 6C-1750s of Tazio Nuvolari and Achille Varzi, who came first and second, but the result exacerbated the already strained relations between the two men. The excitable and mercurial Nuvolari and the quiet, introspective Varzi both considered themselves as the top Italian driver and the mutual antipathy that had begun in 1927 now fuelled the rivalry. Nuvolari had abandoned his own Scuderia at the end of 1929, knowing that it was not going to beat the works entries.

Jano realised that Nuvolari was in a quandary, looking for a drive, so apparently on his own initiative approached him and suggested that he should drive regularly for Alfa Corse in 1930. The Portello management agreed and a parallel deal was also arranged with Enzo Ferrari, though this was not formalised with a contract until June.

The first circuit event in which the Scuderia ran cars was at Alessandria on 20 April where Ferrari himself and Alfredo Caniato drove SSs. Alfa Corse had entered Varzi with a P2 and Nuvolari with an SS. The race was over eight laps, and Georges Bouriano, who had brought his T35B Bugatti from France, led until halfway, but then Varzi, who had made a slow start, was closing up. His task was made easier by a heavy shower that caused Bouriano to slide off the road. After that Varzi ran away with

1930: Two views of the P2 in its final form. The spare wheel mounting caused problems for Varzi in the Targa Florio.

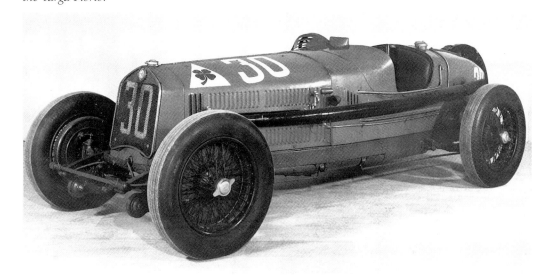

the race, while Ferrari took third place. Nuvolari had the double frustration of going out on the first lap with a broken oil pipe and seeing Varzi win.

Every Italian driver of note was in Sicily on 4 May for the Targa Florio. There is some uncertainty about the entrant of the principal Alfa Romeos. It has been suggested that the P2 was given to the Scuderia to make the entry, together with four 6C-1750s, but Paul Sheldon in his marvellous and microscopically researched series *A Record of Grand Prix and Voiturette Racing* says that Alfa Corse entered the P2 for Varzi and the SSs for Nuvolari, Campari and Maggi, and that there were no Scuderia entries. It seems that the P2 Modificatos had slightly suspect handling; it had been intended that Ferrari should enter them for the Targa, but he decided not to race them on the grounds of safety. At this point Varzi is supposed to have intervened and pointed out to Alfa Corse (or Ferrari) that he had an agreement that he would drive a P2 in the race and he expected this to be honoured.

Apparently the second P2 should have been driven by Campari and the SS was an alternative entry for him. Maybe Campari opted for the SS anyway – after his remarkable drive in 1928 he must have known that the smaller car would perhaps have been more suitable for the Madonie circuit.

The 1930 Targa Florio was a race that would not have seemed out of place in a book of adventure stories for boys. Landslides had damaged the road in the mountains and hasty repairs had left a very rough surface. The cars were started at 3-minute intervals and Varzi immediately dominated the race. Initially he was pursued by Campari and Nuvolari, but it was Louis Chiron with a T35B Bugatti who set up the fiercest chase of the P2. After three laps the spare wheel broke away from the tail of the P2, the mounting damaged by the pounding on the rough sections of road. At the start of the last of the five laps, Varzi led Chiron by 23 seconds, but the fuel tank had cracked when the wheel broke away. Varzi realised that there was a chance

of running out of fuel, so he made a brief stop at one of the depots on the circuit to top up the tank, while Tabacchi, his mechanic, picked up an extra can of fuel as a safeguard. The unexpected stop gave Chiron a chance to snatch the lead, so Varzi now drove faster than ever.

Meanwhile, Chiron's mechanic, anxious about the excessive revs that Chiron was using, started to pump more oil into the Bugatti engine while the car was going down a hill. Fearing that this could oil a plug, Chiron knocked the mechanic's hand off the pump and in doing so inadvertently made the car swerve, clipping a rock on the verge and breaking two of the Bugatti's alloy wheels. The car had two spares strapped on, but Chiron lost valuable minutes while the wheels were changed; in their haste to restart, the damaged wheels, tools and jack were abandoned by the roadside.

It was now Varzi's turn! On the long straight beside the sea, running to the finish, the P2's engine spluttered with fuel starvation. Tabacchi lent across the tail, opened the fuel cap and started to empty the spare can into the tank, while Varzi continued to drive as fast as he could. Some of the fuel splashed on to the exhaust and caught fire, and the back of the car was enveloped in flames. Still Varzi did not stop – he could not stop, as not only would the race be lost but the flames would have enveloped the car, which would be lost too. Tabacchi beat out the flames with his seat cushion while trying to hang on to the car. Varzi pressed on at unabated speed and the P2 won the 335-mile (538km) race by 1min 50sec from Chiron after nearly 7 hours of racing.

In the midst of the drama, Campari and Nuvolari also had their problems. Campari's car kept dropping out of third gear and Nuvolari had a broken spring, but both kept going and finished fourth and fifth behind Conelli's Bugatti. This was the last major victory for the P2, the drama and heroics providing a fitting and almost

4 May 1930: Varzi applies opposite lock as he leaves Cerda village during his legendary Targa Florio drive. (Guy Griffiths Collection)

Wagnerian finale for a car that had achieved so much and, at the end, almost literally went out in a blaze of glory.

Both Nuvolari and Varzi were entered in P2s by Alfa Corse for the Premio Reale di Roma on 25 May, while Campari and Tadini were entered by the Scuderia in SSs. Varzi only lasted for six laps before his clutch gave out, but Nuvolari was engaged in a fierce battle with Luigi Arcangeli who had a 'works' Type 26M Maserati. The battle lasted until lap 17 when the P2's engine objected to the demands Nuvolari was making upon it and a piston broke. This left Arcangeli to fight for the three remaining laps to beat Chiron's Bugatti by about 25 metres after 161 miles (258km) of racing. Despite the piston Nuvolari had struggled

on, but the P2's engine objected to the added abuse and gave up on the penultimate lap; the SS was outpaced and Campari finished fifth.

The Maserati brothers had been working steadily in their small factory at Bologna. The mainstay of their business was sparking plugs, but they had now developed a very effective eight-cylinder racing car. By the beginning of 1930 their latest product, the 2½-litre Type 26M, was the fastest car in grand prix racing and was showing up the shortcomings of the obsolescent P2 Alfa Romeo and T35B Bugatti. After Varzi's drive in Sicily, nothing much was being said about the alleged dangerous handling of the modified P2!

There were almost two separate racing

circuses operating in 1930. North of the Alps the French drivers ran in a series of races including the Grand Prix de la Marne at Reims and the Grand Prix d'Europe at Spa. In these races the entry was almost exclusively Bugatti. South of the Alps there was a thriving Italian season. The Italian drivers did not go to the northern races and only a handful of top French drivers went to Italy.

After the Rome race there was a lull in the Italian season, although the drivers were kept busy by the many hill climbs. The circuit racers assembled again on 3 August at Livorno on the Tuscany coast for the Coppa Ciano. By the standards of 1930 this was a comparatively short race, over ten laps of the 14-mile (22.48km) Montenero circuit. The race had a political honour as it was attended by Count Ciano and his wife, Edda. Nuvolari and Varzi in their P2s were

4 May 1930 Targa Florio: Varzi restarts after a pit stop on his last lap. A mechanic shouts encouragement, Jano looks on and Tabacchi, the riding mechanic, shows the strain.

fighting each other as well as the rest of the field, and beating his rival probably mattered more to each than beating the others. This time Nuvolari was entered by the Scuderia Ferrari, while Varzi was running under the aegis of Alfa Corse.

The P2 rivals fought right from the start, with Nuvolari always having a few seconds advantage. Then after five laps Nuvolari stopped with a failed clutch, which left Varzi in front, but he only lasted another two laps before the P2's differential broke. Once again the winner was a 26M Maserati, this time driven by Luigi Fagioli. Campari, who was driving an SS that he had entered himself this time, had been going steadily and came second, 18 seconds in front of Maggi's Bugatti.

Varzi must have realised that, while they were both driving for the same team, the bitter rivalry with Nuvolari was becoming futile. He went to Bologna to talk to the Maserati brothers, they appreciated the problem and were delighted to get the services of a top driver, so Varzi handed in his notice to Portello and was entered in a Tipo 26M by Officine A. Maserati when the drivers came to Pescara for the Coppa Acerbo two weeks later. In the modern grand prix world, when a driver breaks a contract there are hysterical threats of litigation and huge claims for compensation, but in 1930 Varzi's defection probably engendered little more than sharp words and shrugged shoulders.

Varzi arrived in Bologna at an opportune moment. There was a vacancy at Maserati, as Borzacchini had left the team and joined the Scuderia Ferrari. He was a friend of Nuvolari and wanted to work with him, and the pair working together probably made Varzi feel isolated in the Scuderia. The personal rivalries and politics of Italian racing at that time had an operatic quality that was hard to comprehend, but is readily understandable by today's racing standards. The rivalry among the drivers must have been one of the biggest problems for Aldo Giovannini, who was now team manager for Alfa Corse. He went with the team to the races but, rather like Giorgio Rimini, he was a slightly shadowy figure.

The Pescara race had a grid start and Nuvolari's P2 and the V-16 Maserati of Luigi Arcangeli went to the front from the start. Arcangeli led for three laps, then Nuvolari passed him. The big Maserati now fell back, but Fagioli and Varzi, with their more nimble 26Ms, were putting pressure on the P2 and Fagioli took the lead when Nuvolari stopped on lap six to change plugs out on the circuit. Nuvolari stopped again and finished fifth, while Fagioli led until a few miles from the finish, when his back axle broke. As he took the flag, Varzi must have felt that the change of allegiance had been well worth any of the agonies and anxieties involved. The sun was now setting fast for the P2.

Everyone was at Monza for the Gran Premio di Monza on 7 September. Nuvolari, Campari and Borzacchini had Scuderia-entered P2s, so all three Modificatos were in action. Count Florio had devised a new circuit that used the main grandstand straight, the Curva Grande, Lesmo and Vialone sections. On the back straight behind the pits it crossed from the road circuit to the track section by a short link road, went round the south banked curve, then back again to the main straight. This gave a lap of 4.26 miles (6.86km) and it was called the Florio circuit. The race was run in three 14-lap heats and a 35-lap final; for those who came lower than fourth in the heats, all was not lost – they had a second chance to qualify in a 7-lap répêchage.

The three P2s ran in heat two, which started at 11.15am. The pace was more than the tyres could stand. Nuvolari had a savage battle with Varzi and Arcangeli, both driving 26M Maseratis, and everyone had a turn at leading, but Nuvolari had to stop to change his rear wheels, as did Campari. Borzacchini, perhaps prudently, ran slower and came up to second at the end, behind Arcangeli, Nuvolari and Campari qualified to run in the répêchage. There they were chased hard by Lehoux's T35B Bugatti but came first and second, so qualified for the 149-mile (239km) final.

At 3.15pm the Crown Prince Umberto, resplendent in full uniform, dropped the flag. It was a disastrous race for the P2s. From the start Nuvolari hounded Arcangeli's leading Maserati, but within eight laps all three cars were out with tyre failures. Varzi, who had made an early stop, charged through the field and caught Arcangeli on the line to win by one-fifth of a second and score a first and second for Maserati. Borzacchini's P2 was being tended by an 18-year-old mechanic Consalvo Sanesi, who had previously worked for Brilli Perri, but after the Tripoli accident had joined Alfa Romeo at Jano's suggestion.

The P2s ran their very last race at Brno in Czechoslovakia on 21 September. The race was over 17 laps of the Masaryk circuit, a distance of 307 miles (493km). Two cars were entered by the Scuderia Ferrari for Nuvolari and Borzacchini and, almost inevitably, Nuvolari's car could not stand the pace, or probably more accurately his driving. He retired after six laps with a burned-out clutch while in the lead, then took over Borzacchini's car when it stopped for fuel and tyres and was leading again on the last lap when the water pump burst. While limping to the finish the P2 was passed by the Bugattis of von Morgen and Burggaller.

It was significant that by the end of the season the question of who was entering the cars seemed to have been resolved: Alfa Corse had handed the reins over to the Scuderia Ferrari. Two cars were entered for the Gran Premio d'España at San Sebastian on 5 October, but did not turn up as it was probably realised that there would have been little chance of beating Varzi's Maserati, which won by 22 minutes. So the astonishing and protracted career of the P2 came to an end; not until its last season did it begin to show its age and give way to the faster and more modern Maserati.

Chapter 6

Jano's new 8C

Vᴵᴛᴛᴏʀɪᴏ Jᴀɴᴏ's ɴᴇᴡ ᴅᴇsɪɢɴ is regarded by many as one of the greatest of all time, though perhaps it is iconoclastic to observe that the new engine developed 165bhp in racing trim when it was introduced in 1931, about 10bhp less than the output of the P2 in its final form. The new engine owed much to the earlier design of the 1750. It had twin overhead camshafts and the bore and stroke were the same, 65mm x 88mm, but the two extra cylinders increased the capacity to 2336cc. The engine was, in effect, two four-cylinder units with separate blocks and joined by a central gear train that drove the camshafts, supercharger and auxiliaries. The blocks and head were cast in light alloy and the two-piece crankshaft ran in ten main bearings. The supercharger was set low down on the offside of the engine; lubrication was dry-sump. A four-speed gearbox was integral with the engine.

The chassis was conventional with semi-elliptic springing at the front and rear, and the braking system was similar to the 6C but the drums were much larger. The chassis came in two wheelbase lengths: the Lungo was 10ft 2in (3100mm) and the Corto was 9ft (2750mm). The track was

1931: The off-side of the 8C engine showing the supercharger.

4ft 6in (1380mm). The Lungo was intended to carry a four-seat body and would comply with the regulations for the Le Mans 24-hour race, while the Corto was to have a two-seat sporting body and, when in two-seat racing body form for grand prix events, was called the Spyder Corsa.

The prototype 8C was being tested in January 1931, but Jano must have had doubts about its chances in grand prix racing, so he began work on an alternative racing design at the end of 1930. This was a remarkable machine. It used two supercharged 1750 6C engines mounted side by side in a chassis similar in general arrangement to the new 8C. Each engine had its own gearbox and propshaft and drove separate differentials in the rear axle. One lever changed the gears in both boxes, so if the linkages slipped the driver could find himself uncomfortably busy. The driver sat over the propshafts and the car was a genuine single-seater with a rather wide body. It was also relatively heavy at 900kg, and the combined engine output was 230bhp. Jano saw that the side-by-side engine arrangement was effective in the V4 Maserati, so he must have been confident that this new car, called the Tipo A, would work. Much of the detail work was done by the chief of the design department at Portello, Gioacchino Colombo, who was then 27 years old.

On 5 October 1930 Nuvolari signed a contract with the Scuderia Ferrari for 1931, though he was still retained to drive for Alfa Corse in the Italian Grand Prix and would be released for other races. He was also permitted to ride in three motor cycle races. Maybe Jano was not certain about the readiness of the new 8C for competition, so perhaps as a face-saving precaution it was the Scuderia that entered two of the new cars for the Mille Miglia on 11 April. The cars were driven by Nuvolari and Arcangeli, but although both led the race they were slowed by continuous tyre troubles. Arcangeli crashed, Nuvolari finished well down the field and victory went to a German Mercedes-Benz SSKL driven by Rudolf Caracciola. The result was not popular in Italy; doubtless there were political enquiries about the failure, there were recriminations between Portello and Modena about the responsibility, and both parties must have expressed themselves forcefully to Pirelli.

Two racing 8Cs were entered for the first major grand prix of the season at Monaco, but were withdrawn as the tyre problems had allegedly not been solved. On 26 April the Scuderia sent a big team to the Circuito di Alessandria. Nuvolari had a rather rough-looking 8C prototype with an angular radiator cowling and a ribbed oil tank between the dumb-irons, and there were four SSs for the lesser lights. Varzi abandoned Maserati after his brief flirtation during the second half of the 1930 season, and signed up with Ettore Bugatti during the winter. He now appeared at Alessandria with one of the new T51 Bugattis, a development of the T35B with twin camshafts, and led from start to finish. Nuvolari held second place for a while, but was falling back and dropped out on lap ten with a broken differential. It has been suggested that the Scuderia assembled its own 8Cs from parts supplied by Portello, and to distinguish these from the factory cars they were given an 'SF' chassis number.

It was a different story in the Targa Florio three weeks later. Heavy rain caused the road to collapse in the mountains, so Count Florio decided that the race would revert to the old long Madonie circuit with a 90-mile lap; this would be covered four times so the distance was 370 miles (595km). The entries were made by Alfa Corse, and the team comprised Nuvolari and Luigi Arcangeli with 8Cs, while Campari, Borzacchini and Guido d'Ippolito had 1750 SSs. There was a full works team from Maserati with three 26Ms, and Varzi turned up with a solitary T51 Bugatti, which was painted red instead of the usual blue.

Jano, who was managing the team, concluded that it would rain during the

10 May 1931: The seconds are counted down as Nuvolari waits for the start of his winning Targa Florio drive in the new 8C. Amedeo Bignami, the passenger, exchanges a word with Jano, who is standing on the right. The mudguards played a crucial part in the victory.

race, so the Alfa Romeos were fitted with front mudguards, although Arcangeli declined these for his car, which he was sharing with Goffredo Zehender. Nuvolari's 8C had long touring front wings. On both cars the rear of the body was removed and the spare wheels were strapped behind the exposed fuel tank; the cars were probably the pair that ran in the Mille Miglia. Jano also had another vital innovation: he equipped the refuelling posts in the mountains with two-way radios so that information could be relayed round the circuit to the drivers when they stopped. No doubt mindful of the Mille Miglia, the Alfa Romeos were running on Dunlop tyres.

The cars started at 5-minute intervals and Varzi was the first to go. The first lap took over 2 hours and Varzi led Borzacchini by 3 minutes, with Nuvolari in third place. During the second lap the expected rain started to fall, the road turned to a quagmire of mud and all three Maseratis went off the road. The mudguards now began to pay dividends. At the start of the last lap Varzi still led, but Nuvolari was only 2 minutes behind; even more important, he knew the problems that Varzi was having, and just how far ahead he was. W. F. Bradley described the last lap dramatically in his biography of Ettore Bugatti:

'With mud and stones flying in every direction, the brilliant red Bugatti soon became unrecognisable; its numbers disappeared. Goggles were useless and were thrown away. Varzi drove through seas of mud, he sat in mud, he swallowed mud, he was blinded by mud just when the utmost precision was essential to avoid disaster – but he hung on grimly … Varzi had finished first as he had started first. They lifted him out of his car; they stripped from him the once blue overalls; they sponged his face and placed a lighted cigarette between his lips but the Lone Wolf remained grim and silent. Only a dozen yards away, a muddy, olive-skinned, exuberant Italian was clutching the black hair of two stalwarts who held

him aloft and "Victory" exuded from every pore of the vociferous Nuvolari.'

After more than 9 hours of racing Nuvolari had won, giving the 8C its first victory. Varzi, suffering from the conditions, had dropped 7 minutes behind Nuvolari on the last lap, and had even lost his second place to Borzacchini, finishing only just ahead of Campari. Arcangeli had paid the penalty for his decision and his mudguardless 8C was sixth, three-quarters of an hour behind. That evening Count Florio found Nuvolari standing outside his hotel in Palermo. He congratulated Nuvolari, who replied, 'Well, I'm glad I beat Varzi.'

So far in 1931 the T51 Bugatti had been the car to beat. For Bugatti, the failure of Varzi in Sicily was probably attributable to the conditions, but the 8C was now going properly and was to meet the T51 on equal terms in the Gran Premio d'Italia. To be a proper grand prix in 1931 a race had to be of 10 hours' duration, and only the Italian, French and Belgian épreuves satisfied this daunting requirement. The Italian event was held at Monza on Sunday 24 May and was

to be the début of the Tipo A. The new car was to be driven by Nuvolari and Marinoni and was backed up by two 8Cs for Campari sharing with Arcangeli, while Borzacchini and Goffredo Zehender shared the other car, Minoia was the reserve driver. The team of three cars was entered by Alfa Corse.

The Tipo A was finished on 18 May and was first tested round the factory roads by Bazzi and Campari, when it was found difficult to get each engine to run slowly at the same speed. The team of cars was driven from Portello to Monza the following morning; there they were tested and the Tipo A showed it was fast and the drivers said that it handled well. The testing continued and the second Tipo A, which was to be the race car, was finished at the factory.

At the end of the official practice on the morning before the race, Arcangeli took the second Tipo A round the circuit as he was curious to find out how it went. Jano became concerned that he was going too fast and hung out a 'Slow' sign. After a few laps Arcangeli went off the road at Vialone bend, the same point where Sivocci had crashed in 1923. The Tipo A hit a tree and Arcangeli

24 May 1931: Campari in his 8C waits for the start of the GP d'Italia at Monza.

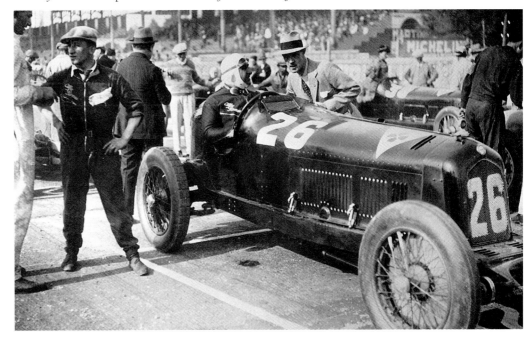

was killed when he was thrown out. He was 29 years old, a much-liked member of the team and respected for his forceful driving. Alfa Corse wanted to withdraw from the race but the political masters who now held the reins had other ideas. That evening, Prospero Gianferrari received a telegram from Mussolini's office directing the team to race – '… according to the perfect Fascist style he orders you to compete and win'. The crashed Tipo A was too badly damaged to race, so the mechanics worked through the night to prepare the first test car. It was driven to the track at 7.00am.

The race started at 8.00am and the flag was dropped by Italo Balbo, now a Marshal of the Regia Aeronautica, a considerable elevation for the man who had led the *squadristi* in the streets of Milan ten years earlier. There were 14 cars in the field. The Maserati team was absent, saying that their cars could not be repaired in time, but there were four T51 Bugattis and several fast private entrants. Marcel Lehoux (Bugatti) led the field away, but after a lap Varzi's Bugatti was in front, followed by Campari's 8C and Lehoux. The Tipo A was not running well, and although Nuvolari worked it up to fourth, on lap 33 he pulled off on the grandstand straight and stopped; one of the engines had run its bearings.

Varzi still led and came in for his first pit stop at the 2-hour mark. He handed over to Chiron, but Campari had already taken the 8C into the lead. Gianferrari and Jano were managing the Alfa Corse pit and they did not bring in Campari for another nine laps. When he stopped, Nuvolari took over the car. Meanwhile Chiron had regained the lead, but only for a lap as he came slowly into his pit with a broken differential bearing – the T51 was out. Shortly after this the Lehoux T51, now being driven by Phillipe (Phi-Phi) Etancelin, stopped abruptly with a broken con-rod, so the main Bugatti challenge was down to one car. Minoia had started with the second 8C, and when he stopped Borzacchini took over. The 8Cs now commanded the race, stopping regularly at 40-lap intervals and cruising on to victory. With about 15 minutes to go, Borzacchini's car struck a pheasant and he stopped to check if the radiator had been damaged.

At the end the Campari/Nuvolari car had

24 May 1931 GP d'Italia: Nuvolari on the starting grid in the Tipo A. Marinoni leans on the back wheel and Borzacchini (with goggles) is on the far side of the car. (Guy Griffiths Collection)

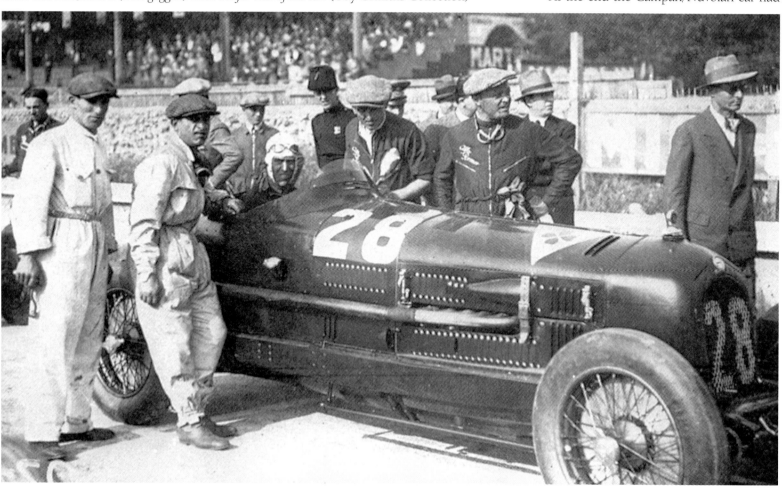

covered 155 laps (967 miles/1556km) and was two laps in front of the car of Minoia/Borzacchini. The Divo/Bouriat T51 was a further two laps behind. In fourth place was a T51 Bugatti being shared by a French amateur pair, Jean-Pierre Wimille and Jean Gaupillat. There were nine finishers. *Motor Sport* said prophetically of the 23-year-old Wimille: 'He looks like becoming famous one day.' Thereafter the racing-bodied 8C was always known as the 'Monza'.

After the race, Gianferrari sent a telegram to Mussolini's office. It said tersely, 'We have obeyed.' Arcangeli's funeral was held the next day; the cortège went from Portello to a local church before he was taken to Forli, his home town, for burial.

Following the Monza race, the Monza Alfa Romeos were rested, or more likely extensively rebuilt. The entries for the Grand Prix de Genève were not taken up and the cars also missed the Premio Reale di Roma. Energies were being reserved for the Grand Prix de l'ACF (French Grand Prix) at Montlhéry on 21 June, which was to be another 10-hour marathon. The Alfa Romeo team had not been back to France since the tragic race at Montlhéry seven years before, when Ascari had been killed, but they now came back in force. Alfa Corse entered three Monzas to be driven by Minoia with Zehender, Campari with Borzacchini and Nuvolari with Giovanni Minozzi. They were up against full teams from Bugatti and Maserati as well as a big field of private entrants, some with the latest cars. The Monzas were identified by white bars painted on the radiator cowl; Minoia's had one bar, Campari's two and Nuvolari's three.

There was a crowd estimated at 10,000 watching the 8.00am start. On the first lap the Maseratis of Fagioli and Dreyfus led, followed by a horde of Bugattis, while the Monzas were near the back, realising that there was a long way to go. After four laps Chiron's Bugatti went to the front, Fagioli repassed and led again for three laps, but thereafter the Bugatti, which Chiron was

24 May 1931: Monza 9.35am, Campari has made his first pit stop. Nuvolari, whose Tipo A has already retired, refuels the car and will take it over later in the race. Jano gives instructions to the driver.

sharing with Varzi, stayed in the lead and was not headed again during the race. At 9.00am Campari and Nuvolari were seventh and eighth, while an hour later the Nuvolari/Minozzi car had come up to fourth. By noon Nuvolari held second place briefly while those in front of him made pit stops. Campari had dropped a long way behind, having lost time while new front brake shoes were fitted to his Monza. At the 5-hour mark, the Nuvolari car was fifth, followed by Minoia/Zehender, but Campari was down to 13th place.

It had become an intensely hot day and the drivers were suffering, while the spectators had become bored with the race and many were sleeping in any shade they could find. The correspondent of *The Motor* noted that half the spectators in the main grand-stand were asleep soon after noon. Now it was Nuvolari's turn to lose time while the brakes of his Monza were rebuilt, and Campari joined him in the pits as he needed some more front brake drums. Perhaps the new drums did the trick, as Campari and Borzacchini were now going faster and began to climb through the field; at 4.00pm they were third behind the Divo/Bouriat T51 Bugatti, but the engine mounting bolts of the Bugatti worked loose and 40 minutes before the end the Monza took second place and finished the race 31 miles (50km) behind the winning Bugatti of Chiron and Varzi, which had run on happily throughout the race when all the others were having troubles. The Minoia/Zehender car was sixth and Nuvolari and Minozzi trailed home in 11th place, their car having virtually no brakes left. It had been a tough and rather unattractive event where the ability to survive had mattered as much as the ability to race. Jano and Gianferrari were realising that although the Monza was a good car, it was not quite fast enough to dominate grand prix racing, and, perhaps more to the point, the results were not pleasing the political masters.

The first Monza to be sold to a private owner now went to the French driver Phi-Phi Etancelin, and he took it, painted blue, to the Grand Prix de la Marne outside Reims on 3 July, where he came fourth. A week later it was the turn of the Belgians to stage a 10-hour grande épreuve at Spa-Francorchamps. A surprisingly small field turned up; the Maseratis stayed away, so it was the three Alfa Corse-entered Monzas that were to do battle with the three works T51 Bugattis. At the 7.00am start, Nuvolari and Varzi showed that all the old rivalry had not abated. For the first 2½ hours they fought wheel to wheel, evenly matched drivers with evenly matched cars. When the time came for the first pit stops, the Alfa Romeo and Bugatti came into the pits together. Chiron took over the Bugatti and Borzacchini the Monza.

Chiron now drove superbly and lapped 5 seconds faster than Nuvolari or Varzi had been able to manage, which must have irked both of them and was some indication of who was top driver at that time. Four laps later he had a 2-minute lead over Borzacchini, but then stopped on the circuit with a broken magneto coupling; he ran back to the pits for spares but nothing could be done. This left Nuvolari and Borzacchini sitting on a lead of nearly two-thirds of a lap from the T51 of 'Williams' and Conelli, but they now lacked some support as Campari's Monza had dropped out after catching fire. Pitwork was now vital and the Bugatti team must have been doing some useful practice as they were gaining a lot of time. Their three stops only took a total of 5 minutes, while the Alfa Romeo stops took 9 minutes. 'Williams'

and Conelli were gradually eating into the lead and at the last stop the T51 was fitted with new brake shoes, giving 'Williams' the advantage he needed. He caught and passed Borzacchini, who came into the pit immediately complaining of fuel starvation, but after a time-wasting inspection it was found that the coil was faulty. The Bugatti was now a lap ahead, but Nuvolari took over and managed to pass 'Williams' and get back on the same lap. It was too late, however, and the Bugatti came home the winner by a margin of 7 miles (11km). Minoia and Minozzi, who had run a relatively quiet race, were third. Presumably more political telegrams were received at Portello asking 'Why?'.

The racing circus now moved on to the Nürburgring for the Grösser Preis von Deutschland on 19 July. The Germans were having nothing to do with 10-hour races – this was going to be 22 laps of the 14.2-mile (22.7km) circuit, a distance of 311 miles (500km). Surprisingly, only two Monzas were entered for Nuvolari and Borzacchini, this time the entrant was the Scuderia, and only Nuvolari's car appeared. As a reserve driver to Nuvolari, the English amateur Sir Henry Birkin was nominated. He had been having a very successful season with a sports 8C with which he had won the Le Mans 24-hour race and finished fourth at Spa.

The 'Ring was renowned for its poor weather and just after the start it began to rain heavily. Fagioli took the lead with his Maserati, but Rudolf Caracciola with a big SSKL Mercedes, surprisingly carrying a riding mechanic, went to the front halfway round the first lap and went on to win convincingly. Nuvolari was driving with less fire than usual, perhaps not liking the wet, but he worked his way up from eighth on lap one to second at the end of lap six. Nuvolari now battled with Fagioli and had got the better of him only to be passed by Chiron's Bugatti. Towards the end of the race the rain stopped and Varzi, who had been following Nuvolari, speeded up and

took third place, so the Monza came fourth; it was suggested after the race that the car was wrongly geared for the circuit.

Probably to the relief of the drivers and the rest of the team, the action now moved back to the Italian sunshine. Realising the need for more power, the Scuderia brought out the Tipo A for the Coppa Ciano at Livorno on 2 August. Since Monza the car had been modified with freewheels behind the gearboxes to compensate for differing engine speeds. Campari took the car to the Susa-Montcenisio hill climb on 28 June. He calculated that if he stopped the 'inside' engine on the corners it would improve the drive of the other engine to the outside wheel and benefit his time. This strange scheme seemed to be working, but at a crucial moment both engines cut out and Campari was reduced to pushing the car to restart it, an activity to which his physique was well-suited. After all the drama he made the fifth fastest time.

Campari, who after his hill-climb endeavours presumably knew a thing or two about the peculiarities of the Tipo A, now drove it again at Livorno, while Nuvolari and Borzacchini were driving the Monzas. Ranged against them were the works teams from Maserati and Bugatti, a field as good as any grande épreuve. The cars were started with time intervals and Fagioli's Maserati led the Bugattis of Varzi and Chiron with the Alfa Romeos following. Varzi passed Fagioli, who fell back, and it looked like another Bugatti win, but then Varzi damaged a wheel and lost 5 minutes getting back to his pit. This gave Nuvolari his chance and he ran on to win, followed by Chiron and Fagioli. Campari was fourth with the Tipo A; history does not relate if he tried cutting engines to assist cornering on the tighter parts of the Montenero circuit.

The same leading runners went to Pescara a fortnight later. The Arcangeli Tipo A had been rebuilt so now both cars were handed over to the Scuderia and were entered for Campari and Nuvolari. They were backed up by Borzacchini and Francesco Severi with Monzas. The race was 12 laps, a distance of 187 miles (300km), and Campari set off into the lead, followed by Fagioli's Maserati. Campari went on happily to win, but after a lap Varzi was second, closely followed by Nuvolari with the second Tipo A. The pair fought their usual bitter battle, which only ended when Varzi's Bugatti had a puncture. Near the end of the race one of the engines of Nuvolari's car blew a head gasket and he slowed, dropping behind Chiron's Bugatti to finish third, but probably delighted that he was still in front of Varzi.

While the dramas of the Bugatti/Alfa Romeo battles had continued from race to race, Phi-Phi Etancelin had been quietly going about his business with his new Monza. Staying in France, he scored wins in the grands prix at Dieppe, Grenoble and Comminges after seeing off strong Bugatti challenges. He now brought his car to Monza for the Gran Premio di Monza on 6 September. This had an enormous entry of 41 cars. There were four works Maseratis, two of which were new cars with the engine bored out to 2.8 litres, and they were backed by the 16-cylinder V4. Bugatti had sent two 4.9-litre T54s, with evil handling but capable of over 150mph. For this race the entries were back with Alfa Corse; Campari and Nuvolari had the Tipo As, while Borzacchini, Minoia and Minozzi had Monzas. Once again it was organised by Count Florio, who realised that the public wanted to see cars racing against each other and not struggling to finish after 10 long hours. Using the short Florio circuit, there were three 14-lap (60-mile/96km) heats, with a répêchage for the unfortunate, then a 35-lap (149-mile/239km) final. It was a full day's racing: there had already been an 1100cc race when the first heat for the 2-litre cars began at 11.30am.

However, the crowd were waiting for the entry of the gladiators with the 3-litre heat. It was clear that the extra 300cc had given Maserati an advantage. The Maseratis of

16 August 1931: Campari with the Tipo A during his winning drive in the Coppa Acerbo at Pescara. (John Maitland Collection)

Fagioli and Dreyfus ran away from the Monzas and T51 Bugattis with ease. Minoia's Monza was third, 1min 23sec behind, while Minozzi, Etancelin and Borzacchini finished humbly in sixth, seventh and eighth places, so needed to

16 August 1931: Campari's Tipo A waits at the finish of the Coppa Acerbo while the timekeepers check their watches. The Duke of Abruzzi holds the chequered flag and thinks of other things.

redeem themselves in the répêchage.

It was then the turn of the bigger gladiators. Varzi and Chiron with T54 Bugattis were matched against the Tipo As of Nuvolari and Campari, while Ernesto Maserati was driving his own V4. Chiron led at the start, but Varzi was soon in front pursued by Nuvolari. The rivals now fought wheel to wheel, lapping at over 100mph (160kmh) and passing the grandstands at 145mph (235kmh). The Bugatti was faster on the straights but the Tipo A handled better, so Nuvolari caught up again on the fast curves. On lap nine, when in front, the Tipo A threw a tread and came into the pit. The wheel was changed in 15 seconds, but Nuvolari's chances were gone and Varzi came home to win from Chiron by 27 seconds. Nuvolari was third, 46 seconds behind Varzi, and Campari was fourth.

After this the crowd must have expected the répêchage to be rather tame. Borzacchini and Minoia jumped the start but were not penalised. Etancelin started to catch up, but in his efforts he slid off the road at the Lesmo curve. Some spectators had broken down the fence and were sitting on the edge of the track. They were mown down by the Monza, three being killed and ten injured, but Etancelin was unhurt. The accident caused the start of the final to be delayed until 5.00pm. Campari did not bring his Tipo A to the start as the gearbox linkages had tightened up, and all the 2-litre qualifiers decided not to race, knowing that they would merely get in the way.

Fagioli beat the field away followed by Chiron, but at the end of the lap Varzi was running second. Nuvolari had made a slow start but now came past Chiron to challenge Varzi and the battle began again. On lap six they went by the stands side-by-side, but then Nuvolari came into the pits. He did another lap, then stopped with a broken piston. Despite all Varzi's efforts, Fagioli still led. Varzi and Chiron then threw treads and Dreyfus came up to second place, so the Maseratis were now heading the field. Even this did not last as it was

now Fagioli's turn for thrown treads, so the crowd were getting their money's worth. Meanwhile Minoia had been pulled in, and was ordered to hand his Monza over to Nuvolari. The Alfa Romeo chances looked a little brighter when Dreyfus stopped for plugs, then gave up with a broken piston. Borzacchini, who had been going along quietly keeping out of trouble, was now in second place, but Fagioli was still out in front and won by 1min 15sec from Borzacchini. Nuvolari had been pushing the Monza to its limits but was unable to take third place from Varzi. The excited crowd invaded the course as Fagioli was flagged off, but there were no more mishaps.

It was a chastened team that went back to Portello. The new 2.8 Maserati had the legs of the Monza, and rumours were already seeping through from Bologna that the 2.8 engine would be a full 3 litres in 1932. Doubtless the enquiries were already coming again from Rome asking why Alfa Romeo was not conforming with 'the perfect Fascist style'. Jano knew that the answer lay with him, so he set to and 15 days later presented the outline of his new project to Gianferrari and the management team. What he laid on the table were the first design studies for one of the all-time classic grand prix cars, one that would outshine the Monza and even the P2.

It is unlikely that Jano went to Brno, in Czechoslovakia, for the last big race of the season. Alfredo Caniato went with the team and had an accident when his 1750 touring car collided with a horse and cart. Caniato was unhurt, the car was slightly bent, but the wretched horse suffered total and irremediable damage. The Monzas were in the hands of Nuvolari and Borzacchini, and were entered by the Scuderia again. The Masarykuv Okruh was run on 27 September, and it was being taken seriously, as all the teams were there. Not only were the Monzas facing the usual Bugattis and Maseratis, but Mercedes-Benz had joined in with two SSKLs.

A huge crowd saw Fagioli take his usual

lead at the start, but then everything happened. As he completed his first lap he ran wide on a bend and clipped the supports of a footbridge. The bridge collapsed and Borzacchini, who was following, passed under it as it fell. Nuvolari and Varzi, side by side, swerved off on opposite sides of the road; Nuvolari's rear axle was smashed and Varzi's car was almost undriveable. Following them were Caracciola's SSKL and Chiron's Bugatti. Both went into the ditch; the Mercedes's shock absorbers were broken, but Chiron, by astonishing brilliance, drove along the ditch and came out of it at unabated speed. Their rivalry temporarily forgotten, Varzi gave Nuvolari a lift back to the pits.

Chiron was chasing Fagioli and took the lead, but soon after the Maserati engine blew up, which left Chiron with a commanding lead. Meanwhile, Nuvolari was chafing in the pit insisting that Borzacchini be called in. When the Monza stopped there was a long altercation between the two drivers before Nuvolari climbed into the driving seat. The race regulations required the engine to be started on the handle. It was swung but nothing happened, so, breaking the regulations, the mechanics pushed the car nearly 500 metres, but still nothing happened – the battery was flat. Nuvolari had to abandon it, and stalked back to the pit where presumably the altercation with Borzacchini was resumed!

It had been an incredible season of motor racing with an absorbing three-cornered fight for grand prix supremacy, and cars racing at speeds never attained in grand prix racing before. The sport was also attracting large crowds and was becoming a major attraction on mainland Europe. There were three rivals for driving supremacy. Varzi perhaps had a slight edge on Nuvolari, who was yet to reach his prime, but maybe better than both in 1931 was Louis Chiron. However, for Alfa Romeo the promise of success in the early part of the season had not been properly fulfilled.

Chapter 7

Two seats good, one seat better

THE DEPRESSION OF 1929, which ran on into the early 1930s, affected Italy less than some countries, probably because, apart from the two major industrial cities of the north, it was still almost a peasant economy. As a result Jano was able to proceed with his new design relatively unhampered by financial stringencies, and doubtless receiving encouragement in his work from the Palazzo Veneto. It was much the same story with the Maserati brothers at Bologna. North of the Alps, however, it was a different picture. Mercedes-Benz, which had gained some remarkable successes with Caracciola and his SSKL in 1931, was badly affected by the economics of the Weimar Republic, now in its dying throes, so withdrew its support from Caracciola and decided that in 1932 its competition programme would be very limited. Bugatti kept going, not yet introducing a new design and relying as much on those customers who could still afford to race as on a factory team.

The design that Jano showed to the Alfa Romeo management in September 1931 had one fundamental difference from the Monza that preceded it: profiting from the experience of the Tipo A, the new car was a single-seater. As there was no requirement that a mechanic should be carried, no seat was provided for one. The engine was the logical development of the 1931 8C, though Peter Hull has suggested that as the layout of the new engine had a striking similarity to the 1100cc eight-cylinder Salmson designed by Emil Petit in 1928, Jano may have been influenced by it.

The new engine was a straight-eight with a bore of 65mm and a stroke of 100mm; the capacity was 2654cc. It was in effect two 'fours'. The cylinders were cast in alloy in two blocks of four and, unlike the Monza, the heads were fixed; there were two valves per cylinder at an angle of 104 degrees. The blocks were mounted on an electron crankcase, which had ten main bearings for the two-piece crankshaft. Two helical gears were driven from the centre of the crankshaft. One drove the two overhead

1932: The Tipo B (P3) engine, showing the two superchargers.

camshafts via two intermediary gears, while the other drove the superchargers, magnetos, and oil and water pumps. There were two Roots superchargers mounted on the nearside of the engine, driven by the helical gear at about 1.1 engine speed; each had a Memini carburettor. The boost pressure was about 10lb (0.7 bar). The compression ratio was 6.5:1 and it developed 215bhp at 6500rpm. The engine drove a four-speed gearbox with a central change, through a multi-plate dry clutch.

It was at this point that the design became wholly unconventional. A differential was attached to the rear of the gearbox where it gave the advantage of being part of the sprung weight of the car. Two shafts diverged from the differential, each driving a crown wheel and pinion in an alloy casing adjacent to each back wheel; an empty axle tube joined and supported the two casings. Various theories have been advanced for Jano's reasons in embracing such a complicated and unusual transmission. It has been suggested that it enabled the driver to sit lower in the car, but a study of the car does not support this. It has also been suggested that the system was lighter than the conventional axle, but any weight saving would have been marginal. Another theory is that it made it easier for the axle ratio to be changed, but this is debatable and a small advantage for such a complication. Apart from the transmission, the chassis was entirely conventional. The rear frame was upswept and there were semi-elliptic springs all round.

This new car was known by Jano and his team as the Tipo B, but as the heir and successor to the earlier cars it quickly became known as the P3 and was also called the 'Monoposto'; here it will be called the P3. Six of these cars were built at Portello in the spring of 1932.

While Jano had been busy at Portello, there had also been developments at Modena. Alfredo Caniato had resigned as president of the Scuderia Ferrari and his place was taken by Count Felice Trossi.

Trossi was 23 years old, a keen driver and a rich man, his fortune derived from the wool trade and the Banco Sella, which was owned by his family. He lived in almost feudal splendour in the Castello Gaglianico, outside Biella, about 60 miles (100km) from Milan. He had started racing with a Mercedes in minor events in 1928, and although relatively inexperienced he was keen and had talent as a driver. Trossi brought with him to the Scuderia another aristocratic driver, the Marquis Antonio Brivio. Brivio, who was 27 and lived in Biella, already had some serious racing experience with the Scuderia Materassi 1500cc Talbots and with a 6C Alfa Romeo. While Trossi and Brivio were paying for their drives, Enzo Ferrari had signed up Piero Taruffi, who would join Nuvolari as one of the 'professionals' in the Scuderia. Taruffi, a 26-year-old Roman, had made for himself a big reputation as a motor cycle racer. Ferrari had given him a trial in some minor hill climbs at the end of the 1931 season and he had acquitted himself well.

By the end of 1931 the nature of racing had changed, and the cult of the 'ace' driver was emerging. In the 1920s some drivers had been regarded as better than others, but these were not particularly sought out for their virtuosity; teams were keener to recruit steady 'old hands' rather than hot 'aces'. Now the full racing circus had evolved and it was realised that drivers of the calibre of Nuvolari and Varzi could get results for a team, even when the car was inferior to its rivals. It became important for teams to get the services of these top drivers, who would not only win races but could also command better starting money, an essential commodity for a team to pay its way.

With the withdrawal of Mercedes-Benz, Rudolf Caracciola was looking for a drive and Alfa Corse wasted little time in signing him up. His victories in the Mille Miglia and the German Grand Prix in the previous year, driving an unsuitable car, had marked him out as a driver of considerable talent. Aldo

Giovannini went to see him at his home in Switzerland and offered him a contract. While he would have a Monza, prepared at Portello with very favourable terms concerning prize and starting money, the contract stipulated that he would not be a full member of the Alfa Corse team and his car would be painted white, the German racing colour. Caracciola questioned Giovannini about this, who revealed rather grudgingly that Campari did not want him in the team, so the deal offered was a compromise. Apparently Campari had stated forcefully that Caracciola was not up to the standard that the Alfa Corse team expected. Campari's view was not, however, shared by *Motor Sport*, which described Caracciola 'as probably one of the world's four best drivers'. Prudently, it did not identify the other three!

It must have been a considerable disappointment, but the new P3 was not ready for the start of the season. The Scuderia sent Eugenio Siena with a single Monza to the Grand Prix de Tunisie on 3 April to back up Etancelin. This was on the Anfa circuit outside Carthage and the Bugattis were in force and on form, so the best Etancelin and Siena could manage was third and fourth. The next weekend the sports 8Cs redeemed the honour of the marque and the Scuderia in the Mille Miglia, but after driving 1000 gruelling miles on Italian roads the drivers only had seven days to recover their breath before the next performance, when they made the short trip along the French Riviera coast to Monte Carlo for the first major épreuve of the season, the Grand Prix de Monaco.

This was only the fourth time the race had been run, but already it was considered a major classic, perhaps because of its unique ambience. In 1932, as a concession to the needs of motor racing, the tramlines had been taken up. Once again it was going to be a three-cornered fight between Alfa Romeo, Bugatti and Maserati. Alfa Corse entered Borzacchini, Campari and Nuvolari, who were backed by the private entries of

Etancelin, Zehender and, most significant of all, Caracciola. In practice Chiron's Bugatti was fastest at 2min 4.0sec, while Borzacchini's Monza was next with 2min 4.8sec. To some extent this was wasted effort as the grid was by ballot, and of the likely front runners Chiron was best placed on the second row. Nuvolari was in the middle, while Caracciola and Varzi were one row from the back. Before the 1.30pm start, the course was opened by Sir Malcolm Campbell, the current holder of the Land Speed Record.

Chiron jumped the start and was level with the front row as the flag dropped. He was in the lead at the end of the first lap, followed by two more Bugattis. Meanwhile the Monzas were working their way through the field, and after ten laps Nuvolari was second, behind Chiron. He then applied the pressure and on lap 30 Chiron clipped a sandbag wall as he lapped a back-marker going through the Chicane and the Bugatti overturned. He escaped with a shaking but Nuvolari was in the lead, though only 6 seconds in front of Varzi's Bugatti. Borzacchini and Caracciola were next, and when Varzi's rear axle broke Caracciola came up to second and it was now Nuvolari's turn to be pressured. The white Monza closed right up, but then seemed to ease off and Nuvolari won by 3 seconds; in the closing laps he had almost run out of fuel and switched to the reserve tank just in time.

Afterwards the crowd booed Caracciola, thinking the result had been arranged, and his mechanic asked why he had not taken the lead. A rather embarrassed Caracciola seemed lost for a reply, but was clearly thinking about the contract and his chances of a place in the full team. It seems that Giovannini wasted no time, offering him a full team place as they talked in the pits. The doubts of Campari, who was tenth, had been answered.

Monzas were now coming on to the market and being bought by private owners. Some, like Etancelin, were nearly as quick as the team drivers, but others were

17 April 1932: Nuvolari, the eventual winner of the GP de Monaco, is in the centre of the fourth row, and Caracciola, who was second, is behind him.

trundling around at the back of the field, taking the starting money and enjoying a modestly profitable day out.

The Scuderia gave new boy Taruffi a run in the Premio Reale di Rome, a week after Monaco. This race had been moved to a

17 April 1932: Nuvolari's hubcap is about an inch from the wall as he takes the chicane during his winning drive at Monaco. (David Thirlby Collection)

new circuit on the Littorio airfield outside Rome and was a mixture of conventional corners and banked bends. Taruffi, in a Monza, did his stuff and came second behind the Maserati of Fagioli, which was much better suited to the fast track. This was the new V5, built to the same recipe as the V4 but using two 2.5-litre engines combined.

The Targa Florio was still in the calendar but seemed to have lost some of its former glory, though to the Italian drivers it still had a legendary aura of its own; a win in Sicily mattered much more than any number of victories on the short road circuits. The Long Madonie circuit was now unusable, so a link road was built with government funding, which made up the Short Madonie circuit that was used until the last time the race was run in 1973. Once again it was to be a Nuvolari/Varzi battle, with Borzacchini and Chiron in the supporting parts. Nuvolari led all the way followed by Borzacchini. Varzi broke his gearbox on the first lap and thereafter shared Chiron's T51 Bugatti, finishing third 20 minutes behind Nuvolari. The race took over 7 hours – the thought of doing that in the cockpit of a Monza or T51 Bugatti would make most modern GP drivers swoon in horror.

Even without the P3 it was all going Alfa Romeo's way. After the setbacks of 1931, and without any particular improvements, the Monza was proving more than a match for the T51 Bugatti, while the 3-litre Maserati had also been delayed and the 2.8 was not quick enough. However, there was a slight upset to the expected form at the Avus track outside Berlin on 22 May. With its two 6-mile (10km) straights linked by gently banked curves, it was a fast circuit and the race was over 182 miles (292km). Caracciola took his Monza, still painted white, and must have been surprised if not a little peeved that Mercedes-Benz, after apparently withdrawing from racing, entered Manfred von Brauchitsch with a streamlined SSKL. The better shape of that

car made it faster on the straights, but the speed and the weight made its tyres suffer, so von Brauchitsch had to ease off; the Monza was able to hold on all the way and the lead changed several times. The Mercedes won by only 4 seconds and the race average was 120.78mph (194.20kmh). The white Monza stayed in Germany and was taken to the Nürburgring two weeks later for the Eifelrennen. This time ability and road-holding counted more than speed, so Caracciola led for all 14 laps, although he was chased hard by René Dreyfus's T51 Bugatti.

It may have been planned or just fortuitous, but the P3 was ready for the Gran Premio d'Italia on Sunday 5 June. Two cars of the six being built were prepared for the race, which was to run over the full Monza circuit and last for 5 hours. The P3s were given to Nuvolari and Campari, and Alfa Corse had also entered Monzas for Borzacchini and Caracciola. The Scuderia was backing up the entry with Monzas for Pietro Ghersi and Eugenio Siena. The watching crowd was able to distinguish between the different Alfa Romeo entries, as the Corse cars were painted crimson and the Scuderia pair had the usual darker burgundy finish. The opposition was tough, ranging from the V5 Maserati and the T54 Bugatti down to the usual T51 Bugattis and 2.8-litre Maseratis. The crowd was smaller than expected, but AC Milan was playing an important football match that afternoon and the Tour of Italy cycle race was to pass through Milan during the day; perhaps Count Florio had picked the wrong date for the Gran Premio, or perhaps he didn't like football.

When the cars lined up on the grid, the slim monoposto body of the P3 made the rest of the cars look obsolete. Achille Starace, Secretary General of the Fascist Party, dropped the flag, and Nuvolari and Chiron (T54 Bugatti) charged to the front immediately. At the end of the first lap Fagioli (V5) was third, then Chiron eased a bit, leaving Fagioli to chase the P3 while he

and Varzi waited. At ten laps Fagioli was leading Nuvolari by a second. The pair continued to swap places, but when the cars made their first pit stops the P3 gained the advantage. Nuvolari stopped for only 1min 36sec and Campari only took 10 seconds longer, but the V5 Maserati stood at its pit for 3min 25sec. At 30 laps the Bugatti challenge had gone; Varzi's transmission was broken, so he took over Chiron's car, but this seized a piston.

Nuvolari and Campari were now running first and second, separated by 16 seconds and followed by Dreyfus (T51 Bugatti) and Fagioli, who was working hard to make up the time he had lost. Caracciola had stopped in the first few laps to change a magneto. He pressed on at the back, but the second magneto failed at 50 laps. Meanwhile Borzacchini had been hit in the face by a stone and stopped his Monza for first aid, so Attilio Marinoni took the car over, then handed it back to Borzacchini when he was bandaged up. Feeling groggy, Borzacchini came in again; this time the eager and now unemployed Caracciola jumped into the car and began to motor very seriously.

Campari's P3 had lost its edge and was dropping back, but Fagioli had been working very hard and was now hounding Nuvolari, taking the lead just before the second pit stops. Once again all his diligent work was wasted by his pit staff. He lost a lap to Nuvolari and spent the rest of the race trying to make this up and probably having evil thoughts about his crew, but it availed him nothing. Like the P2 before it, the P3 won its first race, having averaged 104.09mph (167.37kmh). Fagioli came in second, a lap behind and only 38 seconds ahead of Caracciola, who had driven superbly, his efforts overshadowed by the P3's victory. Campari was fourth and Dreyfus fifth, having dropped two places in the final laps when he stopped for fuel. It was a famous victory, but, as *Motor Sport* commented, '… if Fagioli's pit work had been as well organised as that of the Alfa

Romeo drivers, he would have undoubtedly won the race …'

The records do not show if Caracciola was still using his original Monza. If he was, the paint shop at Portello must have been busy with the cans of red and white paint, as a fortnight after the Monza race he was at Lwow, in Poland, for the local grand prix. Lwow was at the eastern side of Poland, was incorporated into the Soviet Union in 1945 and is now part of the Ukraine. Caracciola's Monza was white once more, and it did what was needed, giving him an easy win.

While Caracciola was making the long trip back, either to Portello or to his home at Arosa, Jean-Pierre Wimille had forsaken his T51 Bugatti for a Monza and was winning the Grand Prix de Lorraine. He would win some more races with an Alfa Romeo in the fullness of time.

The scene was now set for another 5-hour grande épreuve, the Grand Prix de l'ACF. This race had moved to the classic triangular road circuit outside Reims, which had two long straights linked by a back leg, with fast, climbing curves; it ran across the plains of Champagne, where the fighting had been bitter only 15 years before. The roads were lined with young poplars, planted to replace those shattered by shell-fire, and in honour of the event new rein-forced concrete grandstands and pits had been built. As Reims was the centre of the Champagne vineyards, the local product was always much in evidence at this circuit, so it was not surprising that it was a popular venue with the drivers and teams.

To show that he was fully accepted into the fold, a third P3 had been finished and was entered for Caracciola by Alfa Corse. The other two cars were in the hands of Nuvolari and Borzacchini. It seemed to show that the old veteran's status was slipping, as Campari had only been entered with a Monza; although he was at Reims he did not practise and the car was probably not there. It was the beginning of a breach with Portello that would fester for the rest of the year.

19 June 1932: Rudolf Caracciola's Monza is about to lap Stasny's T35B Bugatti during the GP von Lemburg. The crowd protection is minimal.

It was a straight fight between Alfa Romeo and Bugatti as Maserati, still waiting for the new 3 litre, did not turn up. Alfieri Maserati, the head of the family, had died on 3 March and his death had left the small firm bereft and disorganised. With the honour of France at stake, Ettore Bugatti brought out the T54s as speed was essential on such a fast circuit. The Alfa Romeo headquarters was at Thillois, the village on the hairpin at the start of the grandstand straight. As the cars lined up, Nuvolari pulled on a yellow jersey and yellow helmet, while Caracciola was dressed all in white. The Vicomte de Rohan, President of the ACF, dropped the flag and released the field of 16 cars.

Caracciola led Varzi, who was followed by Nuvolari, but on lap nine Nuvolari was up to second place and two laps later passed

3 July 1932: Caracciola wipes the aero screen of his P3 during a pit stop in the GP de l'ACF at Reims. The portly man on the right is 'Toto' Roche, the celebrated race organiser.

3 July 1932: Nuvolari makes a stop during the GP de l'ACF. Campari, the reserve driver, waits hopefully on the pit counter. He did not get a drive.

Caracciola. As he did so there was a lot of fist-shaking, which may have indicated that team orders had been broken and Caracciola should have let Nuvolari through earlier. After that the race for the lead was virtually over. The T54 Bugattis broke their gearboxes and Borzacchini led briefly while his team-mates made their routine stops, but the three P3s, with their notable exhaust boom, ran on to win. At the end of the 5 hours they had covered 92 laps and were less than 45 seconds apart. Jano

walked down to Thillois corner, at the beginning of the finishing straight, and tried to wave Nuvolari down, wanting the cars to cross the line together, but Nuvolari was having none of it; perhaps he did not trust Caracciola not to pull a fast one, and he roared on to the flag leaving Borzacchini and Caracciola to follow him in.

The whole balance of grand prix racing had changed in just four weeks, and when the teams went to the Nürburgring on 17 July for the Grösser Preis von Deutschland, there cannot have been many who would have forecast a win for any car other than an Alfa Romeo; the P3s were now as invincible as the P2s had been eight years earlier. The German race would be the final round of the European Championship, the forerunner of the World Championship; the previous qualifying rounds were at Monza and Reims. The scoring was unusual: a win was worth 1 point, second place 2 points and so on, and the winner was the driver with the least points. Driving a shared car still gained the full points. When he went to the 'Ring Nuvolari had 2 points, Borzacchini had 5 and Caracciola had 6. Provided he finished in the first three, Nuvolari was home and dry, but if not the other two were still in with a chance. The situation was akin to the World Championship dramas that would be enacted in later years!

3 July 1932: The victorious P3 team rounds Thillois hairpin, Caracciola leading Borzacchini and Nuvolari.

Alfa Corse entered a P3 for Campari, but once again he was absent and it was the three Championship contenders who ran. The Bugatti opposition was blunted, as Varzi had injured an eye at Reims and was still unfit. Some of the fire seemed to have gone from Varzi – he was not at the peak that he had attained two years earlier, though the mechanical frailties of Bugatti must have dampened his enthusiasm.

A crowd of 150,000 turned up on race day, no doubt expanded by the hopes of a Caracciola win. They were not disappointed. Jano and Gianferrari had decided that it would make commercial sense to let him win the race, which could be done without jeopardising Nuvolari's championship prospects. Caracciola led at the start, then on lap ten Nuvolari went to the front, but at the pit stops Caracciola's car was replenished in 1min 35sec, while Nuvolari's pit crew seemed to work deliberately slowly and he was stopped for 2min 40sec. It has been suggested that Nuvolari realised that there was a go-slow as he began to threaten the mechanics with a hammer to speed up the stop. Caracciola went on to win, and with two laps to go Nuvolari stopped once more, worried about oil consumption, but he set off again and came second, followed by Borzacchini. Nuvolari was Champion with four points,

17 July 1932: In the GP von Deutschland at Nürburgring, Caracciola launches his P3 into the Karussel on his way to victory.

Caracciola was second with seven, and Borzacchini was third with eight – a clean sweep for the Alfa Corse drivers. If Nuvolari's oil problems had been terminal, it defies speculation what would have happened – who would have been ordered to hand over their car, and what bloodshed would have ensued?

The motor racing circus then moved to Italy, and first came the Coppa Ciano at Livorno on 31 July; 10 laps of the 12.4-mile (20km) rough and hilly circuit. Although it was a relatively local event, Alfa Corse took it seriously and presented three P3s driven by Nuvolari, Borzacchini and, surprisingly, Campari. After some early opposition from

14 August 1932: The start of the Coppa Acerbo at Pescara. Caracciola (No 2) holds the rear wheel of his P3 to stop it rolling forward. With him on the front row are Silvio Rondini (OM, No 4) and Baconin Borzacchini (Monza, No 6).

August 1932: Nuvolari's Pescara-winning P3 has been taken to Rome to be inspected by Mussolini in the grounds of his residence, the Villa Torlonia. He sits in the car, Nuvolari, in a pale suit, stands beside the cockpit, and Borzacchini is on the extreme right.

Varzi's T51 Bugatti, the trio finished in that order. A fortnight later they all went to Pescara for the Coppa Acerbo. Although racing for the Coppa, the winner knew that he would not receive it, as it had been stolen by a burglar two weeks before the race. Again Campari was entered with a P3, but he did not turn up. Nuvolari and Caracciola drove P3s, while this time Borzacchini had to be content with a Monza. It seems that if six cars had been built as has been stated, it was never possible to make more than three raceworthy, and sometimes only two. Ghersi and Taruffi had the Scuderia Monzas, which could only hope to be among the supporting cast.

In the race the P3s swapped places at the front and Nuvolari won by 15 seconds. The team were racing on Pirelli tyres; it seems probable that in the previous races in the season they were racing on Dunlops. This was certainly so in the French Grand Prix.

After the Livorno race, Nuvolari and Borzacchini were summoned to visit Mussolini in Rome, taking a P3 with them. They met at Mussolini's residence, the Villa Torlonia in the Via Nomentana, where he congratulated them on their results and the Mussolini family inspected the car.

Everyone was going to be at the Gran Premo di Monza on 11 September, so it seems likely that Portello was working hard to have the P3s in perfect condition. As a result only one was sent to Brno for the Masarykuv Okruh the week before on 4 September. For this race the entries were made by the Scuderia and surprisingly it was Baconin Borzacchini who had the P3, Nuvolari and Brivio having to make do with Monzas. At last Maserati had readied the new 3 litre, the 8C-2300. This had a new engine but still carried a two-seat body; Fagioli was the driver. The other opposition came from the works T51 Bugattis.

Siena demolished a Scuderia Monza in practice and Borzacchini set the fastest time, but it all went wrong in the race, which was run in terrible conditions. Borzacchini fell out with a broken differential early on, while Nuvolari had ignition problems, probably caused by the wet, and spent nearly half an hour in the pits, so Chiron won, giving Bugatti its first major win of the season; the new Maserati was second.

The Monza race had the usual three 10-lap heats and a répêchage, with a 20-lap final. As Paul Sheldon points out, the entry was magnificent, better than any grande épreuve during the season. This time Alfa Corse had prepared four P3s, driven by Nuvolari, Caracciola, Borzacchini and Campari. Maserati had brought out the V5 again and Bugatti was running the T54s. The rest of the field was impressive and the Scuderia Monzas were handled by Siena and Taruffi. It was also a royal occasion, as Crown Prince Umberto and his wife, Princess Marie, were there.

In the first heat, at 10.30am, Caracciola led all the way, followed by Minozzi's works Tipo 26M Maserati. Varzi seemed content to conserve his Bugatti for the final, and ran home in third place. The second heat produced the fireworks. Both Nuvolari and Fagioli drove as if it was the final. For six laps the lead changed continuously, then Nuvolari came in to change a buckled wheel. He did not lose second place, while Taruffi's Monza was third catching Chiron's T54 Bugatti when he too stopped for a damaged wheel. Campari and Borzacchini ran away with the third heat, which was run at a much higher average speed than the second, though Fagioli probably eased right off when Nuvolari stopped.

While the répêchage was being run, it was announced that Prospero Gianferrari had lodged a protest for Alfa Corse alleging that Fagioli had forced Nuvolari off the road and demanding that Fagioli should be disqualified from the final. Nuvolari said that he had tried to pass the Maserati on the Curva Granda and Fagioli had 'closed the door', forcing him on to the verge where he hit a culvert. Fagioli replied that he had merely held the racing line and Nuvolari had tried to pass without enough room – a dialogue that sounds very much like World Championship racing in the 1990s. Little has changed! Gianferrari said that the P3s would be withdrawn from the final unless Fagioli was disqualified.

When the cars were pushed out to parade in front of the stands before the final, the P3s were not there. The crowd began to jeer and catcall. Meanwhile, the chief race commissioner, appointed by the RACI, the Marchese Pietro Parisio, had considered the protest and indicated that he did not support it. Gianferrari was adamant that the cars would not start despite the pleas of Parisio and Count Florio. At this point Roberto Farinacci, the Secretary of the Fascist Party, intervened. As Charles Faroux told it in L'Auto: 'Gianferrari, his engineer Jano and his team manager Giovannini, conscious of their duty and of the wrong done to their man, were greatly affected and finally Gianferrari consented.' In reality it is more likely Farinacci pointed out to Gianferrari that he who paid the piper called the tune. If the Party said they would race, they would race.

To the cheers of the crowd the P3s were therefore pushed out to join the parade, although Campari's car was missing, having been robbed of a front axle to repair Nuvolari's car. After all that, the final was a slight anti-climax. The three P3s pulled away from Fagioli, Caracciola and Nuvolari swapped the lead several times, and Fagioli moved up to third when Borzacchini made a short stop. Nuvolari fell back with a punctured float chamber and was passed by Fagioli, but kept third place to the end, while Caracciola ran on to an unchallenged victory.

It was not quite the end of the season. Alfa Corse sent Nuvolari to the Grand Prix de Marseille, which was run on the Miramas track, the unusual, flat oval in the Camargue where the cars ran in a continu-

11 September 1932: Nuvolari's P3 is wheeled out for the start of the second heat of the GP di Monza. Behind the car, from left to right, are Amedeo Bignami, Consalvo Sanesi and Vittorio Jano.

ous curve, as there was no proper straight. Fagioli was there with the V5 and for the first ten laps he and Nuvolari battled. The V5 then made a long stop and Nuvolari seemed to have the race in his pocket. When he made a leisurely stop his pit staff made a miscalculation, believing that Raymond Sommer's Monza was a lap behind. Sommer gained nearly a lap on the P3 and when the error was realised Nuvolari drove so hard that he burst a tyre and had to stop again, so Sommer went on to a deserved and unexpected win. A young Algerian driver, Guy Moll, was third with a T51 Bugatti, and his performance must have impressed the Alfa Corse team. It would not, however, be the last time that Alfa Corse would think Sommer was a lap behind.

Alfa Romeo had dominated grand prix racing throughout the season and the 8C sports cars had been equally successful, winning every major event. Nuvolari was

Italian Champion as well as winning the European title. The success of the Alfa Corse drivers earned the firm the first prize in the fund set up to accompany the European Championship, and FF75,000 went to Portello. In the picture that was soon to emerge, this must have been manna from heaven. In November 1932 the Sporting Commission of the AIACR (Alliance Internationale des Automobile Club Reconnus), the international governing body of motor racing, met to decide upon the next grand prix formula. It was worried that cars were getting too fast. The 150mph being achieved on circuits such as Monza had to be curbed. The Commission believed that if a weight limit was imposed, the heavy and fastest cars like the V5 Maserati would be kept out and so, in its wisdom, it decreed that in 1934 the new formula would limit grand prix cars to a maximum weight of 750kg, satisfied that this would keep speeds down.

Chapter 8

A brave new world?

O^N 30 January 1933 Adolf Hitler was appointed as Chancellor of Germany, an event that was to change the face of the world totally and irrevocably. It was an event that was also to have a decisive effect on the fortunes of Alfa Romeo and its motor racing aspirations. At the beginning of 1933 Alfa Romeo had major problems. Although the company was loosely controlled by the Istituto Liquidazione (IL), the directors were responsible for the day-to-day running of the company and its financial affairs. In January the Istituto per la Ricostruzione Industriale (IRI) took over the holdings of the IL, which meant that the state grip was even tighter. During 1932 582 cars had been built, but how many were sold is not known. The world was still in the grips of the Depression that had begun in 1929, and trading prospects for 1933 did not look any brighter. The company had contracts to build aero engines, but even so it was making a loss. The factory at Portello was out of date and needed re-equipping, but there was no capital to do this.

In racing the P3s had swept the board in 1932 and it was likely that they would do so again in 1933, but the 8C-3000 Maserati, now a monoposto, looked promising and there were rumours of a wholly new 2.8-litre Bugatti. To win again in 1933 could be harder and any failures could tarnish the superb reputation built up in 1932. It cannot have been difficult for the directors when they made the decision in January that Alfa Corse would not race in 1933. Money would be saved and the Scuderia Ferrari would continue to keep the Alfa Romeo name in the public eye. Furthermore, there seemed little likelihood of any marque toppling Alfa Romeo from its pinnacle in sports car racing; the victories there would ensure that the reputation was maintained, and would be more likely to sell production cars.

When Enzo Ferrari was told of the withdrawal, he assumed that the P3s would be handed to him so that the Scuderia could carry on where Alfa Corse had left off the previous autumn. The loan of a P3 for the Czech race seemed to indicate that this would be a foregone conclusion. As well as casting his plans into confusion, it must have been a tremendous blow to Ferrari's pride when he was told that he would not be having the P3s, which would remain stored at Portello and not race at all. He made several trips from Modena to Milan to plead his case, but the Alfa Romeo directors were adamant. The cars remained stored at Portello. Perhaps in the hope of applying more pressure, it was rumoured that Ferrari had been negotiating with the Maserati brothers about the possibility of running a pair of Maseratis instead, but the story did nothing to soften the collective Portello managerial heart.

The decision not only discountenanced Ferrari, but the four Alfa Corse drivers were out of a job. Nuvolari and Borzacchini decided to join forces with Ferrari – he had cars and a well-organised team. Alfa Romeo suggested that Caracciola should go with them, but he had already decided to join up with Louis Chiron. Chiron's relations with the Bugatti team had become strained and matters were brought to a head after a row about hotel accommodation for the Gran Premio di Monza. There were also additional problems as Meo Costantini, the Bugatti manager, was taking a lot of interest in Chiron's mistress, 'Baby' Hoffman. She had been married to Freddie Hoffman, who had sponsored Chiron's early racing and also made the Nerka sparking plug used by the Bugatti team and several drivers; she had left Hoffman to live with Chiron and her marriage had recently been dissolved. Chiron and Caracciola formed a new team, Scuderia CC, which would race two Monzas, bought from Portello. In the light of what was to come, it was significant that the small team was given a diesel lorry by Mercedes-Benz to carry the cars.

Campari had other ideas. It seems that disillusion had set in and he must have realised that if he went to the Scuderia he would be playing third fiddle to Nuvolari and Borzacchini, so he went down the road to Bologna and negotiated with the Maserati brothers. He was talking of making 1933 his last season, as he was coming up to his 41st birthday.

Enzo Ferrari knew that he had to find more power if he was to beat the Scuderia CC Monzas and cope with the stronger challenge likely to come from Bugatti and Maserati. Modifications were made to the

Scuderia Monzas devised by Luigi Bazzi, though it is probable that most of the development work was carried out by Giulio Ramponi, who was now the chief engineer at Modena. The principal modification was to bore the engine out to 68mm, which increased the swept volume to 2556cc. The supercharger was modified and a double-choke Weber 55 replaced the Memini carburettor. The porting of the cylinder head was improved, larger inlet valves were fitted and attention was paid to the lubrication system. After the improvements, the engine output was increased to 180bhp at 5600rpm. The CC cars were also fitted with 2.6-litre engines, but it is not known whether these engines came from Modena or were supplied by Portello when the cars were delivered.

The 1933 motor racing season began unseasonably early. The first event was the Grand Prix de Pau, held on a round-the-houses circuit on 19 February. It was run in a snowstorm and Etancelin would probably have won, had he not stopped to have accumulated snow removed from his Monza's plugs! Monzas were now being sold to the keen amateurs and three found their way to Sweden, where Per-Viktor Widengren used his to win the Sveriges Vinter Grand Prix. A second Swedish race, the Svenska Isloppet, was won by a Monza driven by the German driver Paul Pietsch, who would later have more to do with Alfa Romeo, and indirectly would have a profound effect on the life of Achille Varzi.

The season proper started when most of the leading players went to Tunis on 29 March for the local grand prix. Nuvolari had the first Monza to be enlarged by the Scuderia, while the second car, driven by Borzacchini, was still a 2.3. Borzacchini led for the first few laps, then let Nuvolari through and the pair went on to finish first and second separated by 0.2 second at the end, though 13 minutes ahead of Zehender's Maserati. The opposition must have wondered why Ferrari was so anxious to have the P3s.

A week later it was the Grand Prix de Monaco. The story of the 1933 race has rightly passed into heroic legend. Paul Sheldon has described it 'as one of the greatest races of this or any other age'. The mechanics must have been too busy preparing the cars at Modena to find the time to bring another car up to the 2.6 specification, so Borzacchini, Siena and Trossi had the Scuderia 2.3s, while Nuvolari was given the 2.6. The Scuderia CC had their new Monzas, Chiron's in blue with a white stripe, Caracciola's in white with a blue stripe. There was a full team of T51 Bugattis led by Varzi, and two of the monoposto 8CM Maseratis, driven by Sommer and Zehender. The race was significant as it was the first where the starting grid was decided on practice times. Varzi was on pole, sharing the front row with Chiron and Borzacchini, while Nuvolari was the fastest on the second row.

On the first day of practice Caracciola set the fastest time, then, trying to improve on this, he locked a brake at the Tabac and struck the wall. His right femur was fractured and the Monza was wrecked. His accident also wrecked the Scuderia CC, as he would not race again for 15 months, and when he returned to the wheel it would be in very different circumstances. The Tabac corner also caught out Nuvolari later in the morning, and the Monza's back axle was damaged.

When the flag fell Varzi took the lead, and at the end of the first lap Nuvolari was fourth behind Borzacchini and Lehoux's T51 Bugatti. Nuvolari passed these two and by lap four was on Varzi's tail. An incredible struggle now began. Nuvolari took the lead on lap four, held it for three laps, then lost it for two. Varzi took the lead on lap 13, was passed on lap 17 and went in front again on lap 19. At this stage Borzacchini, Lehoux and Etancelin were not far behind. Nuvolari took the lead again on lap 23, lost it on lap 29 and was back in front again on lap 33. On lap 39 Varzi led again, but a lap later Nuvolari had passed him. For ten laps Nuvolari was in front, then Varzi was back there on lap 50. The crowd watched enthralled, realising that a legend was being

3 April 1933: Nuvolari's Monza behind the pits before the start of the GP de Monaco. (Robert Beaver)

3 April 1933, Monaco: Varzi's T51 Bugatti shares the front row with the Monzas of Chiron and Borzacchini. Nuvolari is behind Varzi. (John Maitland Collection)

made. In the midst of all this excitement, Etancelin had passed Borzacchini and was chasing the leaders, but spoiled it when he hit the chicane sandbags and lost time.

Nuvolari and Varzi were probably slowing each other down during their battle, and Etancelin had caught Borzacchini again and passed him on lap 55, so at 60 laps only 4 seconds covered the leading four cars. On lap 65 Nuvolari led from Varzi, but Etancelin was only a few lengths behind,

then a halfshaft broke and he dropped out, while Borzacchini's engine had lost its tune and he fell away from the two duellists. Varzi was in front again on lap 81, but two laps later Nuvolari went by. He now began to pull away, and by lap 90 he had a 4-second lead. Varzi was not yet done, however. Perhaps he had indulged in a few laps' relaxation, conserving his energy for the final laps, as now he closed the gap again and on lap 98 the cars crossed the

line level. Varzi took the lead again, but lost it as the cars took the Gasworks Hairpin to finish the 99th lap.

So the last lap began. Varzi knew it was all or nothing, and allegedly took his engine up to 7500rpm in third as they went up the hill from Ste Devote to the Casino. This took him past Nuvolari once again. Nuvolari responded instantly and, savagely over-revving, tried to pass in the tunnel, but the Monza's engine had had enough and a piston broke. Nuvolari emerged from the tunnel with flames coming from the exhaust manifold where oil had sprayed on to it. He coasted to a halt and began to push the car, and a mechanic ran to help while Varzi completed the lap and received the flag. Nuvolari had led for 66 laps and Varzi for 34. Borzacchini came in second, his engine expiring as he crossed the line; he was the only driver on the same lap as the winner.

Poor Nuvolari gained nothing as he was disqualified when the mechanic helped to push the car, but he probably preferred to have ended the race amid flame and smoke, a symbolic pyre, than to see Varzi take the flag a few lengths ahead. It had been a truly great race, where both drivers had driven impeccably and had always given their rival

3 April 1933: Nuvolari and Varzi come out of the Gasworks Hairpin during their epic duel.

room to pass. For Varzi, the festering bitterness of the Targa Florio had been avenged, but for Nuvolari there was a growing disenchantment with Ferrari. The relationship between the two was beginning to sour and Nuvolari was also frustrated at the absence of the P3s.

There was now a brief interlude while the Scuderia Ferrari Monzas raced at Alessandria and took the first three places, led by Nuvolari. Varzi did not take part as his entry was made too late. At about this time, in deepest secrecy, Nuvolari visited Bologna and began negotiations with the Maserati brothers; his first move was to buy the 8CM Maserati that Sommer had driven at Monaco, but it was kept under wraps at Bologna for the time being.

Those who thought that the pool of racing drama had been drained dry at Monaco were now proved wrong. The Gran Premio di Tripoli was to produce just as much drama, but in a different form. The race on 7 May not only had a big prize fund, but was combined with a national sweepstake and the holder of the winning ticket would become very rich. The object of the lottery was to stimulate interest in the Italian colony of Libya, in which Tripoli was situated, in the hope of increasing immigration to it and also to give a boost to government funds. The counterfoils were sent to Tripoli and 30 tickets were drawn by the Governor of the colony, Marshal Badoglio, on the day of the Alessandria race. Each ticket was allocated to a driver in the race, so the lucky ticket holders knew who was carrying their chances.

There was now frantic activity. Nuvolari seems to have been a prime mover, but a meeting was held at which, it is alleged, Nuvolari, Varzi and Borzacchini were present, as also were the ticket holders who had drawn those drivers, accompanied by lawyers for all the parties. A deal was struck that all three would drive to win, but the drivers would have a cut of the lottery prize and share the race prize money, while the three ticket holders would all share in the

winnings. It was assumed that the race winner would be one of the trio of drivers; afterwards, Campari may have been brought into the plot. All would be well unless a driver outside the ring went too fast and won the race.

Both the Scuderia Monzas were now 2.6 litres and there was also a stripped sports 8C entered for Mario Tadini. The rest of the top runners were there and Campari was making his début in a Maserati. But the best laid plans … The grid was balloted and on the front row was Sir Henry Birkin with a new 8C Maserati, who took the lead from the start and held it for three laps. Campari then went past, but the English driver held on, and when the cars made their first stops he and Campari were in the pits together. Birkin had arranged for Maserati to provide him with a mechanic, but no one was in his pit when he stopped so he had to refuel himself, losing time that he was unable to make up. Meanwhile Campari had been delayed by a loose oil tank, so Nuvolari had taken the lead, followed by Varzi in his usual T51 Bugatti.

A repetition of the Monaco battle now began, but Varzi was able to go through non-stop and Nuvolari had to make a quick refuelling stop on lap 23. He was stationary for only 23 seconds, then set off in pursuit, catching Varzi on the last of the 30 laps; at that crucial moment the Bugatti faltered with fuel starvation and in the brief moment while Varzi switched to the reserve supply, Nuvolari went past. However, as the cars came up to the line Varzi was in the Monza's slipstream and pulled out just as they crossed the line to win by 0.2 second after 244 miles (392km) of racing. Birkin was third. He had burned his arm on the Maserati exhaust while refuelling and died in a London hospital six weeks later, reportedly of blood poisoning. This may have been caused by mosquito bites he received in Tripoli, to which he had an allergy after contracting malaria during the 1914–18 War, rather than as a result of the burn.

It has been suggested that the finish

between Varzi and Nuvolari was rigged, as there would have been no financial gain for either, but both were out-and-out racers and in the heat of the battle to be the winner would have been all that mattered, especially remembering their previous fights. What happened to Birkin's mechanic is a question that was not asked at the time.

The teams now went to Berlin for the Avusrennen on 21 May, where the races were watched by the new Reichschancellor, Adolf Hitler. Hitler had a great interest in motor racing and, like Mussolini, felt that racing successes were tangible evidence of the virility and mechanical ability of a nation. It must have irked Hitler that the race was a fierce struggle between the T54 Bugattis of Varzi and Czaikowski, the products of what he considered to be a decadent France. Varzi won and the 2.6 Monzas of Nuvolari and Borzacchini were almost lapped, finishing 5 minutes behind after 182 miles (292km). They crossed the line together, being given an equal third place.

After the Berlin race the Scuderia sent two cars to the Nürburgring for Nuvolari and Taruffi to drive in the Eifelrennen the following Sunday. The importance attached to motor racing by the National Socialist Party was highlighted by the presence of Hermann Goering, the President of the Reichstag and the Reich Minister for Aviation. Goering saw Chiron lead the race with his Scuderia CC Monza until he dropped back and Nuvolari went on to win; he was presented to Goering after the race. German hearts must have been lifted by the performance of von Brauchitsch, with a Mercedes SSKL, who was second.

That weekend the main force of the Scuderia seems to have been at the Targa Florio, now rapidly fading in importance, the clash of dates with the German race indicating its falling prestige. Borzacchini's Monza led for four laps until he hit a wall and broke a rear spring, after which it was left to Brivio to drive steadily to win.

The next major event was the Grand Prix de l'ACF at Montlhéry on 11 June, but a

28 May 1933: Brivio during his winning drive with his Monza at the Targa Florio.

week earlier Nuvolari had taken his Monza to Nîmes, on the edge of the Camargue, where he won the local grand prix, leading home the Monzas of Etancelin and the promising new boy Guy Moll, who had now abandoned Bugatti and bought a Monza. Moll's driving in this race impressed observers and he finished well ahead of Raymond Sommer, who was fourth in yet another Monza. Many of the rich amateurs were now disposing of their Bugattis to buy Monzas, which were readily available from Portello and were faster than the T51.

The Scuderia entered Nuvolari, Borzacchini and Taruffi for the French race, but morale at Modena had slumped and there were doubts as to whether the cars would be at Montlhéry. The entry for the race looked a bit thin as the Bugatti team did not appear; they had been hoping to have the new 2.8-litre T59 ready, and in anticipation of this had done no work on the T51s. When the T59 was not ready, there was no alternative but to scratch their entries.

Practice was held over four days and it was not until the last day that the Scuderia

Monzas turned up. Nuvolari broke the lap record on his first flying lap, but then pressed on, seeking even better times, and broke his supercharger drive. Until the morning of the race there was still a doubt about the Scuderia participation and it was an indication of their problems that it was not possible to repair Nuvolari's car, so Borzacchini stood down and handed his car over to him.

It was a cloudy day and the crowd was smaller than expected. M Perouse of the ACF flagged the cars away, and at the end of the first lap Nuvolari led from Campari's earlier two-seat 8C Maserati, while Taruffi with the other Scuderia Monza was third. Nuvolari kept ahead of Campari, who was bulging out of his car like Mr Bibendum, the Michelin advertisement character, and chasing hard; he was followed by Taruffi, who was balking the Monzas of Chiron and Etancelin. On lap six both Nuvolari and Chiron stopped. Chiron's rear axle was broken and Nuvolari set off with new rear tyres, but stopped on the circuit on the same lap, also with a broken axle. This left Campari with a 32-second lead over Etancelin. The Maserati then stopped and

Taruffi, now in front of Etancelin, took the lead. When Etancelin stopped for fuel and tyres, Campari was able to chase Taruffi and took the lead again on lap 19.

At half distance Campari led Taruffi by 19 seconds, with Sommer third and Etancelin fourth, so it was one Maserati holding off three Monzas. Shortly afterwards Taruffi made his pit stop. Four wheels were changed, the tank was filled, then Taruffi was ordered out of the car and Nuvolari took his place. In his autobiography, *Works Driver*, Taruffi mentions his 'bitterness', particularly as Nuvolari managed to break the transmission in the next four laps. Although Campari still led, Etancelin was keeping the gap constant, and when the Maserati stopped for tyres again, Etancelin's Monza took the lead.

Campari was 31 seconds behind with 12 laps to go. He cut the deficit back until he was only 3 seconds behind on lap 36, but then he stopped again for more tyres and now it began to rain. This put him a minute behind Etancelin again, and he had also contravened the race regulations by having a push start after his stop. But Etancelin was also in trouble and had to ease off as his clutch was giving out and he could not engage gears. At the start of the last lap the blue Monza led by 24 seconds, but halfway round the lap it came to a halt while Etancelin struggled to engage a gear. While he was doing this, Campari roared past and went on to win, giving Maserati its first grande épreuve victory. Etancelin got going again slowly and crossed the line in second place, 42 seconds later. There was a suggestion that Campari would be disqualified for his offence, but he was fined FF1000 instead. There were only six finishers; behind Etancelin were the English amateur George Eyston, later to hold the Land Speed Record, Sommer, Moll and Julio Villars, all driving Monzas. After the race Taruffi might well have wondered what the result would have been if he had been left in his car. The bitterness rankled and a few days later he resigned from the Scuderia and, like Campari, went to have discussions at Bologna.

The morale of the Scuderia was now at rock bottom and once again Enzo Ferrari pleaded with the Alfa Romeo directors to release the P3s. Their reply may have been that if private owners could win races with their Monzas, why did the Scuderia need the P3s? The gloom was compounded by more sad news. After his crash, Caracciola's care had been undertaken by Aldo Giovannini as his personal responsibility. Giovannini had moved Caracciola to the Rizzoli Institute at Bologna where his recovery could be supervised by Professor Putti, a specialist in orthopaedic injuries. Caracciola was beginning to recover, but now Aldo Giovannini was admitted to the same hospital with kidney failure. The days of transplants and dialysis were nearly 50 years ahead, and Giovannini died shortly after his admission. In the spring of 1933 Sir Henry Birkin had published his memoirs, *Full Throttle*, and he unwittingly wrote Giovannini's epitaph:

'... only the very greatest of team managers could control them [the Alfa Romeo team] and only the very greatest of team managers did. His name was Giovannini; his position was that of an impresario producing an opera in which all the leading roles are taken by temperamental stars. Yet he contrived to satisfy everyone and calm every storm. He had a deep insight into the qualities of men and of cars; he speaks Italian, French, German Spanish and English, and needs them all; he possesses the most delightful sense of humour; and that he also needs.'

Truly, his death was a blow to Alfa Romeo.

The week after the Montlhéry race, Nuvolari and Sommer took an 8C to victory in the Le Mans 24-hour race, which was won on the very last lap when Nuvolari overtook Luigi Chinetti's similar car to take the lead and win by about 400 metres. This must have been a substantial consolation for the failure at the Grand Prix. Seven days later the Scuderia sent Nuvolari with a Monza to the Gran Premio de Pena Rhin on a circuit in the Montjuich Park in the centre of Barcelona. It was another debacle. He led for a few laps, then fell right back with carburation problems and finished fifth. The race was, however, an Alfa Romeo victory, the Monza of the Chilean driver Zanelli coming first and that of the Portuguese Samiero second.

The happenings at Reims a week later showed that the Scuderia was now only on a par with the private entrants. The grid for the Grand Prix de la Marne was decided on practice times. The 8CM Maseratis of Campari and Zehender shared the front row with Lehoux's Bugatti. Nuvolari had arrived too late to practise and was at the back. This seemed to make little difference as he was second, behind Lehoux at the end of the first lap. Next time round, he was in front followed by Campari and Etancelin. Campari then stopped, his eye injured by a stone, and Nuvolari went on his way, pulling out a minute's lead over Etancelin by lap 12. On lap 22 Nuvolari stopped for fuel and was passed by Etancelin, Moll and Wimille, all driving Monzas. Nuvolari soon disposed of Wimille and Moll, and was closing on Etancelin when the back axle broke and he was out.

Etancelin now led, but then he stopped for fuel, which let Moll go by to lead, but only by 10 seconds from Etancelin and 18 seconds from Wimille. With two laps to go Moll had to stop for fuel, which left Etancelin in front, but only a few lengths ahead of Wimille. As the two Monzas, the all-blue of Etancelin and the blue with red stripe of Wimille, rounded Thillois for the last time and started the dash up the straight to the flag, Wimille was about half a length behind. He pulled out of Etancelin's slipstream and tried to pass but could not make it and was 0.2 second behind as they crossed the line. Moll had been disqualified for having outside assistance at his stop, so Sommer's Monza was third.

Sommer had been busy. He had practised at Reims on the Friday, flown to Spa and driven a sports 8C Alfa Romeo in the Spa 24-hour race starting at 4.00pm on the Saturday, raced through the night at Spa, then flown back to Reims at 8.00am on the Sunday. As his co-driver, Stoffel, took second place at Spa, Sommer must have been one of very few men to be placed in two races over 100 miles (160km) apart at the same time!

The relations between Nuvolari and Enzo Ferrari now broke down. Nuvolari felt that he deserved a car that matched his talents, and this Ferrari could no longer provide. Ferrari knew about the Tripoli sweepstake 'deal' and was bitterly hurt that it had not been discussed with him. The biggest blow to his pride, according to the journalist Giovanni Canestrini, came when Nuvolari proposed that the Scuderia should be renamed the 'Scuderia Nuvolari-Ferrari'. The secret deal that Nuvolari had made with Maserati now came out into the open. For the Grand Prix de Belgique at Spa on 9 July Nuvolari took over the 8CM Maserati that Campari had driven at Reims, which was available as Campari's eye had not yet healed. Whether Nuvolari let Ferrari know that he had already bought another Maserati is not known, but if he did it cannot have helped the deteriorating relationship.

One of the stranger aspects of this dispute was that the Maserati was entered at Spa by the Scuderia Ferrari. Ferrari seemed likely to be losing his ace driver, something that could have a serious effect on the existing fuel, oil and tyre contracts, so he was probably willing, despite everything, to try and accommodate Nuvolari. Hurt pride is one thing, but losing good income is another. The retainer being paid to Nuvolari may also have been a matter of contention. According to Guidotti, Nuvolari said to Ferrari, 'Who races, who wins, who risks their lives?', and went on to demand that he should get an equal 'cut' with Ferrari. At Spa the Scuderia 2.6 Monzas were entered for Borzacchini and Siena; Sommer's car was now also a 2.6. To add to the humiliation of Ferrari and complete the rupture of the relationship, Nuvolari's Maserati ran away with the race. Borzacchini dropped out, while Siena finished fifth and Sommer was seventh.

After their sojourn north of the Alps the Italian drivers now went home for the traditional series of races in August. First it was the Coppa Ciano at Livorno, and Nuvolari now produced his own Maserati. Baconin Borzacchini, whose loyalty to Nuvolari was stronger than his loyalty to Ferrari, secretly helped him prepare the Maserati for the event. Nuvolari walked away with the race once more, and the best Scuderia Monza, driven by Brivio, was second. Borzacchini, sharing the second car with Tadini, was fifth.

There was now yet another twist to the tale, in which the dramas and intrigues were beginning to seem more like grand opera than motor racing. Luigi Fagioli was severely discountenanced by the arrival of Nuvolari at Maserati – he had been their

No 1 driver, but now found himself sidelined by the *arriviste* Nuvolari. A proud man, Fagioli immediately went to Modena and joined the Scuderia Ferrari. Whether Ferrari discovered that Borzacchini had been helping Nuvolari is not known, but at the same time Borzacchini left the Scuderia and joined Nuvolari at Maserati. Borzacchini had raced for the Maserati brothers three years earlier and had retained a considerable affection for them and their cars.

When the cars arrived at Nice for the Grand Prix de Nice on 6 August, although Nuvolari and Campari had the two works Maseratis, Campari had been demoted to driving a 4CM Maserati voiturette bored out to 2 litres; he was in much the same position as he had been with the Scuderia a year before. Fagioli was now in a Scuderia 2.6 Monza. Nuvolari won, but only after a splendid battle with Etancelin who was driving right at the top of his form in his Monza, which was still a 2.3. Fagioli had a quiet race and was fourth behind Moll, who was now showing real promise. Brivio had not been at Nice with the Scuderia as he

had been sent to enjoy the midnight sun in Sweden, where he won the Sveriges Sommar Grand Prix at Vram with a Monza after avoiding an eight-car crash on the opening lap, which eliminated Chiron's Monza.

While Fagioli was at Nice, Enzo Ferrari had been busy. He had made yet more entreaties to the Alfa Romeo board, pointing out that because of their intransigence not only had he lost his best driver, but he also could no longer win races. Furthermore, the private owners of Monzas could no longer win races either. Alfa Romeo was in danger of becoming an also-ran in grand prix racing, especially as the new 2.8 T59 Bugattis were imminent. Ferrari timed his pleas perfectly; the commercial situation at Portello had become desperate and the directors were now worrying about the problems of sheer survival, so it is likely that when Ferrari arrived to present his arguments he received the reply, 'Oh yes, take the cars and stop bothering us.'

In the first week of August six P3s were taken from Portello to Modena, together with all the spares needed. Luigi Bazzi, who had been dividing his time between Modena and Portello, was released and became the chief technician of the Scuderia. Several mechanics came with the cars, including Attilio Marinoni, whose experience would be invaluable; Guidotti remained at Portello and was elevated to become chief technician and chief tester.

At about this time Giulio Ramponi left the Scuderia. It was suggested that he fell out with Ferrari and may also have offended the Fascist bosses. It was also said that he had made an appreciable sum from fringe dealings in the Tripoli affair. He came to England, where he began work with the Anglo-American driver Whitney Straight, who was then running a 2.5 Maserati in grands prix. Not everyone made a 'killing' from Tripoli, however; the mechanics were given a small cash bonus and Guidotti said that he received a case of Lambrusco and a

6 August 1933: Both spinning their wheels, Etancelin (No 24) and Wimille (No 6) lead the field at the start of the GP de Nice. Behind are Nuvolari (Maserati, No 2), Sommer (Monza, No 4), Lehoux (Bugatti, No 10), and Moll (Monza, No 8).

zampone, a stuffed pig's trotter and Modena speciality!

Ferrari was not the only man who was busy in the week after the Nice race. Campari was upset by the arrival of Nuvolari and Borzacchini at Maserati, and had probably also heard that the P3s had been released to Ferrari, so he arrived back in Modena and rejoined the Scuderia in the seven days between the Nice race and the Coppa Acerbo at Pescara. The Scuderia entered two P3s for Fagioli and Campari, who were matched against four Maseratis led by Nuvolari, while Bugatti sent two T51s for Varzi and Dreyfus. Campari beat the field away, but on the long 15.27-mile (24.5km) lap Nuvolari had forged to the front and led Campari by a few lengths as they crossed the line. Taruffi's Maserati was next, followed by Fagioli and Varzi. For eight laps Nuvolari and Campari passed and repassed, then the Maserati came past alone – the P3 had expired.

Fagioli then took up the chase of Nuvolari, who seemed to be in command of the race, but on lap 11, with one to go, Nuvolari came into the pits with an overheating transmission universal joint. His mechanics tried a cure born more of desperation than high technology and threw a bucket of water over it, but Fagioli swept past and completed the remaining lap to win. Nuvolari started again and was second, 2min 26 sec behind and followed home by Taruffi and Varzi. As he saw Fagioli take the flag, Enzo Ferrari must have thought, 'What price Scuderia Nuvolari-Ferrari now?' Suddenly the fortunes seemed to have reversed; the following Sunday Fagioli had a P3 at the Grand Prix du Comminges in South West France. The Maserati team were promised but did not turn up. Fagioli had an initial tussle with Etancelin, who once again drove his Monza superbly, but the P3 pulled away and won easily, followed in by the Monzas of Wimille and Moll.

Louis Chiron had been having a dismal season with his Scuderia CC Monza, which reached its nadir when the car was badly damaged in the eight-car accident during the Sveriges Sommar Grand Prix on 8 August. Some of the magic seemed to have gone from Chiron's driving, perhaps caused by crises in his personal life, where his relationship with 'Baby' Hoffman was becoming increasingly stormy. Having left her husband for Chiron, she wanted marriage, but he preferred to leave the relationship as it was.

He must have felt that things were looking up when Ferrari offered him a P3 for the Grand Prix de Marseille at Miramas on 27 August, where he would be joining Fagioli who stopped at Miramas on his way back from Comminges. This time the Maseratis were there. A prize was offered for the race leader on every fifth lap of the 100-lap race, and a crowd of 50,000 watched Chiron take the lead at the start. Dreyfus's T54 Bugatti also had a turn at the front, but Nuvolari always seemed to be in the lead on every fifth lap! At half distance the Maserati was starting to pull away, although Fagioli came up to contest the lead for a while. Just when it seemed that Nuvolari was going to win, his back axle broke, and Chiron, who had passed Fagioli, now led. The two P3s went on to win, thanks to Nuvolari's axle. The race was marred by an accident to the Swiss driver Karl de Waldthausen, who was killed when his Monza overturned after a tyre burst.

Once again the circus now went to Monza for a remarkable festival of racing. On the morning of 10 September the Gran Premio d'Italia was being held over the usual combined circuit. This was a 50-lap, 310-mile (498km) race, which would normally be a good day's racing in itself, but after lunch the cars were to come out for the Gran Premio di Monza, with its customary three 14-lap heats and a 14-lap final. It was an indication of the healthy state of motor racing that the full Gran Premio attracted 26 entries and the afternoon event 30 entries. The Scuderia entered Campari, Fagioli and Chiron with P3s in the Gran Premio, but when a military band struck up and the cars were wheeled out for the parade in front of the grandstands, Campari's P3 was missing; it was being held back for the afternoon. There were three 8CM Maseratis and numerous supporting Monzas and T51 Bugattis.

It was a wet day and the correspondent of *Motor Sport* commented, 'And mud! Mud everywhere – nasty sticky yellow-brown mud.' Nuvolari took the lead followed by Fagioli, and they swapped places several times, but after six laps Fagioli came in to refuel so he probably started with a half-full tank to seek an early lead. This left Nuvolari in front, though he was led by Taruffi for a short time. Taruffi then went off the road and broke a wheel, leaving Nuvolari to take on Fagioli and Chiron. The lead changed as each made pit stops for fuel and tyres, but by lap 40 Chiron had pulled out nearly 2 minutes lead over Nuvolari. Chiron then made a long stop to mend a broken exhaust so Nuvolari went ahead again. With two laps to go he had a 30-second advantage over Fagioli, but the Maserati then threw a tyre tread and Nuvolari limped in on the canvas to change a wheel. He set off to chase Fagioli, but the gap was too great to make up in two laps, and the P3 won by 40 seconds. The pace had been so hot that Zehender's 8CM Maserati, which was third, was more than two laps behind.

Everyone then settled down for lunch. T. G. Moore, *Motor Sport*'s correspondent, went to one of the circuit's restaurants and complained that he was overcharged for a third-rate meal. The track was still damp when the cars were paraded for the first heat of the Gran Premio di Monza. Crown Prince Umberto was among those watching when Count Czaikowski, the emigré Pole living in France, took the lead in his T54 Bugatti from Count Trossi. Trossi was driving a 4½-litre track-racing Duesenberg, which he had commissioned for the Scuderia Ferrari from the American manufacturer, feeling that it would be just the car for Monza. For nine laps the Bugatti led the Duesenberg, which then stopped, allegedly because a con-rod had broken, leaving an oil slick on the banked South Curve. This left Czaikowski to win from the Monzas of Moll and Felice Bonetto. Moll was a hard man, as he had already finished eighth in the morning's Gran Premio.

When the cars were paraded for the second heat, Campari got an extra loud cheer from the crowd, who knew that he was probably going to retire from the sport after this race. Campari waved to the crowd and gave Crown Prince Umberto an exuberant Fascist salute. The front brakes had been removed from his P3 to cut drag and give more speed. Borzacchini had the only works 8CM Maserati as Nuvolari and Zehender had withdrawn. When the flag fell Campari and Borzacchini shot away, but at the end of the lap it was Renato Ballestrero who appeared in his Monza, signalling that there had been an accident. Campari had passed Borzacchini going into the South Curve, but had slid and a wheel had ridden up on the retaining wall; the car had run along the wall for 100 metres, then plunged over the wall and overturned. Borzacchini had braked hard to avoid hitting the P3, but had locked a wheel, and he too had mounted the wall and overturned. Campari was killed instantly and Borzacchini died a few minutes after the crash.

The stunned crowd knew there had been a dreadful accident, and the announcement that Campari had been killed was followed shortly by the news of Borzacchini's death. After a 2-hour delay the third heat was run, then the cars came out for the final. Czaikowski's Bugatti took the lead and led for nine laps, but then entered the fateful South Curve slightly too fast. The Bugatti ran wide, mounted the wall as the others had done and overturned, catching fire. The driver was trapped and died of burns. The remaining drivers finished the race and

10 September 1933: Campari fastens his helmet before the GP di Monza, his last race.

24 September 1933: Fagioli with his P3 at the GP de España at San Sebastian. Chiron's P3 is behind.

Lehoux won from the Monzas of Moll and Bonetto, but the result had little meaning to the drivers or the crowd. History has always blamed an oil slick from the Duesenberg for the fatal crashes, but Giovanni Canestrini reported that he looked at its engine after the race and there were no holes in the crankcase or sump, so it is possible that the accidents were caused by driver error, compounded by a still damp track.

Giuseppe Campari was 41 and had been a father figure to a generation of Italian drivers. Large, happy and full of life, he seemed indestructible and it was particularly poignant that after nearly 20 years of motor racing with no serious accidents, he should die in what he declared to be his last race before retiring. 'El Negher', the 'Dark One',

was mourned in Modena and at Portello; the whole of Italy had lost a loved and respected figure. He had driven Alfa Romeos from the early days of the modified touring cars before the War, had persevered with the first Grand Prix car and had come to share in the great glories of the P2, the Monza and the P3. His first loyalty had always been to Alfa Romeo and he had only been driven away for a short while by an unwillingness to be involved with the tensions and drama between Ferrari and Nuvolari. He was buried in Milan with the full honours of the Fascist Party and the cortège was followed by the drivers and the old team companions from Portello and Modena.

Mario Umberto (or Baconin) Borzacchini was 34. His parents had christened him Baconin after a Russian revolutionary, but after meeting the Crown Prince at Monza, he changed his name to Mario Umberto. He was fine driver verging on greatness, and it was his misfortune to be racing when the talents of Nuvolari and Varzi were shining so brightly, but his performances showed that on his day he could live with the very best. Although his heart had always remained with Maserati, where he had gained his first successes, he had driven hard and well for Alfa Romeo and had been the very best type of second-string driver. His funeral at his home town of Terni, some 60 miles (100km) north-east of Rome, was simple. Nuvolari led the mourners walking behind the coffin, carried on a farm cart. Borzacchini was not a rich man; he had been a party to the Tripoli agreement and shortly afterwards told Giovanni Canestrini that the 'cut' he had received was a source of great pleasure to him as it had enabled him to make provision for his wife and children.

The racing circus had little heart for the remaining events of the season. Chiron and Fagioli took the P3s to Brno on 17 September for the Masarykuv Okruh, which they had little trouble in winning in appalling conditions of wind and rain. Guy Moll offered some opposition until he crashed his Monza, and Wimille finished third. Nuvolari had been deeply affected by the deaths of Campari and Borzacchini, but he recovered sufficiently to go to the Gran Premio de España at San Sebastian on 24 September, the last important race of the season. It was significant as the new T59 Bugattis finally made an appearance, but the fears that they would be a match for the P3 were soon allayed – they were not fast enough.

The race settled down to be a typical struggle, with Nuvolari battling against the P3s of Fagioli and Chiron. Nuvolari led from the start and pulled out a big lead, even keeping it when he refuelled, then stopped again to tighten a loose filler cap. It began to rain, and despite a particularly slippery surface Nuvolari pressed on. Then the inevitable happened; he went off the road and the Maserati overturned. He escaped with cuts and a shaking, but it left a stylish Chiron, driving with all his old skill, to win from Fagioli by nearly 5 minutes. The best Varzi could do with the new T59 was to come home fourth behind Lehoux's T51 Bugatti, an unhappy drive that must have made him ponder on the wisdom of staying with Bugatti.

It had been a momentous racing season with probably the most intense and exciting competition that there had been since the sport began. Although not quite so dominant as they had been in 1932, the P3s were still the cars to beat, and without the extraordinary brilliance of Nuvolari the Maserati challenge would have been minimal. The deaths of Campari and Borzacchini had been a cruel blow, but there was a new generation of drivers waiting to take their places. Enzo Ferrari knew that even with the P3s it would not be easy in 1934; there were rumours coming from Germany of government-supported teams being prepared by Mercedes-Benz and by a new consortium of manufacturers called Auto-Union, which would compete in the grands prix run to the new 750kg formula.

At Portello the contrast with the success of the P3 on the race track could not have been greater. Only 408 cars had been built during the year, and the production of aero engines for the Regia Aeronautica had been minimal, with only 103 turned out. There was an agreement to build Deutz and Bussing diesel lorries under licence, but production was slow and limited. The factory was completely run down and the financial deficit was enormous: 93 million lire, or about £37 million in the values of the late 1990s. Giovanni Agnelli, the President of Fiat and probably the most powerful industrialist in Italy, recognised that a solution was needed and also knew that the resources of Alfa Romeo would be a useful addition to his empire.

On 22 September Agnelli wrote to IRI suggesting two alternatives: the Alfa Romeo company could be closed down and the assets liquidated, or the company could be absorbed by Fiat and the assets utilised in the Fiat empire. The proposal for closure was rejected by the Ministry of Finance and IRI in a joint submission to Mussolini, but a

week later, in circumstances that have not been revealed, Prospero Gianferrari left the company, resigning as managing director, and was replaced by Corrado Orazi, who came from OM, a Fiat subsidiary. Orazi assessed what he found at Portello and immediately reiterated the proposals for shutting down the company. Mussolini again rejected this proposal, declaring that 'the maker of the best Italian product' should be preserved. He may also have been listening to the local Fascist leaders who were expressing concern about the impact on Milan if Portello was closed. With this decree from the top, IRI had to find an alternative solution, so Orazi was dismissed and on 1 December Ugo Gobbato was appointed as managing director.

Gobbato was 45 and had trained as an engineer; when he was discharged from the Italian Army in 1919 he had joined Fiat, where he was put to work studying and advising how to put the company's car division back on to a peacetime footing. He was given the responsibility for the equipping and layout of Fiat's new Lingotto factory in Turin; at this time he met Mussolini, who was impressed with his talents. Gobbato soon became one of Italy's leading experts on industrial organisation, and in 1929 was sent to reorganise Fiat's new purchase, the NSU works at Neckarsulm in Germany; a year later he did the same task in Spain with Fiat España. The Agnelli family had a controlling interest in the RIV ball and roller bearing concern, and between 1931 and 1933 Gobbato was in the USSR organising a joint Agnelli-Soviet project to build and equip a ball and roller bearing plant in Moscow. In recent years his career would have seemed commonplace for an industrial high-flyer, but in 1933 such a man was a rarity. He was exhausted on his return from Russia when he was appointed to Alfa Romeo.

Chapter 9

Deutschland Über Alles

WHEN UGO GOBBATO ARRIVED at Portello, the workforce was inclined to greet him as their saviour. Vittorio Jano, on the other hand, was very wary of the newcomer, but there was an element of jealousy as Jano probably felt that he should have been the new managing director. Griff Borgeson, in *The Alfa Romeo Tradition*, says that Jano was on a downward path; '… his luck had already turned'. There was soon concrete evidence of this, when in April 1934 Gobbato issued a directive reorganising the top management at Portello. Previously Jano had been responsible for all the technical development within the company, but now the duties were divided. Gobbato himself took overall responsibility for the technical side, while Giustino Cattaneo, who had come from Isotta-Fraschini and was an old student friend of Gobbato, took over the responsibility for aero engines, aircraft propellers and trucks; Jano was left only responsible for the cars.

Jano's attempt to design an aero engine, the nine-cylinder radial D2, had been unfortunate. It was underpowered, developing approximately 290hp, and the design must have had fundamental faults, as the Bristol Jupiter from which it had been copied developed 425hp. When a supercharger was fitted to the D2 there was no improvement; indeed, the power output fell to 275hp. The British Armstrong-Siddeley Lynx was also being made at Portello under licence; similar in many respects to the D2, it was another slap in the face for Jano

when the Alfa Romeo-Meridionali aviation subsidiary picked the Lynx for its light aircraft. On more familiar territory, Jano had designed a new production model, the 6C-2300, which was shown to the world at the Milan show in April 1934, but this was only to be produced in small numbers and there were no other major projects planned. Cars were now of little importance.

Gobbato had been assured by IRI of adequate funds being available to re-equip the factory and meet the costs of new developments, but it was clear that the main purpose of Alfa Romeo was now to produce aero engines and military trucks. Mussolini wanted Italy to be a powerful military nation; at that time his ideas of military conquests in Africa had probably not crystallised, but there was a need to show that Italy had military muscle, and for this a large air force was planned. The Regia Aeronautica was being expanded and Savoia-Marchetti and Caproni had new bomber designs on the drawing board. To respond to this need, a new 18-cylinder engine was devised at Portello, the 135 RC 34 Tornado. On the commercial truck side, there was co-operation with Fiat and a range of unified, identical vehicles were produced, intended primarily for the Italian Army. All this meant that Jano's status was substantially diminished.

Then the rumours coming from Germany about new racing cars became hard facts. Mercedes-Benz and Auto-Union were building cars that would race in 1934 and would

be revolutionary in design. As the stories of their specifications reached Italy, Jano must have realised that the P3, already a two-year-old design, would be obsolescent, but in the new climate there was little he could do about it. From Gobbato's point of view the racing side had been handed over to Enzo Ferrari and was no longer a drain on the company's finances. If the cars continued to win, well and good, but if they failed he would then consider what to do, but any plans would have be tailored to the new financial structure he had created, and the military projects had complete priority. With the interest that he took in Alfa Romeo and his strong grip on all aspects of Italian life, it seems certain that the marginalising of the car side of the company, and hence its racing activities, must have had Mussolini's full approval.

At Modena Enzo Ferrari was enthusiastic about Gobbato's appointment. On 30 November 1933 Gobbato announced what everyone already knew, that Alfa Romeo would no longer be racing, but would entrust all its racing activities to the Scuderia Ferrari. In October it had been reported that a batch of 25 P3s would be built for sale to customers, but this decision was now rescinded. No cars would be going on sale and several drivers who had ordered cars had their deposits returned. Orders had already been taken for two cars from Guy Moll and Marcel Lehoux, but Ferrari was told that these drivers must be taken under the banner of the Scuderia in 1934 so that the obligations to them could be met. It may seem strange that the pair had preferential treatment, but they were probably the most talented of the potential customers and worth keeping.

Seven new cars were built during the spring of 1934 at Portello under the supervision of Guidotti, and two additional cars were built during the 1934 season. The principal modification to the P3 during the winter was the enlargement of the bore to 68mm, which increased the engine capacity to 2905cc. The compression ratio was raised from 6.5:1 to 7:1 and the supercharger pressure was slightly boosted. The modifications increased the power to 255bhp at 5400rpm. Apart from the weight restriction, the new grand prix formula stipulated that the body at its widest point could not be less than 85mm, so the scuttle and cockpit sides were widened. According to Guidotti, when the first 2.9 engines were bench-tested the cylinder blocks cracked after about 2 hours' running. The foundry had used a new alloy of aluminium and magnesium that expanded unevenly when hot, but Guidotti said that this was cured by making small expansion cuts in the top of the castings.

Enzo Ferrari found himself with an enviable driving strength at the beginning of 1934. Nuvolari had gone – he seemed undecided whether his loyalties lay with Maserati or Bugatti – but in his place there was an equally strong player. Perhaps prompted by the evident weakness of the T59 Bugatti, or happy to go back to his roots now Nuvolari was not there, Achille Varzi had returned. Louis Chiron was continuing the relationship he had formed with the Scuderia at the end of the 1933 season. The missing member of the cast was Luigi Fagioli; with a decision felt by Ferrari to be disloyal, Fagioli had taken part in the testing of the new prototype W25 Mercedes-Benz at Monza in February and had liked what he found, so had signed a contract with the German team. Backing

April 1934: Trossi's P3 in the pits during practice for the GP de Monaco, with Chiron's car behind. (Motor Racing Tradition, Graeme Simpson)

Varzi and Chiron were ex-customers Marcel Lehoux and Guy Moll. Lehoux had shown himself to be a highly competent driver with Bugatti. Although not quite at the pinnacle, nevertheless on his day he could put in a performance that could make the very best work hard. Moll was only 24. He came from Algeria and had a French father and a Spanish mother. His drives with his Monza had shown that he had an exceptional talent, and he was certainly the most promising of the rising generation of grand prix drivers.

The serious season began on 2 April at Monaco, which was to be a race like so many others had been in 1932 and 1933, a triangular match between Alfa Romeo, Bugatti and Maserati, although soon the Germans would come and upset a comfortable apple-cart. The Scuderia had entered five P3s, with Trossi backing up the four professionals. The main opposition would be from three works T59 Bugattis accompanied by Nuvolari in a fourth car that he had entered himself, while the Maserati entries were a bit thin. The course was opened by Rudolf Caracciola, still limping and in pain, but already signed up by Mercedes-Benz. During his convalescence his wife had been killed in an avalanche while skiing, but as he recovered from his grief he began to cultivate a close friendship with 'Baby' Hoffman, a situation that was affecting Chiron.

Dreyfus's T59 led at the start, but at the end of the first lap Chiron was in front followed by Dreyfus. Behind them the rest of the field was having all kinds of dramas and problems, but Chiron stayed in front for the next 98 laps. Moll, who was driving a quiet, unobtrusive race, moved up to pass Dreyfus on lap 65, then, with two laps to go, Chiron spun at the Station hairpin and, while he dragged his P3 out of the sandbags, Moll went by. Moll, who had run through the race non-stop, covered the remaining two laps to win an unexpected victory, while a furious Chiron got going again to come second. Ferrari must have felt

it was fortuitous that he had been forced to take on Moll who was clearly moving quickly into the top class.

Moll was given a rest when the Scuderia went to Alessandria three weeks later. It was a very wet day, the race was in the usual two heats and a final, and Chiron and Varzi each won their heat. Nuvolari was now in his 8CM Maserati, but could not match the P3s. In the final he skidded in the wet and hit a tree – there were allegations that he had been balked by Trossi and went off the road to avoid a collision. His leg was broken and for most men that would have been the end of the 1934 season, but not for Nuvolari. The result was an easy Scuderia victory with Varzi, Chiron, Tadini and Comotti taking the first four places. Trossi crashed and his P3 caught fire, but he escaped with minor burns.

After all the intrigue of 1933 the Gran Premio di Tripoli was a model of respectability. There was a sweepstake again, but this time the draw was made only 30 minutes before the start. When practice ended the day before the race, Dreyfus was asked by Costantini, the

Bugatti team manager, to drive his T59 round the circuit accompanied by a mechanic to collect Brivio's T59, which had broken down, and tow it back to the Bugatti garage. The towrope was tied to Brivio's car and the two Bugattis began to cross the circuit when Varzi's P3 came round a bend towards the two Bugattis going flat out. Varzi swerved and mounted the bank at the side of the road, just missing the two T59s, bounced back and stopped in the middle of the track. There was a heated and abusive conversation between the three drivers, Varzi accusing them of nearly killing him, and the Bugatti drivers pointing out that practice was over and that he should not have been going at the speed he was! The accident had broken a halfshaft on the P3 and may have done some damage to the engine, as a spare engine was flown from Milan to Tripoli that night and fitted to the car before the race. Maserati had brought out the V5 for Taruffi, as the course had been speeded up with the corners eased, so maximum speed was at a premium.

The V5 led for four laps until Taruffi

2 April 1934: Guy Moll, about to gain an unexpected victory at Monaco, follows Dreyfus's T59 Bugatti through the Station hairpin.

locked a brake and motored off the road through a beer advertisement hoarding, suffering a broken arm and leg injuries; a few days later he received a letter from the brewery expressing pleasure that the hoarding had slowed the car down, but asking him to pay for the damage! With Taruffi out, Chiron took command followed by Varzi, who now closed on Chiron and took the lead on lap 20. The pair then became so absorbed battling with each other that they forgot about Moll who was closing fast. With three laps to go, Moll passed Chiron then set Varzi in his sights. He tried to pass Varzi on the last bend of the last lap, but could not get through; it was suggested that Varzi 'closed the door', forcing Moll to run wide on to the verge, and he crossed the line 0.2 second behind.

There was little doubt now that here was a new star who was a match for anyone. It is interesting that there seems to have been no attempt to enforce any kind of team orders within the Scuderia, and the drivers seem to have been free to fight each other to the death. Ferrari, in his wisdom, probably realised that it would be a wasted effort trying to tell Varzi and Chiron that one should win and the other should follow home in second place. After the race the three Scuderia drivers were presented to Marshal Balbo, now the Governor of Libya.

For old times' sake the Scuderia sent two P3s to the Targa Florio on 20 May; awakening memories of earlier races, they had spare wheels strapped to the side. The race was now but a feeble thing compared with its glory days. Varzi won easily, but the other P3 driven by Pietro Ghersi, who was usually seen in a Maserati voiturette, was only sixth. On the same day three more P3s were sent to the Anfa circuit, near Casablanca, for the Grand Prix du Maroc. Chiron led throughout, but Lehoux had a series of battles with the Maseratis of Etancelin, Hamilton and Straight and was third, while Comotti finished fifth.

Meanwhile the motor racing world waited for the German teams to appear. Probably with a true sense of the dramatic, the teams chose to make their début at the Avusrennen on 27 May, in the presence of the Führer. Unfortunately for Mercedes-Benz, there was trouble with the fuel system in practice and the team was withdrawn on the morning of the race; Caracciola, now recovering from his Monaco crash though still in pain, was a member of the team with Fagioli. It was left to the Auto-Union team to show the 200,000 crowd how the face of motor racing had changed. With V-16 rear engines, independent suspension all round and slim, smooth bodies, the cars made the rest of the field look antiquated.

Realising that speed was the essential factor at Avus, a dramatically altered P3 was produced at Portello. Guidotti suggested to Jano that an aerodynamic body was the answer, and proposed that he should talk to Ing Pallavicino, who was the aerodynamicist with Società Italiana Caproni, the aircraft manufacturers at Bergamo. Pallavicino had served with Guidotti's brother during the 1914–18 War, and some authorities state that he worked for Breda, the aircraft manufacturers in Milan, but Guidotti's account seems more likely. Pallavicino said that he was keen to beat the German cars, but there was an enquiry about payment. Jano was not keen to release funds as he was not convinced that the result would be effective. After discussion, Pallavicino said that Caproni would design the body free of charge, and the drawings were sent to Guidotti in about ten days.

The outcome was a rather lumpy, streamlined body with a rounded radiator cowl, a fin incorporating a head fairing for the driver, fairings behind the front wheels and fairings both before and behind the rear wheels. To save weight smaller rear brakes were fitted, and to gain more power the engine was bored out even more, to 71mm, which gave a capacity of 3165cc and increased the power to 265bhp. Guidotti wanted to rebody three cars, but Jano only agreed to one. Just before the Avus meeting the car was taken to the Milan–Varese autostrada on 24 May and tested by Varzi and Moll. It did 175mph (280kmh), but Varzi had no liking

6 May 1934: A poor-quality photograph, but it shows the narrow margin between Varzi and Moll as they cross the finishing line of the GP di Tripoli.

for the way it did it. When it came to the race, Varzi was emphatic that he would drive a conventional P3, so it was left to Moll, who was younger and therefore braver, to take the streamliner. Chiron also had a conventional P3.

Apart from the excitement of the Auto-Unions, the crowd was amazed to see Nuvolari in a new 8CM Maserati, driving with his leg still in plaster. It was wet when the race started and Hans Stuck took an immediate lead with his Auto-Union; going impossibly fast in the conditions; he had almost a minute's lead at the end of the first lap and was followed by Chiron, Varzi and Moll. As the track dried, Moll speeded up, passing Varzi on lap four and Chiron on lap seven. Stuck's pace played havoc with his tyres, and when he stopped for new ones after ten laps Moll took the lead. The clutch of the Auto-Union gave out two laps later, and Moll went on to win, averaging 127.56mph (205.11kmh) for the 182 miles (292km) of the race.

The Scuderia split its forces a week after the Berlin race. Chiron and Tadini went to the Nürburgring for the Eifelrennen, while Moll, Varzi and Trossi went to Switzerland for the Grand Prix de Montreux. They were all using conventional-bodied cars again; the streamliner had been taken back to Portello. At the 'Ring Mercedes had solved the fuel problems and the cars were making their début, though Caracciola was still not fit to drive. The two remaining Mercedes drivers, Fagioli and von Brauchitsch, took an immediate lead at the start, followed by Stuck's Auto-Union; Chiron was third and losing ground. The Mercedes team seemed to have the race in the bag, but Fagioli had been told that von Brauchitsch must win and there was a big row when the two cars refuelled. It was resolved when Fagioli had a sulk and parked his car by the roadside, so von Brauchitsch went on to win and Stuck was second. Chiron trailed in third, 6 minutes behind the winner. The writing was on the wall!

It was much more like old times at Montreux. Etancelin was still showing excellent form, but had replaced his Monza with an 8CM Maserati. He took the lead, followed by Whitney Straight's Maserati, while the Scuderia P3s of Moll, Varzi and Trossi followed. Moll speeded up, passed Straight and was about to do the same thing to Etancelin when his back axle broke; this also happened to Varzi, but he was able to struggle on. Meanwhile Trossi took up the chase, and when Etancelin's brakes weakened he took the lead and won from Etancelin and Varzi. At this stage of his career, Etancelin was showing a talent that would have justified a place in a factory team, and it is surprising that Ferrari did not give him an occasional drive.

After Montreux, Varzi, Chiron and Lehoux took the P3s to the Montjuich circuit in Barcelona where, after some opposition from a fast-recovering Nuvolari, they took the first three places. Two days before the Montreux race, on 1 June, there had been a rare event, a British road race run through the streets of Douglas in the Isle of Man. This race, the Mannin Moar, had a wholly British entry. Noel Rees, a rich British sponsor, arranged, with Gobbato as a go-between, to hire a 2.6-litre P3 from the Scuderia, having given a security of £2500. The car was driven by Brian Lewis, then possibly the best British driver. Against thin opposition, Lewis had an easy victory and the car was then returned to Modena.

The next race was the big one, the Grand Prix de l'ACF, once again at Montlhéry on 1 July. It was the first real test of strength as there were five full works teams taking part, and it would show if the German teams really meant business. Matched against the Scuderia P3s with Varzi, Chiron and Trossi were Auto-Union, Bugatti, Mercedes and Maserati, each running three cars. In a throwback to the attitudes of 1924, the organisers decided that private entrants were not wanted.

For the first part of the season the logistic management of the Scuderia Ferrari at races had been handled by Mario Lolli. Lolli was

24 May 1934: The unpainted P3 aerodinamica is tested by Moll and Varzi on the Milan–Varese autostrada. Standing by the front wheel, from the left, are Pallavicino, who designed the body, Moll and Guidotti.

17 June 1934: The Scuderia Ferrari P3s line up at the pits at Barcelona for the GP de Pena Rhin. No 2 is Lehoux, No 12 is Chiron, and No 16 is Varzi. (Motor Racing Tradition, Graeme Simpson)

an amateur doing the job for the fun of it, but Ferrari realised that it was now becoming tough in the grand prix world, so just before the French race he replaced Lolli with Nello Ugolini, who was a much more forceful personality. Ferrari did not go to Montlhéry, but Ugolini kept him in close touch by numerous telephone calls to Modena. The lure of the German teams brought in a crowd of 80,000 and the shriek of the Mercedes superchargers brought a new sound to grand prix racing.

Against expectations, when the flag fell it was Chiron who took the lead and led for a lap, followed by Caracciola, Fagioli and

Stuck. Stuck now pushed to the front, but Chiron hung on to second place. It was only the P3s that had the pace to stay with the German cars – the Maseratis and T59 Bugattis were already out of breath. Surprisingly, the German teams then began to fall apart. Chiron took the lead again when Stuck stopped for fuel on lap 12, but within the next three laps all the Mercedes had dropped out with mechanical problems. Stuck began to fall back; he was making regular stops for tyres and fuel, and the water pump was leaking. On lap 32 he retired, the last German car to go.

That left Chiron in front followed by Varzi

and Trossi. Trossi had been trundling round with only two gears; becoming fed up with this, towards the end he handed his car over to Moll, and so they finished. The Scuderia had scored a remarkable and unexpected victory; Benoist's Bugatti was the only other car to finish. After the race the more complacent believed that the German threat had been exaggerated. *Motor Sport* commented, 'Experience has triumphed over experiment once again.' It seemed to have been overlooked that when they were running, the Mercedes and Auto-Unions were much too fast for the opposition.

Any complacency must have been encouraged a week later at Reims, where after an initial burst from Nuvolari, the P3s

1 July 1934: The Scuderia Ferrari team line up before the GP de l'ACF at Montlhéry. Left to right, they are Varzi, Chiron and Trossi. On the extreme right, Alice Hoffman leans over the fence and talks to an official.

ran home in the first three places, with Chiron leading Moll and Varzi, who had shared his car with Marinoni.

In the wider world relations between Mussolini and Hitler were not wholly cordial at this time. They had met for the first time on 14 June at Padova, but there had been no meeting of minds. Afterwards Mussolini said of Hitler, 'He's quite mad', and 'He is just a garrulous monk', so when the Scuderia went to the Nürburgring for the Grösser Preis von Deutschland on 15 July they were not greeted as close allies by the National Socialist dignitaries attending the race. Those dignitaries, together with a crowd of 200,000, were expecting to see a German victory, and they were not disappointed. Caracciola and Stuck battled for

the lead, followed by Fagioli, while Chiron could only follow and wait. Caracciola's engine eventually expired and Stuck won from Fagioli, while third was the best that Chiron could do, 8 minutes behind the winner. He had driven for much of the race without third gear; the P3 gearboxes were giving trouble and Varzi and Moll had dropped out with this problem.

Unlike the German teams, the Scuderia was a commercial venture and had to make ends meet, so while Chiron was hoping for the best and losing gears in Germany, Trossi and Lehoux were bringing in the starting

money and the prize money by running in the Grand Prix de Vichy in South West France. Trossi won after a fierce struggle with Straight's Maserati, but Lehoux dropped back after he buckled a wheel.

It was Ferrari's policy to race as often as possible, and during July the P3s ran at Dieppe and in the Coppa Ciano at Livorno. Etancelin got the better of them at Dieppe but Varzi and Moll saw off Nuvolari's Maserati at the Italian race.

On 29 July the Scuderia was at Spa for the Grand Prix de Belgique. To their surprise when they arrived there were no

1 July 1934: Chiron leads Caracciola (W25 Mercedes) and Varzi at the start at Montlhéry. (John Maitland Collection)

German teams. The excuse was that the drivers needed a rest, but the more likely reason was a demand from the Belgian customs for an extortionate amount of duty on their racing fuel. The race was a straight fight with the T59 Bugattis. Chiron and Varzi roared away into the distance and the result seemed certain, but at half distance Chiron clipped the verge at Eau Rouge corner; he went off the road and the P3 overturned, but he escaped unhurt. Varzi then stopped in a cloud of blue smoke, allegedly from a broken oil pipe though more likely from a broken piston, and what

1 July 1934: Caracciola leads Varzi, but the Mercedes is blowing out oil and will retire shortly afterwards.

seemed a foregone conclusion had disappeared in clouds of dust and blue smoke. To the surprise of everyone, probably not least the Bugatti team, Dreyfus's T59 won. Sadly it marked the end of an era, for it was the last grande épreuve that Bugatti would ever win.

On the political front German-Italian relations had now taken a turn for the worse. On 25 July German agents assassinated the Austrian Chancellor, Engelbert Dollfuss, as the start of a plan for the German annexation of Austria. Dollfuss's wife and children were the guests of Mussolini at the time of his death, so Il Duce's reaction was fierce. Three Italian army divisions were moved to the Austrian frontier as a warning to Hitler, and Mussolini expressed his support for Dollfuss's successor.

It may have been a gesture of goodwill or a piece of an olive branch, but both German teams turned up at Pescara on Wednesday 15 August for the Coppa Acerbo. As the Scuderia was there in force, as well as the works Bugattis and Maseratis, the field was as good as any grande épreuve. The P3s were being driven by Varzi, Chiron, Moll and Ghersi. The road was wet at the start but began to dry out, though there were several showers that fell on parts of the long circuit.

Caracciola's Mercedes led after the first lap from Stuck's Auto-Union and Varzi; chasing this trio were Fagioli and Moll. Caracciola stayed in front for seven laps, then he had an enormous accident that wrecked the car, though he was unhurt. Stuck dropped out and Fagioli's Mercedes led, but when he stopped for tyres and fuel, Moll was the new leader. At this point Chiron made a refuelling stop and, while in the pit, the P3 burst into flames. Chiron was dragged out of the car with slight burns, but the car continued to burn and the pit also caught fire. The pit fire was extinguished but the car was well ablaze and burned itself out. Varzi had already retired with a broken spring, so he took over Ghersi's car. When Moll stopped for fuel, Varzi took the lead, but then he stopped to change a wheel. This left Fagioli in front, but Moll was chasing hard, eating into Fagioli's lead and realising that he could win the race.

When Moll came up to lap Henne, who was driving the third Mercedes and finding the pace too much for him, there had been a rain shower. The road was wet, and as Moll drew level with the Mercedes, running along the fast straight beside the sea leading to the main grandstands and pits, the Alfa Romeo began to snake, perhaps caught by the wind. Moll struggled for nearly 300 metres to try and regain control, but the car clipped the edge of a bridge, then struck a house beside the road. The car overturned and Moll was thrown out, dying within a few minutes. Fagioli won the race and Varzi finished fourth, but the result was irrelevant.

Enzo Ferrari was deeply affected by the death of the young Algerian. In later years

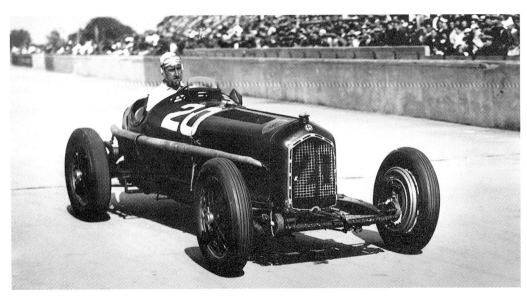

1 July 1934, GP de l'ACF: A tired-looking Moll, his goggles up, coasts in at the end of the race. (Motor Racing Tradition: Graeme Simpson)

8 July 1934: The start of the GP de la Marne at Reims. Varzi leads Etancelin (No 2, 8CM Maserati) and Moll (No 16). (John Maitland Collection)

he said of Moll, 'I rank him with Stirling Moss as the only driver worthy of comparison with Nuvolari.' During the race the cars were timed over a flying kilometre on the straight, just before the point where Moll crashed. The fastest was Caracciola's Mercedes at 179.6mph (288.8kmh), the fastest P3 was that of Chiron at 168.7mph (271.2kmh), and on the fatal lap Moll had done 161.2mph (259.2kmh).

A chastened team was in Nice for the grand prix the following Sunday. The races without the German teams were now becoming second-division events, but sizeable crowds came to watch and the organisers were still paying good starting money. Nuvolari and Etancelin with their 8CM Maseratis provided the opposition to the Scuderia, but Nuvolari burned a piston and Etancelin ended as the ham in a Varzi/Trossi sandwich. It was an intensely hot day and Varzi burned his legs on the gearbox. Trossi ran out of fuel just before the end, but pushed his car 200 metres to the pit, added fuel and drove to the finish.

Motor racing had become so popular that even the sober Swiss now decided to run a grande épreuve. This first event was in the Bremgarten, a wooded park on the outskirts of Berne, and the circuit ran through the woods for almost its entire length. It was fast with no appreciable straights but many very fast curves. Once again it was Mercedes versus Auto-Union, with the Scuderia P3s leading the also-rans over the 70 laps of the 316-mile (508km) race. Stuck's Auto-Union led from flag to flag, but it was a bad day for Mercedes and they all fell out. This should have given the P3s their chance, but they too had an off-day, the best of the trio being Varzi, who came fourth, sharing his car with Trossi; Chiron was fifth and Ghersi seventh. It must have been especially galling that Dreyfus, with the only T59 Bugatti, managed to come third. The race was marred by another fatal accident. The British driver Hugh Hamilton, driving one of the Whitney Straight 8CM Maseratis, went off the road on the last lap and hit a tree.

On the same day as the Berne meeting, Comotti and Lehoux took their P3s to Comminges; Comotti won but Lehoux dropped out. This was his last race for the Scuderia. It is possible that his contract expired with the Comminges race or it may be that the Scuderia, now that defeat was commonplace, was no longer a happy place in which to work.

As an interlude before the Gran Premio d'Italia, the Scuderia went to Biella, Trossi's home town, on 2 September for a race through the streets of the town on a 1.36-

19 August 1934: It was a hot day for the GP de Nice and the cowling has been removed from Trossi's P3 to keep him cool. He finished third. (Robert Beaver)

mile (2.19km) circuit. The race was in three heats and a final, and the circuit was so tight that only seven cars ran each time. Nuvolari ran in the first heat and won it driving a borrowed Monza. The car was outclassed in the final and, fittingly, Trossi won by 0.2 second after what may have been a staged battle with Varzi. At the Gran Premio a week later, the organisers had remembered the tragedy 12 months earlier. Anxious to avoid another accident, they had devised an emasculated circuit using only the Vedano curve on the road section and the southern curve on the banked track, with the Florio link road. The cars came round the Vedano curve, along the main straight past the pits, then rounded a straw bale hairpin and doubled back along the straight; two chicanes were also added to cut down the speed. The circuit was 'fiddly', the cars never reached full speed, and it was very tiring for the drivers who had 116 laps to cover to complete the 310 miles (500km).

The Auto-Unions and Mercedes fought it out for the prizes and the Scuderia P3s could only hope for the scraps from the table. This time it was a Mercedes win; Caracciola, still not fully fit and sharing his car with Fagioli, won after wearing down the Auto-Unions. Trossi and Comotti, sharing a P3, managed to rise to third at the end when some of the German cars fell out. Chiron, who drove all the way without relief, was fourth, and Varzi broke his gearbox.

A fortnight later the teams were in Barcelona for the Gran Premio de España. For this race Nuvolari was back with Bugatti, but as an indication that he was looking for alternatives he tried an Auto-Union in practice. By now it seemed that the Scuderia was flagging and morale was dropping. Nuvolari by sheer brilliance managed to beat all the Auto-Unions,

driving the T59 Bugatti as it had never been driven before and coming a close third to the Mercedes of Fagioli and Caracciola, but Varzi could only manage fifth while Chiron was tenth.

Much the same thing happened when the circus moved on to Czechoslovakia for the Brno race on 30 September. Once again Nuvolari tried an Auto-Union in practice, but in the race he shifted his allegiance back to Maserati. This time Stuck's Auto-Union beat Fagioli's Mercedes, though hounded by Nuvolari all the way; he now had a new car, the Maserati 6C/34 with six cylinders and 3.7 litres; which was much quicker than the 8CM he had been using. Once again the Scuderia drivers were mobile spectators of the racing at the front; the best Varzi could do with the P3 was fifth, while Chiron and Comotti fell out.

On 14 October it should have been a busman's holiday for the Scuderia when they turned out in force for the local race, the Circuito di Modena. Five P3s and a Monza were produced from the Via Trento Trieste workshops, and it seemed that it would be a pleasant end-of-season demonstration in front of the loyal locals. Unfortunately, perhaps with a malign sense of humour, the Maserati brothers and Nuvolari had other ideas. The 6C/34 was brought out again and it ran away from the field. To make matters worse for the Scuderia, Varzi was having an off-day and gave no opposition to Nuvolari; he may just have been tired at the end of the season or he may have felt that he was now fighting for a lost cause. Nuvolari won easily, while Varzi and Tadini brought their P3s home a long way behind in the places. Enzo Ferrari now rarely went to races, but he watched this one and must have realised that he not only had a problem with obsolete cars, but also needed some more driving strength, and there was only

one person who could fit the bill.

The season was nearly over, the German teams had gone home to their winter quarters, and the remaining races should have been there for the Scuderia's picking, but it did not work out as hoped. Nuvolari and the 6C/34 put it across the Scuderia again at the Coppa Principessa di Piemonte, which was run round a tight circuit in Posillipo, a suburb of Naples, on 21 October. In this race Giuseppe Farina, who had been one of the most successful voiturette drivers during the season, ran his 4CM 1500cc Maserati and went so well that he beat Comotti's P3 to fourth place. Enzo Ferrari must have considered that here was a talent worth spotting.

The final race was the Grand Prix d'Algèrie. The Scuderia sent two P3s for Chiron and Brivio. It was a race run in two heats with the results aggregated to find the winner. Wimille was another showing a rapidly emerging quality in his driving and he drove his T59 Bugatti so well that he won both heats; the P3s had no answer. Chiron and Brivio ended up sharing a car in the second heat and came a distant second. After the race some of the drivers went to the Maison-Carée cemetery in Algiers to see Guy Moll's grave and were touched to find it was still covered in flowers and wreaths.

On the financial side, it had been a reasonably successful season for the Scuderia Ferrari. The Scuderia's winnings amounted in total to FF2,117,000, or £28,225, which, converted to modern-day figures, would be about £1.12 million. The policy of seeking out the smaller races had paid off well. Although the income had probably paid all the bills, it cannot have been a great comfort to Enzo Ferrari. His cars were now also-rans, and he was no longer a big-time player. He needed better cars and a new driver, or more accurately one particular driver.

Chapter 10

The P3 bows out

Although the exhausts are stilled and the circuits are empty at the end of a racing season, for some the activity in the close season is just as frenetic as when the cars are racing, if not more so. For Vittorio Jano, 1934 had been a bitter and frustrating year. The 6C-2300 had appeared and was being built in limited numbers – 692 were completed in 1934. The 8C was now phased out – only eight were built in the year. It was still dominating sports car racing although obsolescent in the eyes of the factory, but its front-line competition days were numbered as the AIACR was considering barring superchargers in international sports car racing.

Jano's passion for motor racing remained

1935: A P3 fitted with the experimental swing axle rear suspension designed for the 8C 35.

unabated and he knew that something had to be done to put back some muscle into the Scuderia Ferrari. He intended to design a new car, but with the constraints apparently being placed on him this would take longer than he wanted. As a stopgap, a P3 was brought back to Portello and Jano threw away the rear suspension, fitting reversed quarter elliptic rear springs instead. The layout was almost pure Bugatti, but when tested it worked and the car handled better; it also probably saved some weight. Jano then looked at the front suspension.

André Dubonnet, the French millionaire whose fortune was derived from the aperitif bearing his name, had been a competitor in the 1920s with various cars including Hispano-Suiza and Bugatti. In the early 1930s he financed the building of a few luxury sporting cars bearing his name; their design was done by an engineer, Chedru, who evolved an unusual system of independent front suspension employing an axle beam bolted to the frame. At each extremity of the axle there was a short swinging arm compressing an enclosed spring. The system worked quite well and had the advantage of minimal unsprung weight. To adapt the Dubonnet system to the P3 was simple as the front dumb-irons were cut off and the Dubonnet axle was clamped to the frame. It looked neat and gave the front of the car a business-like appearance.

Jano also changed the brakes, fitting the Ariston hydraulic system in place of the former mechanical brakes; these were made by the Farina coachbuilding firm in Turin as a sideline and had the unusual feature of maintaining the fluid under constant pressure to prevent air leaks. In 1934 the gearbox had demonstrated regular fragility, so first gear was now removed and the car was left with three speeds, but with wider gear teeth and modified ratios. The final modification, which only seems to have been done to two cars, was to bore out the engine to 78mm, increasing the capacity to 3822cc. Four Scuderia P3s were fitted with the Dubonnet suspension.

The chronology of events becomes somewhat obscure at the beginning of 1935. In *When Nuvolari Raced*, Valerio Moretti says that Jano showed the fully modified P3 to Nuvolari at Portello in February, but at the Grand Prix de Pau on 24 February a P3 ran with the modified rear suspension only and it was not until the La Turbie hill climb on 18 April that the Dubonnet suspension made its first appearance. When the 6C-2300 was announced early in 1934, it had semi-elliptic front and rear suspension, but during the year Jano devised an independent system for the car; at the front he used double trailing links with enclosed coil springs incorporating shock absorbers. This system had been designed by Ferdinand Porsche and Alfa Romeo negotiated a licence from Porsche to use it; it was similar in layout to the suspension fitted to the Auto-Union, although on that car torsion bars provided the springing. At the rear Jano used swing axles operating torsion bars, another Porsche idea. The 6C-2300 was purely a touring car and long-chassis versions carried limousine bodies and large tourers suitable for Fascist Party dignitaries, including Mussolini himself. The short-chassis cars were modified and ran in sports car events such as the Mille Miglia and the Targa Abruzzo. The new version of the car appeared at the Milan show in the spring of 1935. From the bits he had devised for the uprated 6C-2300, Jano had the chassis for his new grand prix car. It will never be known if this was fortuitous or whether he modified the 6C-2300 with the intention of using the design and parts for a racing car. Having regard to the regime that Gobbato had imposed, the latter possibility cannot be dismissed.

The press had been talking about a new grand prix design. In December 1934 *Motor Sport* said that, 'Work has begun on nine cars having 4-litre 12-cyl engines and independent suspension fore and aft.' Jano had intentions of building a V-12, but this would be an expensive task and it would be more than 12 months before it was ready. Jano knew that the modified P3 would only be a temporary measure – it could not hope to offer real resistance to the German teams and a new design was needed even before the V-12 could be ready. He must have persuaded Gobbato that he could produce a new design with the minimum of expenditure using modified suspension from the 6C-2300 and the enlarged P3 engine.

By now, with the firm financial controls that Gobbato had imposed and the income from the military contracts, the situation had probably improved to a point where Jano could be given some freedom and a little money to start work on motor racing projects again. Relations with Germany were still cool and it is almost certain that there was political pressure to do something about the German dominance of grand prix racing. The design that Jano proposed could be built quickly and comparatively cheaply with very little disruption at Portello. The only major new

casting would be the gearbox casing.

The outcome was the 8C-35, a considerable advance on the P3. It had the bored-out 3.8-litre P3 engine and a welded-up tubular ladder-frame with modified 6C-2300 front suspension and swing axle rear suspension, with radius arms and a transverse leaf spring mounted under the combined gearbox/final drive. It had a well-rounded body, the work of Lucio Fontana, and was quite a large car in which the driver sat high over the propshaft. It is not known when construction began, but as it did not race for the first time until September 1935, it is unlikely that work began until the spring. The rear suspension was tested on a modified P3 during the early spring of 1935.

Jano was not the only person thinking about new Alfa Romeos in the early months of 1935. Luigi Bazzi pointed out to Enzo Ferrari that the races at Avus and Tripoli were not governed by the rules of the 750kg formula. These were true formula libre events and any car, however big and fast, was eligible to run. It is said that Bazzi put the original proposal to Ferrari at the Scuderia's annual dinner in Modena during December 1934. Large quantities of Lambrusco, the local sparkling red wine, were consumed at these dinners, and the machine that subsequently evolved could well have been spawned by a heavy intake of the wine. Ferrari liked Bazzi's ideas and early in 1935 Bazzi set to work aided by Stefano Meazza, the workshop foreman.

They took a P3 frame and extended it by 15cm. It was fitted with Dubonnet front suspension but retained the semi-elliptic springs at the rear. One P3 engine was fitted in the normal place in front of the driver, but another was installed in the frame extension behind the driver, which drove forwards into the back of the gearbox. The drive was split as in the P3, and the two splayed propshafts each drove a back wheel. The transmission was designed by Arnaldo Roselli, and the driver sat above the gearbox. Two cars were built, the first using two 3.2-litre engines and the second two

2.9-litre units. The outcome was a quite well-proportioned car that in appearance gave little indication that an eight-cylinder engine nestled behind the driver. As the place normally taken by the fuel tank was now the rear engine bay, the fuel tanks were placed outside the frame. Although called the Alfa Romeo Bimotore, it has been said that this car could truly be called the first Ferrari, and it carried the prancing horse badge on the front of the radiator cowl.

Not only was it 'all change' with the cars, the driver line-up changed too. Ferrari wanted René Dreyfus and Chiron was asked to woo him. The overtures were successful and Dreyfus agreed to join the Scuderia after the Barcelona race. Chiron's great talent now showed only fitfully, certainly affected by his personal life, where 'Baby' Hoffman's friendship with Caracciola was growing into something stronger, but he accepted Ferrari's offer to stay on for another year. In November Varzi, who had been declared to be Italian Champion for 1934, announced that he would be leaving the Scuderia as he had signed a contract to drive for Auto-Union in 1935. This must have been particularly satisfying for Varzi as he had secured the drive despite Nuvolari's tests during several race practice sessions. Indeed, he had gone one better, as in his contract was a clause that Nuvolari would not be in the same team, so he had effectively shut the door on his great rival.

Ferrari knew that now Nuvolari had missed out on the Auto-Union drive, he would be on the market again; furthermore, he knew that Nuvolari offered him the chance of beating the Germans and putting Alfa Romeo back on top. Even if the cars were not as good, Nuvolari's incredible, impossible skill could bring the chance of victory. The stumbling block was the fierce unbending pride of both men; both felt the bitterness of the previous parting. It was Vittorio Jano who now became the honest broker; he persuaded, cajoled and had continual meetings with both the parties, pointing out that they were being pig-

A photograph of Alice Hoffman taken after the Second World War. She had a great effect on the lives of Louis Chiron and Rudolf Caracciola. (Rodolfo Mailander, Ludvigsen Library)

The 1935 season began in February at Pau, and two P3s were sent for Nuvolari and Dreyfus. Nuvolari's had the new quarter elliptic rear springs, and there were press comments that his car seemed to have better road holding. It was a fine spring day and the two drivers dominated the race, swapping places until Nuvolari went ahead to win. Without the Germans the improved P3s were still better than the rest.

On Sunday 31 March most of the Italian drivers and other racing personalities went to Terni, where a memorial to Baconin Borzacchini was unveiled. It was a bas-relief of the driver set in stone and mounted at the end of an avenue of trees.

The real racing began at Monaco on 22 April, but while the Mercedes team was there in force, the Auto-Unions stayed away, considering that their long cars were unsuited to the tight circuit. The Scuderia entered four P3s; the two entered for Chiron and Nuvolari had the Dubonnet suspension, while Dreyfus and Brivio made do with the earlier cars. *Motor Sport* commented on the spotless blue overalls of the Scuderia mechanics.

Fagioli's Mercedes led from start to finish, and it must have been somewhat galling that it was not the improved P3s that gave him the strongest opposition but Etancelin's 6C/34 Maserati. The Ariston brakes were fierce and unpredictable in operation, which is probably why Nuvolari buckled a wheel then retired with what was reported as 'braking problems'. It was only near the end, when Etancelin's brakes gave out as well, that Dreyfus and Brivio moved up to second and third. This result was little better than the Scuderia had been achieving in 1934, although it was probably a slight consolation that Brivio and Chiron took first and second places in the Targa Florio a week later. This was now so insignificant that to make up the field there was a posse of Fiat 508S Balilla sports cars.

At the beginning of May Nuvolari and Comotti took two P3s across the Mediterranean to Carthage for the Grand

headed and stubborn and each needed the other. Finally they agreed to meet on neutral ground at Piacenza, halfway between Modena and Mantua, Nuvolari's home town. Once face-to-face, terms were agreed quickly; it was suggested that it was the attraction of the Bimotore that finally decided Nuvolari to return, and a contract was signed on 31 January. It was announced to the press immediately that Nuvolari would drive for the Scuderia in 1935.

While Jano designed, Bazzi and Meazza built and Ferrari and Nuvolari negotiated, there had also been significant happenings in the political world. In December 1934 there was a clash between Italian border guards and Abyssinian tribesmen in the colony of Italian Somalia. Somalia, in East Africa, had become an Italian protectorate in 1889, and Italy had then cast covetous eyes on the adjoining kingdom of Abyssinia. The Italian army invaded

Abyssinia in 1896, but was routed in the battle of Adowa. This was at a time when other European nations were rapidly extending their influence in Africa and making considerable accretions to their colonial empires. In Italy the Adowa defeat was felt to be particularly humiliating, and nearly 40 years later the Fascist Party felt that the defeat should be avenged. Abyssinia was the last potential colony in Africa and was regarded as a primitive country that would benefit from Italian rule. Mussolini had wanted to invade Abyssinia in 1932 but had drawn back, fearing British opposition, so the frontier skirmish was regarded by many as the justification needed for armed intervention. Mussolini was making bellicose speeches and the country began to prepare for a conflict with Abyssinia; at Portello this had a noticeable effect, as the demands for aero engines and military vehicles suddenly increased.

Prix de Tunisie. It should have been another profitable starting and prize money trip, but unfortunately Auto-Union sent Varzi, who during practice was 4 seconds a lap quicker than Nuvolari and this form was repeated in the race. Nuvolari broke a piston and the best Comotti could do was fourth place, while Varzi, just to rub salt in the Scuderia's wounds, had enough time in hand to smoke a cigarette during a pit stop.

On Thursday 4 April the Scuderia took the first completed Bimotore with the 2.9-litre engines to the Milan–Brescia autostrada for a test. Ferrari and Jano came to watch and the road was closed. Marinoni tried the car first, then Nuvolari took it out. He did several runs at about 175mph (280kmh), then tried hard. He was hand-timed at 212mph (340kmh) and the test showed that the car was just as quick as

had been hoped, as well as quite stable, but even in this short test it was showing a voracious appetite for tyres; to reduce drag the rear wheels had been fitted with discs.

The big test of the Bimotore came on 12 May in Tripoli. For this Nuvolari had the 6.4-litre car and Chiron was entrusted with the 5.8-litre. It was not only the Scuderia Ferrari that expected tyre trouble; all the teams had established auxiliary tyre depots halfway round the 8-mile (13km) circuit, and the Mercedes team had been in Tripoli since 29 April testing tyres. The corners had been eased and speeded up so the cars were now lapping much faster. The Scuderia had already tried the Bimotore on

Dunlops, but that firm felt unable to guarantee that its tyres would last out, so a switch was made to Engelbert, which turned out to be a disaster. Nello Ugolini made a quick calculation and found that Nuvolari would possibly have to make 13 tyre stops during the race!

Marshal Balbo dropped the flag and Fagioli, with a good position from the balloted start, took the lead. At the end of the first lap it was Caracciola in front followed by Fagioli and Nuvolari, but after only two laps the Bimotore was in for tyres. When it was going the car was as fast as the Germans, but on lap seven it was in again. The order changed continually as the cars

5 May 1935: On the front row at the GP de Tunisie, Nuvolari is sandwiched between Varzi's Auto-Union and Wimille's Bugatti. Sommer's P3 (No 16) is on the second row and Comotti's P3 (No 6) is on row three. (John Maitland Collection)

12 May 1935: Nuvolari's Bimotore leads Fagioli's W25 Mercedes in the GP di Tripoli.

dashed in and out of the pits for new tyres. At half distance it was Varzi leading Fagioli, while Dreyfus, being spared the tyre problems, had worked his Dubonnet P3 up to third in front of Caracciola. As the race neared its end, Ugolini gave Nuvolari and Chiron the flat-out signal, throwing discretion to the wind. Caracciola, knowing the tyre situation, let Nuvolari through and he chased Varzi.

The Bimotore caught the Auto-Union and for a lap they ran wheel to wheel, but it did not last and on lap 34 Nuvolari was changing tyres again. The duel had wrecked Varzi's chances as he now burst a tyre and had to hobble for half a lap. This left the guileful Caracciola to sail on and win, followed by Varzi and Fagioli. Nuvolari was fourth, Chiron fifth and Dreyfus sixth; Dreyfus would have finished in front of Chiron if he had not misread a pit signal on the last lap. Corrado Filippini said in *L'Auto Italiana*, '... as for Chiron there is nothing worth saying, as he raced without the necessary determination.' Brivio had a fortunate escape. On lap 13 he was hit in the face by a stone and lost control; the P3 somersaulted off the road and he was thrown out and concussed. After the race he was taken to Prof Putti's clinic at Bologna to convalesce.

As soon as the Bimotores were shipped back from Tripoli they were on their way to Berlin for the Avusrennen. Between these two major races the Scuderia supported the first Coppa Citta di Bergamo, run on a tight street circuit of 1.8 miles (2.9km). Surprisingly, Nuvolari had a beam axle P3 for this race and Pintacuda had the Dubonnet car, but it made no difference as Nuvolari won anyway.

Dreyfus was sent to Berlin with a P3 to back up Nuvolari and Chiron. Practice showed once again that if the Bimotore was run flat out, the tyres gave up immediately. There were four Mercedes and four Auto-Unions, two of which had enveloping bodies with closed cockpits. The race was run in two five-lap, 61-mile (98km) heats and a 10-lap final. Nuvolari ran the 6.4-litre car in the first heat and was out of contention immediately as he stopped for tyres on lap two. He finished sixth, and as only four qualified for the final, that was that; sometimes Nuvolari's intense competitiveness seemed to over-ride prudence and sense. Dreyfus, meanwhile, came in third and qualified. Chiron, with the 5.8-litre car, was in the second heat and sensibly held his speed down so that he would qualify, coming fourth.

26 May 1935: NSKK troopers are much in evidence as Dreyfus's P3 and the two Bimotores receive final preparations for the Avusrennen.

In the final the German teams, although trying to conserve their tyres, fought each other fiercely. Chiron drove a watchful race, deliberately easing off on the long straights, and at the end he finished second behind Fagioli's Mercedes, having moved up as the others stopped. Another lap and he could have won, as Fagioli's tyres were down to the canvas. Chiron had given Filippini an answer. It was said that Georges Engelbert thanked Nuvolari personally for not making an issue of the tyre failures after the race.

A full team went to Biella on 9 June to support Trossi's local race. Nuvolari won his heat and the final after a fierce battle with Trossi, fuelled, it was suggested, by the circumstances of the accident the previous year at Alessandria. Trossi, to the disappointment of the crowd, had to stop when he felt unwell. It was reported that he had heat stroke, but this could have been the first signs of the ill-health that was to dog him in the coming years. Trossi was now starting to mature as a driver and would soon move up towards the front rank.

The Scuderia only sent Chiron and Dreyfus to the Eifelrennen. Nuvolari was busy with another venture that weekend and the team was probably more concerned to have the cars on top form for the Grand Prix de l'ACF the following week. Once again, Chiron delivered a smart riposte to Filippini. Both German teams were running four cars each and both teams were determined to win; after the Grösser Preis, this was the most important German race. Driving for Auto-Union was newcomer Bernd Rosemeyer, a German motor cycle champion. His first race had been at Avus, but now he showed that he had an uncommon talent. He fought with Caracciola and beat him, only to be passed on the last lap just a kilometre from the finish when his engine went off tune. Caracciola won and Rosemeyer was second, but Chiron, driving a quiet, low-profile race, came third ahead of the Mercedes of Fagioli and another newcomer, Hermann Lang. As Chiron had an old beam-axle P3, his drive was impres-

26 May 1935: Chiron looks nervous as he fastens his helmet.

sive. His sensible driving at Avus and his quiet skilful effort at the 'Ring showed that he could still deliver the goods. His problem was that the delivery could sometimes be uncertain. After the race he was congratulated on his drive by several members of the German teams.

On Saturday 15 June, the day before the race at the 'Ring, Nuvolari was at Altopascio, outside Lucca on the autostrada

that runs from Florence to the seaside town of Viareggio. His task was to take the International Class B (5001–8000cc) flying mile and kilometre records with the 6.4-litre Bimotore. On 14 February Hans Stuck had used the same road to take the Class C (3000–5000cc) records with an Auto-Union, and while Nuvolari was not strictly after Stuck's records, this was the unofficial target and there were undoubtedly matters

26 May 1935: Nuvolari rounds the Nordkurve during the Avusrennen in his Bimotore.

9 June 1935: Nuvolari leads the field at the Circuito di Biella. His P3 is fitted with small rear wheels to gear it down for the tight circuit.

of national prestige at stake. Dunlop knew more about high-speed tyre design than any other maker, having a monopoly of supplying tyres for the World Land Speed record and also producing tyres for very heavy cars running at high speeds at Brooklands, so it was not surprising that the Bimotore was again fitted with Dunlops. The racing side tanks were removed, the head fairing was fitted, there was a wrap-round Perspex screen and the rear wheels had discs.

At 8.30am Nuvolari made a first run, but soon turned back to the depot as the oil pressure was fluctuating. Bazzi, who was in charge of the team, changed the oil tank and at 9.30am the Bimotore set of again. Nuvolari did two runs. There was a side wind and the car swung and skidded badly as it passed under a bridge, but he kept his foot down. The car skidded again on the return run, but he had taken the records and, better still, had beaten Stuck's figures. The average of his times gave the result as the mile record at 200.66mph (323.12kmh) and the kilometre at 199.60mph (321.42kmh). His fastest speed was on his return run over the mile at 208.81mph (336.25kmh). A jubilant and impromptu party took place on the road as Nuvolari climbed out of the car.

Next day the Bimotore was brought out again and Nuvolari attempted to improve on the records, but the cross wind was stronger and after five runs he gave up. The Dunlops had given no trouble at all and it must be speculated what the outcome would have been if the Bimotores had raced on Dunlops at Tripoli and Avus. A month later, on 7 July, Nuvolari went to Rome where Mussolini presented him with the Gold Medal 'Al Valore Atletico' in honour of his achievement.

The Scuderia only entered Nuvolari and Chiron for the Grand Prix de l'ACF at Montlhéry on 23 June. Both had the

Dubonnet P3s fitted with the 3.8-litre engines for the first time, and when the cars were weighed at the scrutineering there were no problems – at 739kg both were well within the 750kg limit. Apart from the P3s, opposition to the German teams was negligible and the French public, knowing a home win was impossible, stayed away, so the crowd was much smaller than in previous years. Nuvolari made the second fastest practice time. The circuit had been modified with straw bale chicanes, the first of which was just after the start; the cars were given a clear run for the first lap, then the chicane was hastily constructed by white-coated workers after the cars had rushed past.

At the end of the first lap, as the cars came to the rapidly finished chicane, Nuvolari led the field followed by Stuck's Auto-Union. The P3 stayed there for five laps with Caracciola's Mercedes now giving chase. The Mercedes then took the lead, but two laps later Nuvolari was in front again. Chiron had risen to third after three

laps, but now he stopped and struggled on for a lap with the car making 'unpleasant grinding noises'; he retired with broken transmission. Nuvolari was pulling away and set a lap record that was not beaten, but on lap 14 he slowed, Caracciola passed him and the P3 came into the pit. The back was jacked up, there was an agitated discussion with Jano, and the car was pushed away. His transmission had been making 'unpleasant grinding noises' too; the extra power of the 3.8 engine had proved too much for the ageing P3 transmission. Although the result had been disappointing, for Jano there was a glimmer of hope, for he had seen that the 3.8 engine seemed powerful enough to tackle the German teams. With the new 8C chassis, which would have stronger transmission, perhaps it could be a return to the good old days … In the sports car racing arena the fortunes of Alfa Romeo were declining; after four successive victories, the 8Cs had been defeated by a 4½-litre Lagonda at Le Mans.

15 June 1935: The crowd cheers as Nuvolari sets off along the Lucca–Firenze autostrada on his record-breaking run with the Bimotore.

15 June 1935: The Bimotore, showing both engines. For the record attempt the car was fitted with wheel discs, a head fairing and a Perspex wind deflector.

The Dubonnet cars were in no state to race the next weekend in Barcelona, so Nuvolari and Brivio had to make do with two beam-axle P3s for the Gran Premio de Pena Rhin. At least the Scuderia was able to produce cars; after Montlhéry Auto-Union scratched, saying that they had problems that needed time to solve and would not be racing again until the Grösser Preis von Deutschland in July. Nuvolari tussled with the Mercedes of Caracciola and Fagioli, but eventually they pulled away and he had to settle for third place. The same day Chiron and Comotti went to Nancy for the Grand Prix de Lorraine. This was a useful starting and prize money outing and Chiron won by a lap from Wimille's T59 Bugatti, with Comotti in third place.

It was now the height of the season and the races came thick and fast. To prepare for

the weekend of 7 July the mechanics at Modena must have been working round the clock. Seven P3s were made ready and the efforts were split by races 400 miles (600km) apart, both centred on ancient cities. As another P3 had been converted into a quasi-sports car, this must have brought nearly the full force into action. The French drivers were sent to France, where Chiron and Dreyfus ran in the Grand Prix de la Marne outside Reims. The result was all that could be expected. In a race of two 15-lap heats and a final of an hour's duration, each won a heat, and in the final Dreyfus won from Chiron. In third place came Raymond Sommer driving a 1932 P3 that he had bought from the Scuderia before the season began. He had been having mixed results with the car; it was outclassed in the major épreuves but he

had gained several places in minor events and had won the 50-mile (80km) Grand Prix de l'UMF at Montlhéry.

The Italian element was at Turin for the Gran Premio del Valentino, which was run in the Valentino Park in the centre of the city beside the River Po on a twisting 2.5-mile (4.0km) circuit. The Dubonnet P3s had been mended and were driven by Nuvolari and Trossi, but were only running with the 3.2-litre engines, while Tadini, Brivio and Pintacuda had to make do with the older cars. It was a race of three 20-lap heats and a 30-lap final. Tadini won the first heat, Trossi and Pintacuda were first and second in the second heat, and Nuvolari led Brivio home in the third heat. When the cars came out for the final, five of the ten runners belonged to the Scuderia. Nuvolari won from Brivio and Pintacuda, while Tadini let the side down a bit, being beaten into fourth place by Farina's Maserati. Trossi had dropped out as his eye was injured when he was hit by a stone thrown up by Nuvolari's car.

The French expeditionary force of the Scuderia had an extended sojourn in Northern Europe. Their next stop was a short trip across the Belgian frontier to Spa for the Grand Prix de Belgique. Auto-Union had kept its word, so it was the two Scuderia P3s against the Mercedes team, while Bugatti supplied the chorus with three T59s. It was a scorchingly hot day, and the three Mercedes led the field followed by Wimille's Bugatti. This blew up, but then there was drama. Caracciola was leading, but von Brauchitsch stopped with a burst engine. Fagioli was called in and Neubauer, the Mercedes team manager, ordered him to hand his car over to von Brauchitsch; there was a fierce row in the pit and Fagioli climbed out of the car and stamped away. The delay let Chiron and Dreyfus up into second and third places. Von Brauchitsch gave chase and caught both P3s, but only went past Chiron after a struggle.

Both the P3 drivers complained that the Mercedes fuel contained a noxious element that made them feel unwell. Dreyfus had to stop and hand over to Marinoni, but Chiron carried on and the two cars finished third and fourth. After the race Chiron collapsed, but the press were unimpressed by the allegation. Harold Nockolds, writing in *Motor Sport*, said, 'If the smell of the fuel is so potent, why are not the Mercedes-Benz drivers themselves affected by it?'

The wandering team's next destination was the Grand Prix de Dieppe on 21 July. Here they raced against a field with many English amateurs, among them Richard Shuttleworth with a wide-bodied 1934 P3 that he had bought from the Scuderia at the start of the season. The race result was not unexpected. Dreyfus, despite suffering from a severe cold, won from Chiron; they were pursued by Wimille's T59 Bugatti, while Shuttleworth was fourth. As some compensation for Chiron, at about this time an announcement appeared in the Paris *Journal Officiel* that he had been appointed

as a Chevalier of the Legion d'Honneur, so now he wore the small symbol in his buttonhole that all Frenchmen recognised and respected.

After Dieppe the two P3s were taken back to Modena, but Chiron went to the Nürburgring where he met the main team, which had brought two Dubonnet cars and an ordinary P3 for the Grösser Preis von Deutschland. Chiron and Nuvolari had the Dubonnets while Brivio was the third driver. The race was on Sunday 28 July and the Mercedes team, which had entered five cars, arrived for practice the previous Tuesday. The four-car Auto-Union team appeared the next day, but it was not until the Friday that the Scuderia cars turned up for practice, when Chiron complained that the steering of his car was not to his liking.

Race day was overcast with rain threatening. Much to the disappointment of the 250,000 crowd, Hitler did not attend, but the former Crown Prince Wilhelm, the son of the deposed Kaiser, was among the dignitaries. A light rain was falling when the race was started at 11.00am, and instead of a flag, lights were used to send the cars on their way. Caracciola led all round the first lap, followed by Nuvolari and Fagioli; next time round Nuvolari had fallen back to sixth behind a phalanx of Mercedes and Auto-Unions. Brivio soon dropped out with a broken differential and Chiron passed Nuvolari into fifth place, but then he too went out with a broken differential. The hopes of the Scuderia seemed to be fading, then Nuvolari became inspired. Between lap six and lap nine he moved up to second place at the expense of Fagioli, Rosemeyer and von Brauchitsch. On lap 10, to the astonishment of the crowd, the red P3 was in front – he had lapped the circuit for the first time at under 11 minutes, having passed Caracciola.

For two laps Nuvolari led, then the four leading cars came into the pits to refuel at the same time. The Mercedes mechanics had von Brauchitsch out again in 47 seconds, while the Auto-Union mechanics did the same for Stuck in 49 seconds. In

the Scuderia pit there was chaos. The handle of the refuelling pump, which should have delivered 30 gallons (135 litres) in 16 seconds, had broken; Nuvolari screamed and shouted, jumping up and down with frustration as he saw his chances slipping away while churns of fuel were poured into the car. After an agonising 2min 14sec he was on his way again, getting an ironic cheer from the German mechanics, but now down to sixth place.

It has been said that Juan Manuel Fangio's drive at the Nürburgring in the Grösser Preis von Deutschland in 1957, when he closed a seemingly impossible gap to beat the Ferraris of Hawthorn and Collins, was the greatest grand prix drive of all. The drive that Nuvolari now began probably surpassed that. Fangio was driving a 250F Maserati, which was the technical equal of the Ferraris. Nuvolari was driving an uprated 1932 car prepared in a workshop in a small Italian town, and he was chasing the latest grand prix cars coming from superb modern factories, backed by massive resources and hundreds of technicians. Within a lap he had caught and passed Fagioli, Rosemeyer, Caracciola and Stuck and left them in his wake looking like amateurs. There were nine laps to go and he now began to pursue von Brauchitsch. The German was alive to the situation and speeded up, lowering the lap record to 10min 30sec. The crowd watched and waited, enjoying the race and not worried, for a German victory was certain.

Then nagging doubts started to intrude. The P3 was catching the Mercedes inexorably. The gap fluctuated; lap 13, 1min 9sec; lap 14, 1min 26sec; lap 15, 1min 27sec; lap 16, 1min 17 sec; lap 17, 1min 3sec; lap 18, 47 seconds; lap 19, 43 seconds; lap 20, 32 seconds. As the two cars began their last lap, the gap was 35 seconds. At Adenau, halfway round the lap, Nuvolari was only 27 seconds behind, but at the famous banked Karussel the gap was visible to the astonished crowd – Nuvolari was only 200 metres behind. Von Brauchitsch could

28 July 1935: A frantic Nuvolari supervises the refuelling of his P3 from churns after the pressure pump broke during the GP von Deutschland at the Nürburgring. (Ludvigsen Library)

see the red Alfa Romeo closing on him, and in his desperation now he tried too hard. A rear tyre was down to the breaker strip; he should have stopped on the previous lap, but knew that a stop would cost him the race. With 7 kilometres to the finish, the nearside tyre of the Mercedes burst, and Nuvolari swept by the German driver who was weeping tears of bitter frustration. The huge crowd waited in the grandstands craning to see who would win; there was a stunned silence as the P3 came down the straight to the finish, then a deafening roar of cheering. The German crowd knew that they had seen the impossible happen – although their teams had been beaten, the driving brilliance that had been demonstrated received the reception it deserved.

The jubilant team, led by Ugolini, hoisted Nuvolari from his car. He went to the winner's rostrum where an enormous garland was hung round his neck – it was so large it came down to his knees. Reichskorpsführer Huhnlein, the Nazi official in charge of motor racing, had expected to make a speech extolling a German win, so he now made a rather stilted, impromptu address saying suitably nice things about Nuvolari, Alfa Romeo and Italy. The organisers were so certain of a German win that they could not find a recording of the Italian anthem 'Marcia Reale', so Nuvolari's mechanic Decimo Compagnoni obliged – he always carried one in case it was needed!

The drivers were staying in the Eifelhof Hotel adjoining the paddock, and after the race Nuvolari went to commiserate with von Brauchitsch in his room and gave him some flowers from the garland. Enzo Ferrari heard of the victory when Ugolini telephoned him; while the triumph must have been sweet, he knew that the prospects of repeating it were slim. The P3, even with Nuvolari's driving, was a spent force; everything now depended on the 8C-35, but even if the car was fast enough, the resources he had to maintain it and keep it racing were woefully meagre.

The Scuderia mechanics must have worked with remarkable speed during the next seven days. The three cars came back from Germany and were ready the following Sunday for the Coppa Ciano at Livorno. Three Dubonnet cars, fit and repaired, were driven by Nuvolari, Brivio and Dreyfus, while Trossi had the older P3. Count Ciano, the Italian Foreign Minister, was there with his wife Edda, Mussolini's daughter, and before the race he bestowed suitable and deserved praise on Nuvolari. In the race Nuvolari was unbeatable and won by 2 minutes, so he then received some more praise; Brivio was second, followed by Trossi and Dreyfus.

While the Cianos were enjoying Nuvolari's win, Chiron and Comotti had gone to the French South West for the Comminges race. Both had the older P3s, and the race was run in two heats and a final. In his heat Chiron had a puncture and could only manage third after changing a wheel; the heat winner was Sommer's P3. In the second heat Comotti led all the way. The final was not what the Scuderia wanted. Chiron had to stop twice and change plugs to cure a misfire, while Comotti went out with the almost inevitable broken rear axle. This left Sommer to take an easy win in his P3, followed home by another P3 driven by 'Georges Raph', the pseudonym of Raphael Bethenod de Las Casas, a rich French amateur who had bought his 1932 car from the Scuderia earlier in the season and was improving as he got to know it.

'Raph' was having a busy month as he took a stripped sports 8C to Montlhéry with a team of drivers including Luigi Chinetti, the Le Mans winner, with the intention of taking the World 48-hour record. A broken piston defeated the principal aim, but during the attempt they captured a number of Class D records including the 6 hours at 113.94mph (183.21kmh) and the 12 hours at 112.47mph (180.85kmh).

The Indian summer of the P3 came to an end at Pescara in the Coppa Acerbo on 15

August. This race was always held on the 15th to coincide with the Ferragosto public holiday. The Mercedes team stayed away, but two Auto-Unions turned up and were just too fast for the P3s. The team was out in force: Nuvolari, Chiron and Brivio had the Dubonnet cars, backed by Comotti, Tadini and Pintacuda. Nuvolari chased Varzi, but never looked like catching him, then the 3.8 engine dropped a valve; after that Varzi and Rosemeyer cruised home to win, with the Scuderia P3s following meekly behind.

Three P3s were entered for the Grand Prix de Nice the following Sunday and presumably these cars were resting at Modena while the team battled in vain at Pescara. Apart from the Modena team, the field was mostly made up of the enthusiastic French circus. It was the height of the Riviera season and a large and fashionable crowd saw Nuvolari, Chiron and Dreyfus take the first three places, followed by Sommer. Richard Shuttleworth had kept his P3 up with the Scuderia cars, at one time leading Nuvolari and Dreyfus, but fell out with a broken gearbox.

After the drubbing they had received from Nuvolari at the 'Ring, the German teams went to the next grande épreuve at Berne in a very determined mood. It stood them in good stead, for the Bremgarten circuit, with its fast curves, gave Nuvolari less chance to out-drive his rivals than the endless corners, rises and dips of the 'Ring. He only had a 3.2 engine and the extra power of the 3.8 might have made a difference, but at the end it was rather a let-down after the German victory and he could only manage fifth place behind two Mercedes and two Auto-Unions, with Caracciola the victor. Chiron fought with von Brauchitsch's Mercedes until he crashed heavily, knocking the Dubonnet P3 about and bending the front axle severely. He was thrown out but escaped badly shaken.

The military pressures at Portello must have hampered the completion of the new 8C-35, but the car was tested by Marinoni

and Guidotti in August, running in unpainted aluminium, at Monza and on the Milan–Como autostrada. After the first trials, extra apertures were cut round the radiator grille, so it may have been running hot. It seems that financial stringencies forced Jano to fit the 3.8-litre engines that the Scuderia had been using in the P3 during the season, which may explain why these engines were not being fitted to the P3s after the German victory.

Fittingly, the new car appeared at the Gran Premio d'Italia at Monza on 8 September. Two had been finished and were driven by Nuvolari and Dreyfus, while Marinoni had a Dubonnet P3. The circuit had been changed again, and this year it went back to the Florio layout, although five straw-bale chicanes were included to keep speeds down. For the German teams it was a three-line whip; each had brought out four cars. Maserati had been threatening a new car all season and now it appeared. Although it had a V-8 engine, it was a sad effort and already out-dated. Italian hopes were high – perhaps the 8C-35 could emulate the feats of the P2 and

P3, winning first time out.

It was a lovely autumn day and a huge crowd turned up; the Scuderia pit must have been crowded, for the top brass including Ferrari, Jano and Gobbato had come to see the 8C-35 in action. The cars were paraded before the start, each being preceded by its national flag, and the new 8C-35s were given a massive ovation. At 11.00am the race was started by a blue flag. Caracciola led from the start, followed by Varzi and Stuck's Auto-Unions, then came Fagioli's Mercedes and the two 8C-35s, Nuvolari leading. The Auto-Unions had the legs of the Mercedes that day and Stuck went to the front on lap three, followed by Varzi. Varzi then passed Stuck, but on lap 14 he pulled into the pits with a broken piston. Caracciola was still second behind Stuck, with Nuvolari straining every sinew in trying to close on the Mercedes, while Dreyfus was running in fourth place. The effort paid off when Caracciola dropped back before pulling out with a broken transmission, then Nuvolari nearly threw it away when he spun at one of the chicanes, but he did not stall his engine and carried on.

28 July 1935: This poor photo is one of the very few showing Nuvolari's remarkable victory at the Nürburgring – presumably the German agencies felt it was imprudent to keep them! The aeroscreen has been put flat, always an indication that Nuvolari was driving on the limit.

Stuck now made his routine stop, so to the ecstatic cheers of the crowd Nuvolari was in the lead for a lap before he too made his pit stop. Back in second place after the stop, Nuvolari was trying desperately to close on Stuck, then the crowd groaned as he came into the pit and climbed out of the car – a piston had broken.

Gobbato now took command, and on his instructions Dreyfus was called in and ordered to hand his car over to Nuvolari. With hindsight this was probably a misguided decision that may have cost Alfa Romeo the race, but the crowd loved to see Nuvolari in action and if the car won, an Italian driver would be a good thing politically. Stuck's brakes were weakening and Dreyfus was not pleased to be pulled out of the car, as he felt confident that he could catch the Auto-Union. However, Nuvolari began chasing again, but in doing so he caned the brakes of the 8C-35 and had to make a brief stop for brake adjustment. He carried on again at unabated pace, but the chance had gone. Stuck won by 1min 41sec and the shared 8C-35 was second. Marinoni, who had driven steadily, was fourth with his P3 behind Rosemeyer's Auto-Union. Under the terms of the drivers' contracts, Nuvolari and Dreyfus should have shared the second place rewards, but Nuvolari insisted that Dreyfus should have it all, hinting that if he had remained in the car he might have taken the winner's prize money instead. As Ferrari and Jano pondered on the race afterwards, they must have felt that for a first outing the 8C-35 had put up a creditable show; with better judgement it might have won. Soon it would have the new V-12 engine and, with that installed, it would surely be a winner. It was probably a comfort to Jano that the car had not let him down in front of Gobbato.

A week later the 8C-35 scored its first victory, albeit against the thinnest opposition. The Circuito di Modena was almost an exclusive Scuderia benefit. The team ran six cars, and matched against them were a T51

Bugatti and Farina with the new V-8 Maserati; Nuvolari romped home followed by Tadini and Pintacuda. It was probably with high expectations that the team went off to San Sebastian for the Gran Premio de España on the tough and narrow Lasarte circuit. Nuvolari had the 8C-35 and Chiron, nearly but not quite recovered from the Berne crash, had a Dubonnet P3. This time it was the turn of the Auto-Unions to have an off-day and Mercedes took the first three places led home by Caracciola, a win that secured him the 1935 European Championship. Unfortunately, the Scuderia had an off-day too. The 8C-35 never really got into its stride and stopped after seven laps with broken front suspension. While running it had not been particularly impressive, staying behind Wimille's T59 Bugatti and Chiron. Chiron lasted until the penultimate lap of the 30-lap race then dropped out, feeling off-colour.

Throughout 1935 a wave of nationalism had been building up in Italy. To foster this was very much part of the creed of the Fascist Party and it had been centred to a great degree on Abyssinia and the frontier dispute of December 1934. This fervour had also spread to motor racing. René Dreyfus said in his autobiography, *My Two Lives*:

'By September 1935, after the Grand Prix of Nice, I had begun feeling quite uncomfortable as a Frenchman on an Italian racing team. There had seemed to me to be an uneasiness all through the season, the sense of a nationalism growing that was not hospitable to a foreign presence usurping glory that should accrue only to Italy and Italians.'

After the Monza race Dreyfus told Enzo Ferrari how he felt and it was agreed that he would not drive for the Scuderia again in 1935. It seems that there was also pressure on Ferrari from the Fascist Party to engage only Italian drivers. Ferrari had striven to keep out of politics, which had little inter-

est for him – his only passion was motor racing and the success of the Scuderia. He had joined the Fascist Party in 1934, largely because it was expected of him and it made his position easier when dealing with Gobbato, who was a keen Fascist, and with other members of the Party.

At the end of the month, on 29 September, the team divided again. Nuvolari with the 8C-35, accompanied by Chiron and Brivio with Dubonnet P3s, went to Czechoslovakia for the Masarykuv Okruh on the Brno circuit. Mercedes stayed away; perhaps now that Caracciola had become European Champion the pressure to compete was less. Auto-Union sent four cars, however. The Auto-Unions ran in team order until Stuck dropped out when he was hit in the face by a bird. Varzi's gearbox then broke, but Rosemeyer carried on to win by 6½ minutes from Nuvolari, who had only been able to make any progress up the order as the Auto-Unions fell out. Chiron and Brivio were third and fourth. The race showed again that although the 8C-35 was not a bad car, it was not the winner that had been hoped for and was no real match for the German teams. Driven by anyone but Nuvolari its results would probably have been no better than the Dubonnet P3s; as it was, Chiron was only 4 seconds behind Nuvolari at the finish.

The rest of the Scuderia with the older P3s went to the delightful walled city of Lucca where the Coppa Edda Ciano was run on and through the walls. The Contessa Ciano attended to give away her Coppa and Prince Borghese, the vice-president of the RACI, dropped the flag. The race was in two heats and a final. Pintacuda won the first heat, Tadini and Comotti came first and second in the second heat, and in the final the Scuderia P3s took the first three places. Tadini received the Coppa from the Contessa, leading home Comotti and Pintacuda.

The following Wednesday, 2 October, Italy invaded Abyssinia. The national conscience was salved by the suggestion that it was a pre-emptive strike to protect the Italian colonies of Somalia and Eritrea from a planned invasion by Haile Selassie, the Emperor of Abyssinia. The effect in Italy was dramatic – nationalist fervour was whipped up to an even higher intensity, parts of the Italian economy went on to a war footing, and at Portello car production was stopped. Only 83 cars had been made in 1935 while the rest of the factory had been making aero engines and lorries, but now even this trickle was halted.

Dreyfus now had his mind made up for him; he would have to leave the Scuderia, so he began negotiating with Anthony Lago to drive in the French Lago-Talbot team in 1936. Enzo Ferrari accepted this decision, but acknowledged the driver's ability and was reluctant to lose Dreyfus's services altogether, so suggested that he should drive for the Scuderia in some events on a race-by-race basis without a formal contract. Chiron was also feeling the pressure and he too decided not to renew his contract with the Scuderia, so he went to Unterturkheim to talk with Mercedes.

International opinion condemned Italy for the invasion. The Council of the League of Nations, meeting in Geneva, voted that there should be economic sanctions against Italy and these took effect on 18 November. The economic effect of the sanctions was minimal, as it was agreed that there should be no oil embargo; however, the political effect of the sanctions was considerable, as Italy was now affronted and isolated. The ties that Britain and France had fostered as part of an anti-German front were now severed irrevocably and Mussolini, needing support, knew that he would have to look elsewhere for an ally.

All this would take time to have an impact on the Scuderia Ferrari in Modena. For the time being it was business as usual, and four days after the invasion, on Sunday 6 October, Brivio and Pintacuda took two of the earlier P3s to Cosenza, in Calabria deep down in the Italian South. Here they raced in the Coppa della Sila against thin

August 1935: Guidotti waits for a tow-start of the new 8C 35 during the first trials on the Milan–Como autostrada.

opposition. The race was in three heats and a final, and Brivio won the final after Pintacuda made a mistake and crashed, damaging the car but not himself. The day before the Cosenza race, the Donington Grand Prix was held in England, a full-length grand prix of 306 miles (492km); it was the first 750kg formula race to be held on the British mainland. Initially the race was led by Farina's V-8 Maserati, and when he fell out with a broken halfshaft, Sommer's P3 took over the lead, but he also broke a halfshaft and retired. With the foreign aces out, it was left to the British drivers to share the spoils. The winner was Richard Shuttleworth with his P3, who defeated two ex-works T59 Bugattis driven by Earl Howe and Charles Martin.

Enzo Ferrari knew that 1936 would be a challenging season. The 8C-35 was not up to the task and the V-12 was an unknown quantity, but he still held the ace card in Nuvolari. Now that Italy was in the middle of a war, the need for a boost in national prestige by racing successes was even greater, not only for the morale of the people but also to show that Italy was a strong country in every field. Mussolini had declared, 'My objective is simple – I want to make Italy great, respected and feared.' No doubt this message was relayed to Portello, where Jano was now getting every encouragement to finish the V-12 engine and make it work properly.

Chapter 11

The lean years

DURING THE WINTER OF 1935/36 Scuderia Ferrari evolved into a full and complete professional racing organisation. The days when it was a club catering for the racing activities of rich amateurs had gone. At the annual celebration dinner of the Scuderia in November 1935, Count Trossi resigned as president and Enzo Ferrari took his place. Trossi's last race had been at Livorno at the beginning of August, so the breach had been developing for some months, but now he severed his links with the Scuderia completely and became a leading light of the Scuderia Torino, which to show its independence purchased Maseratis; he would soon become a member of the Maserati works team. Trossi's departure was not wholly amicable and it was reported that he did not like the complete professionalism that was now sought in the Scuderia.

Dreyfus and Chiron had also gone. *Motor Sport* reported that Chiron's friends had commented that it was better he should win races in a German car than be beaten in an Italian car! There was now the policy of Italian drivers only; Nuvolari signed up again and Ferrari also engaged Giuseppe Farina, who had driven voiturette and grand prix Maseratis with considerable verve and skill during 1935. He was generally accepted, together with the British driver Richard Seaman, as the best of the voiturette drivers of the 1935 season. Farina was 29 years old, a doctor of engineering and a member of the renowned coachbuilding family. Brivio, Pintacuda and Tadini still

remained with the team. None of them was a top-flight driver, but all could be relied on to give a workmanlike performance. Ferrari was not short of drivers as he could also call on Marinoni and Severi, and there was the informal arrangement with Dreyfus for races outside Italy.

More 8C-35s had been built at Portello during the winter; it is difficult to give a figure with certainty, but it seems that seven cars were built, though probably only four were ready at the beginning of the 1936 season. The faithful old P3s were sold; three of the four Dubonnet cars went to England and the older beam-axle cars also found new homes. A 1932 P3 was presented by Alfa Romeo to the car museum being established by Count Biscaretti in Turin, which seems to indicate that the P3s were still in the nominal ownership of Alfa Romeo, so presumably the Scuderia had to account for the proceeds of any sales.

The V-12 engine was not ready in the spring despite Jano's efforts, but war material was now the principal product of Portello. Jano had devised a new road car, the 8C-2900A; the chassis frame was welded box section and the suspension owed much to the 6C-2300 as it had the same trailing arm and coil spring units at the front, while at the rear there were swing axles with trailing links, but a transverse leaf spring similar to that of the 8C-35. The first few cars used spare P3 engines with the twin superchargers, but in the later cars

there were noticeable differences in the detail engine design. In its final form as the 8C-2900B it would be regarded by many as the ultimate sports car built between the wars. The first four 2900As had bodies that were virtually widened versions of the 8C-35 fitted with cycle wings. These were intended for sports car racing, but could be stripped of road equipment and run as racing cars.

For some time the French had been disgruntled at seeing every race for grand prix cars in France being won by German or Italian cars. It had been hoped that Bugatti would build a new car that would restore the glory and honour of France, but nothing happened. The Delahaye company built very effective sports cars that had gained a number of successes in 1935, while Delage and Lago Talbot were going to introduce new sports racing cars in 1936, and Dreyfus had been engaged by Lago-Talbot as its works driver. The Automobile Club de France had announced in October 1935 that the 1936 Grand Prix de l'ACF would be for sports cars, and that it would not support a race for the 750kg grand prix cars. In line with this momentous decision, many of the French provincial clubs, which had regularly organised minor grands prix, now announced that their races would also be for sports cars.

This decision was significant news at Modena, as it ended the profitable starting and prize money forays into France that had made a substantial contribution to the

Scuderia coffers. The Scuderia entered three 8C-35s for the Grand Prix de Pau, one of the few French races that was still catering for grand prix cars. Two cars were taken to Monza on 20 February to test the suspension; the fairings had been removed from the front suspension and there was provision for varying the roll stiffness at the rear. The cars were tested over the 1935 Gran Premio circuit and Nuvolari did some of the driving. The Pau race was on 1 March, but when the Scuderia lorries carrying the cars reached Ponte San Ludovici, the frontier post between Ventimiglia and Menton, the team was told that a directive had been received from Rome that they were to return to Modena – Italian cars would not be allowed to race in France as a response to the trade sanctions.

This rule was, however, finely interpreted as the lorries were allowed to roll through the frontier post six weeks later en route to the Grand Prix de Monaco. Monaco had not voted for the sanctions in the League of Nations, but as it did not have an indepen-

13 April 1936: Nuvolari (8C-35) is on the front row for the GP de Monaco between Chiron (Mercedes W25, No 10) and Caracciola (Mercedes W25, No 8). (John Maitland Collection)

13 April 1936: Chaos at the Harbour chicane during the GP de Monaco. Farina's 8C-35 has been shunted by von Brauchitsch's Mercedes, and Farina is inspecting the damage. Brivio (8C-35, No 28) had avoided Trossi's Maserati and will carry on to finish fifth, sharing the car with Farina.

dent foreign policy and took its lead from France, the distinction was fine indeed. Four cars ran, driven by Nuvolari, Brivio, Tadini and Farina. While the 8C-35 was a better car than the P3, the German teams had not been standing still during the winter. The W25 Mercedes was faster and slimmer with an enlarged 4.7-litre engine developing 490bhp, while the C-type Auto-Union now had an 6-litre engine developing an impressive 520bhp.

The race was run on Easter Monday and it was wet. Charles Faroux, the clerk of the course, gave the drivers a special briefing, warning them of the perils of a wet track for the first time at Monaco. Nuvolari had given a typical performance in practice and made second fastest time in 1min 53.7sec, behind Chiron's 1min 53.2sec in his Mercedes. Caracciola took the lead at the start, followed by Nuvolari. At the rear of the field Tadini slowed immediately after the start as his 8C-35 had broken an oil pipe. He did not stop but motored blithely on round to the pits, leaving a trail of oil on the track. Caracciola and Nuvolari had passed him before reaching the chicane where the oil slick became thicker. The next car was Chiron's Mercedes, which lost control on the oil and hit the sandbags lining the corner. Farina also hit the sandbags, and his 8C-35 was then struck hard by von Brauchitsch's Mercedes. Siena managed to miss the others, but his Maserati hit the sandbags.

Nuvolari seemed to be the only driver who could cope with the oily circuit and he passed Caracciola's Mercedes on lap 10 entering the Tunnel. Fagioli's Mercedes and Rosemeyer's Auto-Union had also spun and crashed, so there was only one Mercedes left. Nuvolari's brakes then began to fade and Caracciola closed the gap, retaking the lead on lap 27; at half distance, 50 laps, he led by 1min 21sec. Nuvolari was now passed by Varzi and Stuck and dropped back steadily; he finished fourth, a lap behind the winner Caracciola and two laps in front of Brivio's 8C-35, which had been

handed over to Farina at half distance. It had been a disappointing result but, in the light of the crash, somewhat inconclusive.

There was a lull of four weeks before the next race, the Gran Premio di Tripoli. During this time the V-12 engine was considered ready to race and three 8C-35s were fitted with it for the race; the chassis remained unchanged, financial constraints preventing the building of new cars. The V-12 engine had dimensions of 70mm x 88mm and a capacity of 4064cc. The alloy blocks with fixed heads were mounted on a common crankcase at 60 degrees, and the crankshaft ran in seven main bearings; both main and big-end bearings were plain. Each block had two camshafts driven by a train of gears from the rear of the engine; there were two valves per cylinder. The single supercharger was driven off the front of the crankshaft drawing from a pair of horizontal Weber carburettors, and the magneto was mounted above the supercharger and driven by a spur gear. This engine developed 370bhp at 5800rpm, which would have been a race-winning output in 1934 or 1935, but was now at least 100bhp short of what was needed. It must be wondered if Jano was running out of ideas, as in some respects the V-12 was little more than two 6C-2300 engines on a common crankcase. Much of the detail design of the V-12 was done by Bruno Trevisan, an old friend of Gobbato who had previously worked on aero engines at Fiat; Trevisan had some slight competition experience and had driven an unusual car in the 1931 Mille Miglia, an Ulster Austin Seven.

There was another testing session at Monza, and Farina was hurt when his car overturned after a tyre burst. The Scuderia went back to Engelbert tyres for the 1936 season, a puzzling choice in the light of the problems of 1935 and the prevailing all-Italian policy. It is not known if Farina was driving the 12C-36 or the 8C-35; as he was entered for Tripoli in an 8C-35, it was probably the latter, while Nuvolari, Tadini and Brivio were entered with the 12C-36s and

Pintacuda had an 8C-35. However, Farina's entry was scratched as he was still unfit; perhaps to honour the entry and, much more important, get the starting money, Severi was taken along with a P3.

Half an hour after the first practice session began on Friday 8 May, Nuvolari ran off the edge of the road and over the rough kerbing stones, bursting a rear tyre. The 12C-36 overturned, but fortunately he was thrown out and landed softly. Several ribs were broken and he was taken to hospital where the doctors who examined him decreed that he was unfit to race and wrapped him in a plaster cast. Undaunted, Nuvolari discharged himself from hospital and appeared at the circuit for practice the following morning. He did two practice laps, with a time of 3min 46sec, which was better than those achieved by Tadini or von Brauchitsch, although 18 seconds slower than the fastest car, Rosemeyer's Auto-Union. Nuvolari said that he would race, so Ugolini and the Scuderia mechanics, whatever their misgivings, now had to repair the crashed car. To ensure that Nuvolari had a reasonable car, Brivio gave him his car and took over Tadini's, while Tadini, who presumably did what he was told, drove the repaired machine.

The race became a bitter battle between the Auto-Unions of Stuck and Varzi. Varzi won, but it was suggested that Stuck had been told to give way to ensure an Italian victory. This greatly upset Varzi and it is said that to calm him that night, his mistress Ilse Pietsch, the wife of driver Paul Pietsch, gave him an injection of morphine. This incident began an addiction that Varzi was unable to beat for several years.

Nuvolari held third place for the first lap, then dropped back through the field, unable to stand the pace. By the end he was in eighth place behind the other Scuderia runners. Surprisingly, Pintacuda with the 8C-35 was fifth ahead of the 12C-36s of Tadini and Brivio. It was a result that cannot have brought much satisfaction to Ferrari or to Jano. Probably more to the point, Ugo

Gobbato was unhappy that the new engine was not competitive.

After Tripoli some of the team went back to Modena, but Pintacuda and Brivio stayed in Africa and travelled along the coast to Tunis for the Grand Prix de Tunisie seven days later. Pintacuda brought the 8C-35 into second place, although two laps behind Caracciola's Mercedes, but Brivio fell out when the 12C-36 caught fire.

Nuvolari was resilient and four weeks after the Tripoli race he was fit again; he now began a sequence of races that certainly flattered the capabilities of the 12C-36 Alfa Romeo, but emphasised his astonishing ability. First he went to Barcelona where the Gran Premio de Pena Rhin was held on 7 June. It was surprising that this race took place. In February 1936 a populist, left-wing Government was elected in Spain; it was opposed by the right-wing parties and the army, and there was considerable unrest. Five weeks after the race took place, the Civil War began.

Nuvolari was accompanied by Brivio and Farina with 8C-35s. Caracciola's Mercedes led at the start, but on lap five Nuvolari took the lead and started to pull away. A refuelling stop on lap 39 dropped him back to second, but he went to the front again when the Mercedes made its stop. Despite another stop for a wheel change, Nuvolari held on to the lead. Near the end the V-12 engine was fluffing with carburation problems and Caracciola closed up, but Nuvolari just held on to win by 3.4 seconds at the end of the 80-lap race. Farina, three laps behind, was third.

A week later Nuvolari was at the Nürburgring with Brivio and Farina for the Eifelrennen, which was run in mist and rain. Nuvolari took the lead on the second lap followed by Rosemeyer's Auto-Union, but the German driver seemed to have a extraordinary sixth sense in the mist and was driving at unabated speed. His pace in the conditions was something that even Nuvolari could not match and he caught Nuvolari at the end of lap six and took the

May 1936: The 12C-36 engine made its début in the GP di Tripoli. The supercharger is mounted at the front.

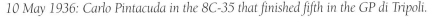

10 May 1936: Carlo Pintacuda in the 8C-35 that finished fifth in the GP di Tripoli.

14 June 1936: Brivio finished third in his 12C-36 in the Eifelrennen at the Nürburgring.

lead in front of the main grandstand. While Nuvolari and the others floundered in the mist, Rosemeyer forged on, and the Auto-Union won by over 2 minutes, its driver thereafter being called the 'Nebelmeister', the 'Cloudmaster'. However, it was a good day for the Scuderia, which finished second, third and fourth, Nuvolari's 12C-36 leading Brivio's similar car and Farina's 8C-35. Most satisfying, they finished in front of all the Mercedes team and the rest of the Auto-Unions.

The Scuderia mechanics must have become expert at negotiating the highways of Europe and having to cover long distances in a short time. The following week they took two 8C-35s all the way to Hungary where the Magyar Nagy Dij was

being run at Budapest on a tight circuit in the Nepliget Park in the centre of the city. It was decided to use the older cars as it was felt that the extra power of the V-12 might be excessive on a tight circuit. The race became a straight fight between Nuvolari and Rosemeyer, by then probably the two most talented drivers in the world.

The Mercedes team, which was having a disastrous season, fell by the wayside, Caracciola and von Brauchitsch both crashing while trying to keep in front of Nuvolari, while Rosemeyer was happily in the lead. However, on lap 35 Nuvolari overtook him on the inside of a corner, then, in the best modern idiom, 'shut the door' for the rest of the race and won by 14 seconds. Tadini brought the second car home in

fourth place. The English amateur Austin Dobson was sixth with his new purchase, the P3 with which Nuvolari had won the Grösser Preis von Deutschland the previous year.

The Scuderia now went back home to Modena, but there was no rest for the mechanics as a 12C-36 and two 8C-35s were at the Sempione Park in the middle of Milan the following Sunday for the Circuito di Milano on a twiddly 1.6-mile (2.6km) circuit running between the ornamental flower beds. The park was only about 2 miles (3km) from Portello and was behind the Castello Sforzesco, the inspiration for

21 June 1936: Two views of Nuvolari's 8C-35 at the unpretentious pits at the Magyar Nagy Dij in Budapest. The oil cooler is below the exhaust pipe.

28 June 1936: The front row of the grid for the Circuito di Milano is shared by Brivio (8C-35), Nuvolari (12C-36) and Varzi with the only Auto-Union in the race. Nuvolari was the winner.

the marque's badge. Once again Nuvolari showed consummate skill, his principal opposition being a single Auto-Union entered for Varzi, who was very keen to run in a 'home' event.

The race began at the late hour of 5.30pm. Nuvolari beat Varzi away at the start, but after two laps the Auto-Union was in front, and by lap 10 Varzi had opened out an 11-second gap. Nuvolari then began to motor and closed up until, by lap 32, he was on Varzi's tail. He squeezed by and although Varzi hung on and tried every gambit, Nuvolari won by 9 seconds to the delight of a highly partisan crowd, many of whom must have worked at Portello. At the end both drivers were acclaimed; it had been a re-run of the duels of six years before.

The conquest of Abyssinia had been completed in May 1936, so on 15 July, by a decision that in hindsight could be called cynical pragmatism, the League of Nations lifted the economic sanctions against Italy. The Italian Government now had no objection to the Scuderia running in French races again, so no time was wasted, and four days later Farina was at Deauville to join forces with Dreyfus for the local grand prix. It was the height of the season at the fashionable resort and Bugatti, perhaps thinking about possible publicity for his T57 road cars in front of a lot of potential buyers, sent two T59s to match the two Scuderia 8C-35s. Marcel Lehoux, who had driven for a number of private teams since leaving the Scuderia, had joined the English ERA team and had been competing in voiturette races

during the 1936 season. At Deauville he appeared in an ERA with a 2-litre engine.

The course was opened before the race by Ettore Bugatti driving a T41 Bugatti Royale. Farina took the lead at the start and was chased by the Bugattis of Wimille and Benoist, while Dreyfus soon stopped with a broken gearbox. When Farina stopped for fuel at half distance, he was passed by Wimille and Lehoux. Farina now caught Lehoux and, in trying to get by, the front wheel of the Alfa Romeo hit the rear wheel of the ERA. Both cars spun and rolled; the ERA caught fire and Lehoux was killed instantly, Farina escaping with slight head injuries. Farina was developing a reputation for arrogant, forceful driving that could have been a factor in the accident. It was an unhappy meeting altogether, as Raymond Chambost, a French amateur, was also killed when his 8CM Maserati overturned.

At 48 Lehoux was older than most

drivers. He was a 'nearly' man, never quite achieving the success his ability deserved, either with Bugatti or Scuderia Ferrari. He had given great encouragement to fellow Algerian Guy Moll at the start of his brief career, and was a popular and respected man. His funeral in Paris was attended by many of his fellow drivers.

The 2900A sports cars was used with great success in the Mille Miglia in April, and took the first three places driven by Brivio, Farina and Pintacuda. Soon after that two 2900As were shipped to Brazil for the Gran Premio di Rio de Janeiro, on the Gavea circuit, held on 7 June. Pintacuda and Marinoni went with the cars, but it is puzzling why the Scuderia troubled to send members of the team with mechanics such a long way for a relatively minor race during the middle of the European season. It is possible that the first prize, £60,000 at modern values, was a lure. It may also have been hoped to encourage the sales of Alfa Romeos, but as car production was at a standstill, this would have been somewhat pointless.

The 2900As ran stripped of road equipment, but the race was a disaster as Marinoni broke his transmission on the first lap and Pintacuda fell out with the same problem while leading on lap 21. The race was so popular that it was decided to hold another at Sao Paulo, the 'Gran Premio Cidade de Sao Paolo', on 12 July. This was a 60-lap race on a 2.6-mile (4.25km) circuit and the prize money was only the equivalent of £30,000, but this must have been worth staying for, as both 2900As were entered; presumably Pintacuda and Marinoni had an enforced five-week holiday!

Pintacuda led from the start, but Marinoni lost a lot of time when he spun. He subsequently caught up and was running second when he spun again and was unable to restart the engine. Pintacuda put the nose of his car against the tail of Marinoni's and gave him a push-start, so both cars went on to take first and second

places. The French woman driver 'Helle-Nice' had taken her Monza out for the two races, and was having a fierce battle for third place with the Brazilian champion Manuel de Teffe, also driving a Monza. On the last lap, with 200 metres to the finish, she pulled out to pass de Teffe and the crowd, anxious to get a better view, pushed against some straw bales that moved into her path. The Monza somersaulted into the crowd, killing seven spectators and injuring 33; 'Helle-Nice' was badly hurt. Her real name was Helene Delangle, and she was a dancer and striptease artiste in a Paris night club. For many years she was the mistress of Marcel Lehoux, whose death she heard of while in hospital. The race organisers did not approve of Pintacuda's push-start, so his share of the prize money was given to a fund for the victims of the accident.

The day before the Deauville race, the Spanish army in Morocco revolted against the new republican government and the Civil War began. On 24 July 1936 the nationalists, as the rebels were known, established an insurgent government in Burgos and the Moroccan army began moving to the Spanish mainland, where fighting had started. It was some months before Italy formally recognised the insurgents as the Government of Spain, but already Mussolini had offered his support. He was anxious to secure the use of Spanish bases for his fleet and also hoped that if the insurgents were successful in overthrowing the republican government, there would be another Fascist state in Europe, which then would be a natural ally of Italy. Mussolini agreed to supply arms to the nationalists, so dashing any hopes at Portello that the company would go back to a peacetime footing with the end of the Abyssinian War.

The European racing circus now moved to the Nürburgring for the Grösser Preis von Deutschland on 26 July. With the stupendous form being produced by Nuvolari, hopes were high that he might repeat his 1935 success. The 12C-36s were

entered for Nuvolari and Dreyfus, who was standing in for the injured Farina, while 8C-35s were driven by Brivio and Severi. At the end of the first lap Rosemeyer was leading and Nuvolari was sixth, but gradually the 12C-36 worked up the field and on lap six Nuvolari was third. When Rosemeyer came in for a stop at half distance it seemed possible that Nuvolari would take the lead, but it was not to be, as he had stopped halfway round the lap with a broken back axle. Dreyfus had gone after seven laps with magneto trouble and Severi's oil pump broke on lap 17 after Dreyfus had taken over the car, so it was left to Brivio, who had driven an excellent race, to bring his 8C-35 home in third place behind the Auto-Unions of Rosemeyer and Stuck, while Hasse's Auto-Union was fourth. Once again, Mercedes had a terrible day with fifth and seventh places.

Mercedes were so chastened by the 'Ring result that they scratched from the Coppa Ciano, leaving it open, as it seemed, for another Auto-Union demonstration. Nuvolari and Brivio had the 12C-36s and Dreyfus signed up for the race, being given an 8C-35; the second 8C-35 was driven by Pintacuda, reappearing after his South American trip. The Auto-Union team were so confident that the cars were taken straight from Nürburg to Livorno with only routine maintenance. The old mountainous Montenero circuit had been abandoned and a new 4.3-mile (7km) circuit on the outskirts of Livorno had taken its place.

On the first lap Nuvolari stopped with a broken back axle, which left Varzi and Rosemeyer to conduct an Auto-Union demonstration. The crowd were baying for Nuvolari, who had walked back to the pits. Count Ciano, who had come to watch his race, went to the Scuderia pit and urged Bazzi and Ugolini to call in one of the cars so Nuvolari could drive again. It was decided that Brivio should be sacrificed, but Nuvolari demanded Pintacuda's 8C-35 so he was called in instead, and Nuvolari took over. Rosemeyer stopped, feeling unwell,

2 August 1936: Nuvolari (8C-35) shares the front row of the Coppa Ciano at Livorno with the Auto-Unions of Rosemeyer and Varzi. No 50 is Brivio (12C-36), No 60 is Dreyfus, and No 64 is Pintacuda, both the latter driving 8C-35s. No 52 is Calamal's 1750, which remarkably finished fifth, three laps behind the victorious Nuvolari. (John Maitland Collection)

and handed over his car to Stuck, but Varzi was still in front, followed by Brivio and Dreyfus. Nuvolari stormed past Dreyfus, but Brivio was catching Varzi, whose brakes were failing. On lap 20 the crowd were hysterical; Nuvolari passed both Brivio and Varzi to take the lead, while Brivio went by the Auto-Union as well. A lap later Varzi was out and Dreyfus was in third place. The trio now reeled off the remaining laps to take the first three places and receive a tumultuous reception. A Scuderia Ferrari 1–2–3 – it must have seemed that the good old days were back again!

The Coppa Acerbo at Pescara was held on the Ferragosto holiday on 15 August, and after the Livorno debacle Auto-Union had worked hard on its cars. This time Nuvolari and Brivio had the 12C-36s, while Dreyfus and a recovered Farina had the 8C-35s. In the hope of giving the Alfa Romeos more chance, the organisers had put chicanes in the fast straights, which would reduce the straight-line speed advantage of the Auto-Unions. Once again Mercedes stayed away.

Nuvolari led for five laps then Rosemeyer went by him on the long straight. The cars were timed through a kilometre, but speeds were slower than in previous years because of the chicanes: Nuvolari did 151.05mph (243.24kmh) but Varzi's Auto-Union did 174.65mph (281.25kmh). Nuvolari held on to second place until lap eight, then fell out with burnt valves; Dreyfus and Farina had already gone, so it was left to the steady Brivio to follow the Auto-Unions home in fourth place.

With the lifting of the sanctions, Dreyfus was almost back as a permanent member of the team, and the Italian-only policy was now conveniently overlooked. He was therefore entered for the Grösser Preis der Schweiz at Berne on 23 August, driving a 12C-36, as was Nuvolari, while Farina had an 8C-35. Nuvolari was holding third place on lap two but then fell back and was out on lap 18 with engine problems. Farina had already gone and Dreyfus only lasted until lap 26. Once again the result was a clean sweep for Auto-Union.

There was now a little interlude when Brivio, Tadini and Pintacuda were sent to Lucca for the Coppa Edda Ciano with 8C-35s. The three drivers played for the lead on the delightful circuit until Brivio's fuel pump failed, but the others carried on playing and Tadini won by 5 seconds. As a further indication that the all-Italian policy was over, at about this time it was reported that Jean-Pierre Wimille had received overtures from Enzo Ferrari suggesting that he should join the team. Wimille confirmed the reports but rejected the offer.

For Mercedes the season was becoming a complete debacle. Having failed again at Berne, they did not go to the Gran Premio d'Italia at Monza on 13 September, probably surmising that it would be yet another humiliation. Without Mercedes it was a straight fight between the Auto-Unions and the Alfa Romeos, with four Maseratis providing the background music, racing over the Florio circuit as in 1935 with the straw bale chicanes. This time Nuvolari, Farina and Dreyfus had the 12C-36s and Pintacuda made do with an 8C-35. Nuvolari chased the Auto-Unions over the whole 308 miles (495km). He was able to dispose of Stuck after seven laps, but Rosemeyer was uncatchable and Nuvolari was 2min 5sec behind at the end. Dreyfus was fourth and Pintacuda was fifth, while Farina, who had been in third place for a while, bent his car on the straw bales at the Lesmo chicane.

By now Enzo Ferrari must have been pondering on the glories the season might have held but for the brilliance of Rosemeyer, who was all that had stood between the Scuderia and a string of wins. There was one Italian race left, the Circuito di Modena, and here on 20 September Nuvolari with the 12C-36 led Tadini, Farina and Severi home; the latter was using a stripped 2900A.

Early in September the Scuderia had sold an 8C-35 to the Swiss driver Hans Ruesch. He took it to England for the Donington Grand Prix, the only 750kg formula race run in England in 1936, sharing the car with Richard Seaman, who had just finished a triumphant season with a 1927 Grand Prix Delage in voiturette racing and was about to sign a contract to drive for Mercedes in 1937; the pair ran home to an easy win. Seaman's remarkable season with the Delage owed much to Giulio Ramponi, who prepared the car.

In the 1930s there was almost an unbridgeable gulf between motor racing on both sides of the Atlantic. In the United States track racing, with Indianapolis at its pinnacle, reigned supreme. Millers and Duesenbergs had raced in Europe but were dismissed as fast but unreliable. Europe stuck to road racing, and the odd grand prix car that had gone to the United States was mostly unsuitable for the American style of racing. To redress the balance, in 1936 a road-style circuit was built at Westbury on Long Island, and called the Roosevelt Raceway; it was the site of the airfield where Charles Lindbergh had taken off for his Atlantic flight in 1927. The

organisers invited European drivers to race against the best of the Americans for the George Vanderbilt Cup, an enormous example of the silversmith's art made specially for the race by Cartier, the New York jewellers.

The Scuderia entered three 12C-36s for Nuvolari, Brivio and Farina, and they were shipped from Genoa to New York on the liner *Rex*, the flagship of the Italian merchant fleet. Matched against them were Wimille's works T59/50 Bugatti, Etancelin with a V-8 Maserati, and a large number of English and French amateurs with Maseratis, Bugattis and ERAs. The American drivers entered in force with their track racing cars and there were 58 entries in all, of which 43 came to the start for the 75-lap, 300-mile (482km) race.

The 4-mile (6.4km) circuit was too tight, with 16 corners and a loose surface. In

practice, the Scuderia tried running with locked axles, but replaced the differentials for the race. Nuvolari led nearly all the way, but the American driver Billy Winn, with a Miller, harried Brivio and kept in front of Farina who went off the track on lap 18 when the rear suspension broke. Winn eventually fell out with axle failure, which must have been a relief to the Europeans, whose credibility was in some danger. There was a $100 prize for the leader on every lap, and Nuvolari lost this only once when he refuelled and tried to cure a misfire that dogged him throughout the race. Near the end Brivio fell back and was caught by Wimille's Bugatti, but came third, followed by Sommer's P3.

It was a much richer team that returned on the *Rex* with a cheque for $32,000, approximately £320,000 at today's rates, and the enormous trophy as well. Moreover,

12 October 1936: Brivio's 12C-36 shares the front row with Wilbur Shaw's Stevens-Miller (No 3) and Billy Winn's Well-Miller (No 7) for the George Vanderbilt Cup race on Long Island, NY. Nuvolari won and Brivio was third. (Guy Griffiths Collection)

1936: The trailing link and coil spring front suspension that was fitted to all the Grand Prix Alfa Romeos from 1935 until 1938. The coil spring is concealed in the cylinder and is worked by a vertical rod. This example is on the Bimotore that came to England in 1937. (John Maitland Collection)

the takings had been increased by the sale of an 8C-35, taken as a spare car, to the American driver Rex Mays, who prevailed upon Marinoni to stay on in the United States for several weeks to advise him on the tuning and setting-up of the car. *La Gazetta dello Sport* reported that the total earnings of the Scuderia during the season had been the modern equivalent of £650,000.

On 18 November 1936 Italy and Germany formally recognised the nationalist government in Spain and began giving it military support. Eventually Italy would supply 50,000 troops and 600 aircraft to bolster the nationalist forces. Germany encouraged Italian participation, for large Italian forces in Spain drained Italian military strength, thus ensuring that Italian opposition to German plans for Austria would be more subdued, but despite this Germany needed Italy's friendship. In March German troops had reoccupied the Rhineland, the area between the Rhine and the French frontier, which had been demilitarised since 1919. This resulted in diplomatic protests from the French and resigned regret from Britain, but it meant that Germany had alienated Britain and France and needed allies. Hitler had also recognised the conquest of Abyssinia, while Mussolini, suitably flattered, talked of a 'Rome-Berlin Axis'.

All this put pressure on Ugo Gobbato, who had to ensure that Portello maintained the supply of military hardware. Only 18 cars had been made in 1936, but there was now more pressure from Rome. With Germany gradually becoming an ally, there was an even greater need to show that Italy could produce racing cars as good as the German machines; effective racing cars were regarded as a microcosm of effective armies and armaments. Awkward questions were coming from Rome about the 1936 season – there had been victories in Italian national races, but in the major international épreuves the cars had failed, and without Nuvolari the results would have been negligible. If a Roman headmaster had been writing Gobbato's report, it would have read 'Must try harder next term'.

Chapter 12

Pride and prejudice

A MOST CONTROVERSIAL CHARACTER now enters the Alfa Romeo racing story. In the summer of 1936 Gobbato engaged Wifredo Pelayo Ricart y Medina to work at Portello as a 'Consultant for Tests and Technical Themes'. Ricart was Spanish, having been born in Barcelona in 1897. He had designed the Ricart-España car, which had been built at Industria National Metalurgica in Barcelona in the late 1920s, and after that he may have been working for Hispano-Suiza in Barcelona on aero-engine design (the company was building a nine-cylinder radial and a V-12, which were used in the aircraft of the Spanish Army Air Force). Ricart's views did not sit comfortably in Spain once the Civil War began; Barcelona was a stronghold of the republican government and Ricart was a supporter of the nationalist insurgents. He therefore had to leave the country in a hurry, and Italy was the obvious haven; the Fascist political climate was more congenial, and he knew Gobbato. Their friendship had begun when Gobbato was working for Fiat in Barcelona and had collaborated with Ricart-España; he had a high regard for Ricart's abilities. At Portello Ricart was employed initially to work on aero engines, but soon turned his attention to a V-6 diesel. His talents were considerable, not only as a technical designer, but also as an administrator.

The introduction of this new influence made Vittorio Jano's position even more uncomfortable. The 12C-36 had not lived up to its expectations and now, in desperation, he did a rushed revision of the design. Both the bore and stroke were increased to 72mm x 92mm, which brought the capacity up to 4495cc. Roller bearings replaced the previous plain mains and big-ends, two superchargers replaced the single unit of the earlier design, one feeding each bank of the engine, and the power went up to 430bhp at 5800rpm, which was better, but still a poor figure when compared with the German opposition. This time Jano went further and designed a new chassis. This kept the trailing link front suspension and the rear swing axles of the earlier car, but had a ladder tubular frame that made the car much lower.

Gobbato now made a fundamental move that changed every aspect of Alfa Romeo's approach to motor racing. In March 1937 Alfa Romeo bought 80 per cent of the shares of Scuderia Ferrari. When the Scuderia had been established in 1929, Enzo Ferrari held 25 per cent of the shares; how the ownership of the remainder of the shares devolved subsequently is not known, but presumably Count Trossi had bought some and probably invested additional capital, reducing Ferrari's personal holding to 20%. Gobbato must have approached the other shareholders surreptitiously to acquire their shares, thus presenting Ferrari with a fait accompli. The immediate effect was that the racing activities, although still run from No 11 Via Trento Trieste in Modena, were now under Gobbato's full control, so he could ensure that the energies of the Scuderia were wholly focused on the major events and on the main aim of beating the German teams.

Sympathy must be felt for Ferrari. The Scuderia had been sold out behind his back and this must have been a bitter blow for such a proud man. From being the complete boss, he was now reduced to being merely the paid racing manager. He had kept the Alfa Romeo flag flying since 1930 and the lack of success during the three previous seasons had been no fault of his, but had been caused partly by lack of funding for new cars and partly by the withering of Jano's inventive talent.

Nuvolari was persuaded to sign again for 1937, but he did so reluctantly as he was now admitting privately to his friends that he had little faith in Alfa Romeo or in the abilities of Jano. He wanted to drive for one of the German teams and had his eye on a seat with Auto-Union. Varzi was now deeply in the throes of his morphine addiction, so there was a vacancy, and Nuvolari visited the factory at Zwickau for discussions with Ferdinand Porsche. Nothing came of the visit, but it seems that there may have been political pressure to make him stay at Portello for the time being. The old faithfuls, Brivio and Tadini, signed too, together with Farina. After his year in the Maserati wilderness, Trossi came back, but was not engaged for all the races. A local driver, Emilio Villoresi, was also engaged; 24 years old, he had shown promise in

1936 driving a 1500cc Maserati.

The season began with the usual mass entry in the Mille Miglia, in which Pintacuda and Farina were first and second with 2900As. Running under the Scuderia banner in the 1100cc sports class was a Fiat Balilla driven by Ugo Gobbato. He did not finish the course, an irony that was probably not missed by Enzo Ferrari.

The new V-12, the 12C-37, was not ready at the beginning of the season, which must have administered a further blow to Jano's prestige. It must have been assumed that it would be ready as steps were taken to sell off at least one 12C-36; Thomson & Taylor, the British Alfa Romeo agents, advertised in the April 1937 issue of *Speed*: 'Alfa Romeo 4.4 litre monoposto 12 cylinder, over 180mph, most successful racing car in the world … £4500'. No 12C-36 ever came to Britain for sale, which is probably not surprising, as at current values £225,000 was being expected for a car that would be obsolete at the end of the season, with the finish of the 750kg formula. As an indica-

tion of the comparative value, in 1937 the average weekly wage in England was under £4, and a new Ford 8 saloon cost £110.

As a preliminary canter, four 12C-36s were entered for the Gran Premio del Valentino at the riverside park circuit in Turin on 18 April. Nuvolari tried too hard in practice and rolled his car. He was taken to hospital and fitted with the almost inevitable plaster cast, but was not fit to race, so his car was taken over by Pintacuda. In the race Pintacuda came fourth behind Brivio, Farina and Trossi, who played for the lead with negligible opposition.

The following Sunday the team was in Naples for the Coppa Principessa di Piemonte, and this time the drives were shared around, with Farina and Clemente Biondetti, who usually drove sports cars, driving the 12C-36s, Siena and Carlo Arzani, a Brazilian, taking the 8C-35s, and Villoresi turned out in a stripped 2900A. Arzani had bought the 2900A which had been left in Brazil after the Scuderia's sortie

in 1936; he had now come to Modena to buy an 8C-35, so was entered by the Scuderia for the Naples race before he took the car back to Brazil. The Scuderia cars took the first five places, with Farina leading Biondetti and Villoresi, while Arzani beat Siena to the line. With the 2900A he had been virtually unbeatable in South America, so he was a driver of some talent.

The first major race was the Gran Premio di Tripoli on 9 May, and the Portello team, crossing the Mediterranean on the *Conte Grande*, cannot have had any great hopes. The race now complied with the 750kg formula and the team no longer had the smaller Bimotore, which had been sold to the English driver Austin Dobson during the winter after the front suspension had been changed to the trailing link system. Auto-Union were racing the same cars as in 1936, though with minor improvements, but Mercedes had a new car, the 5.6-litre W125, and the now obsolete 1936 V-12s could not hope to live with either German car on such a fast circuit. The race ran to form as expected. Nuvolari broke his engine after six laps and the best-placed Scuderia car was Farina's in a humble ninth place.

18 April 1937: Farina (12C-36) leads Brivio during a Scuderia Ferrari 'demonstration' at the GP del Valentino in Turin. Brivio won this minor event and Farina was second.

The Avusrennen was the next meeting on the calendar and it showed that Alfa Romeo had now sunk even below the level of also-rans. Three cars were entered, but they did not go to Berlin and were scratched when it was realised that on the new Avus track with high bankings and race average speeds of around 160mph (260kmh), there would be complete humiliation. However, on that Sunday 30 May the Scuderia cars did have an outing. They were in Genoa for the Circuito della Superba, and against minimal opposition Trossi and Tadini took first and second places with their 12C-36s, while Villoresi was third with a 2900A. The party was slightly spoiled when Biondetti's 8C-35 broke its back axle. Success could now only be found in minor national races.

There was a slight ray of sunshine at the beginning of June, but it appeared a long way from home. The Scuderia sent an 8C-35 and a 12C-36 to Brazil for Pintacuda and Brivio to drive in the Gran Premio di Rio de Janeiro on 6 June. The race was on the twisting 6.9-mile (11.6km) Gavea circuit, which had every kind of hazard from tramlines to 100-foot (30m) drops over cliffs beside the road. Auto-Union sent a car for Hans Stuck and he led the race from the start, but after a lap Pintacuda took the lead; Brivio was third but had to make several stops for new plugs. On lap 11 Stuck went to the front again and tried to give himself a margin for a pit stop to change wheels. Pintacuda hung on and, when Stuck stopped, the 8C-35 led again. Despite all Stuck's efforts, Pintacuda held on and won by 8 seconds, while Brivio was third. It had been a race worth winning, as the prize money for first place was 1½ million lire, which converted to today's values would be £525,000, a useful bonus for the Scuderia's coffers.

Two 12C-36s were sent to the Eifelrennen for Nuvolari and Farina on 13 June. On the twists and bumps of the 'Ring, perhaps it was hoped that Nuvolari's brilliance might redress the balance, but on the day he could only trail home in fifth

place behind two Auto-Unions and two Mercedes, just keeping in front of the German third- and fourth-string drivers. A week later Nuvolari had some consolation when he won the Circuito di Milano on the twiddly Sempione Park circuit. He was followed by Farina, and their 12C-36s were well ahead of Rudolf Hasse, who had been entered with a single Auto-Union, presumably to get experience away from the pressures of the grandes épreuves.

The Scuderia now had a Transatlantic commitment. On 3 July two 12C-36s were sent to the Roosevelt Raceway on Long Island for the George Vanderbilt Cup. Nuvolari travelled on the French liner *Normandie*, which he joined at Cherbourg. During the voyage he received a telegram telling him that his son Giorgio was dead; just 18 years old, he had suffered from rheumatic fever as a child and had a weak heart. Courageously, Nuvolari carried on.

The circuit had been extensively altered since 1936; many of the corners had been cut out and it was now much faster.

Mercedes sent two W125s for Caracciola and Seaman, while Auto-Union ran Rosemeyer and von Delius; the second 12C-35 was driven by Farina and extra support came from Rex Mays, who had entered his 8C-35 with some home-grown improvements, including a large centrifugal supercharger. The race was postponed for two days because of bad weather, but still attracted a big crowd.

Caracciola led until he retired, then Rosemeyer took the lead. While this was going on, Nuvolari burst his engine trying to pass Seaman, then he took over Farina's car. He drove this until it faltered, then handed it back to Farina. Mays meanwhile had always been in the first three, and at the end finished third ahead of von Delius's Auto-Union. Perhaps the Scuderia should have taken note of the modifications! Farina limped on in the over-driven car and came home in fifth place.

While Nuvolari was returning from New York, Trossi and Sommer were at Spa for the Grand Prix de Belgique. Sommer's efforts

July 1937: Nuvolari at the Nürburgring practising for the GP von Deutschland with the 12C-36 in the wet. (Guy Griffiths Collection)

and results with his P3 had been noted and he had been given his first Scuderia drive at Tripoli. There were only eight starters at Spa, with the 12C-36s on the back row of the grid. Trossi retired with a burst engine after five laps and Sommer came last. It was a dismal showing, and all the hopes now rested on the new 12C.

The new car was not ready for the Grösser Preis von Deutschland at the 'Ring on 25 July. It was a further indication of the apparently waning enthusiasm at Modena that only two 12C-36s were sent to the race for Nuvolari and Farina, although an 8C-35 was taken for Marinoni; the American driver Joe Thorne, who had come sixth in the Vanderbilt Cup with a P3, was nominated as reserve driver to Marinoni. Sommer also had an 8C-35, which he entered himself, though it was a Scuderia car bearing the prancing horse badge. The Alfa Romeos made little impact on the race and Nuvolari

came up to fourth place at the end only as some of the German cars fell out. The race had a tragic outcome as von Delius died of the injures he suffered when his Auto-Union went off the road on the main straight as he was passing Seaman's Mercedes. Seaman also went off the road but escaped with facial injuries and a damaged hand. Sommer and Farina had both dropped out and Marinoni was four laps behind, finishing after the P3 that Nuvolari had driven to victory in 1935, now owned by the British amateur Kenneth Evans. Thorne was not given a chance to see if he could do any better.

Nuvolari did not go to Monaco for the Grand Prix on 8 August, and in an impressive show of loyalty missed his starting money, as he was testing the new 12C-37. The car was given a preliminary canter by Nuvolari and Guidotti on the Milan–Bergamo autostrada on Tuesday 3 August.

Nuvolari reported that the new engine had power and was responsive, but the car handled badly and was unpredictable on the curves of the autostrada; he attributed this to the flexing of the frame. Guidotti came to the same conclusion when he tried the car. It was too late for Jano to go back to the drawing board – his credibility and that of Alfa Romeo was at stake and the car could not be held back any longer. It was expected to race and the political masters expected it to win; the political need for parity with the Germans was greater than ever. The gloom at Modena and Portello cannot have been lifted by the results at Monte Carlo, where Farina, Sommer and Pintacuda trailed in at the back of the field many laps behind, while Brivio retired with a burst radiator.

The 12C-37 was taken to Pescara for the Coppa Acerbo on 15 August. Nuvolari did two practice laps and reported that it was not fit to race; apart from the handling problems, when matched against the

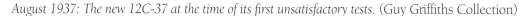

August 1937: The new 12C-37 at the time of its first unsatisfactory tests. (Guy Griffiths Collection)

Germans it was not fast enough. Jano pleaded with him to give it a trial, saying that it would provide valuable data that would enable him to make it fully competitive for the Gran Premio d'Italia four weeks later. To add to the disorder that now seemed to reign, Farina's 12C-36 broke down in practice and could not be made ready for the race. At the end of the first lap Nuvolari was in ninth place with only Vittorio Belmondo's private 8C-35 behind him. He did two more laps and pulled in, handing the car over to Farina. Two laps later it was out with a broken engine. Sommer's 12C-36 also blew up, so it was a totally demoralised team that drove north back to Modena.

Worse was to come. Five days later the teams assembled in Berne for the Grösser Preis der Schweiz. The 12C-37 had been withdrawn for Jano to do what he could to make it race-worthy, so it was assumed that Nuvolari would not be racing. However, when the cars assembled in the pits for the first day of practice Nuvolari went to join the Auto-Union team, with whom he had arranged to drive for this one race. All knew that this was a last warning to Alfa Romeo – if a race winning car could not be produced, he would be going elsewhere.

Once again Sommer and Farina did what they could with the 12C-36s but it was a hopeless cause. Farina went out with a broken back axle and Sommer was eighth after being delayed with a broken gear lever. For Nuvolari the race was not the triumph for which he had probably hoped; it was almost a humiliation. He was pulled into the pit and told to hand his car over to Rosemeyer, who had stopped on the first lap. Later in the race he was put into Fagioli's Auto-Union and finished seventh, a lap down on the winner, Caracciola.

Perhaps hoping that a tight circuit would help the Alfa Romeos and also Nuvolari, the RACI moved the Gran Premio d'Italia from Monza to the Livorno circuit, the home of the Coppa Ciano. Nuvolari returned to the fold, albeit uneasily. Declining the 12C-37, he settled to race a 12C-36, probably remembering his drive on the circuit the previous year. Trossi, Farina and Biondetti were keeping him company, for they too had apparently declined a drive in the new car. The 12C-37 did appear, but very significantly was entered not by the Scuderia but by SA Alfa Romeo, with Guidotti as the driver; a second car had been completed so he had a choice of machines.

Guidotti had never been regarded as having sufficiently high competence to be a regular grand prix driver for the Scuderia, so his practice time must have been slightly embarrassing and possibly indicates that the 12C-37 was not quite as bad as Nuvolari and the rest of the Scuderia drivers

15 August 1937: Nuvolari drives the disappointing 12C-37 in the Coppa Acerbo in Pescara. (George Monkhouse)

were saying with such emphasis. Nuvolari did 3min 20.8sec and Trossi 3min 22.2sec, while Guidotti managed 3min 24.2sec, beating Farina (3min 24.4sec) and Biondetti (3min 24.6sec). To put this in perspective, Caracciola's Mercedes was the fastest with 3min 11sec, but it must be surmised that a truly fired-up Nuvolari could have knocked sizeable chunks off Guidotti's time.

In the race Guidotti lasted for 24 laps, then stopped with various problems. Nuvolari went well at first and found himself battling with Seaman, Muller (Auto-Union) and Achille Varzi, now at least partially recovered from his addiction and driving an Auto-Union, but it was a fight for fifth place, not the lead. After 30 laps Nuvolari seemed to lose interest and handed the car over to Farina, whose 12C had already stopped. Farina finished seventh, followed by Trossi.

To complete the season Nuvolari and Brivio took the 12C-36s to Brno for the Masarykuv Okruh, but it was the same old story and they finished fifth and sixth, both having been lapped on the 18.1-mile (29.1km) circuit. Nuvolari lost time when a rear tyre burst and he had to drive round to his pit on the rim.

11 September 1937: Guidotti clenches his teeth as he tries to get a good practice time with the 12C-37 at the GP d'Italia in Livorno.

12 September 1937: All the fury of grand prix racing in the late 1930s is seen at the GP d'Italia. Just after the start Guidotti in the 12C-37 chases Kautz's Mercedes and the 12C-36s of Trossi, Nuvolari and Farina.

For Vittorio Jano the Livorno race was the end of the road. About two weeks later Gobbato told him that his services were no longer required at Portello so he departed at the end of the month. He went without too many regrets, as the pressures had been impossible. He had been expected to produce new designs with no funds, and had been humiliated first by the arrival of Cattaneo and his demotion to responsibility for a moribund car division, then more recently by the recruitment of Ricart, who was being treated by Gobbato as the 'favourite son'. Jano left Milan and returned home to Turin where he became the director of the experimental department at Lancia. He was not finished with grand prix cars, however; 20 years later in unusual circumstances that neither he nor Enzo Ferrari could have anticipated, his designs would again achieve success.

26 September 1937: At the Masarykuv Okruh at Brno, Alfred Neubauer (on the right) indicates to his Mercedes drivers that there are 10 seconds to go. Nuvolari (12C-36) shares the front row with Lang's Mercedes, with Brivio on the third row. This was to be the last race in which Nuvolari drove an Alfa Romeo. (LAT)

26 September 1937: Nuvolari drives to his pit at Brno after a tyre burst and came off the rim. (Ludvigsen Library)

Chapter 13

A need to win

SINCE THE BIRTH OF motor racing there have been classes for the smaller and lower-powered cars. Early in 1898 the owners of small cars were protesting that they stood no chance in competition with the largest and fastest vehicles, so the organisers of the Paris–Nice race in March of that year included a class for cars that weighed less than 400kg. These smaller competition cars became known as voiturettes; the name being the invention of French designer and constructor Léon Bollée, who patented a three-wheel vehicle in 1895 with that title. The French courts decreed that he had the exclusive right to the use of the word, but it was so admirable and effective that despite the feelings and protests of its proprietor it passed into general usage.

By the time motor racing came to an abrupt halt in 1914, the voiturette class was firmly established. The French magazine *L'Auto* presented the Coupe de l'Auto, which was run annually and attracted as much support from manufacturers as the Grand Prix de l'ACF. For the smallest cars the cyclecar class was evolved, and in 1913 the ACF promoted a cyclecar grand prix the day after the full Grand Prix. Before the First World War the rules defining voiturettes and cyclecars varied between weight and capacity limits, but when racing resumed after the War capacity limits were universally accepted. A voiturette was 1500cc and a cyclecar 1100cc. Throughout the 1920s the voiturette prospered, reach-

ing a high point when 1500cc was the capacity limit for grand prix racing in 1926 and 1927. The effect of those two years was to accelerate the technical development of the voiturette and leave within the class some very advanced designs.

Voiturette racing enabled several manufacturers to flourish; Bugatti had a production racing car with the T37 and the supercharged T37A variant, and the Maserati brothers entered the sport with the 1100cc and 1500cc T26. It also provided a nursery class that enabled drivers to hone their skills before trying to enter the full world of grands prix, and it was a class where the amateur could race with every chance of success without having to compete against the works teams that dominated grand prix racing. By 1930 a regular voiturette 'circus' had developed with numerous races, particularly in France and Italy.

When Jano produced his 6C-1500 it was pressed into service as a voiturette in its MMS version, stripped of road equipment. Alfa Corse entered some events with it, notably the 1928 Targa Florio, and Enzo Ferrari also ran an MMS in this form as an instant racer. The stripped 6Cs competed for the most part in Italian events, while elsewhere the Bugattis and 1100cc C6 Amilcars reigned supreme. With the appearance of the 6C-1750 the 1500 MMS was superseded, although some still raced with amateur drivers and gained minor successes.

When grand prix racing resurged in 1931, the voiturette world expanded with it. At the victorious début of the Monza in the 1931 Gran Premio d'Italia, a 6-C driven by Count Giovanni Lurani and Nino Pirola won the 1500cc class, though their efforts were understandably overshadowed by the win of the big brother. Lurani continued to race his MMS but concentrated mainly on Italian hill climbs. In May 1932 the Swiss driver Henri Taüber entered his stripped MMS with a Monza-like body for the Avusrennen, but dropped out with a broken oil pipe. A week later he had travelled west to the Nürburgring for the Eifelrennen, where he went extremely well, seeing off the attentions of T37A Bugattis and C6 Amilcars to win the 1500cc class.

Taüber went back to the 'Ring in July for the tough 325-mile (522km) Grösser Preis von Deutschland; running in the 1500cc class were most of the faster European voiturettes. Probably the fastest car was the 1927 GP Delage driven by the English driver Earl Howe, who had a considerable reputation and had achieved some success in grands prix with Bugattis as well as winning the 1931 Le Mans 24-hour race with an 8C. Howe led for the first lap and was then passed by Taüber, who kept the 6C MMS in front of the Delage, despite all Howe's efforts. Howe then slowed with problems so Taüber held on to his lead and went on to win, beating a field of 28 cars including many Bugattis and a new Maserati entered by Officine Maserati, the prototype of the four-cylinder Maserati voiturettes that were to be competitive for the rest of the decade. Taüber's victory was a notable effort, but went almost unnoticed at the time.

Just before the Grösser Preis, Taüber and Lurani had been to see Vittorio Jano at Portello. They pointed out the growth of the voiturette class and said that they could achieve much more with a purpose-built 6C, instead of the converted sports cars they were using. They proposed that Jano should build a series of special cars with alloy cylinder blocks, a short chassis and larger brakes, presumably from the 8C. Jano said that he was unable to help; at that time the finances at Portello were causing increasing anxieties and he probably had neither the time nor the facilities available to make the special 6Cs. Nothing came of the proposal; Lurani bought a Maserati and Taüber retired from the sport. Eventually a new generation of voiturettes appeared, particularly the ERA and the 4CM Maserati, so the 6C Alfa Romeo soon became obsolete.

There have been a number of claimants for the honour of being the first to decide that there should be an Alfa Romeo voiturette. Gianbattista Guidotti, when he was interviewed shortly before his death, was emphatic that the honour belonged to Gioacchino Colombo; as Guidotti was as close to the centre of Alfa Romeo racing matters as anyone, his knowledge must be respected. Colombo was born at Legnano, north of Milan, in 1903; when he was 14 he started as a draughtsman in a local engineering firm. In 1923 he won a scholarship awarded by Società Italiana Nicola Romeo and the following year joined Jano's team working on the P2. He worked so well that by 1928 he became head of the drawing office at Portello and was responsible for turning Jano's ideas into practical engineering projects. Jano said of Colombo during this time that he 'began to be my right arm'. There is little doubt that Colombo was responsible for much of the detail

design of the 8C and the subsequent Monza, P3 and 8C-35. Apart from working on Jano's outline designs, Colombo had ideas of his own; Guidotti said of him '... he had a whole heap of designs in his mind, he was always a volcano of ideas.'

Dates on drawings show that Colombo was already working on a 1500cc racing car in 1935. At this time it was probably a means of putting his ideas down on paper as at that time there seems to have been little intention of entering the voiturette field. The 8C-35 was about to appear and the V-12 engine was being gestated. At Portello it must have been assumed that the new car and engine would put Alfa Romeo back on top, so why bother about a minor class of racing?

These assumptions received a sharp jolt in December 1935. On 7 December the Bureau Permanent International des Constructeurs des Automobiles met in Zurich to discuss and put forward proposals for the new grand prix formula that would come into force when the 750kg formula expired on 31 December 1937. The meeting did not reach any firm agreement, but there was some support for the next formula having a limit of 1500cc. Raymond Mays, representing ERA, suggested that the existing formula should be extended for another three seasons, and that a 1500 race should be held as a preliminary before each grande épreuve so that the feelings of the public about a 1500 formula could be judged. Mays's proposal was supported by Alfred Neubauer, the Mercedes team manager. With Neubauer's support such a proposal stood a good chance of being adopted by the AIACR, so it was suddenly realised at Portello that there was a need to start thinking about a 1500cc Alfa Romeo without delay.

When Colombo died on 24 April 1987 a document of considerable significance was found among his papers. It was dated 25 January 1936, and had a printed Alfa Romeo heading. It sets out the specification for a 1500cc racing car in terms that mirror

the specification of the Type 158 that would emerge two and a half years later. Colombo was clearly ready, but the proposals for a 1500cc grand prix formula soon faded and it was decided that the 750kg formula would be replaced by one for 3-litre supercharged and 4½-litre unsupercharged cars. There would be a sliding scale of weight limits dependent upon capacity, which, it was hoped, would give the 1500s a chance. Throughout the 1936 season Colombo's designs remained in the drawer, but as the season passed and the 12C-36 failed to fulfil its hopes, thoughts at Portello and Modena turned to the possibility of finding another new path to glory for Alfa Romeo.

Enzo Ferrari was emphatic that it was his idea that Alfa Romeo should build a 1500cc racing car. In his memoirs he says, 'It was during this period, in 1937 to be exact, that I had the idea of having a racing car of my own built at Modena. This was the one later to be known as the Alfa 158.' Ferrari decided that the car should be built, as Colombo confirmed in *The Genesis of Ferrari*, and proposed this to Alfa Romeo, which now owned 80 per cent of the Scuderia; however, the concept belonged to Colombo who had already done the spade work.

At the beginning of 1937 hopes were still high at Portello that the new 12C-37 would bring success in grand prix racing and thought was already being given to designs for the new 3-litre formula, so the decision to build a 1500 was probably not born of desperation at the failures in grand prix racing; a return to success there was still confidently expected. The decision was probably prompted by the prospect of gaining success in a new field and also getting an early start for the 1500cc grand prix formula, which everyone anticipated would follow the 3/4½-litre regime. Colombo says, 'It was not the most propitious time at Alfa to suggest new undertakings.' Jano was under enormous pressure; his prestige was slipping, he was in the midst of putting together the new 12C-37, and having to think about designs for the new formula. To quote Colombo again:

'... his [Jano's] already difficult task was made absolutely impossible by the fact that Alfa Romeo, deeply involved in its development plans in the aviation sector, allowed him very little of its resources, either in money or in men for the racing section. To make poor Jano's life even more complicated there was the extremely difficult situation that had arisen in the factory – great confusion about roles, too many people all wanting their own way in the matter of planning (and I must include myself in this as well). One certainly can't blame Jano that in these circumstances his 12C-37 failed to attain its objective. In fact, it's a matter for amazement that he managed to build a vehicle at all under those conditions.'

A decision was made to go ahead with the 1500 project in late April or early May 1937, but it was not to be designed or built at Portello. Perhaps to give Jano some breathing space and perhaps so that the project could thrive in a less neurotic and frenetic world, Colombo was sent to No 11 Via Trento Trieste at Modena with his half-finished designs and set to work under Enzo Ferrari's supervision. A small team was assembled to work with Colombo and prepare the detailed drawings under his direction. Luigi Bazzi was the engine man, Alberto Massimimo was responsible for the gearbox, while Angelo Nasi worked on the chassis and front suspension. Ferrari himself was the progress-chaser arranging for raw materials and the supply of components from outside manufacturers.

The masterpiece that took shape, the legendary Type 158, did not contain any great technical breakthroughs; instead it was a combination of state-of-the-art Alfa Romeo design. The true skill lay in how these were put together. The engine was a straight eight-cylinder having two alloy blocks and integral heads, with screwed-in steel liners. The two overhead camshafts were driven by gears from the front of the crankshaft and there were two valves per cylinder at an angle of 100 degrees. There was one plug per cylinder fired by two Marelli magnetos driven from the front of the engine. The crankshaft ran in nine plain main bearings mounted in a magnesium crankcase with dry sump lubrication. There was a single Roots supercharger mounted on the nearside of the engine and driven from the front gear train, drawing its mixture from a three-choke Weber carburettor. The dimensions were 58mm x 70mm and the capacity was 1479cc, and when it first appeared the engine developed 195bhp at 7200rpm. Although Colombo had designed the engine, the lessons he had learned standing at Jano's elbow since 1924 could be seen. According to Griff Borgeson, when Jano saw the drawing of the 158 engine in Borgeson's study, he exclaimed, 'It's one of my engines!'

The drive went through a multi-plate dry clutch and thence to a four-speed gearbox mounted in unit with the final drive. The chassis frame had two main tubular members and four cross tubes and carried the normal twin trailing arm front suspension, while at the back there were swing axles with a transverse spring. The transmission and suspension were similar in main respects to that already used on cars from the 8C-35 onwards. The car was clothed with a neat body that had notably good proportions.

At the end of 1937, while Colombo's team toiled away at Modena working on the 158, which it was intended to race during the coming season, at Portello preparations were being made for the new 3/4½-litre formula. Ugo Gobbato was determined to have complete control of motor racing in Alfa Romeo, so on 1 January he made an announcement that left a dumbfounded motor racing world and a very angry and embittered Enzo Ferrari. With the power that an 80 per cent shareholding provided, he announced that Alfa Corse was being

The 158 engine in early trim with a single supercharger.

revived and would henceforth have sole responsibility for all the racing activities. The Scuderia Ferrari was to be closed down, and Enzo Ferrari was offered the job of racing manager of Alfa Corse, but would be required to work at Portello, to which all the Scuderia staff and equipment would be transferred. Within a few days a convoy of Alfa Romeo lorries carried all the worldly goods of the Scuderia off to Portello, including the partly built 158s, with all the jigs and components for the cars.

Spring 1938: The 308 with bodywork removed.

When the Scuderia was closed, Gioachino Colombo's work on the design of the 158 was virtually finished and the car was now the responsibility of the engineers and mechanics. He returned to Portello where he found a greatly changed world. Wifredo Ricart was now in the ascendant and was being given a free hand by Gobbato to work on new racing designs. While Ricart worked on the designs for the next generation of Alfa Romeo racing cars, Colombo was given the task of doing what he could to cobble together cars that would give a token representation in grand prix racing under the new formula. He had to do his best with the existing designs, some of which were left-overs from the drawing board of Jano, and others Colombo had originated himself before the sojourn in Modena. Whatever he did would be a stop-gap operation, as the real hopes were being pinned on the efforts of Ricart, which were not planned to reach fruition for almost two years.

Colombo paid little attention to chassis design, probably as he had no time to spare; he was having to produce raceable cars with three months to go before the start of the season. The scorned 12C-37 was at hand and he must have felt that its chassis would be adequate, for he did little to change or improve it. It was the engines that concerned him. His first improvisation was to turn to the sports engine that was being used in the 2900 sports car, and which was now in limited production as the 2900-B. The 2900-A had used the P3

engine, but in the B-series the engine was changed in detail, partly for ease of production. To go racing the power output was increased to 295bhp and the engine was installed in a makeshift chassis. Four of the old 8C-35/12C-36 chassis were pressed into service, and virtually nothing was done to them apart from cutting down the scuttles and fitting a new body. Colombo must have known that this car, called the Type 308, would have little chance of

success with such a puny output. Mercedes had already decided that a minimum of 360bhp would be needed, but when the new 3-litre W154 engine was tested at Unterturkheim early in the spring of 1938 it was giving 430bhp. While this intelligence was probably not known at Portello, it would have been realised that on previous form Mercedes would be building cars that would have an impressive power output.

Colombo also looked at the 12C-37, and

Spring 1938: The front suspension and steering of the 308.

Spring 1938: The 312 with the bodywork removed.

in a rapid re-design of the engine the bore and stroke were changed to 66mm x 73mm, which reduced the capacity to 2995cc.

1938: The 316 engine.

Apart from this, the car that now became the Type 312 was little changed, but the output was now 320bhp at 6500rpm.

For his third effort he utilised the experience he had gained at Modena working on the 158. Two 158 cylinder blocks were mounted on a common crankcase to make a V-16. Two superchargers were fitted between the blocks, which was a tight squeeze, and once again the 12C-37 chassis was pressed into service to carry this engine, which had the greatest potential of the trio. The car was entitled the Type 316.

Various outputs have been quoted for the V-16, but having regard to its performance the figure of 350bhp at 7500rpm seems likely. Writing in *La Gazetta dello Sport*, Giovanni Canestrini summed up the situation at Portello in resigned tones: 'It is essential to realise that racing cars are not the products of compromises or adaptations, but of the balanced and original study of the whole.'

During the summer of 1937 the press were told there would be a 1500cc Alfa Romeo, but apart from stating that it would be an eight, no details of the design were revealed. The press continued to publish 'scoops' about the car and also gave it six and 12 cylinders; there were also many reports about the car's possible début. In reality it had been delayed by a rush to finish the three grand prix makeshifts.

After a lot of persuasion and probably some political pressure, Nuvolari agreed to give Alfa Romeo a last chance. Emilio

Villoresi was also given a contract with the primary task of driving the 158 when it was ready, and he was joined by Farina, Sommer and Biondetti. Wimille was contracted for some races, as was Eugenio Siena. Alfa Corse also had Francesco Severi on the factory payroll, a competent driver who could be called on if needed. The faithful Antonio Brivio decided to call it a day and gave up motor racing to concentrate on power boat racing, while Trossi went back to Maserati.

The first grand prix to be run under the rules of the new formula was at Pau on 10 April 1938, and Alfa Corse sent two 308s for Nuvolari and Villoresi. The cars were fitted with a saddle fuel tank in front of the driver to improve the weight distribution. In practice, Nuvolari was trying hard but the chassis frame was flexing; this split the saddle tank and the leaking fuel caught fire. Nuvolari steered off the road and jumped out, receiving slight burns to his legs. The car was too badly damaged to race and Villoresi's car was also withdrawn. The fire was the last straw for Nuvolari; while he was still in the hospital at Pau, he sent a telegram to Gobbato announcing that he was retiring from motor racing. Some negotiation followed, and Alfa Corse accepted that he had made up his mind. It was announced:

'Alfa Corse, while considering the grave damage caused to it by the unexpected decision of its great champion, recognises that a man who has always given so much of himself, with exuberant audacity, to Italian motor sport and to Alfa Romeo has every right to retire from the battle and to leave to others the arduous task of emulating him. At his leave-taking, he fully merits a public recognition of our gratitude.'

Nuvolari went off to the United States for a holiday, but left some resentment behind him as he was very critical of Alfa Corse and said that he had retired as there was no suitable Alfa Romeo for him. He received

Spring 1938: The 316 being built at Portello.

some 'advice' from Fascist dignitaries that he should give no more press interviews.

The next race was the Gran Premio di Tripoli. There was some indecision about which cars should go across the Mediterranean, so a test day was held at Monza on Saturday 7 May. The results were, however, inconclusive, so the team took one 308, four 312s and a 316 to the race, which was on the following Sunday, 15 May. Sommer had the 308, Farina and Siena were in the 312s while Biondetti was given the 316. The Auto-Union team was not ready, so it was Mercedes versus the rest. The rest was quite a big field, as the organisers had included 17 Maserati voiturettes to make up the numbers, and there were also two new 3-litre Maserati 8CTFs driven by Varzi and Trossi. This made an impressive starting grid, but the speed differential on such a fast circuit was likely to cause problems.

In practice Biondetti managed to get the

316 on to the front row beside the three Mercedes, although he was 4 seconds slower. At the start Varzi and Farina took the lead, but at the end of the first lap Lang's Mercedes was in front followed by Farina, von Brauchitsch's Mercedes and Siena. Next lap von Brauchitsch had gone past Farina and on lap five was in the lead, ahead of Lang. Meanwhile Trossi showed that Maserati had learned some lessons and was harrying the leading pair of Mercedes. Siena was holding on to fifth place behind Farina and keeping in front of Caracciola's Mercedes, but on lap eight, as he reached the end of the main straight, he came up to lap Cortese's 1500cc 6CM Maserati. He pulled over and, perhaps caught by a gust of wind, ran on to the left-hand verge. He fought to hold the car but it slid across the road, hit a small sand dune, then slammed into the wall of a house. Siena was thrown out and killed instantly. A few laps later Farina came up to lap Lazlo Hartmann's

7 May 1938: Farina in the 308 at Monza at the test day before the GP di Tripoli.

4CM Maserati. An eyewitness suggested that Farina was impatient to get by and nudged the Maserati, which overturned. Hartmann was thrown out and died of his injuries that night; Farina went off the road but escaped with scratches.

The wretched race ran its course. Trossi snatched the lead for a lap but then fell out, so the Mercedes team cruised home in the first three places. Sommer had driven a steady race and brought his 308 into fourth place, but 8 minutes behind the third Mercedes, while Biondetti had struggled with the 316, which did not show its practice form and fell out before the end.

Eugenio Siena was 33, and had joined Portello as a young apprentice, working in the competition department. He then became the principal test driver for Scuderia Ferrari in 1930. He gained some successes in sports car races, notably winning the 1932 Spa 24-hour race in 1932 with an 8C, and was a reliable and steady third-string driver with a Monza in grands prix. He left the Scuderia in 1934 and was involved with various private teams racing Maseratis with little success, but was noticed again after a voiturette win at Milan in 1937, and some good drives in South Africa in the winter of 1937/38.

There was a notable paucity of grands prix in 1938. The next event, the Grand Prix de l'ACF at Reims, was on 3 July, but Alfa Corse was not there. Maybe after the disasters of Tripoli, time was needed to seek more performance and reliability from Colombo's motley bag of cars or, more likely, all the resources were being devoted to getting the 158s ready. According to Guidotti, the first car was finished at Modena during the last days of 1937 and was tested along the local autostrada by Marinoni. This seems likely as there was an established culture for trying a new car 'up the road' for the first time. Colombo says that it was tested for the first time at Monza on Thursday 15 May 1938, when Enrico Nardi, one of the Portello test drivers, covered many laps without any problems, but this may have been the first track test. After the Second World War Nardi would become a manufacturer in his own right, making a series of lightweight sports racers.

The British press was emphatic that the cars would make their début at the Grand Prix d'Albi in South West France on 10 July, but no Alfa Romeos appeared.

In addition to working on the 158s, Alfa Corse was setting out its market stall. Three 308s were sold, two to Scuderia Torino, a private team run by Piero Dusio, a textile manufacturer in Turin. After the Second World War he would be the progenitor of the Cisitalia racing car. The third car was sold to Renato Balestrero, a keen amateur who had been racing since the mid-1920s with OM and Bugatti before getting a Monza in 1932.

Meanwhile Alfa Corse had not been wholly inactive. Pintacuda and Tadini were sent to South America for the Gran Premio di Rio de Janeiro on 12 June. It seems that they took a 12C-37 and a 308. The race on the Gavea circuit was run in the wet and Arzani took the lead with his 8C-35, but Pintacuda forged ahead and won. Arzani was second while Tadini, who had lost a lot of time changing plugs, was seventh. The drivers returned home but it was a one-way trip for the cars as there were eager buyers for obsolete Alfa Romeo racers in Brazil and Argentina.

Rex Mays had also been busy with his 8C-35. He ran it in the Indianapolis 500 on 30 May; to make it eligible the bore and stroke were diminished to bring it down to 3 litres and the rear suspension was replaced with a Miller axle. Mays led the race for the first 50 miles but retired after 100 miles when the centrifugal supercharger seized.

Alfa Corse sent Farina and Biondetti to the Nürburgring with 312s for the Grösser Preis von Deutschland on 24 July. To the anger of the team Nuvolari came out of a very short retirement and was driving an Auto-Union. In the view of Alfa Corse he had being playing games. He wrote to Portello on 6 July suggesting that he would like to co-operate with the team again, but sent the letter by registered post, which took several days to deliver. The next day he

July 1938: Attilio Marinoni looks worried as a mechanic works on a 308 being used as a training car for the GP at Nürburgring. (Ludvigsen Library)

sought government permission to drive for Auto-Union, enclosing a copy of the letter to Alfa Corse. By the time Gobbato received the letter and was able to reply, welcoming his return, Nuvolari already had official permission to drive for the German team. It

24 July 1938: Renato Balestrero in the GP von Deutschland in his privately entered 308. (John Maitland Collection)

was inevitable that the race would be a further humiliation; both the 312s dropped out and the private 308s of Balestrero and Ghersi were eighth and ninth. The race was a source of joy for British enthusiasts as the winner was Richard Seaman driving a Mercedes.

Sunday 7 August 1938 was a turning point in the history of Alfa Romeo and also in the history of motor racing. Six 158s had now been built and three were taken to Livorno for the Coppa Ciano Junior. The drivers were Emilio Villoresi, Severi and Biondetti. The main rival was brother Luigi Villoresi, who was now one of the leading voiturette drivers and the first-string driver for Officine A. Maserati. To meet the chal-

lenge of the 158 the Maserati brothers had produced an up-rated version of the 6CM, which had a light alloy cylinder block, revised rear suspension and a lower, more streamlined body.

The impact of the three 158s was tremendous. Immediately all the other voiturettes were out-dated in appearance, specification and, as practice showed, performance. The cars set the three fastest times, with Emilio on pole position; in the race Severi beat the field away but Luigi's Maserati was in front at the end of the lap followed by Severi, Biondetti and Emilio. Luigi stayed in front for 15 laps but was having to press his Maserati very hard and it began to sound rough. He stopped and

Emilio took the lead, followed by Biondetti. Severi was next, but slightly spoiled the Alfa Romeo demonstration when he spun, and lost two laps when he stopped to change plugs. At the end of the 25-lap (90-mile/145km) race Emilio Villoresi came home to win by 2 seconds from Biondetti; Aldo Marazza with a second works Maserati was third, over a minute behind, and Severi came seventh.

It had been a completely convincing début and for Alfa Corse much of the frustration of the past years was swept away. The European motoring press was suitably impressed by the victory of the 'Alfettas', as the cars were immediately called. To improve the shining hour, after the Alfetta demonstration the grand prix cars came out for the Coppa Ciano. Farina and Wimille

August 1938: The new Tipo 158 has been unloaded from the Alfa Corse transporter at Livorno.

were matched in their 312s against the full Mercedes team and Trossi's impressive 8CTF Maserati. At the start Caracciola and Lang led with their Mercedes, but Trossi and Farina were right behind and after two laps Trossi passed both Mercedes to take the lead. He stayed there for five laps, but then the Maserati's brakes and engine called a halt, leaving the Mercedes in front again. Farina was now behind von Brauchitsch but was hanging on to the German, who spun off trying to hold his place. When Caracciola stopped for fuel and tyres, Farina went up into second place; he was caught by von Brauchitsch but the Mercedes had been push-started by spectators when it spun, so was disqualified. Farina held on to second place until the end, finishing 50 seconds behind Lang;

Wimille, who had shared his car with Biondetti, was third, so it was a happy team that went back along the autostrada to Milan that evening.

A week later the Alfa Corse vans ran down the Adriatic coast to Pescara for the Coppa Acerbo meeting. Severi and Emilio Villoresi were in the Junior race with the 158s while Farina, Vittorio Belmondo and Biondetti had three 312s in the full Coppa race for grand prix cars. This time the opposition consisted of both the Mercedes and Auto-Union teams. The voiturettes ran in the morning, and it must have seemed like a bad dream for the Alfa Corse team. Brother Luigi took the lead with his 6CM

Maserati and was chased by Emilio, but the changes of altitude between the mountains and the long straight beside the sea upset the 158's carburation and Emilio stopped at his pit after a lap, then retired. Severi took up the chase, but then he too had a long stop and fell to the back of the field; Luigi Villoresi swept on to win and the best Severi could do was fourth. All very reminiscent of the recent past.

When the grand prix cars raced it was a disastrous day for Auto-Union and all four fell out. Three of the four Mercedes also retired, but Caracciola kept going and won by nearly 4 minutes. Farina was second, but gained his place by virtue of survivorship

August 1938: Francesco Severi testing the new Tipo 158 at Livorno before official practice for the Coppa Ciano Junior.

7 August 1938: Emilio Villoresi (158) takes the lead in the Coppa Ciano Junior at Livorno followed by Luigi Villoresi (6CM Maserati, No 22) and the 158s of Severi and Biondetti. (George Monkhouse)

and never offered a challenge, while Belmondo was third. The result looked quite good on paper but in reality the 312s had only hung on.

In the voiturette world the Prix de Berne, which preceded the Grösser Preis der Schweiz, was regarded as the premier race of the year. It was the event where the British ERAs, which were almost unbeatable north of the Alps, met the Italian circus, who raced frenetically throughout the season in their own local races. Two 158s were entered for Raymond Sommer and Emilio Villoresi and there was great disappointment when the cars did not turn up for the race on 21 August – the motor racing world felt robbed of the expected showdown. The official reason was that the cars were not ready, but some observers hinted that the morale of Alfa Corse was still fragile and the prospect of a defeat could not be countenanced, especially if

this came from a foreign marque. As a result, the rising stars of the 158s never met the now fading stars of the works ERAs.

Although the 158s did not go to Berne, Alfa Corse sent two 312s for Farina and Wimille who ran in the Grösser Preis. It was a very wet race and neither made much impact. Farina came up to fifth at the end after some of the German cars fell out and Wimille was seventh; they sandwiched Taruffi's Scuderia Torino 308. It must have been a small crumb of comfort to the team that Nuvolari, who seemed very unhappy with his Auto-Union, finished ninth, four laps behind.

Alfa Corse were certainly coy about bringing out the 158s again. Two cars were entered for the Coppa Edda Ciano on the Lucca circuit on 4 September; one was to have been driven by Villoresi and the second driver was not nominated, but the cars were not there on the day. All the

efforts were being reserved for the Gran Premio d'Italia and its supporting race, the Gran Premio di Milano, the following Sunday, 11 September.

While the mechanics worked on the cars at Portello, in the wider world events were moving at a pace that made it increasingly unlikely that the race would happen. Italy and Germany were gradually coming closer at a halting pace of two steps forward, one step back. In March 1938 Hitler annexed Austria; though this had been opposed by Mussolini, in the event he acquiesced because he knew that Italy was not strong enough to oppose the annexation by force. Hitler needed Mussolini's support, or at least the knowledge that he would not oppose German plans for territorial expansion into Czechoslovakia, so he now began to woo the Italians and Mussolini in particular. Hitler visited Italy in May where he received a welcome full of pomp and military ceremony. Despite Italy's commitment in Spain, where the republican forces were relentlessly being ground down by the nationalists, Italy was still weak in military terms and Mussolini confided in his son-in-law Count Ciano, 'If war breaks out in Germany, Prague, Paris and Moscow, I shall remain neutral.'

Encouraged by his reception in Rome and by the knowledge that Italy, on his southern flank, would remain neutral, Hitler now demanded that the Czechs hand over the Sudeten territories that formed the western part of Czechoslovakia, adjoining the German frontier and with a predominantly German population. Throughout the summer of 1938 Hitler's demands grew more insistent, and the fear of war increased as Britain and France supported Czech resistance. Mussolini found himself in the role of neutral mediator, wooed by

Britain, which was prepared to forget Abyssinia, and by Hitler, who still wanted him as a inactive supporter. By the beginning of September Hitler had declared that if he did not get the Sudetenland by negotiation he would use force, giving as his justification the right of the Sudeten Germans to join the Reich and vague allegations of Czech brutalities against the population. The British population were issued with gas masks while the Royal Air Force and the French Armée de l'Air painted their silver aircraft with camouflage and briefed their crews on potential German targets.

It was in this tense atmosphere that the

Monza meeting was run. The Gran Premio d'Italia had returned to the Florio circuit at Monza after its brief migration to Livorno. The RACI had hoped for a representative foreign entry for the voiturette GP di Milano, particularly the British ERAs, but the international situation and the Italian currency regulations, which forbade starting or prize money being taken out of the country, were strong disincentives to take part, so there were only two outside entries. Alfa Corse ran four 158s driven by Emilio Villoresi, Sommer, Severi and Marinoni. The main opposition came from the works Maseratis. The Minister of Propaganda, Dino Alferi,

September 1938: Marinoni tries the 316 during practice for the GP d'Italia at Monza, while a lounge-suited Colombo stands beside the cockpit.

11 September 1938: The three 158s take the lead at the start of the GP di Milano.

inspected the cars and drivers on the grid and the only British driver, Arthur Dobson, the brother of the Bimotore purchaser, who was driving an ERA, gave him an exaggerated Fascist salute that delighted the crowd.

Sommer led for a lap from Marazza's Maserati and Severi, but then came into the pits for a plug change. Luigi Villoresi was now leading with his 6CM Maserati from brother Emilio and Severi. The Maserati was being driven harder than it liked to stay in front, and after four laps a piston rebelled. This left Emilio Villoresi in front followed by Severi, and the two 158s stayed there for the rest of the 25-lap race. Severi took the lead on the penultimate lap but was repassed by Villoresi and they finished 1.2 seconds apart; for a few laps Marinoni was running in third place, but he stopped at the pits, then retired on lap 20. The ERA had offered no challenge, Dobson having broken a halfshaft at the start. It was a satisfying result for Alfa Corse, but one that was tragically marred.

Sommer had carried on after his stop, although two laps down, and as he crossed the line his 158 emitted a huge cloud of smoke, probably from a broken piston. Sommer carried on round his slowing-down lap and was followed by Aldo Marazza, who had finished fifth. When Marazza reached the Lesmo bend, the smoke from the 158 may have caused him to misjudge the corner and he went off the road; the Maserati overturned and Marazza was thrown into the air and impaled on a tree, dying of his injuries a few hours later. He was 24 years old, and his efforts with Maserati had marked him as a driver of great promise; Alfa Corse had already approached him with suggestions that he should drive a 158 in 1939.

For the Gran Premio in the afternoon, Alfa Corse entered Farina and Biondetti with 316s while Taruffi and Wimille had 312s. The race was a fierce Mercedes/Auto-Union battle, and at the end only one Auto-Union and one Mercedes survived, but it

was Nuvolari's Auto-Union in the place where it mattered, coming first. Farina, by dint of keeping going in the 316, was second; though two laps down, he was ahead of the surviving Mercedes shared by Caracciola and von Brauchitsch. Biondetti was fourth, but both 312s had dropped out.

Although the 158s had been victorious at Monza, their reliability was still suspect. The last race of the Italian season was the Circuito di Modena on 18 September, and it seemed that it would be a close thing whether the race took place or a War began first. The Alfettas were driven by Villoresi, Severi, Sommer and Biondetti, and apart from Dobson's ERA this was to be an all-Italian show, with the Maserati team spoiling for revenge after the defeat at Monza. At the start the Maseratis of Luigi Villoresi and Cortese led Biondetti, brother Emilio and Severi. Then after four laps Biondetti went by the Maseratis and took the lead, but stopped almost immediately with poor oil pressure, dropping right to the back. Villoresi

11 September 1938, GP d'Italia: Biondetti's 316 leads a W154 Mercedes in the early laps.

now broke the gear lever of his Maserati, which left Emilio in the lead being chased by Cortese and Severi.

Meanwhile Sommer had a long stop while his mechanics wondered where his 158's oil pressure had gone; when he restarted he joined Biondetti at the back of the field. It was now Severi's turn to stop with fading oil pressure, but he too got going again and joined the other 158s at the back, running in formation together. Emilio Villoresi was still in front, but his brakes were failing and on lap 27 Cortese passed him; the 158 then came into the pits and retired with the contagious oil pressure ailment. Biondetti retired too, followed by Severi, whose rear suspension

had broken as well. Sommer's 158 was now the only one left, but on lap 37 his oil pressure went for good and he was out, so Maserati won, leaving the score at two-all. It was a dismal performance for Alfa Corse, and not the note on which to finish the season.

The 158 had shown that it was much the fastest voiturette when it was going, but its reliability left much to be desired. While Colombo and Guidotti pondered about the problem as the cars were brought back to Portello, Europe seemed about to be enveloped by war. On 28 September Hitler issued an ultimatum to the Czechs threatening military invasion if his demands were not met. Neville Chamberlain, the British

Prime Minister, flew to Munich on 30 September to seek a compromise with Hitler and was joined by Edouard Daladier, the French Prime Minister. Both now turned to Mussolini as a mediator and a compromise was agreed that effectively gave Hitler all he wanted; the next morning German troops rolled into the Sudetenland. For Britain and France a few vital months had been gained to prepare for the war, which all knew was now inevitable. Mussolini returned to Rome to be acclaimed as a peacemaker and still believed that if war came he could maintain Italy's neutrality. With the threat of war lifted, at least for a while, Alfa Corse prepared for the 1939 season confident that if reliability could be found, the 158s would be unbeatable.

Chapter 14

The summer before the storm

BY 1939 WIFREDO RICART had become established at Portello. Initially his title had been Consultant for Tests and Technical Themes, but in this guise he had, with Gobbato's support, begun the reorganisation of the design and experimental departments. The design department was split into three sections, one for cars, one for trucks and one for aircraft, while the experimental department served all three sections. Griff Borgeson says, 'Ricart's compelling ambition seems to have been

the creation of high-performance engines and vehicles of advanced design.' In pursuit of this ambition, by the summer of 1938 he had started work on two new racing car designs. Probably wisely he was backing it both ways, the first being a supercharged 3-litre that would be eligible for the current grand prix formula, and the other a 1500, a possible replacement for the 158. Either way he was determined to look ahead and prepare for any likely changes. As a further insurance he intended that the 3-litre

engine should be usable in sports car racing, much as Jano had done with his 8C nearly ten years before.

Ricart's design for the 3-litre car was called the Tipo 162; it was a V-16 and owed nothing to the 316 gestated by Jano and Colombo. The engine had two light alloy cylinder blocks with wet liners, incorporating a split crankcase that bolted together along the centre line of the crankshaft at an angle of 135 degrees. There were ten plain main bearings and roller big-ends. The bore and stroke were 62mm x 62mm and the capacity was 2995cc. The cylinder heads were detachable and each had two overhead camshafts operating four valves per cylinder, the camshafts operating the valves through fingers, with hairpin springs. The camshafts were driven from a gear train at the centre of the engine, a feature that was reminiscent of Jano's practice.

The major advance of the design was the use of two-stage supercharging. There were four three-lobe Roots superchargers, two first-stage and two second-stage, mounted between the two banks of cylinders and driven from the centre gear train. Each first-stage supercharger drew from a triple-choke carburettor. When it was given a first bench-test on 12 March 1940 this engine developed 490bhp at 7800rpm, which was comparable with the 1939 W163 3-litre Mercedes. The chassis of the 162 was tubular and had trailing link front suspension with coil springs and De Dion rear suspension with longitudinal torsion bars. The

Autumn 1938: Wifredo Ricart tries a 158 at Monza.

four-speed gearbox was mounted behind the final drive.

The 1500cc racer was the Tipo 512, and this too owed little to earlier designs, having no similarities to the 158. The 512 engine was a flat-12 with a bore of 54mm and a stroke of 54.2mm. It had two magnesium alloy blocks with wet liners, joined on the centre line, the cylinder heads being detachable. There were two valves per cylinder, with the finger operation and hairpin springs of the 512. The two overhead camshafts on each bank were driven by a gear train from the front of the engine. The bearings at each end of the crankshaft were plain, but the five inside mains and the big-ends were rollers. There was two-stage

1940: Two views of the Tipo 512. The two-stage superchargers can be seen above the engine.

supercharging with one first-stage and one second-stage two-lobe Roots superchargers drawing from a triple-choke carburettor. When bench-tested this engine gave 335bhp at 8600rpm.

Ricart must have been impressed by Auto-Union for the engine was mounted behind the driver. There was a tubular chassis with unequal-length double wishbones at the front operating longitudinal torsion bars, while at the back there was De Dion suspension similar to the 512, the triangulated De Dion tube being pivoted at the rear extremity of the chassis. The five-speed gearbox was in unit with the final drive and behind the centre line of the driveshafts. The driver sat well forward of the centre point of the car and between him and the engine was a large fuel tank.

The 512 was in many respects a milestone in racing design, but when tested at Monza it was said to have serious handling defects. Consalvo Sanesi, who drove it, told Borgeson that although it developed 100bhp more than the 158, it lapped 2 seconds slower, but it has to be wondered if this was a fair test, for by then the 158 was fully developed in every department whereas the 512 was raw and untested. With serious development perhaps it could have been turned into an effective racing car and could have brought forward the 'rear-engine revolution' in grand prix racing by ten years; in many respects it was a design of the 1950s rather than the final flowering of the inter-war years. The 512 may have been a victim of Portello's antipathy to anything connected with Ricart.

Ricart seems to have been incapable of doing anything right in the eyes of the old hands. In his autobiography Ferrari devotes several pages to a vicious diatribe against the Spaniard, criticising everything from his abilities as a designer to his style of dress and his handshake. There are probably several reasons why Ricart was unacceptable at Portello. The Italians feel an inherent superiority to the Spanish, dating back to Roman times when Spain was a mere colony that had slightly inferior citizens. This view was prevalent in Italy in the 1930s when the country was pulling the nationalist chestnuts out of the civil war fire and looked down on Spanish Fascism as a second-rate example of the Italian original. It was also a bitter blow to the in-house pride at Portello that a Spaniard had been employed to put the design house in order when the local talent had been found wanting. Ricart's cold and detached manner was alien to the cheerful and rumbustious approach of many of his fellow workers and caused misunderstandings – even his sense of humour was incomprehensible to some, including Ferrari. Ricart always wore shoes with thick crepe rubber soles.

Ferrari recalls one conversation: 'One day I could not help asking him the reason for his extraordinary shoes with their huge soles. He replied quite seriously that this was an obvious precaution "because a great engineer's brain should not be jolted by the inequalities of the ground and consequently needed to be carefully sprung". Nonplussed I broached the matter with Gobbato …'

Ricart may have seemed proud and arrogant to those who worked with him at Portello, but correspondence has recently emerged from the Alfa Romeo archives and from the archives of Ricardo Consulting Engineers Ltd at Shoreham in England showing that he was willing to seek advice from others and let them make substantial contributions to his designs. In July 1938 Ricart approached the British engineering consultant Harry Ricardo and asked his advice about the design of the 162. Many of the features of the design seem to have been introduced by Ricardo, including the four valves per cylinder, the hairpin valve springs, the wet liners and the use of a detachable head made from aluminium bronze where the valves could seat directly on to the bronze. Ricardo also suggested to Ricart that he should use Jano's central gear train to drive the camshafts. To Ricart's critics, his use of foreign consultants to advise on the design of his engines is additional ammunition to show that he was a charlatan, but equally it could be argued that he knew his limitations and went to the best sources available for advice and ideas. With the nationalist fervour of the times it is unlikely that the political masters knew that Ricart was seeking advice and ideas from England.

Vittorio Jano had been a designer liked and respected by the staff, but who did not have the confidence of the management. With Ricart there was now a designer who had the confidence of the management but was disliked and mistrusted by the staff. It was an unhappy situation, but it was to become insignificant in comparison with the events that were emerging in the real world. In the early months of 1939 much happened both in European politics and in motor racing politics. The political tensions were increasing, Italy was in the throes of an anti-French campaign and was making claims that Tunis, Nice and Corsica should be ceded by the French.

On 15 March German troops occupied the remainder of Czechoslovakia. Mussolini, being courted by Hitler and invited to join in a German-Italian Axis, was angered by this, but decided that he must have a territorial expansion of his own. On 7 April the Italian Navy bombarded the sea ports of Albania, then Italian troops landed and effected an almost bloodless conquest of the country within a week.

Meanwhile the RACI decided that there would be no motor races run to the 3/4½-litre formula in Italy during 1939; all races including the Gran Premio d'Italia would be for 1500cc cars. This was done not only to ensure Italian victories and isolate the German teams, whose wins would have less impact, but also to prepare for the next grand prix formula, which was now certain to be for 1500cc cars. As a reflection of the political crisis, Mussolini decreed that no Italian teams or drivers would compete in France during 1939.

At Portello, under the slightly embittered and mutinous management of Enzo Ferrari, the 158s were prepared for the forthcoming season. To prevent a recurrence of the humiliating bearing failures at Modena, the oil flow to the main bearings was improved and the plain big ends were replaced by needle rollers. A further directive came forth that it was back to an all-Italian policy for drivers, so Sommer was told that his services were not needed. He still found work driving for Alfa Corse in sports car events, and a 308 was available for him in grands prix, which if not a works entry still had a lot of factory influence. Emilio Villoresi and Farina were the first-string drivers, supported by Biondetti, Severi and Pintacuda. A newcomer was signed up, Giordano Aldrighetti; 33 years old, he had been 500cc motor cycle champion of Italy in 1933 and 1938 and was well known to Enzo Ferrari, having raced Rudge motor cycles under the Scuderia Ferrari banner.

Between January and March 1939 the British motoring press was full of rumours that Mercedes was working on a 1500cc car that was variously described as a six, a straight-eight and a V-12, but Mercedes said nothing. There must have been consternation in Tripoli, Rome and Portello when Daimler-Benz AG sent in two entries for the Gran Premio di Tripoli, which was now a 1500cc race intended for the exclusive delight of Alfa Romeo and Maserati. It has been suggested that the move to build a 1500cc Mercedes was done with Nazi encouragement as a means of putting down Italian pretensions, but there is no evidence for this and it seems that the directors of Mercedes had an impish sense of humour and were also wanting to be prepared for the expected 1500cc formula.

All six 158s were prepared for Tripoli, and the drivers were Villoresi, Farina, Severi, Pintacuda, Biondetti and Aldrighetti. The cars were taken to Monza on Sunday 30 April and tested; all seemed well so the cars were shipped to Tripoli for the race. When Gobbato engaged Ricart, he also secured the services of Bartolomeo (Meo) Costantini, the Venetian who had been the

Bugatti team manager for many years. Costantini's main task was to help Ricart, but he was sent to Tripoli as team manager. The 158 had a pressurised radiator and, according to a subsequent account given by Colombo, Costantini feared that the heat might cause the cooling system to burst, so during practice he instructed the mechanics to reduce the pressure in the system.

The Maserati brothers had been busy during the winter and had produced a new car, the 4CL, which had four valves per cylinder and was also known as the '16 valve'. A 4CL was specially prepared for the race with an aerodynamic body that covered the wheels and was built by Stabilamente Farina, the family firm of Giuseppe Farina.

In practice Luigi Villoresi, with the streamlined 4CL, was fastest, but the two W165 Mercedes were next and Farina, with the fastest 158, was 3.5 seconds slower than the Maserati and over 2 seconds slower than Caracciola's Mercedes. Despite the press rumours, the W165s were V-8s

and looked like miniatures of the full Grand Prix W154 Mercedes.

Marshal Balbo dropped the flag and Lang's Mercedes went off into the lead, followed by Caracciola. Villoresi's Maserati was left with gearbox problems, so the two German cars were chased by Farina, who caught and passed Caracciola after five laps, though Lang was now 70 seconds ahead. Farina seemed to be the only 158 driver capable of giving the Mercedes drivers a race, and the other five cars gradually fell back. At ten laps Farina stopped and retired with an overheating engine and was soon joined in the pits by Biondetti, Aldrighetti, Severi and Pintacuda, all with the same overheating problem. Only Emilio Villoresi was left, and as the two Mercedes ran on to a spectacular and legendary victory, he kept going and finished third, but he was nearly 8 minutes behind Lang and over 4 minutes behind Caracciola. Mercedes had the last laugh at the expense of Alfa Romeo and the result was a bitter humiliation.

If Colombo's account is correct,

7 May 1939: Lang and Caracciola (W165 Mercedes) are on the front row with Farina (158) for the GP di Tripoli. (Guy Griffiths Collection)

7 May 1939: Just after the start of the GP di Tripoli the Mercedes have already gone; Emilio Villoresi (158, No 48) and Giordano Aldrighetti (158, No 34) follow, with Luigi Villoresi (Maserati 4CL Aerodinamica, No 38).

Costantini's decision to alter the cooling system was the cause of the failure of the 158 at Tripoli, but this may not be the whole story. Soon after the race Ricart wrote to Ricardo seeking help with the overheating problem. The correspondence is incomplete but it seems that Ricardo gave advice about the water flow in the cylinder head and around the valve seats and cylinder liners. The engines were modified immediately and the pressure in the radiator was increased again. It has to be wondered if Colombo was loath to admit that the original design was less than perfect, and Costantini was a useful scapegoat!

7 May 1939: Emilio Villoresi makes a pit stop with his 158 during the GP di Tripoli.

Two weeks after Tripoli, on Sunday 21 May, Count Ciano went to Berlin and the German-Italian Axis was created by the signing of what Mussolini called the 'Pact of Steel'; the war was coming ever closer. In the motor racing world, the calendar had contracted sharply with the fear of war and the 158s were not brought out to race again for over two months. However, the cars were not completely inactive. On Monday 20 June there was a day of what would now be called corporate hospitality at Monza, when Alfa Romeo dealers and trade representatives were invited to lunch and to inspect the cars, including a 158.

As a team driver, Emilio Villoresi was present to meet the customers, and after lunch Enzo Ferrari asked him to take the 158 out and do a few laps to please the visitors. Villoresi declined, saying that he had drunk too much wine at lunch, but Ferrari insisted and Villoresi was pushed off in the 158. After a few laps the car went off the track at high speed and overturned, and Emilio Villoresi was killed. It was reported that he had been killed 'testing', but the accident was the cause of much bitterness for Luigi Villoresi, who never forgave Ferrari. As an added cause of bad feeling, the insurers of a policy on Emilio's life refused to pay out, saying that the policy was void as he was not fit to drive, and Enzo Ferrari did nothing to support the claim of the Villoresi family against the insurers.

At the end of that week two Alfa Romeos appeared in the Grand Prix de Belgique at Spa. Farina had a 316 and Sommer a 312, but both were private entries, though it was evident that the cars had come from Portello. The race was run in appallingly wet conditions and Richard Seaman was killed when his Mercedes went off the road while in the lead. At the beginning of the race Farina had been in fifth place in front of Seaman, but he retired with a broken gearbox and Sommer came fourth after most of the German cars had dropped out. A month later Sommer took the 308 to the Nürburgring for the Grösser Preis von Deutschland, but only lasted a lap.

The 158s came out again at Livorno on 30 July for the Coppa Ciano, forming a four-car team of Farina, Aldrighetti, Pintacuda and Biondetti. The main opposition came from the 4CL Maseratis, which had won every mainland European voiturette race since Tripoli. Such was the popularity for the class now that there were two races, with the slower amateurs running in a 'junior' race. When the 158s appeared it was seen that the cars had been fitted with new bodies, which enclosed the front suspension, and a slim head fairing; the cars' appearance would now remain unchanged until the last season of their racing life.

Before the race there was a minute's silence in memory of Emilio Villoresi, and

9 July 1939: Sommer in his privately entered 308 at the GP de l'ACF at Reims. He finished fifth. (Ludvigsen Library)

there was much sympathy for his brother Luigi, who was carrying on with his racing despite the loss. Farina took the lead at the start and was followed by a phalanx of Maseratis driven by Villoresi, Cortese and Taruffi. Farina was pulling away steadily and Biondetti now came up to battle with the Maseratis but his 158 ran out of breath as it passed them. Biondetti stopped at his pit while the car was put right and Pintacuda was called in and told to hand over his 158. Biondetti's car had now been mended and Pintacuda was told to drive it, but he refused, so after a long delay Severi, who was the reserve driver, climbed in and drove off. Villoresi stopped with a broken half-shaft, leaving Biondetti chasing the Maseratis of Cortese and Taruffi; he caught Taruffi and finished third behind Farina's 158 and Cortese. Farina had won by over a minute and in doing so broke the lap record set by Lang's W154 Mercedes the previous year – a 1500cc 158 was now faster than the best grand prix car of the year before. Severi had brought the other car home into fifth and last place, but the

158s were still not quite right, as Aldrighetti had dropped out on lap 31.

One 158 had been written off in Villoresi's accident, but four cars were entered at Pescara for the Coppa Acerbo on 15 August. There were three days of practice, and on the first morning Aldrighetti went off the road outside Spoltore village on the winding, hilly section of the circuit; his 158 overturned into a ditch and caught fire. Aldrighetti was trapped under the car and was badly burned before he could be released; he died the following day. After some discussion it was decided that the team would race, so Pintacuda was nominated to take the place of Aldrighetti and drove a car with the earlier body style, joining Farina, Biondetti and Severi. This time the 'juniors' had competed in a preliminary heat and the first three raced with the 'big boys'. There was another tragedy when Catullo Lami, who was third in the heat, was killed on the first lap of the main race when his 6CM Maserati crashed.

Once again it was 158s versus 4CLs. Villoresi took the lead at the start but was

15 August 1939: The four 158s wait at the pits at Pescara before the start of the final of the Coppa Acerbo. This was the second appearance of the cars with the restyled bodywork, which they would keep for the rest of their career. The third car, Pintacuda's, still has the earlier bodywork with the exposed front suspension.

passed by Farina before the end of the first lap; the pair were being chased by Biondetti, Cortese (4CL) and Pintacuda. On lap three Villoresi spun and dropped behind Biondetti, but Farina then had a long stop to change a plug so now Biondetti was in front and trying to keep the two Maseratis at bay. Both 4CLs were hot on his heels at the start of the last of the 15 laps, but astonishingly both ran out of fuel just before the finishing line, so the 158s came home to an unexpected 1–2–3–4 victory with Biondetti leading Pintacuda, Farina and Severi. It was a much more convincing victory on paper than on the track and, as an indication that the 4CL Maserati was offering a serious challenge at that time, Villoresi had been the fastest of all through the usual Pescara time-trap at 147.14mph (236.6kmh).

Throughout the summer of 1939

Germany made belligerent claims upon Poland, centred on the Danzig corridor, a strip of land that gave Poland an outlet to the Baltic at Danzig, but cut off East Prussia from the rest of Germany. It was an invention of the Treaty of Versailles in 1919, and had been a cause of German grievance ever since. Hitler insisted that if Poland did not surrender Danzig and the corridor, he would take it by force; as Britain and France had guaranteed Poland's frontiers, war seemed inevitable if the German threats were realised.

In this atmosphere the teams gathered at Berne for the Grösser Preis von Schweiz and the Prix de Berne on 20 August. The British competitors in the Prix de Berne were ready to load their cars and dash across France to avoid being trapped on the mainland if war began. The Prix de Berne for the voiturettes was also a heat for the Grösser Preis, and

the first six finishers would qualify to run in the main race. Alfa Corse had only entered two 158s, driven by Farina and Biondetti. The Prix was a 20-lap race and Farina went straight into the lead and stayed there to the flag. Biondetti was behind the Maseratis of Pietsch and Rocco for five laps, then broke away to follow Farina across the line in second place.

The two 158s had qualified comfortably and now ran in the full race against the 3-litre Mercedes and Auto-Unions. It began to rain just before the start, which gave Farina an advantage. He made a superb start and at the end of the first lap was running in second place, 2 seconds behind Lang's Mercedes. Farina held second place for six laps, but then the rain eased off and Caracciola's Mercedes passed the 158. As the road dried out the other German cars went past Farina and at the finish he was back in sixth place, with Biondetti eighth. The performance of the 158, with an engine half the size of the German cars, astonished the crowd and probably the German teams as well. It must have been frustrating for

Alfa Corse that the 1500cc W165 Mercedes had not been in the race, as the 158, with its improved form, would surely have run it close. However, Farina's drive had gone a long way to redeem the embarrassment of Tripoli.

Twelve days later, at dawn on Friday 1 September, German tanks rumbled into Poland and the Second World War had begun. Mussolini had changed his position constantly during the summer, swinging continuously from peacemaker to warmonger; in the last days of August he tried to persuade Hitler to call off or postpone his plans to invade Poland, and as late as the evening of 31 August he suggested that he should be mediator. Once the war started he was still undecided if Italy should remain neutral or enter it on the German side; the economic advantages of neutrality were many, but he was certain that there would be a German victory and wanted to share in the territorial spoils. Initially, however, Italy remained neutral and as 1940 began there seemed every chance that motor racing could continue, at least within Italy itself. A calendar of events was drawn up with a series of 1500cc and sports car races culminating in the Gran Premio at Monza in September.

At Portello hostilities of another kind came to a head. In November 1939 the tensions surrounding Enzo Ferrari and his virtual hatred of Ricart reached a crisis. Gobbato found that Ferrari was becoming unwilling to accept his authority and, in Ferrari's own words, 'The rift became unbridgeable and led to my dismissal.' Ferrari returned to Modena with substantial compensation; he agreed not to revive Scuderia Ferrari for four years or engage in motor racing during that time. Back to Modena with him went Enrico Nardi and Alberto Massimimo, but Colombo and Bazzi preferred to stay at Portello.

With the prospect of a season's racing ahead, Alfa Corse took stock; with the fatal crashes of Villoresi and Aldrighetti, two 158s had been destroyed, so during the winter a further six cars were built. These were similar in specification to the original cars in their final 1939 form and it seems that the four surviving 1938/39 cars were broken up and parts probably incorporated into the new cars. The problem of employing foreign drivers was no longer a burning issue; the two most likely, Sommer and Wimille, were otherwise engaged, Sommer in the French Army and Wimille as an officer in L'Armée de l'Air. Farina, Pintacuda and Biondetti were still on the books and they were now joined by Trossi. There were a number of reasons for his return: he may have been unhappy with the changes at Maserati where the easy-going firm run by the brothers had been taken over by Adolfo Orsi, a rich industrialist who was running it on much more commercial lines; the departure of Ferrari may also have been relevant, as there was still bad feeling about their split in the autumn of 1935.

The first event in the 1940 Italian calendar was the Mille Miglia. In 1938 the race had been won by Biondetti with a 2900A, but there had been a serious accident when a Lancia Aprilia had crashed into the crowd and ten spectators were killed. As a result the race was not held in 1939, but now it was to be revived and run over nine laps on a 104-mile (167km) closed circuit between Brescia, Cremona and Mantua. Despite the war, a full factory team of BMWs came from Germany and two Delages from France, albeit with Italian drivers. Most significant of all were two 1500cc sports cars that were just called '815s'; these were entered by Auto-Avio Construzioni of 11 Via Trento Trieste in Modena. Enzo Ferrari was back in business. The cars had eight-cylinder engines based on two Fiat 1100 blocks, and in the race they were driven by Lothario Rangoni and Alberto Ascari, son of the great Antonio; both retired, but a new legend had begun. Just to show that nothing had changed, a BMW was the winner, leading home a 6C-2500 driven by Farina, but afterwards no German flag was flown, nor was the German national anthem played.

Alfa Corse now prepared for Tripoli and received an unexpected approach through Rino Parenti, the Fascist Party secretary in

12 May 1940: Farina acknowledges the crowd after his victory in the GP di Tripoli. Beside him is the bearded Balbo, who a month later would be killed when his aircraft was shot down.

Milan; Nuvolari wanted to drive a 158. The events of 1938 had not been forgotten or, more important, forgiven at Portello, so the overture received a brief but pointed reply: 'Today, given our present situation, we are not able to provide Nuvolari with a car worthy of him and of his great fame.' Nuvolari's links with Alfa Romeo had been finally and irrevocably broken.

The Gran Premio di Tripoli was held on Sunday 12 May, and two days before the race German forces invaded Holland and Belgium preparatory to the invasion of France; Northern Europe was in the grip of total war and blitzkrieg reigned supreme. Practice showed that Villoresi's 4CL Maserati was likely to be the only threat to the 158s, and at about the time that the Alfa Corse mechanics were making the final checks to the 158s on the morning of the race, Flying Officer Garland and Sergeant Gray of the Royal Air Force were winning posthumous Victoria Crosses by diving their Fairey Battle on to a bridge across the Albert Canal in Belgium in a vain attempt to halt the German advance. In Tripoli the race seemed important, but it was now of complete insignificance compared to the awful events that were unfolding.

The 158s were driven by Farina, Trossi, Biondetti and Pintacuda. Villoresi led from the start and stayed there for a lap, then was passed by Farina. However, the 158 ran wide on a corner and Villoresi went to the front again and stayed there until lap 10. Farina went by again and on lap 16 Biondetti also caught the 4CL. On lap 17 all three stopped for fuel, and as they halted Villoresi was only 17 seconds behind Farina. The pitwork won the race for Alfa Corse. Farina was away in 24 seconds but the Maserati mechanics took 57 seconds to do the job and Villoresi had lost the race; while stationary he was also passed by Trossi. Farina won, followed home by Biondetti and Trossi, while a frustrated Villoresi was fourth; in ninth place was Alberto Ascari with a 6CM Maserati. Farina's average speed for the 244-mile (392km) race had been 128.22mph (206.17kmh) and his time had beaten that set by Lang in 1939 by almost 5 minutes. Two weeks later an emasculated Targa Florio was held on a short circuit in a park in Palermo and was won by Villoresi's 4CL

Maserati, and that was the end of the 1940 Italian season.

By the end of May the British Army was being evacuated in small boats from the beaches of Dunkirk, and the French Army, demoralised and offering little resistance, was being swept back across France by the German Panzer divisions. To Mussolini it seemed that the war was virtually over – France would be defeated and Britain would sue for peace on what terms it could get. If he was to sit at the conference table and share the victor's spoils it was time to act. On 28 May he met Marshal Balbo and the Chief of Staff of the Italian Army, Marshal Badoglio, and told them that he was going to war. With commendable foresight, Badoglio said that it would be suicidal for Italy, but his views were swept aside with the reply, 'I can tell you that everything will be over by September and that I only need a few thousand dead so that I can sit at the peace conference as a man who has fought.' On Monday 10 June Italy declared war on Britain and France.

Meanwhile at Portello 373 cars were made in 1939 and 103 in 1940 before everything stopped to make way for War production. While the rest of the factory set to making aero engines and military vehicles, in the racing department the Alfa Corse staff carried on much as before. Perhaps it was assumed that it was going to be a short war as Mussolini had promised and there would be racing again in 1941. There were reports that there would be a victory grand prix in Berlin as soon as hostilities stopped.

A 158 was fitted with the front and rear suspension from the 512, and on 18 June Attilio Marinoni tested it on the Milan–Varese autostrada. Coming in the opposite direction was a lorry whose driver had dozed off. The lorry ran into the path of the 158, the car caught fire in the collision and was burned out, and Marinoni was killed. A native of Lodi, outside Milan, he was 48 years old and had been a faithful servant of Alfa Romeo, first as a mechanic, then as a

18 June 1940: The burning wreck of the experimental 158 in which Marinoni was killed in a collision with a lorry on the Milan–Varese autostrada.

Autumn 1940: Sanesi tests the 512 at Monza.

riding mechanic to Franchini and Campari in 1919/20. Later, when he began to drive, he had a penchant for long-distance sports car racing and won the Belgian 24-hour race three times. In grands prix he was usually a reserve driver, and several times he brought home a limping car into a place. His death was used as further ammunition by Ricart's critics, who reported inaccurately that he had been killed in a 512, his death caused by the ill-handling.

The 512 did not have its first test until 12 September when Consalvo Sanesi, now head test driver after Marinoni's death, took it round Monza and, as previously mentioned, reported unfavourably on its handling. Sanesi, who was then 28, had started work as an apprentice mechanic with Gastone Brilli Perri; after Brilli Perri's death at Tripoli in 1930, he had joined Alfa Corse, first as a riding mechanic and later as a production test driver.

Ricart's other project, the 162, had already been finished and was given a preliminary run-out on 19 April; later, in June, it was given more intense tests, presumably in expectation of the victory grand prix. Development work was still

being done on the 158 and it was during this time that the first two-stage superchargers were fitted to the car. Guidotti says with grudging admiration that the installation designed by Ricart was taken off the 512, it fitted the 158 with virtually no

1940: A workshop mock-up of Ricart's Tipo 162.

modification, and worked perfectly.

During the ten days between Italy's entry into the War and the capitulation of France on 22 June, 99 Squadron of the RAF flying twin-engine Wellington bombers was sent to Salon on the edge of the Camargue, its task being to bomb Genoa and Turin; though several raids were attempted, the crews ran into severe storms over the Alps and the damage caused was minimal. For the next two years the inhabitants of Northern Italy slept quietly in their beds, their nights unbroken by the air raids that became the lot of those who lived north of the Alps. The industrial centres of Milan and Turin would have been tempting targets for the RAF, but they were 750 miles (1200km) from the bases of Bomber Command in Lincolnshire and East Anglia and the journey was outside the range of the Wellington, Whitley and Hampden bombers with which the RAF was equipped until the end of 1941. However, by the beginning of 1942 the Halifax was already in service and the Lancaster was just reaching the squadrons; with four engines, both these types had the range to reach Northern Italy.

The first major raid on Milan was on 24 October 1942. It was not a popular target for the crews, being further to fly than Berlin and involving a climb to over 20,000 feet (6000 metres) to cross the Alps, both factors reducing the bomb load. Portello was not damaged in this first raid, but Ricart realised that further raids were inevitable, so the special projects, design and experimental departments went to the Hotel Belvedere at Lago d'Orta, about 50 miles (80km) from Milan, and the experimental workshops were set up at Armeno, about 11 miles (18km) from Orta, where work continued on Ricart's major aero engine project, the 28-cylinder Tipo 1101. The six 158s were stored in the garages in the Monza paddock.

On 14 February 1943 there was another major raid on Milan, and this time Portello was hit. The RAF was still having problems hitting targets accurately in night raids. The Pathfinder technique and bombing with radar using the H2S system had not been fully developed, but despite this much damage was done. For Italy the War was proving as disastrous as Badoglio had

feared. Abyssinia and the East African colonies of Eritrea and Somalia were taken by the British in 1941. The army in Albania had attempted to invade Greece but had suffered a costly repulse, and was only saved from humiliation by German intervention. The Italian army had been defeated in Libya and hundreds of thousands of troops were now in British prison camps. Libya and Tripolitania had only been held by the efforts of the German Afrika Korps and this was now being swept away by the British 8th Army after the victory at El Alamein. By the middle of May 1943 the German forces had been expelled from North Africa and all the erstwhile Italian Empire was in British hands. On 10 July British and American forces invaded Sicily.

Since the beginning of 1943 the Italian generals led by Badoglio had been discussing with King Victor Emmanuel how Mussolini could be deposed and Italy could withdraw from the War, and even Mussolini's own Fascist supporters joined in the clandestine discussions. On 24 July the Fascist Grand Council met in Rome and a substantial number of its members sided against Mussolini. The following day King Victor Emmanuel summoned Mussolini to the royal residence at Villa Savoia and, after a short audience, he was dismissed. As he walked out to his car, he was arrested. Marshal Badoglio was appointed as Head of the Government.

Negotiations now began with the Allies to enable Italy to withdraw from the War. During August, while the discussions continued, Milan received several heavy night raids. It has been suggested that this was done to speed up the negotiations, but the Italians had difficulties as German forces were now in Italy in great strength trying to fend off the Sicilian invasion and prepare for the expected assault on the Italian mainland. The Germans were already treating the Italians with hostility and had seized the frontier crossing posts. Monza had been taken over by the German army and was being used as a military vehicle

park; it was realised that the 158s could be in danger either from bombs or from German requisition if they remained there, so in the greatest secrecy the manager of the Milan AC moved the six cars from under the noses of the German guards to a cheese factory in the village of Melzo near Lago d'Orta. This was owned by a keen Alfa Romeo enthusiast and some of the design department staff were working there.

Allied forces landed on the toe of Italy at Reggio di Calabria on 3 September 1943, and on the same day Italy capitulated to the Allies. For the Germans, Northern Italy was now occupied territory and the production capacity of Alfa Romeo was requisitioned. Ricart had many problems in keeping his staff together as they were under constant threat of deportation to Germany. Ugo Gobbato now came into his own; he spoke German fluently, and while he was expected to do everything he could to help the German war effort, he regarded his main task as keeping the Alfa Romeo empire intact so that it would be ready to work again when the War ended.

There was one incident when a group of SS troops discovered a store of metal in the factory at Portello. Gobbato was told that this and any other similar stores would be requisitioned. Immediately Gobbato ordered a test driver, Bonini, to drive a 6C-2500 with an extra fuel tank to Berlin and seek the authority of Albert Speer, the Nazi Minister of Munitions, to keep the stores at Portello. Gobbato knew Speer, and the request was granted, though Bonini had an adventurous drive.

The Germans were not the only problem. Communist partisan forces were now active in Northern Italy, and while the German forces were their principal target, the northern industries were also attacked, ostensibly to deprive the Germans of their use but also to repay old scores, especially against Alfa Romeo, which was regarded as a Fascist-owned company. On 18 June 1944 the partisans razed the Armeno workshops to the ground; some projects were saved from the blaze including a new prototype saloon, the Gazella. With the workshops destroyed, most of the design personnel drifted back to Portello and set up a makeshift office in a monastery a few hundred metres from the factory.

Worse was to come. Just after 11.30am on Friday 20 October a force of USAAF Liberators of the 12th Air Force bombed Portello. More than 30 500lb (250kg) bombs fell within the factory boundaries and almost every building was destroyed or severely damaged. When factories in Germany had been damaged on this scale, astonishing feats of improvisation were achieved and output was restored in a remarkably short time, but at Portello this spirit was absent; there was no enthusiasm for working for a lost Nazi cause and everyone was content to sit out the winter of 1944/45 and wait for the inevitable end of the War. Wifredo Ricart left Alfa Romeo on 29 March 1945; his contract had expired and shrewdly he realised that he was unpopular with too many people. He therefore did not tarry, but returned to Spain almost the next day. It was a journey fraught with problems but he managed it travelling via Switzerland. Although none of his projects came to fruition, his influence left a lasting mark on Alfa Romeo in the years to come.

In September 1943 Mussolini had escaped and with German aid had established a Fascist puppet government in the German-occupied Northern Italy with his headquarters in Milan. However, in April 1945 the German forces in Italy began to crumble and Allied forces advanced northwards rapidly. Modena was liberated on 22 April and throughout the North partisan forces were gaining control, harrying the retreating Germans and waiting for the Allied armies to arrive. On 25 April the Committee of National Liberation, to which the partisans owed a loose allegiance, declared a national uprising and

20 October 1944: The foundry at Portello after the air raid.

the partisan groups took over control of Milan. During the next few weeks old scores were settled and bitter rivalries resolved. People's Courts were set up to try Fascists and on 27 April Ugo Gobbato was put on trial. He received two separate trials on the same day and at both was absolved from charges of collaborating with the Germans.

On the morning of Saturday 28 April he walked from his home to Portello to collect some books. On his return, near the Fiera Campionaria, a Lancia Augusta pulled up beside him. Two men climbed out, one carrying a sub-machine gun and the other a shotgun, and opened fire. Gobbato fell dead on the pavement – his killers were never found. It was an unworthy end for

such a capable man. He had saved Alfa Romeo when he took control in 1933 and had placed it on a firm financial footing; he had also turned it into a modern and competitive concern. His big and fatal mistake was to be too closely allied to the Fascist Party.

Gobbato was not the only man to die that day. Mussolini had been captured by the partisans on his way from Milan to Como, where he intended to hide in the mountains until he could surrender to the Allied forces. He was held captive for two days and was then shot with his mistress, Claretta Petacci, at Dongo, outside Como. Their bodies were taken to Milan and strung up outside a filling station on the Piazzale Loreto, near the central station.

Chapter 15

Happy days are here again

THE CONDITIONS IN EUROPE in the months following the end of the Second World War are now hard to comprehend. Huge bands of refugees were moving around trying to return to their many and varied homelands, their problems compounded by a universal shortage of food. Countless cities had been laid waste and in almost every country where the War had been fought the infrastructure of transport and power had been swept away. The whole of Europe was still a vast army camp. The European War ended on 8 May 1945, and four months later there was a little sign of a return to normality. With the surrender of Japan on 15 August the Second World War ended, and 24 days later the first post-war motor race was held.

This was not the Nazi victory grand prix that had been confidently expected would take place in Berlin, but was instead a modest meeting in Paris over a simple road circuit in the Bois de Boulogne. It was little more than a club meeting, and a wide variety of ancient and modern racing cars were produced. After a voiturette race the main event was the 43-lap, 75-mile (120km) Coupe des Prisonniers, which commemorated, among others, the drivers 'Williams' and Robert Benoist who had been killed while working for the Resistance. Some of the 'names' were back, astonishingly driving works-entered cars: Wimille had a works Bugatti and Sommer a works Talbot, while Etancelin had dusted down his faithful old Monza. Wimille won, followed

home by Sommer, and Etancelin dropped out after a mild crash, but to him must go the honour of being the first to race an Alfa Romeo after the Second World War.

Alfa Romeo now had a new president, Pasquale Gallo, who, now the Fascists had gone, made a triumphant comeback and soon made the decision that the Portello factory would be rebuilt. The rubble was cleared, damaged buildings were repaired and new ones built, and the machine tools that had been dispersed to Lago d'Orta were brought back. Portello would now build cars and lorries; the pre-war emphasis on military aero engines had gone for ever, and while the world was not quite ready yet for luxury cars, the need for lorries was insatiable.

Although the Fascist era had closed with the end of the War, Alfa Romeo was still beset with political pressures. Mussolini had suppressed the Communist Party, and for over 20 years the Communists had gone underground. When Italy joined the Allies in October 1943 the Communist-led partisan bands in the North had received massive support, and when the War ended Italian trade unions immediately became Communist-dominated. Gallo found that he had to tread carefully as the unions had great power and the memory of Gobbato's fate was ever-present; indeed, Gobbato had not been the only victim – Bruno Trevisan had died in a mysterious 'accident' in November 1945.

If Gallo had been minded to appoint

Gioachino Colombo to succeed Ricart, he had to abandon the idea immediately. The trade unions had formed a 'purity' committee with the aim of seeking out Fascists at Portello. Colombo was investigated, his connections with the Fascist party were revealed, and at the unions' insistence he was suspended and sent home to kick his heels. Within a few weeks he was asked by Enzo Ferrari to go to Modena to discuss a new project that would eventually change the face of motor racing throughout the world. During his enforced absence Colombo began the outline designs of the first V-12 Ferrari, but news of this reached Portello and in November 1945 the trade unions thought again, and Colombo was re-engaged as head of the 'Sports Vehicle' section, though he seems to have been moved away from the mainstream of design and also had little to do with the revived racing activities.

Fortunately some good young engineers had been recruited in the years just before the War, and outstanding among these was Orazio Satta. Satta was born in 1910, the son of a medical practitioner in Piedmont. He read engineering at the Turin Politecnico and, after working at the Politecnico for a short time, joined Alfa Romeo in 1938 and during the War years worked as Ricart's

22 April 1946: Sommer (308) leads Chaboud (Delahaye) on to the Promenade des Anglais during the GP de Nice. Sommer finished second. (John Maitland Collection)

30 May 1946: Wimille (308) takes the lead at the start of the Coupe de la Resistance in Paris from the 4CL Maseratis of Sommer and Mazaud. (Guy Griffiths Collection)

assistant. Early in 1946 he was appointed director of the project and experimental department, which in effect made him technical director of the company. Satta had far-reaching ideas of where Alfa Romeo should go with production cars, but racing also came under his aegis and he had ideas about that too; with the full support of Gallo, it was decided that the 158s would race in all suitable races in 1946.

As soon as the Germans had gone, the 158s were extracted from the dusty confines of the deserted cheese factory at Melzo, where they had been dismantled and walled up as an added safeguard against German looting. The retrieval was entrusted to Consalvo Sanesi, who ferried the parts back in several lorry loads, accompanied by Pavesi, the head of experimental testing. The cars were reassembled at Portello and given a preliminary airing along the autostrada during the autumn of 1945.

The manner in which motor racing recovered after the War has never been fully appreciated. Despite the almost insuperable problems caused by the lack of tyres and fuel, there was a full season of racing in 1946 in Western Europe, with almost every car capable of running being pressed into service. Maserati had even managed to assemble some new 4CLs during the War and these were now eagerly sought by those who could afford them. During the early part of the season most races were run to the pre-war formula of 3/4½ litres, though some races were for the supercharged 1500s. Halfway through the season the FIA announced that there would be a new grand prix formula in 1947, which would be for 1½-litre supercharged and 4½-litre unsupercharged cars, and by the end of the 1946 season most races were being run to this new formula, known as Formula A; there was a Formula B for unsupercharged 2-litre cars.

The 1946 season began at Nice on 22 April with a 35-lap, 130-mile (209km) race in which Raymond Sommer ran a 308. His 1939 car had gone to the USA in 1940 to compete at Indianapolis, but he had persuaded Portello to lend him another 308 that was sitting idle in the factory. He led

until he lost first and second gears, so Villoresi's 4CL Maserati won and the 308 was second; Sanesi came from Portello to lend a hand with the 308. At the end of May there was another race in the Bois de Boulogne in Paris. Sommer had lent the 308 to Jean-Pierre Wimille; this time the gearbox behaved itself and Wimille won.

Ten days after the Bois de Boulogne race, on 9 June, there was another event in the Paris suburbs at St Cloud. For an urban circuit the lap was long, 3.72 miles (6km), and the course ran through a tunnel for some 800 metres. For some reason that has never been explained, Alfa Corse chose this small meeting for the return of the 158s, entering two 1940-specification cars for Wimille and Farina. Alfa Corse was free again to chose the best drivers available irrespective of nationality, and it was generally accepted that Jean-Pierre Wimille was now the leading driver in Europe. The two 158s were opposed by a now regular circus of drivers with Maseratis, Talbots and Delahayes, among whom was an ailing Nuvolari with a 4CL Maserati.

Sommer had a 4CL Maserati and set the fastest practice time, nearly 2 seconds quicker than Wimille. After a lap Wimille was in front, followed by Sommer and Farina, while Nuvolari soon fell out. At ten laps Farina passed Sommer, so the 158s were in the first two places, but then Farina stopped and the car was retired with clutch failure. Wimille was still in front, but on lap 19 his clutch also failed, so Sommer went on to an easy win and the 158s were taken back to Portello by worried mechanics.

While the 158s were stripped and examined rigorously at Portello, Wimille continued to have fun with Sommer's semi-works 308 and won at Perpignan and Dijon on consecutive weekends. The big event of the season was the Grand Prix des Nations, which the Swiss had organised at Geneva for supercharged 1500s. Switzerland had remained neutral during the War and emerged prosperous and unharmed, so the race was promoted with an air of pre-war luxury that ensured that every driver wanted an entry. The press called it inaccurately the Swiss Grand Prix, but it had all the importance of a grande épreuve.

The race, held on Sunday 21 July, used a short 1.83-mile (2.94km) circuit in the streets of the city, running past the Palace of the League of Nations. Alfa Corse entered four 158s, two in the 1940 form driven by Wimille and Trossi, and the other two fitted with the two-stage supercharger installation from the 512 that increased their power to 254bhp at 7500rpm. The two-stage cars were driven by Farina and Achille Varzi, who had now completely shaken off his addictions and, according to Guidotti, had worked as a lorry driver for Alfa Romeo during the War, which had prevented him from being conscripted into the Italian Army.

The cars were being run by a small but dedicated team. Though to a casual onlooker it appeared to be a large, well-backed organisation, in reality money was short and the team was being run with minimal resources, able to do little more than keep the cars running but comforted that these were still quicker than the opposition. Giovanbattista Guidotti was the team manager, responsible for the management of the team at events, and the small group of mechanics was led by Alessandro Gaboardi.

Everyone came from Portello to see the cars in action at Geneva. Satta was accompanied by his deputies, including Giampaolo Garcea, now head of the experimental service, and the deputy head Livio Nicolis, who would shortly be given technical responsibility for the racing activities. Also at Geneva was Gioachino Colombo, no doubt keen to see his designs in action but certainly keeping Enzo Ferrari informed about developments in the racing world. In June 1946 Ferrari had announced that he would be going into production with his own Colombo-designed cars in 1947, and a 1500cc V-12 grand prix car would be built.

The four 158s dominated practice.

9 June 1946: The first post-war appearance of the 158 was in the Coupe Rene La Begue at St Cloud, Paris. Wimille leads Sommer (Maserati 4CL) and Farina, but both 158s retired and Sommer won. The tunnel now forms part of the A-13 Paris–Rouen autoroute. (Ludvigsen Library)

Wimille, despite having one of the single-stage cars, was the fastest with 1min 37.5sec, and apart from Villoresi's 4CL Maserati the 158s were the only cars to break the 1min 40sec barrier. The race was run in two 32-lap heats and a 40-lap final,

21 July 1946: Varzi and Farina talk to an official before the GP des Nations at Geneva. Colombo stands behind Varzi.

21 July 1946: Farina leads Harry Schell (6CM Maserati) in the second heat of the GP des Nations. (Ludvigsen Library)

the fastest six cars in each heat qualifying for the final. Wimille and Varzi ran in the first heat; it was raining slightly and Wimille, who jumped the start, went into the lead. Villoresi offered a slight challenge but the two 158s pulled away to an easy win and Villoresi's Maserati was the only car on the same lap at the end. In the second heat, now with a drying road, Nuvolari's 4CL Maserati beat Farina and Trossi away, but after three laps Farina was in front followed by Trossi, and Nuvolari came home third.

By the time the starter waved his flag for the final, the field was on its way to the first corner. Wimille led Farina and Varzi while Sommer (4CL) and Nuvolari were in front of Trossi. Farina passed Wimille on lap three and the pair began to battle for the lead, pulling away from the rest. Varzi made several stops and Trossi was now up to third place. On lap 32 the leading pair

came up to lap Nuvolari, who did not like this and pushed Wimille off on the next corner! Wimille was able to push-start his car and carried on, now well behind Farina and Trossi, while Nuvolari was given a black flag, which he ignored, so eventually the officials put it away in despair. Farina and Trossi finished first and second with Wimille third, a lap down, while the unrepentant Nuvolari was fourth. For Alfa Corse it was a splendid result and showed that there was nothing to fear from the opposition. The motor racing world was ecstatic – real motor racing was back again. The British journalist John Eason-Gibson said, '... this was Grand Prix racing again and it was terrific', while Rodney Walkerley, writing in *The Motor*, said that it was '... one of the most exciting motor races I have ever seen.'

It was significant that even with a single-stage car Wimille had been the equal of

Farina with the two-stage car and had set fastest lap at Geneva. Back at Portello three more cars were now fitted with the two-stage installation ready for the next Alfa Corse engagement at Turin on 1 September for the Gran Premio del Valentino. This was run in the park beside the River Po and was the first race to be run to the new Formula A grand prix rules; while it lacked the title, it was in reality the Gran Premio d'Italia, with an entry that showed the importance of the race. Five two-stage 158s were entered with the same drivers as at Geneva, but now joined by Sanesi. The trade unions at Portello insisted that a 'working mechanic' should have the chance to race and chose Sanesi, which in the circumstances was a happy choice as he was familiar with the 158, having tested all the cars.

The 158s dominated practice, filling the first five places on the grid, and the Alfa Romeo management turned up in force expecting to see an impressive demonstration in the 60-lap race, though it did not turn out quite as hoped. As the flag fell

Farina broke a halfshaft and went no further. Varzi took the lead followed by Wimille, but Trossi was soon in trouble with only top gear and drifted back down the field. Sanesi only lasted eight laps before his magneto ceased to spark, so while Varzi and Wimille swapped places and pulled away from the rest of the field, the 158s looked too fragile for comfort. Fortunately, the opposition was not up to the challenge and the pair ran on to win; in accordance with team orders, Varzi took the flag with Wimille half a second behind, while Trossi limped home nine laps behind in sixth place. It was a result that gave a lot of pleasure; at last Varzi had put the dark years behind him and was up at the top again.

Three weeks later, on 21 September, the team had its last outing of the season at the Circuito di Milano, which was run in the Sempione Park. The 1.7-mile (2.7km) circuit was made up of a combination of roads within the Park; it differed from the pre-war course, but was equally winding. The race was run in two 20-lap heats, the first five cars in each qualifying for the 30-lap final. For this home event Wimille was discarded, but in the first heat Varzi and Trossi took the first two places, both having jumped the start. In the second heat Farina jumped the start so blatantly that the race was red-flagged after a lap and the cars were lined up again; during this abortive lap Sanesi spun and bent the tail of his car, needing a push-start. Some of the drivers protested that he should be disqualified, but as the race was being restarted the protests were overruled. With extraordinary perverseness, Farina jumped the start again and this time received a 1-minute penalty. Although he was first on the road, the penalty put him down to third behind Sanesi and Sommer's 4CL Maserati.

Farina tried to jump the start of the final, but after a lap Trossi led Varzi and Farina with Sanesi in fourth place. Trossi was driving at the top of his form; a habitual pipe-smoker, it was clenched between his

21 July 1946: Farina, the winner in Geneva, is followed very closely by Wimille in the final. (Ludvigsen Library)

teeth, and despite a challenge from Varzi that might have been stage-managed to amuse the crowd, he went on to win, followed by Varzi and Sanesi. Farina, apparently irked that it was Trossi's turn to win, spun off, then abandoned his car in a petulant huff.

For Alfa Corse it had been an excellent season after the initial setback at St Cloud. The cars had shattered the opposition, and with Wimille and a restored Varzi they had the best of the drivers as well. The team at Portello were, however, not complacent; during the winter some detail improvements were made to five of the 158s, pushing the output up to 275bhp. While this

1 September 1946: Wimille leads Varzi in the GP del Valentino at Turin before obeying team orders and letting Varzi through to win. (Ludvigsen Library)

21 September 1946: In the first heat of the Circuito di Milano, Nuvolari (4CL Maserati) on the outside, has jumped the start and draws level with Trossi and Varzi (158s). (Ludvigsen Library)

30 September 1946: Varzi leads Trossi in the first heat of the Circuito di Milano, while Nuvolari and Villoresi (Maseratis) follow. The circuit was tight, running through the city streets near the Portello factory. (Guy Griffiths Collection)

was being done, more development was being done to one of the cars. The low-pressure, first-stage supercharger was enlarged, a fuel tank to give extra capacity was fitted on the right of the cockpit, the supercharger air intake ducting was changed so it now drew from the vent in the front of the cockpit previously used to cool the driver, and the exhaust reverted to a single pipe. All this increased the power to 310bhp, though still at 7500rpm, and the revamped car was called the 158/47. The added tankage was an acknowledgement of a problem that was to become increasingly pressing over the next few seasons: as the power went up, so did the thirst of the engines.

The enthusiasm for motor racing in Argentina and Brazil had continued to flourish while the War raged in the northern hemisphere. In the winter of 1946/47 an ambitious series of races was promoted that attracted some of the leading Italian drivers; partly to cater for the locals, these races were formula libre. Varzi, keen to maintain his rediscovered form, took one or possibly two 308s with him. These were cars that had been kept at Portello during the War and were now obsolete in Europe, and the South American races presented a splendid opportunity to clear them out and also make a useful profit by sales to the local drivers; one may have been the Wimille/Sommer car.

On 9 February the Gran Premio de la Republica Argentina was held in a park in Buenos Aires and the race was honoured by the presence of the Argentine President, General Peron, accompanied by his wife, Eva. It was a 50-lap race over a 1.5-mile (2.4km) circuit and became an Alfa Romeo/Maserati battle. Varzi had his 308, and a second car was driven by Francisco Landi. Villoresi (4CL Maserati) led all the way, while Varzi at first tussled with the Galvez brothers, one with a P3 and the other with a 308 bored out to 3.8 litres. Having got the better of the pair, he pursued Villoresi and nearly caught him, but was balked by a lapped Chevrolet special on the last lap and lost by a second. The race was repeated a week later and Villoresi won again; this time Varzi had a battle with Pessatti's 8C-35, but dropped a valve and retired. The third race of the series was the Rosario City Grand Prix, which confusingly was run in Buenos Aires; this time Varzi won, beating Villoresi by a mere 0.4 second, while Oscar Galvez was third with his bored-out 308.

It was not until June that the 158s were brought out, when on the 8th four cars were taken to Berne for the revived Grösser Preis der Schweiz on the Bremgarten circuit. The race was run in two 20-lap heats, with a 30-lap final. The cars were driven by Wimille, Varzi, Trossi and Sanesi – Farina was no longer in the team, so presumably his behaviour at Milan had been unacceptable. On the first day of practice, Guidotti took the four cars round the circuit and the drivers spent most of the time sitting in the pits, but on the second day the supremacy of the 158s was evident

and the only car to get near their times was Villoresi's 4CL Maserati, now with two-stage supercharging.

On race day, the normally law-abiding Swiss ran amok and crowd control broke down, with spectators lining the edge of the track all round the circuit. It began to rain as the first heat started, but Varzi and Trossi ran away with it, finishing a second apart at the flag. On the slowing-down lap a small boy ran across the road and was struck by Varzi's car; he was reported to have died of his injuries later. There was delay before the second heat while the police tried to push the crowd back, then Wimille led all the way, and it took Sanesi some laps to pass Villoresi and follow Wimille to the flag. During this heat British driver Leslie Johnson driving a 4-litre Talbot-Darracq struck and killed two spectators who were standing on the track. There were more delays before the final, and the drivers were told to ease off to avoid any more accidents. There was a suggestion that the race should be cancelled, but the organisers decided to carry on as it was feared the crowd would react badly to a cancellation.

Wimille led all the way followed by Varzi;

Sommer, in a second two-stage 4CL, was in front of Sanesi and Trossi. The Maserati was thirsty and had to refuel, while the 158s ran non-stop, so when Sommer stopped Trossi moved up to third, but Sanesi could not catch the 4CL and came fifth. As soon as they crossed the line the drivers pulled up as the crowd invaded the course.

Three weeks later the Alfa Corse entourage went to Spa for the revived Grand Prix de Belgique, a traditional-length grand prix again over 35 laps (305 miles/490km). Once more it was Wimille, Varzi, Trossi and Sanesi, and only Sommer's Maserati was likely to offer any opposition. However, things did not go quite as smoothly as the team intended. It was decided by Gallo and Guidotti before the race that it was Varzi's turn to win and he led from the start, but Sommer, driving his blue-painted 4CL faster than the Maserati brothers ever intended it to go, was in second place ahead of Wimille, Trossi and Sanesi. After four laps Wimille got past the Maserati, as did Sanesi, but Trossi came into the pits with a bad cut on what he described as 'my beautiful nose', and while he was patched up Guidotti took over the

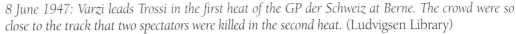

8 June 1947: Varzi leads Trossi in the first heat of the GP der Schweiz at Berne. The crowd were so close to the track that two spectators were killed in the second heat. (Ludvigsen Library)

29 June 1947: In the pits at Spa-Francorchamps Trossi, who has had the cut on his 'beautiful nose' patched, prepares to take over the 158 from Guidotti (in beret) while the mechanics change a plug.

29 June 1947: In the GP de Belgique at Spa-Francorchamps, Varzi lines up for the La Source hairpin, followed by Wimille. The modern circuit has changed out of all recognition, as the pits and startline are now situated at this point. (Ludvigsen Library)

car. Sommer meanwhile had taken back third place from Sanesi and stayed there until lap 13, when he retired with a broken chassis frame, cheered loudly by an appreciative crowd.

Trossi took back his car from Guidotti and was now fourth, so the team were running 1–2–3–4, but Wimille had other ideas about letting Varzi win. He went into the lead and started to pull away, and the team plans fell apart when Varzi made a stop lasting 11 minutes to replace a broken pipe to the nearside rear brake; while this was done he seemed to be smoking several cigarettes at once. He got away before Trossi was able to make up the lost ground, so

7 September 1947: The mechanics tend the 158s of Sanesi (No 24) and Trossi (No 30) on the starting grid before the GP d'Italia at Milan. (Guy Griffiths Collection)

Wimille won amid much disapproval within the team. Varzi was second a lap behind and Trossi was third, but Sanesi stopped on the penultimate lap with rear brake trouble and damaged suspension arms and was not placed. A week before Spa, Biondetti had won a revived Mille Miglia in the old format with a 2900B saloon running without superchargers.

On Sunday 13 July Alfa Corse made a strange commitment to run in the Gran Premio di Bari, a very minor Formula A race at the seaport at the southern end of the Adriatic almost on the heel of Italy. Three cars were entered for Varzi, Trossi and Sanesi, but Trossi did not turn up and Varzi and Sanesi reeled off the 50 laps of the 3.3-mile (5.3km) circuit against negligible opposition to win by a margin of seven laps from the ancient Monza of Renato Balestrero, which was running unsupercharged. Halfway through the race Sanesi nearly upset the demonstration when he spun and stalled his engine, but luckily for him the car finished its spin on a slight downward slope and he was able to restart the engine by pushing the car. While this was going on, Varzi eased up, which enabled Sanesi to catch up again. On the same day the only race meeting to be held on the British mainland in 1947 took place on a disused airfield at Gransden Lodge; the main race of the day over 45 miles (70km) was won by Dennis Poore, driving the ex-Ruesch 8C-35, which at that time was the most powerful racing car in Britain.

As already mentioned, Monza had been used as a military vehicle park by the German Army and the Allied forces had found it ideal for the same purpose. Requisitioned property and armed forces live together uneasily, and even two years after the end of the War Monza was still too badly damaged to be used for the Gran Premio d'Italia. The race therefore moved a few miles to a road circuit in the centre of Milan that ran round the circumference of the Milan Trade Fair park; this was only about a kilometre from the Sempione Park

where the previous Milanese races had been run, and about two blocks from Portello. Despite the move, it was still a tight circuit of 2.14 miles (3.44km), with a premium on acceleration and braking; the race distance was 100 laps.

Perhaps it was a slap on the wrist for the disobedience at Spa, but there was no car for Wimille. Instead, the trade unions had spoken again and Alessandro Gaboardi had joined the team; he had no racing experience but had tested the 158, so at least the car was familiar to him. The other cars were driven by Varzi, Sanesi and Trossi. Sanesi showed that he was learning fast as he made the fastest practice lap. The 158/47 was given a canter round the circuit during practice but was then put away and not used for the race.

At the start Trossi took the lead, but Villoresi's 4CL Maserati was in front of the other 158s for several laps, then normal service was resumed. Varzi caught up with Trossi and the pair swapped places until Trossi began to pull away. At the end he slowed to let Varzi catch up and the pair crossed the line together, with Trossi a length in front, his goggles up and his hands off the wheel; the crowd did not like this and jeered, perhaps feeling that it was an aspersion on Varzi. Sanesi had fallen back but came third, a lap behind, while Gaboardi did all that was expected of him, coming fourth although five laps behind, his position flattered by the fragility of the opposition, which fell to pieces trying to keep up with the Alfa Romeo pace.

That was the end of the season for the 158s. Two weeks later the Grand Prix de l'ACF was run in the outskirts of Lyon, on a makeshift circuit that was a very far cry from the heroic venue of 1924. Two 158s were entered by Wimille, but the cars did not appear, so presumably he was still out of favour at Portello.

Once again Alfa Corse had swept the board, and even the occasional prima donna touch among the drivers had not upset the form. In some respects the

Maserati opposition was not as potent as it had been in 1946, but the French Lago-Talbots were improving and had the great advantage of being able to go through a race non-stop, an improvement highlighted by Chiron's victory at Lyons with one of the cars.

During the winter some of the European drivers made another expedition to South America for the local series of races. The stimulus for these events came from General Peron who was looking for favourable publicity for his regime; while the drivers were in South America, each received an allowance of 300 pesos a day, which was a worthwhile lure as the Argentine currency was strong at that time. The Argentine national oil company financed the races and the cars were required to carry a small company logo. This time Varzi took a car that was probably a 312 with a 4½-litre V-12 engine, and enabled Alfa Corse to dispose of a car that was unsaleable in Europe. This policy of selling obsolete cars in South America was to provide a treasure trove for dealers in vintage and historic racing cars several decades later. Wimille went too, taking the 308 that he had shared with Sommer and 'Raph' in 1946; as a second string he took a 1220cc Simca-Gordini, a car well suited to the short sinuous circuits on which many of the South American races were run.

The first race was the Gran Premio de Buenos Aires on 17 January, run on a 3-mile (4.8km) circuit in a city park and comprising two 15-lap heats and a 25-lap final. In the first heat Wimille broke his gearbox on the first lap, and almost inevitably Villoresi (4CL Maserati) won by some 30 seconds from Varzi. Farina won heat two with a 3-litre 8CL Maserati after a battle with the Tipo 308s of Oscar Galvez and Chico Landi. In the final Landi led for a time until Villoresi went by and carried on to win, and Varzi retired. A week later the circus moved on to Mar del Plata where, in a 40-lap race on a 2.36-mile (3.8km)

17 January 1948: Varzi driving the 312 with a 4½-litre engine in which he took second place in the GP de Buenos Aires. (Ludvigsen Library)

circuit, Farina came out on top leading Varzi home.

The races came thick and fast. Seven days later it was the Gran Premio de Rosario, and this time Wimille showed that his Gordini was suited to the tight circuit and won after Galvez's 308 had retired when in front. Wimille then had a fierce battle with a local driver, Juan Manuel Fangio, who also had a Gordini, though he had driven a 4CL Maserati in the previous races. Fangio blew up his engine but made a big impression on the visiting drivers. Landi's 308 came second behind Wimille, while Varzi did not feature at all. He turned out with a 308 but broke the propshaft at the start. On 25 February there was another park race in Buenos Aires, and this time Villoresi won after a battle with Galvez and Varzi, who had the 312 again; Galvez came second and Varzi retired. The final race of the series was at Sao Paolo in Brazil, and this time Wimille used his 308 and won, while Landi's 308 was second.

While the 158s had been in a different class from the opposition in 1947, the racing had shown a small weakness in the engines – cracks had developed in the crankcase around the main bearings. There was probably no money available to redesign and make new crankcases, so a simple but very effective repair was made; steel tie rods were fitted between the main bearing caps and the cylinder blocks, which cured the problem.

As the existing cars were going so well, they were not modified to the 158/47 specification, so the team went into the 1948 season with still only one car in that form. The team ignored the early races, and surprisingly did not go to the revived Grand Prix de Monaco. Their first outing was the Grösser Preis von Europa, a grandiose title awarded to the Swiss race on the Bremgarten circuit, held on 4 July. The 1947 team had been signed up again and four cars were entered for Wimille, Varzi,

Trossi and Sanesi. In addition to the normal 158s, the 158/47 was taken to the meeting and was used on the first day of practice, Wednesday 30 June.

It was a wet and misty afternoon. Sanesi took the car round for several laps, then handed it over to Varzi. Varzi did several laps, then lost control of the car at Jordenrampe, the section of the circuit after the start that ran beside a quarry; he had almost recovered control when, at low speed, the 158/47 struck a low kerb and rolled over slowly into a ditch. As the car rolled Varzi's head was crushed. Louis Chiron was following in his Lago-Talbot. He stopped, ran to Varzi and helped to lift the car off him, cradling his old friend and rival in his arms, but within a few minutes Varzi was dead.

The Alfa Corse team was shattered. Varzi had been driving Alfa Romeos for 20 years as a team member and a private entrant,

July 1948: The 158/47 is almost undamaged after Varzi's fatal accident in practice for the GP von Europa at Berne.

and had also been one of its greatest rivals. His recovery from his addiction and the post-war return to his best form as a driver had been welcomed with delight. With his struggle back to health, the quiet, elegant Varzi had seemed indestructible, but now he was gone. Satta and Nicolis wanted to withdraw the team from the race. However, Norma Colombo, Varzi's former love whom he had married in 1940, having broken with Ilse Pietsch, and who attended all his races, now intervened and told Satta that

July 1948: Varzi's funeral cortège – his coffin is carried through Milan on a 2500 Alfa Romeo chassis and escorted by the Alfa Corse mechanics. (Guy Griffiths Collection)

the team must race; it would be the best memorial to Varzi and was what he would have wanted. (This was a most distressing time for the Italian motor sporting community, as the day after Varzi's death Omobono Tenni, the leading Italian motor cycle racer, was killed when he crashed his 500cc Guzzi during practice for the Swiss motor cycle grand prix.)

Maserati had produced a new car, the 4CLT/48, which used an uprated 4CL engine but had a new chassis. Two of these cars were entered for Villoresi and Alberto Ascari, the son of the great Antonio, who was developing rapidly as a driver under Villoresi's tutelage. Villoresi went well in practice and was on the front row next to Wimille and Farina, who had also gone well in his older 4CLT. Wimille took the lead followed by the two Maseratis, but Trossi worked his way past them during the first few laps. Wimille then had to make a short stop for water, but did not lose his place to Villoresi; this left Trossi in front, and Wimille now worked to catch up, which he did so that the cars crossed the line 0.2 second apart, Trossi in front. Villoresi was third on the same lap and Sanesi, who had driven a steady race, was fourth one lap short of the distance. To conclude a sad meeting, the Swiss driver Christian Kautz was killed when he crashed his Maserati during the race.

A few days after the race Varzi's body was carried through Milan in a funeral cortège reminiscent of that for Antonio Ascari over 20 years before. Afterwards he was buried at Galliate, his home town, about 30 miles (40km) north of Milan.

Alfa Corse entered three cars for the Grand Prix de l'ACF at Reims on 18 July 1948. Trossi was unwell – his health was beginning to cause concern – so he was replaced in the team by Alberto Ascari. Ascari had already been entered in the race by Scuderia Ambrosiana, which was virtually the Maserati works team, so his 4CLT/48 Maserati was not used; it is surprising that Maserati agreed to release him. The other 158s were driven by Wimille and Sanesi. The 158/47 was almost undamaged in Varzi's accident so it was brought along to Reims and used by Wimille in practice; the team also had a spare 158, presumably the usual fourth car that was now sadly not needed. Writing in *Motor Sport*, T. G. Moore noted that the Alfa Corse team

'... had eight or nine open or closed five-ton trucks, two spare racing cars, one available behind the pits in case any spares were needed during the course of the race, and a mobile workshop. This latter was equipped with a lathe, a drilling machine, welding plant, benches and vices, drawers and lockers for small parts, and an independent petrol engine and dynamo which supplied the power for driving the machine tools.'

The 158s dominated practice and occupied the front row. Surprisingly the second row did not feature Maseratis, but the 4½-litre Lago-Talbots of Etancelin and Chiron.

Excellence was expected, as Pasquale Gallo had driven from Milan to Reims in a new 6C-2500 'Freccia d'Oro' coupé to watch the race. At the start the three red cars romped into the lead. Villoresi (4CLT/48), who had started near the back of the grid, came through and passed Sanesi, but Wimille and Ascari were sailing away into the distance, uncatchable on such a fast circuit. Villoresi paid the penalty for motoring too fast and stopped for new plugs, eventually handing over the ailing Maserati to an equally unwell Nuvolari. After 26 laps Wimille stopped for fuel and to change both nearside tyres, so Ascari took the lead, but the order was restored when he made his stop. On lap 37 Wimille made an unexpected stop and the mechanics spent some time looking at the front of the engine. This gave Ascari the lead again, and he was given a 'slow' signal to let Wimille catch up, which he did on lap 41, but next time

round he came into the pit again for another inspection – apparently a stone had punctured the radiator.

Once more Ascari led, but was slowed for Wimille to pass him. Wimille now made another stop while the water was topped up, but Ascari, obeying team orders, slowed visibly to let Sanesi catch him. Wimille continued to lead and stayed in front to the finish. On lap 55 Sanesi caught Ascari, who tamely followed him to the flag and crossed the line a length behind. It had been a convincing demonstration of Alfa Romeo dominance, only spoiled by the errant stone, and if Ascari had not obeyed orders he would have won.

While Alfa Romeo was unbeatable in grand prix or Formula A racing, there was much more open competition in the lesser Formula B, where Simca-Gordini was battling with the Fiat-based Cisitalia and the Maserati A6G. However, by the middle

18 July 1948: Alberto Ascari enters Gueux village during the GP de l'ACF at Reims. This was his only Alfa Romeo drive, and he finished third. (Ludvigsen Library)

5 September 1948: Wimille and Trossi share the front row for the GP d'Italia at Turin with two newcomers, Villoresi's 4CLT/48 Maserati and Sommer's 125 Ferrari.

of 1948 a new marque was coming to the front. The V-12 Ferrari was becoming the car to beat, especially on the faster circuits, and in the preliminary Formula B race at Reims, Sommer's Ferrari had lapped the field in a convincing victory.

In the late summer of 1947 Colombo left Alfa Romeo and joined Ferrari, where he could direct the development and production of his V-12 design. Perhaps embittered by the treatment he had received, his heart had not really been in his work at Portello,

and he had spent much time 'moonlighting' while he prepared designs for a mini-car, the Volpe, which collapsed in a financial scandal. When this was discovered, his position at Portello was untenable.

The Ferrari factory had moved from Modena to Maranello, and in August 1948 the first V-12 grand prix Ferrari, the Tipo 125, was being completed. The aim was to run the car in the Gran Premio d'Italia, which was held in Turin on the Valentino park circuit on 6 September. Enzo Ferrari arranged for the park to be closed for several days at the end of August and

engaged Farina to conduct private trials of the new car. When these were completed, two more cars were finished at Maranello and a team of three 125s were entered for the Gran Premio. The drivers were Farina, Sommer and the Siamese Prince Bira, who had been an outstanding voiturette driver with an ERA before the War and was still very competitive driving Maseratis and Gordinis.

At Portello all these developments were watched closely – if anyone could end the domination of the 158, it was Enzo Ferrari. Three 158s were entered for the Turin race;

5 September 1948: Wimille, who is leading the GP d'Italia, has lapped Sanesi, who took over from Trossi after he became unwell. (Ludvigsen Library)

Ascari had returned to the Scuderia Ambrosiana Maseratis, so the drivers were Wimille, Trossi and Sanesi. Perhaps prompted by the Ferrari threat, the 158/47 was brought out for Wimille, but Trossi and Sanesi had to make do with the normal 158s. In practice Wimille and Trossi were fastest, but shared the front row of the grid with Villoresi's 4CLT/48 and Sommer's Ferrari.

It was a very wet day and only a small crowd turned out to see the new Ferrari's grand prix début. At the start Sommer beat the rest off the line, but after a lap Wimille was in front followed by Sommer, Sanesi, Ascari, Farina and Trossi. Wimille began to pull away but Sommer and Villoresi battled for second place, while Trossi, who was feeling ill, began to drop back through the field. Wimille cruised on unchallenged and reeled off the 75 laps to win the 225-mile (360km) race by more than 3 minutes. Villoresi eventually got the better of Sommer, but the new Ferrari finished in third place. Sanesi retired after bending his front suspension on a straw bale, so he took over from Trossi, who felt unable to continue. This car also retired after 53 laps when one of the superchargers failed.

At the end of the 1948 season circuit racing had been revived in Britain by adapting disused wartime airfields, notably at Silverstone and Goodwood. The RAC promoted the British Grand Prix at Silverstone on 2 October and invited Alfa Corse to enter, but the negotiations fell through as the RAC did not offer an acceptable amount of starting money. The last engagement for the 158s was at Monza on 17 October. The track had been repaired and the first race was the Gran Premio dell' Autodromo di Monza, which was a virtual re-run of the Gran Premio d'Italia at its proper home. Once again it was Alfa Corse versus Ferrari and Maserati; three 158/47s were entered for Wimille, Trossi and Sanesi, while Piero Taruffi, who had returned to the Alfa Romeo fold for this one race, had an earlier 158.

The circuit had been rebuilt using only the 3.9-mile (6.3km) road section – for the time being the banked track was abandoned. The honour of being the first to use the revived circuit had fallen to Sanesi, who did some laps when testing a 158 on 5 October. The re-opening was accompanied by much pomp and circumstance and Sgr Corbellini, the Minister of Transport, unveiled a plaque and cut a ribbon.

To show Enzo Ferrari that it would not be an easy task to topple Alfa Corse, the 158s had the four places on the front of the grid and Wimille took the lead at the start of the 80-lap race. For a few laps Sommer's Ferrari was running second, in front of the other 158s, but on lap seven he pulled into the pits and retired, suffering from an asthma attack. Farina's Ferrari and Villoresi's Maserati now tried to give battle, but both gradually fell away and eventually retired. This left the 158s in complete command; when Wimille stopped for fuel, Sanesi led for a few laps, but Wimille was soon back at the head of the field. At the end Trossi was second, followed by Sanesi and Taruffi.

Once again the 158s had dominated grand prix racing, and while the Maseratis and Ferraris had tried hard, they lacked the speed and reliability to give real opposition. However, all this was about to change.

General Peron sponsored the usual South American series in January and February 1949, and this time Wimille took a works Simca-Gordini, a familiar car to him as he had driven it often in Formula B races during 1947 and 1948. The first race of the series was the Gran Premio de General Juan D. Peron, run on the Palermo circuit on the outskirts of Buenos Aires. As the roads were used by local traffic during the day, practice was held early in the morning, and on Friday 28 January Wimille was out on the circuit at 6.00am, watched by a large crowd that pressed forward and lined the edge of the track; some went further and seemed to be trying to touch the practising cars as they passed. After five laps Wimille was rounding a fast left-hand curve when the

crowd pushed forward; he swerved to avoid them and, perhaps blinded by the low morning sun, lost control. His car went across the track, hit a straw bale, reared up on to its nose, then fell on to its near side, crushing Wimille in the cockpit as it fell back. He was rushed to hospital but died of head injuries soon afterwards. Four days later his body was flown back to France and he was buried in the Parisian church of St Phillipe de Roule. At the funeral he was awarded a posthumous Legion d'Honneur. Wimille was 39 and right at the peak of his form; all his obituaries concluded that he was the finest grand prix driver of his time.

For Alfa Corse Wimille's death was a heavy blow, and followed equally bad news: Trossi was diagnosed as suffering from incurable lung cancer. He lingered on for a few months, and died in a Milan clinic on 9 May 1949. His career was perhaps enigmatic; there had been times when he seemed to be on the verge of attaining the highest level, and certainly could be as quick as the best of his contemporaries, but he never seemed to have the final bite to his driving that would have taken him to the very top. A rich man, possibly he lacked the economic necessity that would have given him that final edge, and for many years his health had been a problem, so he lacked stamina. Alfa Romeo owed him much for his strong financial support of Scuderia Ferrari in the early 1930s, and he had been a key figure in the post-war 158 team.

With Wimille dead and Trossi dying, Alfa Corse now had a serious shortage of drivers. This was not the only problem; the reconstruction of the company and its factories by Gallo and Satta was about to bear fruit, and a new car, the 1900, had been developed and was going into production. It was to be built in numbers never before contemplated – it would be the first mass-produced Alfa

17 October 1948: Trossi, a sick man, drives in his last race, the GP di Monza. While his 158 is refuelled, a delegation, led by Guidotti, asks if he is fit to carry on. He finished second.

Romeo – and a substantial part of the finance for the project was coming from aid under the Marshall Plan. This was a scheme devised by President Truman of the United States and his Secretary of State, George Marshall, to rebuild European industries and involved some outside control of expenditure. Those who dispensed Marshall Aid looked somewhat sourly at expenditure on a racing programme, which seemed to do little in concrete terms to put Alfa Romeo back on its feet again; the prestige and publicity could not be measured and had already been gained by the results in 1946, 1947 and 1948.

In response to this pressure it was decided that Alfa Corse would only have a limited 1949 racing programme, so Gallo and Satta proposed that only one 158/47 should be raced. When Guidotti was told of this, he protested vehemently, saying that to run only one car would be disastrous and failure was inevitable. If they wanted to pursue this plan they should look for another racing manager – he would have none of it. Guidotti's angry counsel prevailed and it was decided that there would be no racing in 1949. The 158s were put away under dust sheets at Portello, much as the P3s had been in 1933. Such was Guidotti's vehemence that it seems the choice of a driver was never discussed.

The South American races were held under the shadow of Wimille's death. Two races were held on the Palermo circuit, and in the first, the General Peron event on 30 January, Ascari and Villoresi were first and second with their 4CT/48 Maseratis, but Oscar Galvez drove a fine race in his 3.8-litre-engined 308 to come third, beating Fangio's 4CL Maserati. The second race, on 6 February, was the Gran Premio Doña Eva Duarte de Peron, 'Evita' herself. The race was held in a downpour, and the Maseratis of Ascari and Villoresi, and the Ferrari of Farina, all led then blew up, leaving Oscar Galvez with his 308 to battle with Fangio, who now had a new 4CLT/48. Fangio tried too hard and grazed a tree, so Galvez won with the old 308 and Fangio had to settle for second place. At Rosario City on 7 February, the European visitors were in better shape and seventh place was the best that Galvez could manage, but in the final race of the series at Mar del Plata on 27 February, once again the visitors dropped out and Fangio won, while Galvez was third behind Bira's Maserati.

Without the 158s the early races of the 1949 grand prix season seemed to be equally balanced between the new 125 Ferraris, the 4CLT/48 Maseratis and the unsupercharged Lago-Talbots. Villoresi and Ascari abandoned Maserati and were driving for Ferrari, and as the season progressed, this pair gradually established a dominance over their rivals. Ascari had matured rapidly and was now manifestly a faster driver than Villoresi. Ferrari was also not standing still, and by the end of the season the Gran Premio d'Italia at Monza had been won by Ascari driving a long-chassis, two-stage-supercharged 125, which was a greatly superior car to the machines that had appeared at Turin a year before, though his winning speed was lower than that set by Wimille's 158/47 over the same distance in October 1948.

The sensation of the season was Juan Manuel Fangio. He was sent to Europe at the beginning of the season with a 4CLT/48, ostensibly sponsored by the Argentine Automobile Club, though the money probably came from a source much nearer the presidential palace. With the Maserati Fangio won four races, then with a borrowed Formula B Ferrari and a Simca-Gordini he won two more. By the beginning of July the money had run out, so probably to the great relief of the other drivers he went home to Argentina, but this was a new and outstanding talent and he had made his mark.

Chapter 16

Truly champions

IT IS NOT KNOWN when the decision was made that Alfa Corse would race again, but the rumours began to appear in the press at the beginning of 1950 and were confirmed in a low-key announcement in March. The decision may have been prompted by a number of factors: the development of the 1900 was completed and the car was going into production, and the Marshall Aid strings had also been loosened. The United States was now confronted by the Cold War and was concerned that Italy was the Western European country most likely to succumb to the Communist threat; the easing of Aid restrictions could diminish the anti-American stance of the Italian trade unions, which, in alliance with the Italian Communist Party, now formed the most powerful political force in the country. There was also the indomitable Italian passion for motor racing and the fierce pride of Portello, which had been stung by the success of the upstart Ferrari. If Alfa Corse did not race again, all the glory accruing from the newly announced World Championship of Drivers would fall to Ferrari, which would be intolerable. The return was probably the outcome of a number of these factors, just as the withdrawal had been. Some of the cost of the racing programme was met by Alfa Romeo dealers and distributors, who probably felt that the 1900 needed the publicity that racing success would bring.

Once the decision had been made, the drivers were chosen. The driving of Fangio had made a big impression and he was invited to Portello to discuss a contract to drive for the 1950 season. Fangio himself gives two accounts. In *My Twenty Years of Motor Racing* he says that he was offered an immediate contract by Pasquale Gallo and another director, Antonio Allesio, but in *Fangio* he suggests that he was only given a provisional contract to drive for one race at San Remo, and the full contract depended on his performance in that race. The former seems more likely, as Ferrari was also anxious to secure his services if possible. When it was announced that Fangio had joined Alfa Corse, there were some critical comments in the Italian press, which felt that the team should be all-Italian.

Joining Fangio in the team was Giuseppe Farina, who was forgiven his past transgressions. During 1949 he had driven some brilliant races with a 4CLT/48 Maserati and was offering the only real opposition to the Ferraris by the end of the season. The third driver was an astonishing choice in Luigi Fagioli, who had virtually retired from the sport at the end of 1937 and had then driven in a handful of races in 1948. He was now 51 years old, but in his day had been a tough, hard trier. Alfa Corse had chosen a team that in modern grand prix terms would be regarded as geriatric – Fangio, although a new boy, was 38 and Farina was 43, though at that time drivers raced on into early middle age and experience counted as much as youthful exuberance.

The six faithful 158s were overhauled ready for their fifth season of racing. During the lay-off more work had been done to the superchargers and manifolding, raising the power to 350bhp at 8600rpm, and all six cars were brought up to the 158/47 specification. Historians have often speculated about the individual identities of the 158s. Guidotti was asked about this and said that when the first batch of six cars was completed in 1938, they were given factory chassis numbers. However, the cars were dismantled and stripped after each race, and the major components were switched from car to car, so the individual identities were soon lost. When the second batch of six cars was built in the winter of 1939/40, no chassis numbers were allocated, though components were numbered. If the 158s raced outside Italy a plate was affixed to the bulkhead of each to satisfy customs and border controls, stamped with a number '158/…', the number after the oblique being the race number given to the car for the event in which it was competing. For example, when the team went to Reims for the GP de l'ACF in 1948, Ascari's car had the race number 26, so the plate on his car would have been stamped '158/26', and would have been removed when the car returned to Portello. It seems likely that the same policy was adopted before the War. When cars were sold to private owners they had a chassis number, but it is likely that while the cars were being raced by Scuderia Ferrari and Alfa Corse, the identities were speculative.

The European drivers went for another profitable foray to South America during the winter. The locally owned 308s were feeling their age and made little impact on the racing, but in the Gran Premio de General Peron on 8 January, run on the Palermo Park circuit, Clemar Bucci managed to get his 308 into third place behind the Ferraris of Villoresi and Serafini, beating Fangio's Ferrari into fourth place.

Back in Europe the FIA changed the titles of the two racing formulae, which were now known as Formula 1 and 2. The European season began with a Formula 2 race at Marseilles on 19 March. The entry list looked like that of a full grand prix – everyone was there. In practice Farina, driving an OSCA, crashed and broke his collar bone.

The first Formula 1 race of the season was the Gran Premio di San Remo on 16 April in the coastal resort near the French frontier. It was run on a tight town circuit, reminiscent of Monaco, and Alfa Corse intended to run one 158, driven by Farina, to ease the organisation gently back into racing; however, with the Marseilles crash Farina was unfit, so Fangio was substituted. Ferrari, on the other hand, was taking the race very seriously and entered six cars, a mixed bag of 125s and F2 166s. It was a

13 May 1950: The team of 158s lined up in the paddock for the European GP at Silverstone. (Guy Griffiths)

wet day and the upper part of the 158's grille was blanked off to keep the temperature up, a feature that would become familiar in the next two seasons.

Despite being in second place on the grid next to Ascari, Fangio was beaten at the start and for the early laps ran behind the Ferraris of Ascari, Villoresi and Sommer. Over the next few laps he methodically picked off the Ferraris, and by lap 13 was in front, where he stayed until the end. Ascari spun off and bent his car in his efforts to regain the lead. Alfa Corse was delighted. The 158 was still in command and the new boy was as good as the best of the opposition, but the easy pickings of 1947 and 1948 were gone – Ferrari were getting stronger.

If Alfa Romeo still seemed to be the preeminent marque in grand prix racing, it was being supplanted in sports car racing by Ferrari, which had won the Mille Miglia in 1948, then had repeated the victory in 1949, also winning the Le Mans and Spa 24-hour races. The team now began the 1950 sports car racing season by winning the Mille Miglia for the third time.

The first round of the new World Drivers' Championship was held in England on the converted airfield circuit at Silverstone on Saturday 13 May. To add some extra dignity to the race, as well as being the RAC British Grand Prix it was given the title Grand Prix d'Europe. Four 158s were entered; it had been intended to run the fourth car for Sanesi, but he had damaged his arm when he crashed an experimental 3-litre coupé in the Mille Miglia, so the car was offered to the English driver Reg Parnell. Parnell, who had started racing in the 1930s, had been the most consistent British driver since the War and had gained a number of wins and places driving 4CL and 4CLT/48 Maseratis; on the form he had shown he would be capable of keeping up with the pace. Surprisingly, Ferrari did not enter; he was hatching new plans. The race therefore appeared to be a reversion to the form of

13 May 1950: Farina, the winner of the European GP, poses in front of the pits at Silverstone. (George Monkhouse)

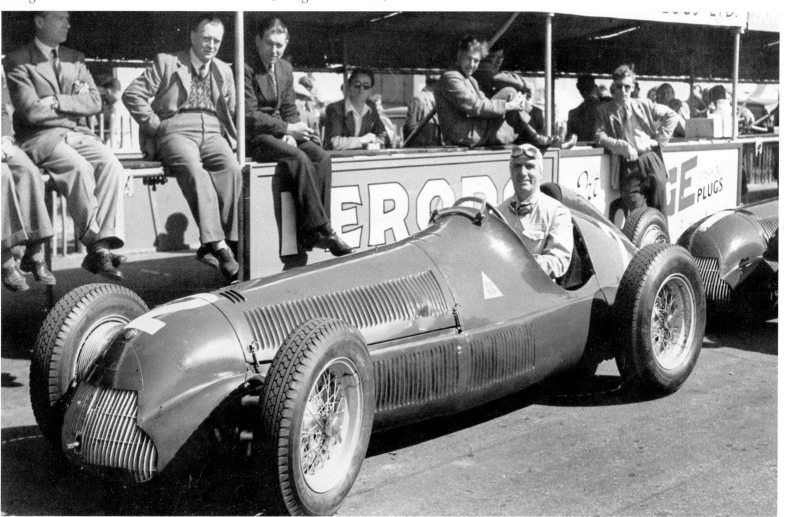

1947 and 1948, with the Maseratis and Talbots offering little opposition, and that was how it turned out.

The 158s dominated practice and the 70-lap, 202-mile (324km) race, winning as they pleased – all the opposition was at least two laps behind. They swapped places among themselves, but the demonstration was spoiled when Fangio stopped after 62 laps with a broken con rod. Parnell hit a hare, which dented the front of his car but did not delay him, and Farina was the winner from Fagioli and Parnell. The race was watched by King George VI and Queen Elizabeth, who, like the crowd, must have found it an impressive but dull demonstration. Before the race began the BRM, the British grand prix hope, was demonstrated by Raymond Mays, its main progenitor; the Alfa Corse mechanics crowded to the trackside to watch what was hoped would become an effective British rival to the 158s.

A fortnight later the teams were at Monaco, and this time the Ferraris turned up. The starting grid was a muddle as only the times recorded in the first practice session counted. Fangio and Farina were on the front row, but Villoresi, who should have been with them, was back in row three. There was a strong wind, and waves had been breaking over the harbour wall and had wetted the course at the Tabac corner.

Farina led at the start, but by the time the cars reached the Tabac Fangio was in front. Farina hit the wet patch and spun, initiating an enormous multiple crash that eliminated nine cars, including Farina himself and Fagioli. On the second lap Fangio realised that something was amiss as the crowds were not watching him, but looking the other way, so he slowed and wriggled his way through the mass of mangled cars and

went on his way to win. He was chased by the Ferraris of Ascari and Villoresi, but Villoresi fell out when in second place and Ascari's chances were lost as he had to make two refuelling stops, while Fangio only stopped once.

The Grösser Preis der Schweiz on the Bremgarten circuit was the next Championship round. Once again the 158s dominated practice and shared the front row of the grid. Ascari and Villoresi broke their Ferraris after a few laps and it seemed that it was going to be an Alfa Corse 1–2–3, but then there was a repeat of Silverstone and Fangio dropped out after 33 laps, this time with a cracked valve seat, so Farina won from Fagioli with the rest trailing way behind.

If the team had been growing complacent, it was about to receive a rude shock. In the Paddock at Spa, and entered for the Grand Prix de Belgique on 18 June, was a new Ferrari, but instead of more and even larger superchargers, it was unsupercharged, although only 3.3 litres. It was clear what Enzo Ferrari was thinking: it could be possible to make an unsupercharged 4½-litre engine go as fast as a supercharged 1½-litre, and any speed and power disadvantage would be compensated by fewer refuelling stops. The new Ferrari was not especially fast in practice or in the race, and rather spoiled the concept by stopping for fuel, but Ferrari's theory received an unexpected boost.

The three 158s set off in the race and seemed to be indulging in the usual domination, being followed by Sommer's Lago-Talbot. There may have been an error in Guidotti's lap chart, but when the three 158s stopped to refuel, Sommer, who had been driving the Lago-Talbot faster than it had ever gone before and was running non-stop, moved up into the lead. The Alfa Romeo pit thought Sommer was a lap behind, but then realisation dawned and there was consternation. Fangio and Farina were given the flat-out signal, but it took

21 May 1950: Fangio picks his way past the cars wrecked in the multiple crash at the Tabac on the first lap of the GP de Monaco. The track is covered with fuel from the split tanks. (Stanley Sedgwick Collection, Bentley Drivers Club)

18 June 1950: The crowds look at the 158s in front of the pits before the GP de Belgique at Spa. (Ludvigsen Library)

them four laps to catch Sommer. Unfortunately, the Lago-Talbot protested that it had done enough and blew up, so Fagioli moved up into third place. However, the drama was not quite over, for in his efforts to catch Sommer Farina's transmission had suffered and he began to fall back. Fangio went on to win followed by Fagioli, but Farina was caught by Rosier's Lago-Talbot and could only manage fourth place in front of Ascari, with the new Ferrari. While Fagioli was pursuing Sommer, it was reported that he had been timed on the

Masta straight at 200.75mph (323.27kmh); subsequently it was suggested that the timing may have been suspect, but having regard to the speed recorded by Fangio at Pescara later in the season, it is likely that when geared for the fastest circuits, the 158 was capable of speeds bordering on 200mph (320kmh).

Ferrari must have decided that his new idea needed more thought, so there were no works Maranello entries at Reims for the Grand Prix de l'ACF. In practice, an improved 158 was brought out with more supercharger boost, which increased the

power to 370bhp, and modifications to the brakes. Farina and Fangio both used it for practice and Fangio was able to break the lap record set by Lang's Mercedes-Benz in 1939. This time Sommer's Lago-Talbot was off form and the 158s departed from the front row of the grid and proceeded to dominate the race. Farina was in the lead when he stopped on lap 16 with fuel starvation, but he restarted and caught up his team mates. However, when the fuel pump failed he fell back, and Fangio and Fagioli went on to take first and second places. Farina stopped after 58 laps, when the fuel

2 July 1950: Fangio, Farina and Fagioli share the front row for the GP de l'ACF at Reims. (Ludvigsen Library)

pump finally stopped. At this point in the season, Fangio led the Championship with 26 points, Fagioli had 24 and Farina 22.

On 9 July Alfa Corse again supported the Gran Premio di Bari, sending Farina and Fangio. The opposition was very thin and they had little difficulty in taking first and second places, though the mechanics made an error when Fangio came in to refuel at half distance and put in insufficient fuel, so he had to make an emergency stop on the penultimate lap. Third place was significant– it was taken by a young British driver called Stirling Moss, only 20 years old but already showing an extraordinary talent and

the first of a generation of British drivers who would soon dominate grand prix racing. He was driving an HWM, a British Formula 2 car that was setting a trend for the British teams and would go on to change the face of motor racing within a decade, being made up largely of proprietary parts, a world apart from the BRM on which so many hopes rested.

The Swiss ran the Grand Prix des Nations at Geneva on 30 July, using the 1946 circuit, and attracted an entry that would have looked impressive if it had been a round of the Championship. This time Fagioli was given the day off and the third

car was driven by the Swiss, Baron Emmanuel de Graffenreid, who, like Parnell, had raced in the 1930s and had won a number of races since 1946 driving 4CL and 4CLT/48 Maseratis, including the 1949 British Grand Prix. A fourth car was entered for Piero Taruffi, who had been driving well for Alfa Romeo in sports car races. Ferrari was back again, and this time Ascari had a new car with a 4.1-litre engine, while Villoresi had the 3.3-litre car used at Spa.

Practice showed the way things were going. Fangio was the only 158 on the front row of the grid, the other places being taken by the Ferraris. Fangio led all the way but was pursued by Ascari for almost the full distance and could not afford to relax – the Ferrari was always there and the other 158s

26 August 1950: Farina (158) and Peter Whitehead (Ferrari 125) wait for the start of the first heat of the International Trophy at Silverstone. (Guy Griffiths)

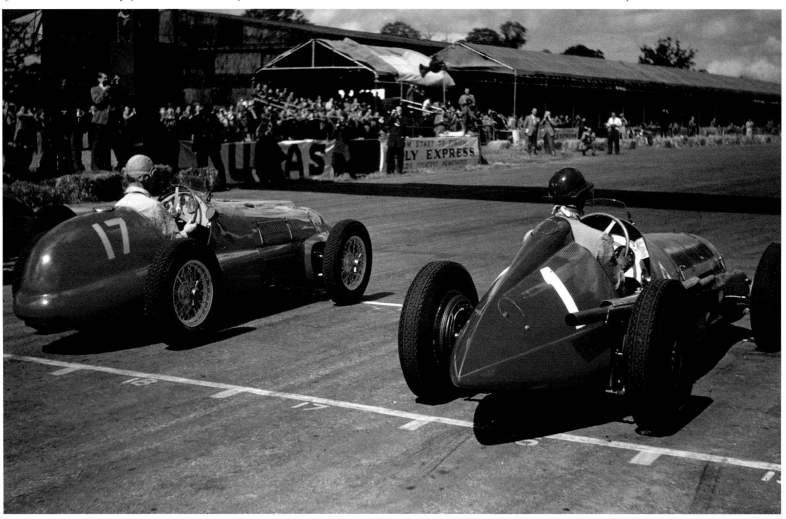

26 August 1950: Fangio wins the second heat of the International Trophy in the rain. (Guy Griffiths)

could not keep up with it. Near the end there was drama when Villoresi slid on an oil slick and his car overturned when it hit straw bales, then some spectators. Villoresi was thrown out on to the road and was badly hurt with a fractured femur and collar bone, and sadly three spectators were killed. Trying to avoid the injured Villoresi, Farina also hit the bales and was out of the race, and a lap later with only six laps to go. Ascari retired with a blown gasket or cracked head. De Graffenreid and Taruffi were second and third and on paper it looked an impressive result, but in reality Alfa Corse had been given a bad scare – the Ferraris were now a real menace.

Pescara had been an old stamping ground for Alfa Romeo for over 20 years, so two cars were sent there for the Circuito di Pescara on 15 August, the traditional Ferragosto holiday, but this time it was

Farina's turn for a holiday. In practice Fangio was timed at 192.84mph (310.08kmh), a speed only as fast as the German cars had achieved more than a decade earlier. In the race Fangio and Fagioli seemed to be having a nice easy outing, leading comfortably and running together until only a few kilometres from the finish. It had been decided beforehand that Fagioli should win and he was in front when he slowed to a halt; a trailing link in the front suspension had broken and the wheel was leaning inwards against the car. Fangio stopped beside him and urged him to drive the stricken car to the finish. Fagioli set off at a snail's pace with Fangio beside him, both looking anxiously behind for Rosier's Lago-Talbot, following in third place. With less than a kilometre to go the

Lago-Talbot appeared and Fangio realised that he could not wait, so accelerated away to take the flag while Fagioli limped on, being passed by Rosier about 300 metres from the line to lose second place by 6 seconds.

Despite quite a modest starting money package – £350 for both cars – two 158s were sent to Silverstone on 26 August for the International Trophy, a Formula 1 race promoted by the British Racing Drivers' Club and run with two heats and a final. In 1949 it had been won by Ascari's Ferrari, which may have stimulated the Alfa Romeo entries. The race was to be the début of the BRM and every British enthusiast hoped that it would show itself as a worthy adversary for the 158s. However, it did not appear for practice and only arrived at the

circuit on race morning, when it did three practice laps in a specially arranged session, driven by Sommer. It then took its place at the back of the grid for the second heat of the race, Farina having already won the first heat comfortably. When the flag fell the BRM did not move – a halfshaft had broken, and the car was pushed off the track while the crowd groaned in despair. It began to rain and Fangio won the heat in most unpleasant conditions. In the final the two cars ran together and Farina won from Fangio by 0.4 second; Fangio said later that his car was not running properly.

The British enthusiasts went home sadly, realising that the possibility of the BRM challenging Italian supremacy in grand prix racing was remote. The BRM failure was not the only sadness at Silverstone. William Lyons, the owner of Jaguar, had invited Nuvolari to drive an XK120 in a supporting sports car race. Nuvolari, now very frail and suffering from rapidly worsening emphysema, was keen to drive and came to the meeting, completing three slow laps in a red-painted car on the first day of practice then returning to the pits. Lofty England, the Jaguar team manager, had the sad and difficult task of telling Nuvolari that he was too slow and was not fit to race. He never drove on a racing circuit again.

The Gran Premio d'Italia was held at Monza on Sunday 3 September. It was the final round of the World Championship and all three members of the Alfa Corse team were in with a chance of becoming Champion; the trio were backed by the additional entries of Taruffi and Sanesi. The Portello trade unions had decided that it was time a union member was racing in the team again, so Sanesi's entry was the outcome. From the management point of view, Sanesi must have been a godsend – his entries kept the unions happy and he was well able to keep up with the pace. If

3 September 1950: Ascari's 375 Ferrari (No 16) has split the 158 team on the front row for the GP d'Italia at Monza. (Ludvigsen Library)

the unions had put a complete tyro in the cockpit, the outcome could have been most unhappy.

The opposition was now getting stronger as there were two Ferraris with full 4½-litre engines. Villoresi was still convalescing, so his place was taken by Dorio Serafini, who had been 500cc European motor cycle champion in 1939, and had raced Formula 2 and sports cars since the War. In practice Fangio was fastest, but only by 0.2 second from Ascari. From the start Farina, Fangio and Ascari battled and on lap 14 the Ferrari took the lead. Ascari then fell back and on lap 21 he was out with a burst engine; two laps later Fangio came into the pits with his engine boiling. He too was out, and his Championship hopes were almost gone, but Satta called in Taruffi and Fangio took over the car, moving it up into second place. A few laps later this car also cried enough and dropped a valve, so Fangio's hopes were dashed.

Meanwhile Ascari had taken over Serafini's Ferrari and was chasing Farina, who was driving along contentedly knowing that if he kept going in front the Championship was his. Ascari had passed Fagioli, but could not catch Farina and the

race ran out with Farina winning the Gran Premio and the Championship. Ascari was second, 1min 19sec behind, and Fagioli was third. Sanesi's 158 had only lasted 11 laps. Farina rejoiced in his Championship, Fangio went back to Argentina slightly bitter, feeling that he had been robbed by the need for an Italian Champion, and Satta, Nicolis and Guidotti realised that they had their work cut out if they were to stay in front of Ferrari in 1951. However, at Maranello Enzo Ferrari presided over an ever-deepening feud.

A week after the Monza finale, Raymond Sommer was at Cadours, near Toulouse, for a minor Formula 2 meeting. Racing a 1000cc Cooper, he crashed while leading the final and was killed instantly at the age of 44. Always at his best fighting ferociously when the odds were against him, he was known to all the French as 'Coeur du Lion'. The historian Paul Sheldon says that the death of Sommer had much the same impact in France as the death of Jim Clark had in Britain. His death was mourned at Portello too, where he was remembered for so many gallant and successful drives for Alfa Romeo, both with racing cars and sports cars.

Chapter 17

'The nearest run thing you ever saw'

AT MARANELLO THERE WAS great tension at the close of 1950. Gioachino Colombo had been demoted, and in his own eyes humiliated, as Ferrari had relegated him to the mundane task of developing a series of production road cars. The glamorous task of designing a new generation of grand prix cars had been given to a newcomer, Aurelio Lampredi. The matter nearly came to a head at the beginning of 1950, but a truce was patched up. However, by the end of the year Colombo was becoming increasingly embittered, particularly when reports of the 'demotion' began to appear in the press. Pasquale Gallo, seeing the reports, approached Colombo and asked if he would like to return to Portello. While Colombo was thinking about it, Ferrari was told by an Alfa Romeo tester that Colombo was returning to Portello, which caused a fierce row between Colombo and Ferrari. In January 1951 Colombo cleared his desk and returned to Alfa Romeo.

Colombo joined a worried team, concerned that the basic 158 design needed to be given an extra lease of life that would see it through one more, perhaps final, season of racing. The superchargers were modified and the boost was increased yet again. The output now went up to 425bhp at 9300rpm, but the penalty was a barely quenchable thirst of about 1.6 miles per gallon (approx 180 litres per 100km) using a fuel that was now 98 per cent methanol. Even more drastic, the money was found to build four more cars, one of

them fitted with De Dion rear suspension, a derivative of that first used on the Tipo 512 and being tested when Marinoni suffered his fatal crash. The new cars had longer tails containing bigger fuel tanks, although in all the cars, including the earlier machines, the drivers now sat surrounded by tanks with one in the scuttle and one beside the driver's seat, so the total fuel capacity was now 66 gallons (300 litres). The four new cars were called the Tipo 159, but to avoid customs and frontier problems all the cars, including the six veterans, were now called Tipo 159s, and when outside Italy carried '159/…' plates on the bulkhead, a point that sometimes confused contemporary journalists. In this account the older six cars will be called 158s and the four new cars 159s. It is not known how much Colombo contributed to the 159 design, but it seems that most of the work was probably done by Satta.

After the War Germany had been in the wilderness, effectively banned from organising or taking part in major motor races, but the ban was lifted in 1950 and Germany was re-admitted to the FIA. Three 1939 W154/163 Mercedes were entered by the Stuttgart firm for the winter series in South America to be driven by Farina, Hermann Lang and Karl Kling, but the race organisers said that they did not want Farina, and that his car must be driven by Fangio. Much argument took place, but Fangio drove, thus keeping in practice, while Farina fumed. The Mercedes were unsuccessful in

the series, but the outstanding driver was another Argentinian, Froilan Gonzalez, who won the main races of the series. He had raced in Europe in 1950 driving a Maserati in Formula 1, and Ferrari and Gordini in Formula 2, but his season had been fitful, interrupted by burns he received when his car caught fire after the big Monaco crash; he was now showing real ability and was about to make a big impression in Europe.

The BRDC International Trophy at Silverstone was brought forward in the calendar and was run on 5 May, providing Alfa Corse with a useful opportunity to give the team a run-out before the serious stuff began. Four 158s were entered for Fangio, Farina, Sanesi and Felice Bonetto. It seemed that the race might be a true pointer to form, as Ferrari had entered Ascari and Villoresi, but they did not appear. There was one fast Ferrari, however, as Tony Vandervell, the British bearing manufacturer who supplied the big-end bearings to Ferrari, had bought a Ferrari fitted with the latest 4½-litre engine, which was entered as a Thinwall Special Ferrari in recognition of his business interests; Reg Parnell was the driver. Vandervell had been one of the major sponsors of the BRM project, but was rapidly becoming disillusioned with its chaotic organisation and was taking the first steps down the path that would end with his own Vanwall Formula 1 cars.

The race was run again in two 15-lap heats and a 35-lap final. Fangio and Bonetto ran in heat one with Parnell. Fangio won, but the Thinwall, after passing Bonetto, who was driving a 'wide' car occupying most of the road, in the modern grand prix manner, chased Fangio all the way, catching up and finishing only 3 seconds behind. Fangio had to work hard, breaking the lap record to stay in front, while Bonetto was left well behind. In heat two, Farina and Sanesi cruised round to take first and second.

As the cars lined up on the grid for the final, the skies darkened, torrential rain began to fall, and the track was awash as the flag fell. Bonetto led at the start but Parnell soon forged in front and the 159s all fell back among the British amateurs. The race was stopped after five laps and Parnell was declared the winner, with Fangio fourth. It was the first time that Alfa Corse had been beaten since 1946, which in the

conditions may not have been significant, but the speed of the Thinwall Ferrari was an indication that Alfa Corse now had real problems – the extra power of the 159 engine might not be enough.

Monaco had been cancelled so the first round of the 1951 World Championship was at Berne on 27 May. Ferrari were slightly below strength, as Ascari was not fully fit – he had been slightly burned in a Formula 2 race at Genoa the previous weekend when his fuel tank split and his car burst into flames. He was racing but was clearly off form, so Villoresi and Taruffi were the main force of the Ferrari attack. Alfa Corse arrived with five cars, three 158s and two 159s, one with swing axles and one

with the De Dion suspension; they were taking the task seriously as there were three mechanics allocated to each car. Fangio and Farina were supported by Sanesi and de Graffenried, who was being given an outing in his national event.

The team seemed undecided about the allocation of cars in practice, but when the cars came out on race day Sanesi had the De Dion 159 while Farina had the other 159. It was raining heavily and the Alfa Romeos were fitted with splash guards behind the front wheels – perhaps the memories of distant Targa Florios had not been forgotten. As the cars completed their warming-up laps, the Alfa Corse mechanics topped up the tanks with jugs of fuel, so

27 May 1951: Farina and Fangio (159s) have been joined on the front row for the GP der Schweiz at Berne by Villoresi's 375 Ferrari. (Ludvigsen Library)

consumption was evidently a worry. At the end of the first lap Fangio led Farina and Sanesi, while Villoresi was next and Taruffi was at the back having nearly succumbed to the conditions. Villoresi passed Sanesi on lap five, but ended in the hedge when he was blinded by spray. Meanwhile Fangio was pulling away from Farina, then he stopped for fuel. He restarted just behind Farina who, with extra tanks, was going through non-stop and soon took the lead again. Taruffi had recovered and was driving way above his class; he caught Farina who hung on to second place for a few laps, then Taruffi went past and Farina fell back. Fangio went on to win by nearly a minute from Taruffi, while Farina recovered from a spin on the last lap and was third. Sanesi and de Graffenreid were fourth and fifth in front of a relatively slow Ascari.

While the rest of the team went back to Portello after the Swiss race, Farina had a date the following weekend in Northern Ireland where a single 158 was entered for the Ulster Trophy, a Formula 1 race on the Dundrod circuit. This was a difficult and narrow 7.4-mile (12km) course, bumpy and ill-surfaced by grand prix standards and running between banks and hedges. It had attracted a reasonable entry with most of the amateur grand prix circus; the opposition to Farina was led by Parnell with the Thinwall Ferrari. The 27-lap race had a Royal presence as Queen Elizabeth (later the Queen Mother) and Princess Margaret, who were making an official tour of Northern Ireland, were among the spectators. Farina led from the start of the 27-lap race and was only headed by Parnell when the 158 made a brief fuel stop on lap 16. Farina was back in front again after two laps and went on to win from Parnell by over a minute. On the difficult road circuit the Thinwall had offered less of a challenge than it had at Silverstone.

After the Irish interlude it was back to the serious business on 17 June for the Grand Prix de Belgique at Spa. As Denis Jenkinson said in *Motor Sport*, the field 'made up in quality what it lacked in quantity'; three Alfa Romeos faced three Ferraris and seven Lago-Talbots. There were no Maseratis, as the 4CLT/48 was now completely outclassed. Fangio had the De Dion 159 and there were swing axle 159s for Farina and Sanesi. The De Dion car now had even more tankage: apart from the tail tank, there was one in the scuttle, tanks on each side of the driver's legs, and a long cylindrical tank on the offside of the engine bay. This gave a total capacity of 70 gallons (320 litres). The usual Pirelli 7.00-18 rear tyres had been replaced by Engelbert 7.00-19s to raise the gearing for the long Masta straight, and the 19-inch wheels had offset spokes, a new feature. Farina's car had the same tank arrangement as Fangio's, but without the scuttle tank, and Sanesi's had the three cockpit tanks, but lacked one in the engine bay; all three cars had bulged side panels, to make room for the cockpit side tanks, and larger tails. It seemed that Alfa Corse was undecided about the tank layout, which indicated to some observers

2 June 1951: Farina (158) sets off for an easy win in the Ulster Trophy at Dundrod. No 3 is Shawe-Taylor's ERA and No 17 Parnell's Thinwall Ferrari.

that the complete self-confidence of the past was now lacking.

Fangio and Farina shared the front row of the grid with Villoresi, while Ascari was in the next row and was already motoring when the flag fell. Villoresi led away, but was passed by Farina on the Masta straight on the first lap. Villoresi was having none of that, and repassed Farina to be in front again at the end of the lap, with Ascari in third place and Fangio fourth. Farina went ahead on the next lap, but Ascari, Villoresi and Fangio continued to swap places until Fangio gradually shook off the Ferraris and started to close up on Farina. Once the fuel load of the Alfa Romeos lightened, they had the edge in performance over the Ferraris. Sanesi stopped to refuel on lap 10 but retired a lap later with a leaking radiator. Farina stopped next and Fangio was in front for a lap, then he also stopped to refuel.

At his stop there was drama. A spoke had broken on one of the rear wheels and jammed behind the splines. The mechanics hammered in vain and eventually the entire brake drum and hub were removed, but still the wheel would not come off, so the tyre was replaced on the rim and inflated, and the other parts were re-assembled on the car. Fangio waited patiently and after 14½ minutes started off again, having lost four laps. Farina was still swinging along happily in front and finished the race over half a lap in front of Ascari, while Villoresi was third, but the unfortunate Fangio was ninth and last.

The battle now moved on to Reims on 1 July for the Grand Prix de l'ACF, which was also the Grand Prix d'Europe. Fagioli, getting his first drive in 1951, now joined the Spa trio, so four 159s were running and this time Sanesi had the De Dion car. Ferrari meant business and entered four cars, the fourth to be driven by the 'new boy', Froilan Gonzalez. In practice Fangio and Farina just had the edge over Ascari.

Race day was sweltering hot and a huge crowd came to see what promised to be a titanic battle. The start was delayed for

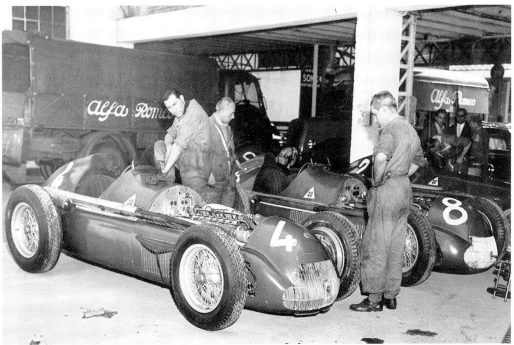

1 July 1951: Two views of the Alfa Corse mechanics working on the 159s before the GP de l'ACF at Reims. (George Monkhouse)

much ceremonial associated with the European title, but when the flag fell Ascari took the lead, pursued by Fangio, Villoresi and Sanesi. The 158s had been headed at the start before, but within a lap the proper order of things had always been restored. Now Fangio was in full pursuit but was

making no impression on the Ferrari – an Alfa Corse nightmare not experienced since Tripoli in 1939. However, to the relief of the Portello team on lap nine Ascari came into his pit with a gearbox problem, but Fangio also slowed and came in with a misfiring engine caused by a defective magneto.

1 July 1951: Fangio out-accelerates Ascari's Ferrari at the start of the GP de l'ACF, while Farina spins his wheels. (Guy Griffiths Collection)

boomed away into the race, now in fourth place. Farina was still in front, followed by Gonzalez and Villoresi, but the smoke thickened and Fangio was up into third place on lap 35. Two laps later Gonzalez came in and handed over to Ascari, so at half distance both aces were back in the race. Farina still led by 90 seconds from Fangio, with Ascari another 20 seconds behind.

Once again as the fuel load lightened the 159s were on terms with the Ferraris, but then Fangio stopped for fuel on lap 44, which moved Ascari up to second place. Now there was drama as Farina limped up the straight with a thrown tread on his nearside front tyre. The tread had wrapped round the suspension and had to be cut away, but he overshot his pit and had to be pushed back so the car was stationary for 3min 15sec. This left Ascari in front on lap 46, but fate had not finished with him, and three laps later he stopped to adjust the brakes, so Fangio now took a lead he was not to lose again. On lap 62 he stopped once more for fuel and a drink – dehydration was a real risk in the great heat – but restarted 38 seconds in front of Ascari. Villoresi's sick Ferrari, smoking and spraying oil over the driver, was still in third place, but still in front of Farina, whose car had now developed the fashionable magneto malady.

Fangio was flagged off as the winner of a heroic race – only his 159 and Ascari's Ferrari had covered the full 77 laps. Villoresi was third, three laps behind, and Parnell, driving the Thinwall Ferrari, had caught Farina to take fourth place. Poor Sanesi's magneto gave up completely on lap 58, so he pushed his car uphill over a kilometre, from the Thillois hairpin to the finish, reaching the line just as Fangio was flagged off; he received a cheer from the crowd far greater than that for the winner and was given tenth place, while Fagioli, who had restarted with Fangio's mended car, was last. The World Championship rules permitted the sharing of a car, with the points split between the drivers, so

Farina now took his chance and went into the lead, breaking the lap record four times in the next eight laps and pulling away until Villoresi was almost a minute behind. Fangio made several stops and was now at the rear of the field, while the same magneto problem was affecting Sanesi.

Villoresi's Ferrari started to smoke, so

Fagioli and Gonzalez moved past him, but on lap 21 Fagioli stopped for fuel and tyres. Fangio was sitting on the pit counter while the magneto was being changed; Satta had a quick word with Fagioli, who then climbed out of his car, shook Fangio's hand and took Fangio's place on the pit counter while Fangio climbed into the cockpit and

1 July 1951: Fangio takes Thillois corner at Reims in the 159 he took over from Fagioli. (Rodolfo Mailander, Ludvigsen Library)

Fangio and Fagioli were the joint winners. The result put 53-year-old Fagioli into the record books as the oldest driver ever to win a round of the World Championship, a record that is probably safe for all time.

For the second race running only one 159 had been running properly at the finish, and the rock-like reliability of the cars was now just a happy memory. The team cannot have gone to Silverstone for the British Grand Prix with a burgeoning optimism, and the more realistic members must have known that it was not *if* Ferrari would beat them, but *when*. Despite his experience of the circuit and his evident form, Fagioli was left out, so Farina and Fangio were backed up by Sanesi and Bonetto. Four 159s were taken to the race –

three, for Fangio, Farina and Sanesi, had the full tankage in the cockpit sides, scuttle and engine bay, but Bonetto's only had the cockpit side tanks and the older-style slimmer body. It was back to Pirelli again: Bonetto had 550-17 fronts and 700-18 rears, while the others were on 550-17 fronts and 750-16 rears. This time it was Farina's turn for the De Dion car. The continuous swapping of this car from driver to driver seems to indicate that any advantage it gave was marginal.

It was Gonzalez, in stupendous form, who was fastest in practice, a second quicker than Fangio; Farina and Ascari had the other front row places. Remarkably, Gonzalez had a car with the 1950 12-plug engine while the rest of the Ferrari team had

the new 24-plug engine. Even the pressure of practice was now telling on the 159s, and the night before the race the Alfa Corse mechanics were seen on the road in front of the garage in Brackley where the team had its headquarters, welding the cracked frame of a partly stripped car.

A huge crowd came for the race, greatly boosted by the presence of two BRMs driven by Parnell and Peter Walker; the pair had not practised but at least they were racing, starting from the back of the grid. Aided no doubt by the lighter fuel load, Bonetto was the surprise leader at the end of the first lap, followed by Gonzalez and Fangio, who soon took over the front places. On lap 10 Fangio passed Gonzalez, but did not pull away and was unable to make the gap wider than 2 or 3 seconds. Gonzalez was driving an inspired race, taking to the verges, going the wrong side

14 July 1951: Before the British GP at Silverstone, the 159s stand beside a Pirelli van in the paddock. (Guy Griffiths)

of the oil drums and straw bales that marked the corners, hanging on to Fangio, and drawing away from Ascari and Farina who followed, only lengths apart. On lap 35 the 159 and the Ferrari crossed the line side by side and five laps later Gonzalez took the lead. Fangio then stopped for fuel and rear tyres, and when he restarted he was 72 seconds behind Gonzalez.

Both drivers were giving an astonishing performance, but Fangio was making no impression on Gonzalez's lead. Farina had stopped for fuel and tyres, letting Ascari into third place. He too made a stop for rear tyres and set off to catch Farina again, but on lap 54 the Ferrari was out with a broken gearbox, so by lap 60 Gonzalez still led followed by Fangio, Farina and Villoresi. On lap 64 Gonzalez stopped for fuel and tyres. When he started to get out of the car to give it to Ascari, the latter waved him back into the cockpit; Ascari knew that he could be no quicker than the incredible Gonzalez that afternoon. The Ferrari went on in the lead and Fangio could do nothing about it. On lap 75 Farina pulled off at Abbey Curve, before the pits, with flames and smoke coming from under the bonnet; the official reason for his retirement was 'clutch trouble'!

Gonzalez completed the 90 laps and beat Fangio by 51 seconds; history had been made by a man who never before and never again drove in such a manner and had made one of the great legendary drives of motor racing. Alfa Romeo's run had been broken after 26 continuous victories, beaten as much by Gonzalez as by Ferrari. Villoresi was third and Bonetto was fourth; to the exuberant delight of the crowd Parnell's BRM was fifth and Walker's car was seventh behind Sanesi; the crowd invaded the circuit to welcome the BRMs.

Enzo Ferrari had been hoping and trying to beat Alfa Romeo since he had left Portello in 1939, and when he heard of Gonzalez's victory he said, 'I wept with joy; but my tears of happiness were blended too with tears of sadness, for I thought that day "I have killed my mother".' He sent a telegram to Satta that said, 'I still feel for our Alfa the adolescent tenderness of first love.' The mother may have been down, but she was not quite out and there were still three rounds of the Championship to be contested. Fangio led with 21 points, while Farina had only 15 and Gonzalez 9.

The team for the Grösser Preis von Deutschland at the Nürburgring on 29 July

14 July 1951: The start at Silverstone. Fangio (159) is already out of the picture, being chased by Gonzalez (375 Ferrari, No 12), Farina (159) and Ascari (375 Ferrari, No 11). (Guy Griffiths)

14 July 1951: Ascari leads Farina at Becketts as they battle for third place in the British GP. (Guy Griffiths)

was Fangio, Farina, Bonetto and Paul Pietsch, whose former wife Ilse had been Varzi's lover. There had been indecision about the choice of Pietsch; as first Willi Daetwyler, the Swiss sports car racer, then Chiron were considered, and as a result Pietsch only managed two practice laps. Defeat had rattled the Alfa Romeo team, and in practice there were many problems. It was the first time the cars had raced at the 'Ring; Fangio hit the bank and bent the nose and tail of his car, there was difficulty in getting the right carburettor settings, the gear ratios were changed several times, then it was found that the notorious bumps and swerves of the circuit were making the chassis frames flex. A car was built up

within hours at Portello with stiffer cross members and rushed to Germany for Fangio to drive; this may have been built up from a 158 and fitted with a 159 engine, as it had a 158 body.

When Fangio tried it during the last practice session, the clutch would not disengage fully; Guidotti stripped the clutch down the night before the race but could not see a fault. On race morning he asked permission to try the car on the circuit, but was refused, so he said that if he did not get permission the team would be withdrawn. The German officials relented and Guidotti tried the car, presumably on the short test course that used the pits straight, the South curve and the return road behind the pits, with a link

road off the North curve between the two straights; drivers used this 2km section of the circuit to test cars before setting out on a lap of the full circuit. Guidotti found that the clutch would disengage at lower revs, but at full revs it was solid. Later it was found that the spring housings had been wrongly machined and only had a depth of 0.5mm instead of 1.5mm, but nothing could be done before the race.

Ascari and Gonzalez took the two pole positions on the grid and the best Fangio and Farina could do was third and fourth. By the time the cars passed the back of the pits, Fangio was in front leading Farina, Ascari and Gonzalez, but by the end of the lap the Ferraris had passed Farina and had Fangio in their sights. With a lighter fuel load, Fangio was able to stay in front until halfway round lap four, despite the clutch

29 July 1951: Just after the start of the GP von Deutschland at the Nürburgring, Fangio leads Gonzalez (Ferrari 375) and Farina out of the Nordkehre. (Guy Griffiths Collection)

problem, then Ascari went by, and on lap six Fangio made his first fuel stop so the Ferraris were first and second. The flexing frame now eliminated Farina with broken oil and cooling pipes, then Bonetto dropped out with a recurrence of the Reims magneto failure. Pietsch, who had been going well in the De Dion car, had an enormous accident at the South Curve, going over the top of the bank on the outside of the corner in full view the main grandstands. Fortunately he was able to walk back to the pits, but this now left only Fangio to battle with four healthy Ferraris.

Ascari stopped for fuel on lap nine and Fangio moved up to second place behind Gonzalez, but Ascari caught up again and took the lead as Gonzalez made his stop. Maybe Fangio was inspired with the spirit that had affected Nuvolari 16 years before,

or perhaps the car was lighter as it used up the fuel, but now he began to motor with grim determination. Setting a series of fastest laps, he went by Gonzalez, then Ascari, and at the end of lap 12 was back in front with a lead of 14.5 seconds. However, it could not last as he needed to stop again. On lap 14 he came in and had difficulty in restarting, struggling to find a gear and stalling. The stop took 44 seconds so Ascari was in front again. It seemed that Ascari was cruising home to win, but on lap 17, with three to go, he came in for new rear tyres, a hub nut jammed and the stop took 39 seconds. Sadly Fangio could not profit from this delay, for the clutch problem had left him with only top gear, so he finished in

second place 30.5 seconds behind Ascari; Gonzalez was third and the Ferraris of Villoresi and Taruffi were fourth and fifth. The prancing horse was beginning to trample on the quadrifolio.

Instead of getting just the usual two cars from Portello to flatten the amateur opposition, in 1951 the organisers of the Gran Premio di Bari found that they not only had the two Alfa Romeos, but also four works Ferraris, so as a change from running a minor event, they had the eyes of the motor racing world upon them on 2 September. When Fangio beat the field away, the team must have felt that it was like old times again, particularly when Farina then moved up to second place; however, it was short-

29 July 1951: Paul Pietsch takes his 159 out of the GP von Deutschland and (right) explains to his mechanics how it was done. (Ludvigsen Library)

lived as he then dropped out with a broken piston, though it was balanced by the retirement of Ascari. When Fangio stopped for fuel, Villoresi went into the lead, but his Ferrari was then shunted by a back-marker, breaking the pipes to the rear oil tank, so his race was run. Fangio was in front again, but after his pit stop he found that he only had top gear left. Despite this he was still pulling away from Gonzalez, and to the delight and relief of the Alfa Corse team he won by 1min 13sec, which gave the team the lift they needed before the crucial Gran Premio d'Italia a fortnight later.

A lot of work had been done at Portello.

16 September 1951: Fangio, Farina, Ascari and Gonzalez leave the start line abreast at the beginning of the GP d'Italia at Monza. (Guy Griffiths Collection)

Three 159s had been fitted with the De Dion rear suspension, and these cars also had twin exhaust systems, the top pipe exhausting cylinders 1, 2, 7 and 8, and the lower cylinders 3, 4, 5 and 6. Instead of the usual huge trumpet-shaped air intake under the bonnet, as before, the superchargers were fed with air from the vent on top of the scuttle, which had previously cooled the driver. Larger front brakes were fitted and the tail of the body was reshaped again.

The team went to Monza well before the race for testing, and during a practice refuelling stop one of the cars caught fire and Sanesi was burned so badly that he was unfit to race, so de Graffenreid was brought in at the last moment and given an earlier 159. As an encouragement Fangio and

Farina were marginally quicker in practice than Ascari and Gonzalez. When the race started, Fangio led for three laps but then Ascari moved ahead. Fangio was not giving up and was leading again on lap eight, but it did not last and when he came in on lap 14 to change tyres a front one burst as he pulled up at his pit. Supercharger bothers had put de Graffenreid out after only a lap, and Farina had gone with oiling problems on lap six, so once again Fangio was holding the fort – but it was all over, as the tyre stop had left Ascari well in front and gaining all the time. Fangio was back in fifth place, but he caught Bonetto and Villoresi only to slow as his engine kept cutting out; he gradually dropped back and stopped for good at half distance with a broken piston.

Meanwhile Farina had taken over Bonetto's car when it was refuelled and he now began a demon drive. He caught Villoresi to take third place and began to close on Gonzalez, then had to stop for fuel again – his rear tank had split and fuel was leaking away. He was eating into Gonzalez's lead once more when he coasted into the pits on lap 70 with a dry tank. Again fuel was poured in and he set off in pursuit, with the fuel visibly pouring out. Ascari completed the 80 laps to the acclaim of the huge crowd, followed in by Gonzalez, while Farina, still gushing fuel, came home third a lap behind. Despite all their efforts with the modified cars, the team had been beaten again, and it seemed that there were no more shots in the locker.

After Monza the World Championship position had changed considerably: Fangio still led with 27 points, but Ascari had 25,

28 October 1951: Early morning practice for the GP de España at Barcelona. There are two No 20 159s, and Farina is about to be pushed off in one of them. (Corrado Millanta)

Gonzalez 20 and Farina 17, and there was still one round to go at Barcelona. On Saturday 29 September Farina was in England at the Goodwood circuit where he ran in the Goodwood Trophy, a 15-lap, 35-mile (56km) Formula 1 race. He took a 158, which the press, looking at the bulk-head plate, called a 159. The field, apart from Parnell's Thinwall Ferrari, was comprised of British amateurs who were unlikely to offer much opposition. Parnell led for a lap then Farina passed him on the outside of a corner and went on to win by 5 seconds. Remarkably, Farina also drove in a five-lap handicap, a peculiarly British institution, where the 158 started from scratch and came through the field to win.

The teams came to Barcelona for the Gran Premio de España on 28 October, run on the Pedralbes circuit through the suburbs of the city and using the Avenida del General Franco, known to the locals as 'el Diagonal', as the main straight. This enabled very high speeds to be reached and became a vital factor in the race. Farina, Fangio and Bonetto had the De Dion cars and de Graffenreid was engaged again with the older 159. Ferrari had fitted his four cars with 16-inch rear wheels, according to most reports to get better acceleration, but Taruffi, in his autobiography *Works Driver*, told a different tale. The halfshafts on the 4½-litre Ferraris were weak and it was feared that the long straight and bumpy surface would put undue strain on them with 17-inch wheels.

Ascari dominated practice and led the race at the start, followed by Farina, Fangio and Bonetto; Fangio then moved up to second and found that he was being hit by pieces of tread from Ascari's rear tyres. He took the lead on lap four, then two laps later the whole character of the race changed. Taruffi was in the pits with a

28 October 1951: Fangio on his way to victory at Barcelona in his 159. (Corrado Millanta)

thrown tyre tread, followed on the next lap by Villoresi with the same problem. Two more laps and the tread bogey hit Ascari, so the Ferrari challenge had dissolved in a shower of rubber chunks. Gonzalez was still going, but when the problem hit him, his pit decided that the halfshafts must take their chance and fitted the Ferrari with 17-inch wheels. Gonzalez was then able to go for the rest of the race with no more tyre bothers and the halfshafts survived. Ascari came in again on lap 17, and yet again on lap 28 with thrown treads; he also was then sent on his way with 17-inch wheels.

28 October 1951: The GP de España was last race for the 158/159. Fangio's mechanics run to acclaim him as he wins the race and becomes World Champion. (Corrado Millanta)

November 1951: Fangio poses at Portello in his victorious 159.

While all this was going on, Fangio was motoring away serenely towards the World Championship and was untroubled by Gonzalez, who managed to take second place when Farina stopped for fuel on lap 55. Fangio covered the 70 laps and came down the Avenida del General Franco for the last time to a huge roar of acclamation from the crowd, taking the flag and doing a lap of honour. As he approached the pit Antonio Allesio ran into the road to be the first to greet him; his exultant mechanics, crying with emotion, lifted him out of the cockpit – he was World Champion. Just as sweet, Alfa Romeo had won and the humiliations of the earlier races had been avenged. Instinctively, the motor racing world knew that a glorious chapter of history had closed, and the era of the greatest grand prix car of all time had ended.

Chapter 18

A faint afterglow

THE DECISION THAT ALFA ROMEO would withdraw from grand prix racing at the end of the 1951 season changed the face of motor racing completely, leaving Ferrari as the only front-line runner in grand prix racing. The only likely challenger was BRM, but the car was still being developed and there were already considerable doubts whether it would ever become an effective racing car. The turning point was the Gran Premio del Valentino held in Turin on 6 April 1952. There was a full Ferrari entry and three BRMs should have run, but they did not turn up and the Ferraris had an unchallenged win. Race organisers now realised that BRM could not be relied on, and the Ferrari team against the also-rans was no race at all. Almost immediately organisers announced that their 1952 races would be for Formula 2 cars, offering every prospect of five or six factory teams, including several from the rapidly growing British motor racing industry. Within a few weeks the FIA announced that the World Championship would be run for Formula 2 cars, and a very active and successful season of racing followed. The Formula 2 racers filled the grand prix gap for two seasons and in 1954 a new formula came into force for unsupercharged racing cars of 2½ litres capacity.

Alfa Romeo toyed with the idea of coming into the new 2½-litre formula and designs were prepared for a car, the Tipo 160. This was an extraordinary confection, as the driver sat behind the rear axle in the style of a sling-shot dragster. If the aviation saying 'If it looks right, it is right' was applied to the 160, it was very wrong. The engine was a flat-12 with dimensions of 68mm x 57mm and a capacity of 2483cc. The flat-12 design was to appear again. A new road car, the Giulietta, with a 1300cc engine, was in full production and was to be the backbone of Alfa Romeo output for the rest of the 1950s, with eventually nearly 200,000 being produced. It was generally accepted that the 160 project did not go ahead because Portello was fully occupied with the Giulietta, but it may have been realised that the design was wrong. If Alfa Romeo had raced again and failed, all the powerful goodwill of the 158 years would have evaporated. Two 160 engines were built, but the chassis got no further than the drawing board.

In 1952 and 1953 a sports racing car was developed. Known as the Disco Volante, it began as a 2-litre four-cylinder and was enlarged to a 3-litre six, but even with Fangio as one of the drivers it achieved little success, and at the end of 1953 all special-

1952: A sad and unworthy end of the road: some of the 158/159s were cut up and scrapped. (Ludvigsen Library)

ist racing was discontinued. For the next 15 years the company would rely on sporting variants of the Giulietta and its larger offspring, the 1600cc Giulia, to keep the Portello flag flying in gran turismo and production car events.

The drivers who had achieved such heights for Alfa Romeo enjoyed mixed fortunes in the years after 1951. Fangio went on to greater glories, winning the World Championship in 1954, 1955, 1956 and 1957. He then retired from the sport and became a revered figure whose record has never been equalled. He died in Buenos Aires on 17 July 1995, mourned throughout the world and regarded by many as perhaps the greatest driver of all. Tazio Nuvolari, who might also have laid claim to that title, lingered on after his final disastrous appearance at Silverstone, his health deteriorating, and died at Mantua on 11 August 1953, deeply mourned in Italy and by all motor racing enthusiasts. Giuseppe Farina continued to race for several seasons driving for Ferrari, but never regained the form of his 1950 season. He retired from the sport in 1955 and was killed in a road accident on 30 June 1960 when his Lotus-Cortina skidded on a patch of ice and hit a telegraph pole in the mountains near Chambery, on the way to the French Grand Prix.

Luigi Fagioli signed up with Lancia for sports car races in 1952, but during practice for the Grand Prix de Monaco he crashed a GT Lancia Aurelia on the exit of the tunnel and was thrown out; though his injuries did not seem serious, he died three weeks later on 22 June. Alberto Ascari, who so nearly deprived Fangio of the Drivers' Championship and Alfa Romeo of the final glory in 1951, stayed with Ferrari and went on to be World Champion in 1952 and 1953. In 1954, still with Villoresi, he left Ferrari and joined the new Lancia grand prix team. It was an unsuccessful venture at first, but in 1955 it seemed that the GP Lancia was about to succeed. At Monaco Ascari was poised to take the lead when he crashed on the harbour front and the Lancia, with him in it, went into the harbour; happily he was rescued unhurt.

However, four days later on 26 May he went to Monza to watch practice for the Supercortemaggiore sports car race. Eugenio Castelotti, the third driver in the Lancia grand prix team, was driving a Monza Ferrari and Ascari took it round the circuit to see if he was fit again. After a few laps he went off the road at the Vialone corner where Sivocci and Arcangeli had crashed, the Ferrari overturned and Ascari was thrown out. He died of his injuries on the way to hospital; like his father he was 36 years old when he died.

When Vittorio Jano was summarily dismissed from Portello in 1938 he went to Lancia, where he worked happily designing a line of successful production cars, including the Aurelia. In the early 1950s Lancia decided that it was time to go motor racing properly; so a series of sports racing cars was built and Jano supervised the last of the line, the D24, which won the 1953 Carrera Panamericana in Mexico and the 1954 Mille Miglia. In the Mexican race one of the D24s was driven by Felice Bonetto, who was killed when he went off the road.

After the D24 Jano carried on directing a design team that worked on the Grand Prix Lancia, which would comply with the 1954 2½-litre formula. Jano's team worked hard: in seven months a car was ready for testing. The result was the Lancia D50, a V-8 that was smaller than its contemporaries and superbly constructed. Ascari and Villoresi were engaged as the drivers. The Lancia was fast but brittle when it first appeared at the end of the 1954 season, then at the beginning of 1955 Ascari had two wins in minor grands prix at Turin and Naples, but his death brought the whole Lancia racing programme to a halt. The cost of the D50 GP car had been crippling and Lancia was almost broke, so a deal was arranged, masterminded by Fiat, for the entire D50 project to be handed to Enzo Ferrari. Ferrari's cars were almost unbeatable between 1951 and 1954, but then Mercedes-Benz returned to grand prix racing and once again became almost invincible.

Ferrari had fallen on hard times; his existing cars were outdated, and he was shuffling parts around trying to make a successful car from the existing bits. His position was reminiscent of Alfa Corse in 1937/38; worst of all, there was a paucity of new designs. When Ferrari took over the Lancias they became the Ferrari Tipo 801s. Jano was fired by Lancia in 1954, as it was felt that he was too old to produce any modern forward-thinking designs, and he went to Ferrari with the cars as a consultant and continued their development. His work on the D50s took Ferrari into the first rank again, and with a Lancia-Ferrari Fangio took the 1956 Drivers' Championship.

While he was with Ferrari, Jano played a major part in the preliminary design of the Dino V-6 engine, which became Ferrari's principal racing engine in the late 1950s and into the early 1960s. This engine was always called the Dino after Ferrari's son, who died in 1958. Ferrari himself suggested to the world that Dino had been the designer, but it seems that if that had been the case, Jano must have sat beside the drawing board and guided the pencil. The Dino V-6 was Jano's last project, and in 1965 he retired to Turin. He believed wrongly that he was suffering from cancer and took his own life on 13 March. He was 74.

His career as a designer had lasted for more than 30 years, beginning and ending with championship-winning cars. Modern designers of Formula 1 racing cars are usually only responsible for the chassis, the engines being the work of many people in complex design departments, but with the P2 and the P3 Jano did the whole task, chassis and engine. Thirty years after he had designed the P2, he was still full of fresh concepts and capable of producing a state-of-the-art design in the D50 Lancia.

After the decision was taken that Alfa

Romeo would retire from the grand prix scene at the end of 1951, Gioachino Colombo left Portello and went to join Maserati. In 1937 the Maserati brothers had sold their firm to Count Adolfo Orsi, a rich industrialist from Modena. The firm had moved from Bologna to an Orsi factory in Modena and the brothers stayed on working for the new management until 1947. Alberto Massimimo then took over the design responsibilities, and in 1952 Colombo joined him. The firm built a Formula 2 car, the A6GCM, which after the change in formula at the beginning of 1952 had been catapulted into the front rank as a grand prix contender. It was a 'nearly' car, not quite good enough to challenge the Ferraris, but Colombo breathed on it and by the end of the 1953 season it was making the Ferraris work very hard.

Maserati also had their sights on the new 2½-litre formula, and for this they produced the 250F, one of the all-time great designs and the last flowering of the front-engined racing car. Fangio used it for half the season when he won the 1954 Championship, and for the full season for his last Championship in 1957. Accounts vary as to the extent of Colombo's contribution to the 250F; some authorities credit him with the major part of the engine design, but others give him little or no credit at all for the car. In fairness, he was with Maserati at Modena during the time of its gestation and it is inconceivable that he was not deeply involved with it. By then he had produced two immortal designs in the 158 and the V-12 Ferrari, but like the 158 the 250F was successful so everyone wanted to claim a share in it; quite a lot of vested interests wanted to diminish Colombo's contribution.

The wanderlust was soon upon him again and in 1955 he took up a commission to design a new grand prix Bugatti. Ettore had died in 1947, leaving a firm that was limping along, eking out a living with industrial engineering; an attempt to make cars for the post-war market had faded away. The firm was being run by Ettore's son Roland, helped by Pierre Marco, who had joined Ettore before the 1914–18 War. They decided that a new racing Bugatti conforming to the 2½-litre formula would help to revive the firm's fortunes. It is said that every great designer has a 'lemon', and this was Colombo's with a vengeance. The design had a straight-eight engine with strong superficial similarities to the P3. It was placed transversely behind the driver, and the suspension was also unorthodox, using a De Dion system both at the front and the back. The car was underpowered and handled oddly; and made only one racing appearance at the 1956 Grand Prix de l'ACF at Reims, lasting only for a few laps, after which it was put away and never seen again. That was Colombo's last effort at racing car design, though he did some effective work for the MV-Agusta motor cycle firm. He died on 24 April 1987, leaving two everlasting memorials in the 158 and the first V-12 Ferrari.

When Alfa Romeo withdrew from grand prix racing at the end of 1951, leaving the field to Ferrari, it was probably reasonable to assume that the love/hate passion that had subsisted between Enzo Ferrari and Alfa Romeo for 30 years had burned itself out. This extraordinary relationship, which had been the spur to such great achievements, had dragged so many people into it, either as willing or reluctant participants, but there no longer appeared to be the need for the constant desertions, recruitments and rapprochements between Modena/Maranello and Portello. Such an assumption was wrong, however; there may have been a truce, but the War was not over.

Joining Jano beside Dino Ferrari's drawing board was a young engineer, Andrea (or Guido) Fraschetti, who became deeply involved in the development of the Dino V-6 engine. The engine started life as a 1500cc unit for Formula 2, and when a car was tested on the Modena circuit on 29 September 1957 it was taken round by Fraschetti, but unfortunately he went off the road and was killed when the car overturned. Ferrari now needed a development engineer and at the suggestion of Giotto Bizzarrini, who had come from Portello to become the control and testing manager at Maranello, Carlo Chiti was engaged.

Chiti, then 32 years old, was a graduate of Pisa University with a degree in aeronautical engineering, and had joined Portello in 1952, working in the special experimental section. Balding and portly, he seemed older than his years, but he had new ideas and wanted to work on racing designs. Chiti set to work on the 1500cc Dino V-6; working quickly, by the beginning of the 1958 season it had been enlarged to a full 2½-litre Formula 1 contender. It ran well, winning races and giving Mike Hawthorn the 1958 World Championship. The original Dino engine had the cylinders in a vee of 65 degrees, but in 1960 it was redesigned by Chiti as a 120-degree unit. Chiti's greatest contribution at Maranello was to persuade Enzo Ferrari that he should abandon the front-engined grand prix car and follow the lead of the British manufacturers by putting the engine behind the driver. It took two years before Ferrari accepted the inevitability of Chiti's view, and the first rear-engined Ferrari appeared in 1960. In 1961 the grand prix formula changed to 1500cc unsupercharged, and the Ferraris now had the engine at the back of a Chiti-designed chassis. It was a good year and Ferrari took the Constructors' Championship, while Phil Hill was World Champion.

Although Chiti had taken Ferrari to the top again, he was not finding life at Maranello congenial. Enzo Ferrari seemed to delight in fostering what management consultants call 'creative tension', setting everyone at each other's throats and hoping that constructive ideas would come from it. By the end of 1961 Chiti had endured enough; in a mass walk-out of senior Ferrari staff he left accompanied by Romolo Tavoni, the team manager, and Bizzarrini. The trio joined a new venture, Società per

Azioni Automobili Turismo Sport Serenissima, which had been established at Bologna by two rich men, Count Giovanni Volpi, who had already been racing Porsches and Maseratis under the Scuderia Serenissima banner, and the Bolivian tin heir, Jaime Ortiz Patino. The first aim was to build a grand prix team, to be followed by a series of exotic road cars, in order to offer a direct challenge to Ferrari. Volpi soon left and the project then became known as Automobili Turismo e Sport, or ATS for short. Chiti designed the grand prix ATS with a V-8 engine and a woefully inferior chassis, inadequate both in design and construction. The ATS raced during the 1963 season and was a disaster; it reappeared once in 1964, but was still completely ineffective. As well as the Formula 1 car, Chiti was busy working on an ATS gran turismo coupé with a 3-litre four-cam V-8 engine, but the whole project was doomed and Volpi reappeared to set up a new concern to market the modified road car as the Serenissima.

In 1962 Chiti joined forces with a friend, Ludovico Chizzola, and formed Delta Auto at Udine, north-east of Venice, with a capital of 1 million lire, to specialise in the tuning and development of the production Alfa Romeos for competition. This firm was immediately adopted by Portello as a competition department and the entries in gran turismo and touring car races soon became recognised as official entries in all but name. The relationship was akin to that which had subsisted with Scuderia Ferrari 30 years earlier. When the Giulia, the 1600cc replacement for the Giulietta, was announced in 1963, immediately the prototype GTZ (Giulia Tubolare Zagato) model was produced at Udine, which, when it went into limited production, was near unbeatable in the 1600cc GT class.

When the ATS project collapsed, Chiti turned all his energies to the Udine concern, and in December 1964 the firm was reformed under a new name, Autodelta, with direct Alfa Romeo sponsor-ship and a capital of 5 million lire. The small factory was moved from Udine to Settimo Milanese, in the suburbs of Milan. Autodelta was still nominally an independent concern and there was a deliberate decision not to bring it within the main factory, where the racing staff would have been bound by union rules and their working hours would have been restricted.

In 1960 Giuseppe Luraghi had become president of Alfa Romeo, and on his appointment he realised that if the company was to be an effective force in car manufacture, a new and completely modern factory was needed. Portello, in the middle of urban Milan, could not be expanded, so a site was chosen at Arese 10 miles (16km) north of Milan and work began at once. A factory of 2.5 million square metres was completed by the end of 1962 and production began in the middle of 1963, which coincided with the introduction of the Giulia. Portello was kept going and now became the centre for engine production, the finished units being transported to Arese.

The desire to get back into the major divisions of motor racing had never been extinguished at Alfa Romeo, and in 1966 the urge could be contained no longer. Autodelta was absorbed into Alfa Romeo and Chiti was appointed as the director of operations. The decision was made that Alfa Romeo would race in sports car events, where success against Ferrari, Porsche and the French Matra would probably have a greater influence on production car sales than the ultimate glory of Formula 1. There was another reason for favouring the sports racers: when Chiti left ATS he took with him, in his mind if not on paper, his designs of the gran turismo ATS engine.

Chiti produced a sports racing car, the Tipo 33/2, with an engine that had a strong family resemblance to the ATS. It had a four-cam 1995cc 90-degree V-8 engine with dimensions of 78mm x 52.2mm, the camshafts being chain-driven from the rear of the engine. There were two valves per cylinder, and the engine developed 270bhp at 9600rpm. The chassis was typical state-of-the-art with a tubular frame and coil spring suspension all round. With the 33/2 Alfa Romeo entered the lists again for the 1967 season and soon found that there was a long hill to climb once more; the opposition was good and the 33/2 was not fast enough.

Meanwhile, Chiti breathed on the design again and the stroke was increased to 64.4mm, giving a capacity of 2462cc and taking the output up to 315bhp. In the 1968 season things began to improve, and though the cars were still not fast enough to win, they gained several creditable places and were also reasonably reliable. Chiti went back to the drawing board and for the 1969 season gave the engine a major redesign; the bore was increased to 86mm, though the stroke remained at 64.4mm, and it was fitted with new four-valve cylinder heads. The capacity was now 2993cc and the output was 400bhp at 9000rpm. The 33 should now have been well in the running, but it was a disastrous season, beginning in March with a tragedy when the Belgian driver Lucien Bianchi was killed testing a T33 at Le Mans. The cars were consistently unreliable and the season ended without any worthwhile results.

The lure of grand prix racing was always nagging at the Alfa Romeo management and an opportunity arose to re-enter the sport in a tentative manner. During the 1960s a full series of races had developed in Australia and New Zealand, becoming known as the Tasman series. These took place during the summer of the southern hemisphere and gave an opportunity for the European drivers, and particularly the British, to keep their hands in during the northern winter. The Tasman races gradually overtook the South American Temporada in importance, but had one peculiarity. They had begun during the life of the 2½-litre grand prix formula, and when this was revised to 1½ litres in 1961 the change was ignored, which gave a fresh lease of life to several obsolete grand prix cars. In 1966 the grand prix formula was enlarged to 3 litres, and again the alteration was ignored in the Antipodes. The races were sufficiently important for the major grand prix teams, including Ferrari, to reduce their engines by 500cc in order to qualify for the series.

In the years since Alfa Romeo had withdrawn from the sport in 1951, grand prix racing had seen dramatic changes. In the late 1950s the British manufacturers had begun to dominate the sport, and the only non-British manufacturer who had offered any opposition had been Ferrari. Coupled with the rise of the British manufacturers had been the rise of the drivers from Britain and the British Commonwealth. Since Fangio retired in 1957, apart from Phil Hill's success in 1961 the World Championship had been the exclusive fiefdom of the British and Commonwealth drivers. The British manufacturers had also led a technical revolution in putting the engine behind the driver and had also changed the nature of the construction of grand prix cars. The British recipe for success was to build a technically advanced chassis and put in it an engine made by a specialist manufacturer. Only Ferrari and BRM were still building the whole car, both chassis and engine, while the rest were deprecatingly described by Enzo Ferrari as 'Assemblatores', making what some commentators called the 'standard British kit car'.

Despite this title, the kit cars were dominating the sport, and the world's major manufacturers were also now taking a strong interest in the sport. Ford had realised the publicity to be gained through racing success and had begun by building sports racing cars that dominated the Le Mans 24-hour race; they had gone on to commission Cosworth, a British specialist tuning firm, to build a Ford grand prix engine, which Ford then supplied to chosen 'kit' manufacturers. The Ford aspect of the victories achieved with these Ford

Cosworth engines was then heavily publicised. It must have occurred to the management of Alfa Romeo that if Ford could do it, so perhaps could they.

Alex Mildren, a successful motor dealer in Canberra, had the Australian agency for Alfa Romeo. Mildren had been an active racing driver for many years, and although he had retired from the sport he still had a keen interest as a racing owner and entrant. During the summer of 1967 he approached Alfa Romeo and suggested that the 2462cc T33 engine, which Chiti had just developed, would be an excellent power plant for the Tasman series. He was supplied with two engines, which reached Australia in September or October; it is not known whether they were loaned or sold to him, but Autodelta announced that the engine would be available to suitable purchasers for £4,300, or £37,000 at today's prices. One of the engines, with Lucas fuel injection, was bench-tested in Australia and developed 285bhp. The disparity with the 315bhp quoted by the factory is puzzling, but dynamometers are variable creatures and the difference may lie in the setting and operation of the particular brake.

To house the T33 engine Mildren bought a new Formula 2 BT23D Brabham, which took the engine, mated to a British Hewland gearbox; to drive the car he engaged Frank Gardner. After Jack Brabham, the 1959, 1960 and 1966 World Champion, Gardner was probably the best driver in Australia at that time, with considerable experience in grands prix, sports cars and touring cars. While not an 'ace', he was recognised as a tough journeyman driver who could make the top drivers work hard. The first outing for the Brabham-Alfa was in the Hordern Trophy on the Warwick Farm Circuit at Sydney on 3 December 1967 and Gardner ran away with the race, winning easily. This was a national race and the Brabham-Alfa was taken to New Zealand for the New Zealand Grand Prix on 6 January, the first race of the 1968 Tasman series. Gardner went very well and finished second

behind the winning Ferrari. In the next race of the series, the Levin Grand Prix, Gardner led for a while but spun off and the car was too badly damaged to continue.

After this race came another change that was to affect the whole of motor racing and was to have as great an effect on grand prix racing as anything in the previous 60 years of the sport. The FIA decided that commercial sponsors would be permitted to have their advertising decals displayed on the cars they were supporting, thus opening the way to full commercial sponsorship of the sport. In New Zealand the decision had an immediate effect and the Lotus team appeared for the next race, the Lady Wigram Trophy, in the livery of their sponsor, the John Player tobacco company. In this newly sponsored world mechanical bothers prevented Gardner from finishing the race as the T33 blew a head gasket. Things improved for the Teretonga International, the final New Zealand round of the series, and Gardner came third behind the New Zealand driver Bruce McLaren, who was now making his own grand prix cars, and the Lotus-Ford Cosworth of Jim Clark, the 1963 and 1965 World Champion, so the T33 engine was showing that it could live in exalted company.

When the series moved to the Australian circuits Gardner had an unhappy start. In the first race at Surfers' Paradise, the T33 engine was down on power in practice and Gardner retired in the race with overheating. During the next week Mildren bench-tested the engine and found that it was lacking 75bhp, so the spare engine was put in the car for the next round at Warwick Farm. Throughout the race Gardner was keeping up with three World champions, Clark, Graham Hill and Denny Hulme, but right at the end of the race the engine made nasty noises and he had to retire. When Mildren's mechanics stripped it after the race they found a broken con rod and a damaged crank caused by a failed oil seal. The first engine, quickly rebuilt, now went back into the car and there was an urgent call to Autodelta for spares.

The scene then moved to Melbourne for the major race, the Australian Grand Prix. This time the T33 performed well and Gardner battled with Hill for third place all the way, losing it by 0.2 second. The final round of the Tasman series was on the Longford circuit in Tasmania. The race was run in heavy rain and was reduced in length; Gardner held second place until the last corner of the last lap when Pedro Rodriguez's BRM nipped past him to snatch the place by 0.6 second. The drivers had been competing throughout the series for the Tasman Championship, and Gardner was placed fourth, tying with Graham Hill.

At the beginning of the British surge to the top of grand prix racing the Cooper company had been the foremost of the British manufacturers, establishing the trend for putting the engine behind the driver and winning the World Constructors' title in 1959 and 1960. By the mid-1960s Cooper had slipped back to being an also-ran and the company had been bought by the Chipstead Group, a London motor distributor that had an Alfa Romeo agency. The results of the Brabham-Alfa in the Tasman series had been noticed and there were reports that a full 3-litre T33 engine would become available during 1968. Chipstead suggested that if the 3-litre engine was supplied to Cooper, a Cooper-Alfa could be a winning combination, and as a preliminary move Autodelta supplied a 2468cc engine to Cooper, which was fitted into a modified Cooper T86C and tested at Silverstone by Lucien Bianchi. Cooper waited throughout the 1968 season for a full 3-litre engine, but Autodelta was too concerned with the problems presented by the development of the T33 and had slowed down work on the larger engine, which did not appear until the end of the year. Cooper withdrew quietly from grand prix racing at the end of the 1968 season, so the project went no further.

For the 1969 Tasman series Alex Mildren decided that he would build his own car, so a Mildren was put together that owed a lot to the Brabham of a year before. It used the T33 engine again and with this very well-engineered and finished car Gardner was at the first race of the series, the New Zealand Grand Prix at Pukekohe on 4 January. Unfortunately as the cars lined up on the grid the fuel pump failed, and by the time this had been replaced Gardner had lost 15 laps. The next race was a week later at Levin, and this time things went much better; Gardner was third, so he had hopes of achieving even more when the third race, the Lady Wigram Trophy, was held at Christchurch. Fate decreed otherwise, however, and the Mildren was pushed off by another car on the first corner of the race and went no further. The final round in New Zealand was at Teretonga, and here Gardner held third place for half the race, ahead of Graham Hill's Lotus, but the engine overheated and he dropped back to fourth at the finish.

The teams then travelled across the Tasman Sea for the Australian races. The first was the Australian Grand Prix at Lakeside in Queensland, and for this Alex Mildren made a big effort; as well as Gardner in the Mildren, he entered Kevin Bartlett, the Australian national champion, with the 1968 Brabham-Alfa, and built another Mildren with a racing specification Giulia engine for a local driver, Max Stewart. Gardner disputed third place with Jochen Rindt's Lotus until half distance when an oil pipe broke and he was out; the Brabham-Alfa blew a head gasket, so the Giulia car was the only finisher in sixth place. Things looked up for the race at Warwick Farm, the Sydney circuit; Autodelta had promised Mildren that he would have a special four-valve 2468cc engine, but *Autosport* commented that this engine was taking as long to appear as that promised to Cooper, so Gardner had to make do with the well-used earlier unit. The race was run in a downpour, but

despite this and the handicap of the older engine, he came a good third and was followed home by Bartlett in fourth place with the Brabham-Alfa. Gardner had found that the engine was down on revs at Warwick Farm and new valve springs came from Milan for the last race of the series at Sandown Park, Melbourne. The Mildren ran in a steady fourth place throughout the race, finishing behind Jack Brabham and ahead of Graham Hill; this result gave Gardner sixth place in the Tasman Championship, two points behind Hill.

The results in the Tasman series must have given a lot of encouragement to Autodelta and the Arese management. The T33 had been keeping up with the Cosworth Fords, in state-of-the-art chassis and driven by World Champions. With a top-rank driver in a chassis designed for the engine, it was not a flight of fancy to believe that Alfa Romeo could be as big a force in racing as Ford – the old days could return.

In the late autumn of 1969 the British press reported that the British manufacturer Lola would be building a Formula 1 car for the 1970 season using a T33 engine, with Andrea de Adamich as the driver. In 1967 de Adamich had driven for Ferrari in Formula 1 but without success, and in 1968 and 1969 he had been the mainstay of the Autodelta T33 team in sports car races. However, either the negotiations with Lola fell through or the reporters had got it wrong. The reports were right in one respect, though – a full 3-litre T33 engine was being put into a grand prix car during the winter of 1969/70, but it was at the Colnbrook factory of McLaren. A deal had been struck between Bruce McLaren and Autodelta that a T33 engine would be provided and fitted to a McLaren chassis, the car would be raced by McLaren as a works entry, and de Adamich would be the driver. Unfortunately for de Adamich, he was not getting the latest M14 chassis that McLaren himself and Denny Hulme, the 1967 World Champion, would be using; he had to make do with an unused 1969 M7

2 February 1969: Frank Gardner contesting the Australian GP in the Mildren-Alfa at Lakeside. (LAT)

monocoque chassis that was at the Colnbrook factory.

To meet the demands of grand prix racing Chiti had done some more development work on the T33 engine. The camshafts were now driven by gears and the power was increased to 430bhp at 10,500rpm, about 10bhp down on the engine that Cosworth was supplying to its customers, though some of the British teams that were especially favoured by Ford were getting more powerful engines. An important factor that would be significant was that the T33 was a 'peaky' engine and lacked the low-down torque of the Cosworth.

The car was not ready for the first rounds of the World Championship in South Africa and Spain. It was entered for the Silverstone International Trophy on 26 April, but sat in the paddock unused, as de Adamich had been busy at Monza the previous day driving a T33 in the 1000km sports car race. De Adamich had shared the T33 at Monza with the British driver Piers Courage; Courage was also entered at Silverstone and he flew back overnight, but de Adamich remained in Italy.

The next entry for the car was at the Grand Prix de Monaco on 10 May. The organisers would only accept 16 starters; ten seeded drivers were guaranteed a start, but the second- and third-string drivers were required to qualify in a special session at the end of practice. De Adamich tried hard in the McLaren-Alfa, painted in the distinctive orange colour of the McLaren team, but the engine's lack of torque was a particular handicap in the streets of Monte Carlo and he was just bumped off the grid, though his time was better than some of the seeded entries.

The next event for the car should have been the Grand Prix de Belgique at Spa on 7 June, but on the Tuesday before the race Bruce McLaren was testing a sports racing CanAm McLaren at Goodwood when he went off the road and was killed. His death shattered the team and the cars were withdrawn from the Spa race.

Despite his death, Bruce McLaren's widow and Teddy Mayer, his co-directors in Bruce McLaren Racing Ltd, made the courageous decision that the team would continue to race, so two cars appeared at Zandvoort for the Grote Prijs van Nederland on 21 June. The T33 engine was installed in a current M14 chassis, but despite this de Adamich did not start; the organisers decreed that the four slowest cars in practice would be excluded. Though he equalled the time of the American Dan Gurney, who had been brought into the team to replace McLaren, Gurney took the last available place on the grid.

Autodelta would probably have been taking a jaundiced view of the career of the McLaren-Alfa had their concerns not been almost certainly wholly focused on the dismal showing of the T33-3s in the World Sports Car Championship. There was little time to ponder on the Formula 1 scene, though no doubt when de Adamich met up with the Autodelta team in sports car races he was able to tell the full tale of woe. There was a slight improvement at the Grand Prix de France, which was held on the demanding Charade circuit at Clermont Ferrand, a miniature version of the Nürburgring. One of the McLaren team M14s had been damaged in a crash at Zandvoort, so the M14 that de Adamich used in Holland was now appropriated and fitted with a Cosworth-Ford engine while the T33 engine was put back into the earlier M7. Despite this, de Adamich had five cars behind him on the starting grid, but on the opening lap he suffered a severe setback when a water pipe broke away on the chassis and he had a long stop on the circuit to make a temporary repair that would get him back to the pits. There the repairs took a long time, and once he was going again he had to make several stops to add water. He finished the race but was 15th and last, having covered only 29 of the 38 laps.

At Brands Hatch on 19 July, in the British Grand Prix, de Adamich should have had six cars behind him on the grid, but as the cars were pushed out of the paddock before the start the rubber bag inside one of the fuel tanks split and there was no time to repair it before the race began. The dismal tale continued at the Grösser Preis von Deutschland; this should have been run on the Nürburgring, but the Grand Prix Drivers' Association was unhappy about the safety arrangements, and at short notice the race was transferred to Hockenheim. McLaren had built another M14, so the T33 engine was back in the earlier M14 again, but this made little difference to the outcome. On the shorter circuit at Hockenheim the entry was oversubscribed and the lesser lights had to qualify; four were unlucky and de Adamich was among them.

The grand prix circus moved on to Austria to the Österreichring for the Grösser Preis von Österreich on 16 August. The

T33 engine was still in the M14 and Autodelta sent Giovanni Marelli, one of their development engineers, to give de Adamich some support. Marelli had been with Ferrari but had left to join Chiti. Perhaps his presence made a difference, but de Adamich went well in practice and was in the middle of the grid. However, it was all to no avail, as he made a bad start and trailed round at the tail of the field gradually picking up places among the stragglers and finishing 12th, three laps behind the winning Ferrari of Jackie Ickx.

Both Autodelta and McLaren pulled out all the stops for the 38th Gran Premio d'Italia at Monza on 6 September. The M14 was produced for de Adamich and the earlier M7 was brought out with a T33 engine for Nanni Galli, who had been working very hard for Autodelta with the T33-3 in sports car races. The organisers said that the fastest 20 cars would qualify for the race, irrespective of the drivers' reputations and records, and practice became a flat-out blind with cars lapping at over 150mph (240kmh). De Adamich qualified comfortably in 12th place, but Galli was off the pace and was out of the list. Just before the end of the last practice session there was an accident when Jochen Rindt crashed his Lotus 49 and was killed. The Lotus team was consequently withdrawn from the race, which let in some of the cars that had failed to qualify, and Galli moved up the list. Just before the race it seemed that John Surtees, one of the qualifiers, would not be starting, so Galli was told to do a warming-up lap and was about to take his place on the grid when the missing Surtees appeared and the frustrated Galli was directed back to the paddock. To compound the frustration, Surtees retired halfway round the first lap of the race. Once again it all went wrong for de Adamich. He had a long pit stop on the third lap, and the cars with which he had been battling until then went by to finish fourth and fifth; by the time the McLaren was on its way again several laps had been lost, and although it ran on to the end of the race it finished in eighth and last place.

The remaining rounds of the World Championship were on the American continent, and the whole circus was flown out. The first engagement was on the Mont Tremblant-St Jovite circuit, north of Montreal, for the Grand Prix of Canada on 20 September. The McLaren-Alfa was in the middle of the grid after practice, and in the race de Adamich ran as high as eighth place, but was slowed by a stop for fuel and

17 July 1970: De Adamich in the M7D McLaren during practice for the British GP at Brands Hatch. In the race the car failed to start when the fuel tank leaked. (Guy Griffiths)

an excursion off the road. He was keeping up with the two McLaren-Cosworths driven by Denny Hulme and Peter Gethin, but retired with 11 laps to go when the oil pressure disappeared.

The circus now moved south in a huge road convoy to Watkins Glen in the Finger Lakes region of New York State for the United States Grand Prix. Twenty-four cars were permitted to start and the prize money was generous, the winner collecting $100,000 and the 24th-placed driver $6,000. Unfortunately de Adamich did not get any chance of the prize money at all. The car suffered a massive engine blow-up in the first practice session. The engine was replaced and in the second session an oil line broke, but there was much delay while it was mended, then there was an electrical fire so the car did not qualify. That was effectively the end of de Adamich's season; the McLaren team had an engagement at the Gran Premio de Mexico, but the organisers said that they would only accept two cars from the team so the McLaren-Alfa was out.

The attempt to re-enter grand prix racing had been an unmitigated disaster, and the Alfa Romeo/Autodelta management considered that the blame lay with McLaren. While the reliability of the engine was not all it might have been, there had also been disappointing preparation and it seemed that the T33-engined car had always been the poor relation at the Colnbrook factory. It was accepted that de Adamich was not a front-line driver – his forte was long-distance sports car racing – but he had been capable of keeping up with the second-string drivers of the other teams and at times had been as fast as Denny Hulme, the McLaren No 1, so with a top driver the T33 engine would perhaps have been quite near the front. At the end of the season Denis Jenkinson, writing in *Motor Sport*, said, 'I enquired if the McLaren-Alfa had ever been driven by a really fast driver and the answer was negative.' The views of de Adamich must have played a part, and at

the end of the season it was decided that the arrangement with McLaren would be terminated. However, the attempt to gain success in Formula 1 would continue.

At the beginning of the 1970 season the March grand prix team had been established. The appearance of this team was greeted by the motoring press with extraordinary publicity and 'hype', and judging by the massive pre-season interest in the team it should have swept all before it. It had been established by a consortium of drivers, engineers and designers. The main driving force was Max Mosley, who would become the President of the FIA, the designer was Robin Herd, who had previously been with McLaren, and the funding came mainly from STP, the oil additive company. Using a Cosworth-Ford engine and a chassis that was up-to-date but conventional, the March was a classic example of the British grand prix kit car

As an augury of what was expected, a March was bought for Jackie Stewart, the 1969 World Champion, by his sponsor, Ken Tyrrell. At first it was notably successful, winning three of its first four races, but as the 1970 season went on the March slipped, and before the end of the season it was an unspectacular mid-field runner, having been abandoned by the Stewart/Tyrrell combine who went off to build a car of their own.

It was a somewhat chastened and much more realistic March team that prepared for the 1971 season. Herd had designed a new car, the 711, which had a distinctive and unusual body, the work of aerodynamicist Frank Costin, who had been responsible for the body of the successful Vanwall in the late 1950s. During the winter Autodelta made an agreement with March to provide T33 engines for one car of the March team during the 1971 grand prix season; the engines would be provided free of charge and Alfa Romeo would also pay March £20,000. Autodelta reserved the right to nominate the driver; Chiti felt that it should be de Adamich, but Barbini, the Alfa

Romeo marketing director, intervened and decreed that the drives should be alternated between de Adamich and Galli. As their No 1, March had signed up Ronnie Peterson, a Swedish driver who had shown exceptional ability in Formula 3 and had driven a privately entered March in some 1970 Formula 1 races. Another car was built so that it could be hired out to local drivers at each World Championship round. Both cars were fitted with the almost inevitable Cosworth-Ford engine. STP still provided sponsorship and the team was entered as the STP-March, the cars painted in a startling day-glo red.

Peterson and de Adamich went to South Africa for the first World championship at Kyalami on 6 March; de Adamich must have reflected that while the team had changed, everything else seemed as before. The March 711-Alfa Romeo was on the penultimate row of the grid, and during the race it trailed round at the back of the field, overheating badly as the new body failed to provide an effective airflow to the radiators, and finished 13th and last. After the race Costin blamed March for the overheating, saying that his drawings had not been followed.

De Adamich did not go to the next Championship round at Ontario, California, the United States Grand Prix West; though the March was entered for him, but he was otherwise engaged. A few days later he gained the first major win for the Autodelta T33-3 in the BOAC 1000 at Brands Hatch, a round in the Manufacturers' Championship for Sports Cars. He caught up with the grand prix circus again in Barcelona, where the Gran Premio de España was held at the Montjuich circuit, on which Nuvolari had dazzled nearly 40 years before. Sadly, even if the driver had shown Nuvolari's talent, the March would have been no vehicle for such skills; as so often happened with Nuvolari, it retired with broken transmission.

On 8 May most of the leading teams were at Silverstone for the International Trophy, but de Adamich was not there as he was working hard in Sicily practising for the Targa Florio with a T33-3, so Ronnie Peterson took over the March-T33. In practice he went some of the way to answering Denis Jenkinson's question and was fastest in two of the sessions. In his book *March*, Alan Henry says that Peterson found that the engine would pull 10,000rpm on parts of the circuit where the Cosworth would only pull 9600rpm. '"Take it to 10,600," grinned Max. "I can't," replied Ronnie. "It makes a funny noise at around 10,400."'

In the race misfortune struck once more. Peterson had a long pit stop, and when he set off again he crashed badly when the throttle jammed at Becketts corner; the nearside front wheel struck him on the head and he was knocked unconscious, though he recovered quickly and was otherwise unhurt. He had shown that the March-T33 could perhaps be competitive with the right driver.

A week later the Targa Florio was a triumph for Autodelta, the T33-3s finishing first and second. During practice a new car appeared, the T33TT-3, the TT standing for Tubolare Telaio or tubular chassis. Chiti was happy to tell the world that it was a prototype that would take the new flat-12 engine he was developing to replace the T33 V-8.

Nanni Galli had missed the Targa Florio as he was recovering from a wrist injury incurred when he crashed a T33-3 in practice for the Monza 1000km sports car race at the end of April. When he was fit again, it was decided that it was his turn to try the March-T33 and it was entered for him at Monaco on 23 May. It was disappointing, however. He did not qualify in practice, as the car suffered from incurable fuel starvation, but as a consolation on 13 June he

was sent to Hockenheim for a non-Championship Formula 1 race, the Jochen Rindt Memorial Race. Apart from the name it was virtually a full grand prix as all the teams were there. March had been so impressed by Peterson's speed at Silverstone that a new car was produced for him, fitted with a T33 engine, while Galli had his Monaco car. This was fitted with a new engine, but when he blew it up in the first practice session, the old engine went back. Peterson also blew up his T33 engine in the final practice session on race morning, so the Cosworth was fitted again. In the race Galli went very well and came fifth, which was the best result yet for the T33 engine in grand prix events.

The cars were then taken from Hockenheim to Zandvoort for the Grote Prijs van Nederland. In practice Peterson

4 July 1971: Ronnie Peterson (March 711) leads Howden Ganley (BRM) just before the March's engine burst during the GP de France at Paul Ricard. (LAT)

tried the March-T33, but though it was faster than his Cosworth-engined car, he settled for the latter in the race. Galli only lasted for eight laps until he collided with Cevert's Tyrrell and went off the road.

The next Championship round was at Le Castellet, on a bleak sandy plateau in Provence, where the French aperitif manufacturer Paul Ricard had built a circuit that was to make its début as the venue for the Grand Prix de France on 4 July. There had been such a demand for overhauled engines that the Cosworth factory had run into difficulties and some customers did not get fully serviced engines in time for the race. March was a victim of this shortage, so Peterson had no alternative but to race his new chassis with the T33 engine, and keeping him company was de Adamich, who was driving the original March-T33 again. During practice the cars were weighed: Peterson's car scaled 582kg and de Adamich's was heavier at 589kg. In contrast, the rent-a-car 711 March provided for the Spanish driver Soler-Roig, which had a Cosworth engine, was only 558kg, indicating that the T33 engine was providing a built-in handicap of approximately 30kg. In the race it was the usual disaster. Peterson's engine blew up and left an oil slick on which several of the leaders spun, while de Adamich stopped soon after when his engine also burst.

Things were just as bad for the British

Grand Prix at Silverstone two weeks later. The March team put a Cosworth engine back in Peterson's car and Galli was also given a Cosworth-engined car, so only de Adamich was left to soldier on with the March-T33. He was the slowest car in practice and, apart from the first lap, ran in last place throughout the race, spending quite a lot of time in the pits mending a broken throttle linkage; at the end he was 12 laps behind. It was a truly dismal showing, but on the sports car front Alfa Romeo fortunes were much brighter, as a week after Silverstone de Adamich and Peterson won the Watkins Glen 6-Hour race with a T33-3.

The Grösser Preis von Deutschland had gone back to the Nürburgring again, the circuit having been modified to meet the drivers' demands about safety, but this did little to help the cause of the March-T33. Galli had a T33 engine in his car again, but blew it up in practice so a new one was fitted before the race. De Adamich lasted for two laps before the fuel injection stopped injecting, while Galli kept going but finished last, two laps behind. De Adamich must have wanted a break from the March-T33, and though he was entered for the Grösser Preis von Österreich, he did not turn up. Galli was there, but he broke two T33 engines in practice and in the race trailed round at the back of the field; he did, however, finish, with a slight improve-

ment, there being one car behind him.

There was a need for a drastic improvement, and Chiti produced a new engine for the Gran Premio d'Italia at Monza on 5 September. This had a stronger crankcase with only three main bearings instead of the previous five and was installed in the hard-used March for de Adamich. It made very little difference – the car stopped after 33 laps and in last place when the engine expired.

The end of the road had been reached. Autodelta and March were mutually disenchanted and, more to the point, Chiti and his engineers had realised that the T33 was never going to make an effective grand prix engine – it was too heavy and there was a lack of torque in the lower rev range. Attempts to increase the power to compensate for the weight and to improve the low-speed torque had resulted in mechanical disaster. March had hoped to keep the relationship alive in the expectation that the flat-12 engine might be a winning proposition, but it was going to be more than a year before this would be ready to race, and then it would only be available initially for the T33TT-3. At Autodelta the decision was taken immediately after the Monza race that the grand prix experiments with the T33 engine would be abandoned; for 1972 there would be a major effort on the sports car front.

Chapter 19

A flicker among the embers

IT TOOK TIME TO MAKE the flat-12 engine raceworthy. It was known as the 115-12, and was not considered to be ready until the start of the 1973 season. The engine had cast magnesium blocks mounted on an aluminium crankcase with light alloy cylinder heads. Each head carried two camshafts driven by gears from the rear of the engine; there were four valves per cylinder at an included angle of 35 degrees, the crankshaft ran in three main bearings, and there was Lucas fuel injection and electronic ignition. The dimensions were 77mm x 53.3mm, giving a capacity of 2995cc. It was claimed that the output was 500bhp at 11000rpm with a compression ratio of 11:1.

The 115-12 engine was put into the T33TT chassis, which had been waiting for it for nearly two years. Called the T33TT-12, it missed the early races of the season, but was sent forth to do battle with the rival sports racing Ferraris and Porsches in the World Championship for Manufacturers in the Targa Florio; a certain win was lost when de Adamich went off the road while in the lead. The rest of the 1973 season was frustrating, the cars being eliminated with a series of minor faults.

The 1974 season began with a most encouraging result as the cars scored a 1–2–3 in the Monza 1000km race, but then it all fell apart; a number of places were picked up during the rest of the season, but there were no more victories. In the autumn of 1974 it seemed that Alfa Romeo had decided to give up; the eight-

year development programme of the T33 had not produced the expected successes and the dividends in technical development and publicity had not been sufficient to justify the continuing expense. Car sales all over the world had fallen, and for Alfa Romeo there was an additional problem. A new model, the Alfasud, had been developed; a complete break with the past, it was aimed at the upper end of the small car market and was being built with large

government subsidies in a huge new factory at Naples. However, as Alexandre Darracq had found nearly 70 years before, that location had problems of its own, with constant delays in production and difficulties with quality control.

It was in this unhappy and rather unpropitious climate that the seeds of the next foray into grand prix racing were sown. After reaching an apogee with two Constructors' World Championships in

1975: The Tipo 115-12 engine supplied to Brabham.

1966 and 1967, the Brabham team had gradually waned and slid back into the ranks of the mid-field runners. Jack Brabham, who had retired from active racing at the end of the 1970 season, had been losing interest in the team and at the end of the 1971 season Motor Racing Developments, the holding company of the Brabham team, was sold to Bernie Ecclestone. At that time Ecclestone was relatively unknown in the sport; he had run a motor cycle dealership at Bexleyheath in South London, raced a 500cc Cooper in the early 1950s, and had then entered an obsolete Connaught in some non-Championship Formula 1 races. Subsequently his motor trade ventures expanded and he made some successful property deals, then he became the racing manager of Jochen Rindt, a venture that ended with Rindt's death in 1970.

When he bought the Brabham team it is probably fair to say that Ecclestone brought a new ethos to grand prix racing. Since Alfa Romeo had withdrawn in 1951, it had been a sport from which the people involved had made a living; this was certainly the case with teams such as Cooper and Lotus, while for Ferrari it was an all-embracing way of life. Ecclestone saw it the other way: it was a business with a sporting element, and the attitude he brought to grand prix racing was to change it totally and fundamentally and would make him the supreme figure in motor racing within the next 20 years.

The Brabham team, like most of its contemporaries, was using the Cosworth Ford DFV, and it continued with this unit in 1972 and 1973. The existing chassis were not as good as the best of the rivals, and the work of designing new cars was entrusted to Gordon Murray, who had been working as assistant to Ralph Bellamy, brought in from McLaren by Ecclestone to act as a stop-gap designer. Bellamy soon left to join Lotus, and while Murray set to work on radical new designs, Ecclestone pondered on the need for another engine that would get the team away from the need to rely on Cosworth and the handicap of having an equal power output to rival teams.

Although it had not been as successful as Alfa Romeo had hoped, Ecclestone realised that the 115-12 engine had potential, and in the lighter format of a grand prix car it could be a potential winner. There was also another attraction: he was paying for the Cosworth DFV engines, but if a suitable deal could be struck he could get a source of free engines. In June 1974 he began negotiations with Autodelta and in the autumn of that year a three-cornered deal was arranged; Ecclestone persuaded Count Rossi di Montelera, whose aperitif firm Martini & Rossi was now the principal sponsor of the Brabham team, to give full support to the project, and even better from Ecclestone's point of view, the engines would be supplied free of charge.

A 115-12 engine was supplied to Brabham, and at the New Haw works, near the old Brooklands track, Murray began working on a new chassis design, the BT45, to take it. The 115-12 was larger than the DFV, 11 inches (28cm) longer and 3 inches (7.6cm) wider; it was also 88lb (44kg) heavier. Consumption figures supplied by Autodelta showed that it was thirstier than the DFV, so Murray had to provide for up to 12 gallons (55 litres) of additional tankage. On the credit side, Autodelta had given the engine larger inlet and exhaust valves, and the camshafts had more lift, while the compression ratio had been raised to 11.5:1; the result was an output of 520bhp at 12,000rpm and a good torque curve.

While Murray worked at his drawing board, the situation at Autodelta was critical. The results in 1974 had been so disappointing that the Alfa Romeo management had decided that all racing activity would stop and Autodelta would be closed down. Chiti argued and pleaded, pointing out that a closure would mean the loss of all the research and development experience in the Settimo Milanese works, arguing also that success was only just around the corner. Another season's racing could give results that would justify all the work his team had done and all the money that had been spent. The board agreed that Autodelta should stay, but working only on production cars; then, after much persuasion, they made a further concession, that the T33 venture could continue for another season provided the bills were paid by commercial sponsors.

Chiti soon found support from drinks-manufacturer Campari and German sausage-maker Redlefsen, while the rest of the bill was picked up by the former German driver Willi Kauhsen, who was the proprietor of a large haulage business and became the entrant of the cars. After early setbacks, the T33TT-12 swept home to seven consecutive wins in the World Championship for Manufacturers, and Alfa Romeo was duly declared the Champion for 1975. The result must have been received with relief by Ecclestone and Murray as it meant that Alfa Romeo participation in motor racing was assured in 1976 and the dangers of their engine supply drying up were averted.

When the Arese plant was constructed, a new test track was also built at Balocco, near Vercelli, midway between Milan and Turin. Among the normal testing facilities was an artificial road circuit with corners designed with the identical characteristics of the Curva Grande, Lesmo and Parabolica at Monza, and a corner at the Dutch circuit, Zandvoort. The first completed BT45 was taken to Balocco in October 1975 and tested by the two drivers of the Brabham team, the Brazilian Carlos Pace and the Argentinian Carlos Reutemann. Reutemann was a competent and effective driver, having won four World Championship rounds with Brabham in 1974 and 1975, while Pace had won one grande épreuve in 1975, so there was no lack of ability in the team.

Both drivers drove the car when it was shown to the press in November and it made a favourable impression. Denis Jenkinson commented in *Motor Sport*: '[It] makes a delightful new noise, a really harsh and brutal sound in contrast to the music of the Ferrari.' As a link with the past the Tipo 512 was brought out of the Arese museum and put on show at the demonstration. Jenks went on to say: 'Talking to the Brabham people, you felt they had designed and built a car round the Alfa Romeo engine. Talking to the Alfa Romeo people, you felt that they had installed one of their engines in a Brabham car! The Martini people were just smiling pleasantly and hoping the alliance would work.'

The BT45 had the usual monocoque hull, but it was extended to provide mounting points for the engine, which was attached from the cylinder heads. The rear extensions of the monocoque gave space for the extra fuel tankage, but the extensions worried Murray who realised that it would not be possible to change plugs without removing the engine. He raised the matter with Chiti who airily assured him that the engines never needed a plug change. Chiti was right – despite all the other problems that were to be experienced with the 115-12, the need to change the plugs was very rare. Like all the other British cars it had a Hewland gearbox, and the suspension, with coil spring/damper units at the front and rear, followed current Formula 1 practice. What no one mentioned at the time was a problem that Murray had not been able to overcome: the 115-12 was a very heavy engine, weighing 385lb (175kg). Brabham was about to find what March had discovered six years earlier, that Alfa Romeo engines had a built-in weight handicap. To remind the driver where the engine had come from, there was an Alfa Romeo badge in the centre of the steering wheel.

The 1976 Formula 1 World Championship season began in South America, but the teams were frustrated at the first race, in Buenos Aires, which was cancelled at the last minute, a victim of cash shortage and political unrest. The teams did get a race on 25 January in the Gran Premio do Brasil, on the Interlagos circuit. The BT45s were finished fittingly in an all-red livery, but to the casual observer it must have seemed that Brabham had taken on the mantle worn uncomfortably by McLaren and March a few years before. In practice both cars banged and popped round the circuit, while the mechanics kept swapping Lucas and SPICA fuel injection units; the hull was also flexing and causing gear change problems. Pace and Reutemann qualified in the middle of the field and made little impact on the race, Pace finishing 10th and Reutemann running out of fuel with three laps to go, having risen no higher than seventh.

The teams then crossed the South Atlantic for the South African Grand Prix on 6 March, but the voyage did little for the Brabham team. Once again both cars qualified in mid-field, during the race blew out all their engine lubricant over the track and the opposition, and were out within 20 laps. The weight problem was now being recognised; Murray used some titanium in the monocoque hulls and there was an increased amount of magnesium in the engines.

Also there was already trouble in the team. Reutemann, who would have preferred the team to stay with the Cosworth engine, had not been enthusiastic about the car when he first drove it; the initial failures confirmed his view that the team had a lemon. The power output of the individual engines differed considerably. Chiti said, 'There was the "Supertigre", the "Tigre", the "Leone", and the least powerful we jokingly called "Bernie".' It was an unsatisfactory situation that would be unfamiliar to Cosworth's customers, who would know that every engine would have a guaranteed output.

When the teams returned to Europe, one car was entered for Pace in the Race of Champions at Brands Hatch. Now fitted with SPICA fuel injection, it ran true to a developing form and was out after seven laps with a defective fuel pump. The whole grand prix circus was then flown out to California for the US Grand Prix West, which was run through the streets of Long Beach on 28 March. A new car, the BT45/3,

Carlos Pace. (LAT)

was built with a revised monocoque that saved 10kg, and Pace tried it in practice. In the race he went back to his original car, but had a dismal time as the brakes wore out and he finished ninth. That was a bit better than Reutemann who was bounced out of the race on the first corner by Vittorio Brambilla's March. Brambilla was known by his fellow drivers as 'Gorilla', a title that he sometimes lived up to.

Back in Europe, Pace was sent to Silverstone for the non-Championship International Trophy. In practice the engine burst after Pace missed gear changes through a gearbox defect. A new engine was flown from Milan before the race, but the car trundled home in ninth place. Denis Jenkinson said, 'It sounds nice and looks a fascinating car but it just doesn't go.'

Things had not worked out as Ecclestone had expected, and it was a slightly dispirited team that arrived at Jarama, outside Madrid, for the Gran Premio de España. In

28 March 1976: Carlos Pace (Brabham BT45) leads Andretti (Parnelli) and Mass (McLaren) in the US GP West at Long Beach. (LAT)

practice Pace broke an engine in the new car, while Reutemann bent his car badly against a post when he went off the road, so he used the spare car in the race. On the second day of practice the technical commission of the CSI, which felt that cars were going too fast, decided that there should be some instant changes in the Formula 1 rules. A number of cars had been using exaggeratedly high air-collecting boxes and these were banned; there were also changes to the rear aerofoils and to the chassis structure in front of the driver. The air box changes principally affected the Cosworth-engined cars; the 115-12s in the Brabhams had smaller boxes on each side of the chassis. Whether the changes made much difference is arguable, but in the race the BT45s put on a much more encouraging performance. Reutemann and Pace kept going steadily, not quick enough to keep up

with the leaders but gradually picking up places to finish fourth and sixth. After the race James Hunt's winning McLaren was disqualified for having the wrong dimensions, so Reutemann moved up to third, only to drop back to fourth place when Hunt was reinstated two months later.

However, any hopes that fortunes were improving were dashed in Belgium at the Grand Prix de Belgique at the Zolder circuit on 16 May. Pace wrecked BT45/3 in practice, while in the race Reutemann stopped after 18 laps with no oil pressure. Pace, driving one of the original BT45s, lasted for 59 laps, then retired with electrical problems.

Although the transmission had been functioning without any dramas, it was decided at Autodelta that an unpromising situation might be redeemed by fitting a new gearbox, so a new six-speed cluster was made up to fit inside the Hewland casing. This was

fitted to Pace's repaired BT45/3 for the Grand Prix de Monaco on 23 May, and he trundled round the streets of Monte Carlo to finish eighth, Reutemann having gone out on the first lap after a collision. The team was getting an unfortunate reputation. In *Motor Sport* Jenks commented, 'At every race there seem to be more Alfa Romeo men than before, fussing around the Brabham-Alfa Romeos, though we ought to call them Ecclestone-Alfa Romeos for Jack Brabham would surely never have got himself involved with such a dead-loss engine.'

For the next grande épreuve, in Sweden, Carlo Chiti appeared, but probably wished he had stayed away. In practice the new gears were causing problems, having distorted the end cover of the box in Reutemann's car. While this was being put right, Pace's engine blew out all its oil, but he seemed to get little sympathy from Chiti. Once the gearbox was working again, Reutemann practised, but went off the road and hurt both the car and his hand. In the race he stopped with a sick engine, but had already found that it was hard to drive with his damaged hand; Pace kept going and came eighth.

The season continued to be a series of ups and downs. Murray worked hard for the Grand Prix de France at Le Castellet, and there were extensive modifications to the BT45s. The front suspension was modified, deep skirts were fitted round the chassis to give more aerodynamic downforce, and the brakes had cooling fans. The air box design was changed and discs were fitted to the wheel centres to reduce drag. The team did a lot of pre-race testing on the circuit and the engines were now oil-tight. In the first practice session Pace was timed at 177.36mph (285.19kmh) on the straight, but, more remarkable, he set the fastest time. In the later sessions he was surpassed by other cars, but at the end of practice was still in sixth place. In the warm-up session on race morning Pace stopped as the clutch was about to burst, but it was changed in time for the race.

In the race the improved form continued and Pace was able to hang on to the battle for third place, eventually finishing fourth, on the same lap as the winner, Hunt's McLaren, and only 25 seconds behind. Reutemann had a miserable race; though the car was now fast enough to be competitive, he had to ease off with failing oil pressure and came 11th. After the race John Watson, whose Penske had been third, was disqualified for a measurement infringement so Pace was uprated to third, only to drop back again when Watson was subsequently reinstated.

In the British Grand Prix at Brands Hatch it was back to the usual form. There was a multi-car crash on the first lap and the race was re-started, but this was little help to the Brabhams. Pace was ninth with a new car, BT45/4, which saved a further 5kg with more titanium and thinner-gauge panels, Reutemann stopped with the inevitable oil leak on lap 49.

More work was done on the cars before the Grösser Preis von Deutschland at the Nürburgring on 1 August. A compressed-air starter was fitted, and in practice Dunlop carbon fibre brake discs were tried. The German driver Rolf Stommelen, who had been racing a BT44-Cosworth for the private RAM team, found himself without a drive as the RAM cars had been impounded during litigation about ownership. Ecclestone offered him the spare BT45, which was fitted with the carbon discs. In the race Niki Lauda, the 1975 World Champion, went off the road at Adenau on the first lap when the suspension broke on his Ferrari; the car caught fire and was struck by two other cars, and Lauda was severely burned. The race was stopped, then restarted over the full distance with a reduced field. Once again Reutemann was out on the first lap with a burst engine, but Pace went well, battling with Regazzoni's Ferrari and finishing fourth. Stommelen, who was probably delighted to get a works drive, fulfilled his part of the bargain and came sixth.

Reutemann had now become so dispirited that he was trying actively to secure a release from his contract with Ecclestone. If he was seeking justification he found it in the next race, the Grösser Preis von Österreich on 15 August. Pace used the new BT45/4 with the carbon discs, and on lap 40 the discs expanded as the car ran on the straight, the fluid boiled and, when Pace tried to brake the car from 180mph (290kmh), it continued at unabated speed, hit the bank and was destroyed; Pace escaped unhurt. Reutemann's clutch failed as he left the start, but the Autodelta mechanics wondered, perhaps unworthily, if the failure had been encouraged.

In the Grote Prijs van Nederland at Zandvoort Reutemann's clutch failed again, and Pace had run no higher than eighth place when he retired with an oil leak on lap 53. After the race Reutemann terminated his contract with the team and bought himself out of his commitment for the rest of the season. He felt that the Brabham was doing nothing for his career and, after being a front-runner and a winner the previous season, he was now a mere also-ran. He went straight off to Maranello and fixed himself a Ferrari drive for the Gran Premio d'Italia on 12 September. Ecclestone was worried that the loss of Reutemann would upset Martini and their sponsorship would be affected, but they were understanding and, realising that nothing would be gained from holding a reluctant driver to his contract, agreed to the move to Ferrari. To fill the vacancy in the team for the Monza race, Ecclestone gave Stommelen a drive again. The remarkable feature of the race was the reappearance of Lauda, who raced despite his severe burns. In practice Pace showed the speed of the BT45, setting third fastest time, but it was the usual story in the race. Pace was out after four laps with a broken piston, and Stommelen's fuel injection stopped working halfway through the race when he was running in mid-field.

To finish off the final three rounds of the World Championship season, the circus now had to travel around the world. The first stop was at Mosport Park for the Grand Prix of Canada. The Formula One Constructors Association had agreed a nominal embargo on any attempt to lure drivers away from other teams before 1 September, but the deadline was now passed and any driver was fair game. However, at this point in the season there was no possibility of getting a leading driver to fill the team vacancy, and Ecclestone had to make do with whoever he could find. He dropped Stommelen and signed up Larry Perkins, an Australian who had been European Formula 3 Champion in 1975 and during 1976 had been driving an Ensign at the back of the Formula 1 field.

A new car was built for the last three races, BT45/5, which had wishbone rear suspension instead of the previous trailing links, more weight was saved on the chassis, and the rear bodywork was revised, with altered ducting for the air intakes. The team were still persevering with the carbon discs. In the race Pace was going well and battling for sixth place with the Ferraris of Lauda and Gianclaudio Regazzoni; Lauda dropped back but the fight continued. Four laps before the end, Regazzoni slid wide on the bend before the pits and Pace tried to pass, but Regazzoni recovered and pushed Pace into the pit wall; both carried on to the finish and Pace took seventh place. After the race Ecclestone protested to the race stewards about Regazzoni's driving, but the protest was dismissed. Perkins had spun on the opening lap, but went on to finish 17th. Before the race Ecclestone had been considering the possibility of offering Regazzoni a contract for 1977, but after the incident the subject was closed.

The United States Grand Prix at Watkins Glen produced no rewards for the team. Perkins stopped when a front wishbone broke away, and Pace was out after a collision with Jochen Mass's McLaren. The last race of the season was the Grand Prix of Japan on the Fuji circuit. The outcome would decide the winner of the 1976 World Championship, which lay between the British driver James Hunt and Niki Lauda, who, despite his injuries, was expected to be the victor. The race was run in torrential rain, which made the circuit slippery and treacherous. The majority of the drivers did not want to race, but the organisers insisted that the race was run, as there was a huge and restive crowd. Within two laps Lauda had pulled off and retired, feeling that his safety was worth more than the Championship. Perkins had already stopped at the end of the first lap, saying that his car was not handling properly, and a few laps later Pace also pulled into the pits; like Lauda, he felt that the conditions were unsuitable for racing.

It had been a dismal season for the Brabham team. In the World Constructors' Championship the team was placed ninth with a mere 9 points, which was a meagre return for all the effort, though there was some encouragement, with Pace finishing in

nine of the 16 races. However, Larry Perkins's performances had not been particularly impressive, and he was not offered a contract for 1977. It seems that unlike the earlier deals that had been made with March and McLaren, Ecclestone was allowed a free hand to recruit the drivers he considered best for the team, and there was little or no Alfa Romeo influence on the subject. Carlos Pace stayed with the team for the new season and Ecclestone was able to fill the second seat by signing the Northern Irish driver John Watson. After success in Formula 2, in 1973 Watson had been given a Brabham drive by Ecclestone for the Race of Champions at Brands Hatch, but had broken his leg when the car crashed after the throttle jammed open. On recovering, he had two more drives with the team in 1973, then raced for the private Hexagon team before joining the Surtees team in 1974. In 1976 he had raced for the American Penske team, and with a Penske had gained his first Championship win in the Grösser Preis von Österreich; however, he was now out of a job, the Penske team having withdrawn at the end of the season after its main sponsor, First Citibank, had lost interest in the sport. As Jenks put it, as soon as he knew that Watson was on the market, 'Ecclestone was in like a ferret'.

In some respects there was surprisingly little co-operation between Alfa Romeo and Brabham. There were considerable differences between the external dimensions of the individual engines, as new castings were used or the existing castings were re-machined. This posed problems at Brabham as the engines were attached to the monocoque chassis by the cylinder heads, and often there could a discrepancy of as much as an inch (2.54cm). The exhaust piping and manifolds were changed continuously and, as delivered, the pipes often interfered with the suspension, so Murray was having to make constant minor alterations to the layout. Teams using the DFV Cosworth could change an engine quickly, confident that each unit had identical dimensions,

but for the Brabham team an engine change was always a voyage into the unknown and the team travelled with a range of spacers, washers and eccentric distance pieces. In later years John Watson commented, 'Frequently there were differences in the output and torque of the engines. I would ask if there had been modifications and be assured that nothing had been done. If I pressed the question, eventually there would be an admission, "Yes, we have changed it, but nothing significant, you won't notice any difference".'

The 1977 World Championship season began with a South American foray. The first race was the Gran Premio de la Republica Argentina, and practice confirmed Watson's comments about the latest state of the BT45 when he drove it for the first time and was surprised with the low-speed torque and flexibility of the engine, which had new cylinder heads and Lucas injection. Watson was on the front row of the grid and only 0.28 second slower than Hunt's McLaren. Pace was frustrated with overheating and also went off the road and bent BT45/1.

Race day was hot – nearly 44 degrees – and after Watson had led for 11 laps he fell back, suffering from the effects of a badly ventilated cockpit. Hunt was in the lead, but the two BT45s ran second and third and moved in to first and second when Hunt went off the road on lap 31. Watson's car was handling oddly as the gearbox securing bolts were breaking, and on lap 41 he stopped. Pace still led but was also suffering from the hot cockpit problem, and on lap 48, with seven to go, he lost the lead to Scheckter's Wolf, which went on to win while Pace was second. The result was disappointing but it showed that the cars and engine were now competitive. The improved form must have been particularly galling to Reutemann, who was well behind

1 August 1976: Pace on his way to fourth place in the GP von Deutschland driving the Brabham BT45. (LAT)

in his Ferrari. After the race BT45/1 was flown home for repairs, but the airline lost the crate and it was over a week before it was discovered at Rome airport!

There were great hopes in the Gran Premio do Brasil two weeks later, especially as Pace was driving in front of his home crowd. He led at the start followed by Hunt, but the double bend after the start, which had been resurfaced just before the race, had become unusually slippery. On lap 31 Pace slid on this bend and Hunt's McLaren, which was close behind, hit the Brabham, damaging the side radiator and knocking off the nose cone; Pace restarted a long way behind. Seven cars went off the road on the double bend, among them Watson's, and near the end of the race Pace also joined them.

Back at New Haw, the Brabham base near Weybridge, BT45/1 was rebuilt into a new car, the first BT45B. The engine was lowered and the rear suspension reverted to trailing links; there was also a new six-speed gearbox. The modifications pared off about 122lb (55kg). As soon as the BT45B was finished, the Brabham team left the New Haw factory and moved to a new site at Chessington near Kingston, about 10 miles south-west of London.

The car was taken to a tyre-testing session at Kyalami before the South African Grand Prix and Watson lapped in 1min 15.2sec, over 2.6 seconds quicker than the lap record. In practice Pace was second fastest, but in the race he was slowed by excessive understeer and had to stop for more front tyres, so finished 13th, two laps behind. Watson kept going, though a bit off the pace, and was sixth, but to show that his testing lap was not a fluke, he made fastest lap during the race. It had nonetheless been an unhappy race, as Tom Pryce was killed when his Shadow struck a marshal who ran across the track.

The team then returned to England for the minor Race of Champions at Brands Hatch, where one car was entered for Watson as Pace had gone back to Brazil for a short holiday. Watson made fastest time in practice, but the evening before the race news came through that Pace had been killed when his Piper aircraft had crashed while he was going to a hunting trip on the Matto Grosso. The team was shattered, and there was little enthusiasm for the race. Pace was 32, and had shown with his results that he had the potential to be one of the top drivers. His efforts in the first races of 1977 indicated that he would be have been likely to have made an impact with the BT45 during the season. The undemonstrative Ecclestone said of him, 'He was a great driver and a lovely bloke.' At Brands, Watson's chances went when he stopped to change blistered front tyres; he finished third.

Ecclestone's immediate problem was to find a driver to replace Pace. All the best had been signed up, so he had to look through the ranks of the rejects for the 1977 season and decided upon Hans-Joachim Stuck. Stuck was the son of the pre-war Auto-Union driver and had shown an erratic form in Formula 1 and 2. He had made a provisional arrangement to drive for the German Hans Gunther Schmid, who had bought the redundant Penskes, but to Schmid's understandable anger he was abandoned for the chance of the Brabham drive.

Stuck's first drive was in the United States Grand Prix West at Long Beach on 3 April, but he retired with braking problems and Watson, who had damaged a tyre in a first-lap multiple collision, was later disqualified for a restart with his mechanics' help just outside the strict confines of the Brabham pit. He had in any event already been slowed with gear selection difficulties.

In the first European round of the Championship, the Spanish event at Jarama, Watson ran as high as third place for the early laps but then fell back and stopped with a defective fuel-metering unit on lap 64. His stop let Stuck up into sixth place at the finish. After Jarama the Brabhams had an extended testing session at Balocco. This paid dividends, and when the teams arrived at Monaco Watson showed not only his ability but the greatly improved performance of the BT45/B, setting the fastest lap in practice. When the race began Scheckter's Wolf beat Watson away, but for the next 40 laps he was never more than a length behind the Wolf. Then the Brabham's brakes began to snatch and Watson took to the chicane escape road, losing second place to Lauda's Ferrari. He carried on in third place for another ten laps until the gearbox seized and he was out of the race. Stuck went out after 20 laps with an electrical fault that caused a small, brief cockpit fire, but the race had shown again that both Watson and the car were potentially the equal of any of their rivals.

There were more frustrations for Watson at Zolder in the Grand Prix de Belgique. Once again he was fastest in practice and started from pole position, but race day was wet and on the first lap, while in the lead, the Brabham was shunted from behind by Mario Andretti's Lotus when Andretti misjudged his braking point in the wet, and both cars were out of the race. Stuck spun off on lap six, then spent a long time in the pits while the car was cleaned up, but went on to finish sixth. It was much the same when the teams went to Sweden for the Sveriges Grand Prix at Anderstorp. Once again Watson was on the front row of the grid. He led for half a lap until passed by Andretti, then became involved in an eight-car fight for second place. This lasted almost the entire race, but on lap 30 Watson was pushed off by Scheckter's Wolf; he recovered but had lost three places and was at the tail of the battle, finishing fifth, while Stuck came 10th.

The Grand Prix de France had moved again, and was now at the small Dijon-Prenois circuit. At the start Watson was second behind Hunt's McLaren, but he took the lead on lap five and stayed there, being chased all through the race by Andretti, the cars rarely more than a few lengths apart. On the very last of the 80 laps, while still in front, the Brabham spluttered with fuel starvation and Andretti nipped past to take the flag by just 1.5 seconds from Watson. Before the race, the team had been concerned about the thirst of the engine, so had put in an additional 3 gallons (13.6 litres) of fuel, but it was not quite enough; the tanks were dry and a frustrated Watson was given a lift back to the pits on the side of Lauda's Ferrari. Stuck again spun off when he was lapped by the group fighting for third place.

Watson seemed to have a permanent lien on a front row place, and he was there again for the British Grand Prix at Silverstone. He made a perfect start and led the race for 49 laps, then fuel starvation set in. He stopped at the pits, then restarted and ran in the middle of the field for another ten laps before retiring. After the race Murray stripped down the fuel system but found no attributable cause of the failure and assumed that it must have been microscopic dirt in the fuel lines. Stuck kept going and finished fifth.

Two weeks later, on 31 July, it was the Grösser Preis von Deutschland at Hockenheim. Again Watson was on the front row of the grid, but this time he only lasted eight laps, the engine bursting just as he was about to challenge for the lead. It was left to Stuck, going well in his home race, to work his way up to third at the end, though it was a close thing as the Brabham was spluttering with fuel shortage as it came up to the line and Stuck swerved from side to side for the pumps to pick up the last vital drops.

The teams then went on to Austria for the Grösser Preis on the Österreichring. Watson was off form suffering from a virus infection and was well back on the grid, but Stuck was keeping the flag flying with fourth fastest practice time. In the race Watson trailed round at the back and Stuck came third after fighting off a late challenge from Reutemann's Ferrari. In the closing stages Stuck lapped Watson, who suddenly came to life, unlapped himself and, in doing so, made the fastest lap of the race.

After the high point in France it was beginning to go awry. At Zandvoort Watson was forced to run wide by a Ferrari on the first corner of the race and the oil sump was cracked on a kerb, so he had to retire a lap later, while Stuck was slightly outclassed and could only manage seventh place. It got worse at Monza in the Gran Premio d'Italia. Alfa Romeo pressure was put on Ecclestone to run a third car for a local driver, Giorgio Francia, who was therefore put into BT45/5B in practice; however, he was so slow that Ecclestone was able to shrug off the pressure with equanimity, even more so when Stuck broke his clutch and needed the car! Neither Watson nor Stuck could set good times in practice as the cars seemed to be unsuited to the tyres, which were overheating – as all the teams were running on Goodyears this was puzzling. In the race Watson, trying hard to pick up places, went off the road on lap two, bounced across a kerb and cracked an engine casting, so his race was over. Stuck made a determined effort and worked his way up to fifth, but his engine burst on lap 31.

By the time the circus arrived at Watkins Glen for the United States Grand Prix, the wheeling and dealing to settle the drives for 1978 was in full swing and Stuck must have realised that his credibility was at stake and something needed to be done. He therefore set to with gusto and made second fastest practice lap, while to show that the cars were running well, Watson was third fastest. As the cars formed up on the grid on race day it began to rain, and it was decided that Stuck would start on rain tyres and Watson would be on slicks in the hope that the rain would stop. Stuck shot into the lead and began to pull away from Hunt's McLaren. On the third lap the Brabham's clutch-operating mechanism failed but Stuck carried on, extending his lead. He stayed in front until lap 15 when the car jumped out of gear as he was rounding a corner and slid off into the catch fencing; Stuck's race was over. Watson had a miserable time on the slicks and was running one from last. On

1977: John Watson. Hans-Joachim Stuck, his team-mate in the Martini Brabham team, is in the background. (LAT)

lap eight he stopped to fit rain tyres, but as the course dried out he had to make two more tyre stops; he was gaining places to lose them again in the stops, and finished in 12th place.

The next race was the Canadian Grand Prix at Mosport Park, and this was another disaster for the Brabhams. The cars did not go well in practice and in the race Watson was out on the first lap when he went off the road after a minor collision with Peterson's Tyrrell; Stuck's engine expired after 19 laps.

The last race of the season was the Grand Prix of Japan. The Brabhams were going better so Watson and Stuck occupied the second row of the grid. Watson ran third until lap 29, then was unable to select any gears so had to retire. Stuck lost a lap when he stopped to change all his tyres, then carried on to finish seventh.

Chapter 20

Hollow victories and dashed hopes

During the 1977 season it seemed that the Brabhams had almost been within grasp of real success, but always it was denied them by problems that were often minor and unnecessary. It had been a

1977:Niki Lauda. His face still shows the evidence of his crash at the Nürburgring in 1976. (LAT)

particularly frustrating season for Watson, who had taken over Pace's role and had shown that he was as quick as the best of his rivals. As the season came to an end, Ecclestone had been active on the business front. The 1977 World Champion was Niki Lauda, but he had been unhappy with Ferrari and relations had deteriorated so much that Lauda, knowing that he already had sufficient points to win, refused to drive in the North American and Japanese rounds. After a test drive in a BT45 at Vallelunga, he agreed to sign up with Brabham for 1978, and this agreement brought a number of changes with it.

Stuck was told that his contract would not be renewed and, more important, the sponsorship with Martini & Rossi was also terminated. Lauda had a personal sponsorship with the Italian food firm Parmalat, with whom it was suggested that Martini should share the team sponsorship, but the aperitif firm wanted an exclusive deal or nothing, so their support of the team ended and Parmalat took on all the bills, including the responsibility of paying Lauda. Gordon Murray had been busy during the summer and autumn, and Lauda admitted that Murray's work had been an additional reason for signing with Brabham.

Murray had been working on a new design that would overcome many of the problems with the BT45, particularly the weight. The new car, the BT46, had been designed during the 1977 season and could have been raced before the end of the

season but was held back to remove the development snags. It had a pyramidal monocoque and the nose section and front wing were a separate foam-filled structure. Carbon fibre brake discs reappeared and there was a comprehensive digital display from which the driver could call up information about all the functions of the car; in addition there was an on-board lap timer, which dispensed with the need for continuous pit signals. More unconventional, Murray dispensed with the usual radiators and relied on surface cooling panels set into the sides of the pyramid. There was an in-built air jacking system using an external air supply. The BT45's suspension remained, but more weight had been saved by a redesign of the Brabham-Alfa gearbox.

While Murray had been finishing the BT46, Chiti had done more work on the 115-12, and a further 5kg was saved with the use of titanium in such places as the connecting rods. The BT46 was given a first run at Balocco in August and was then put away until the end of the season. During the late autumn it was taken to Donington and Silverstone for detailed development, and to the team's dismay it was found that the surface cooling did not work. It seemed that the coolers retained a layer of still air and the coolant just boiled away. To add to the gloom, the vibrations of the car destroyed the digital display systems.

While Murray worked to eliminate the problems with the BT46, the team set off to

South America for the start of the 1978 season. As the new car was unraceable, two more BT45s were built. The design was tidied up with much detail work, and the car was fitted with a distinctive new nose piece having a full-width air intake; the cars were still painted red with the Parmalat name displayed prominently. As World Champion, Lauda's car carried the number '1' throughout the season.

The first race was the Argentina event, and in the early laps Watson moved up to second place behind Andretti's Lotus, being followed by Lauda. On lap 41 Watson slowed and stopped as the cooling system had sprung a leak and the engine was dry, but Lauda kept on going to take second place. The teams then moved on to Brazil where the Gran Premio do Brasil was run on a new short and tight circuit at Rio de Janeiro. In practice Lauda said that his car was almost undriveable, so the old nose

was fitted, which brought an immediate improvement. In the race Watson, who had a severe cold, was nudged off by another car and a tyre deflated; the stop to change the wheel put him out of the running. Lauda, meanwhile, despite the inferior handling worked his way up the field and came third, while Watson was eighth. During the South American tour there were persistent rumours in the Formula 1 world that Alfa Romeo had built a complete car and was going to return to racing in collaboration with Pirelli. The rumours had a firm foundation.

The revised BT46 with a conventional wide radiator set across the nose was ready for the South African Grand Prix at Kyalami on 4 March. Two new cars had been built and Lauda made the fastest time in prac-

tice. In the race he led initially but missed a gear change before the first corner. He ran in third place, slowed slightly by blistering tyres, then on lap 52 the engine expired. Watson was going steadily apart from a spin, and worked his way up the field, moving into third place three laps before the end.

The European season began with the International Trophy at Silverstone. It was wet, and Lauda, who was on the front of the grid, went off the road on the warming-up lap when the throttle jammed, so was unable to start. The scene then shifted to California for the United States Grand Prix West on the tight street circuit at Long Beach. The BT46s were given larger radiators and modified nose pieces. In practice both were fast, and in the race Watson and

15 January 1978: Lauda struggles with the aerodynamically unstable BT45C Brabham at the GP de Argentina at Buenos Aires. (LAT)

Lauda ran second and third behind Gilles Villeneuve, the new recruit to the Ferrari team, until lap 10, when Watson stopped as he had heard a loud bang, seemingly from his engine. It was not the engine, but fumes in the oil tank had ignited and the tank had exploded. Lauda continued to follow Villeneuve, but pulled out on lap 28 with ignition failure.

There was a considerable improvement at Monaco on 7 May. Watson and Lauda were second and third fastest in practice, separated by a mere one-hundredth of a second. In the race Watson took the lead on the first lap and stayed there, followed by Depailler's Tyrrell and Lauda. He held on to the lead until lap 36, when, his brakes beginning to fade, he overshot the chicane, but carried on in second place. At the same time Lauda stopped with a puncture and dropped back to sixth; he charged back up the field and finished second, while Watson, who lost his second place when he overshot Ste Devote corner on lap 65, came fourth.

The Monaco result showed that the Brabhams were a match for the rival teams and, just as important, that the engines were now giving comparable power with reliability, so the team had great hopes of success at the Grand Prix de Belgique on the Zolder circuit. However, with the typical see-saw of fortunes that affected the Brabham team, Lauda was eliminated on the first lap when he was pushed off the circuit by Scheckter's Wolf. Watson, who was unhappy with his car's handling, ran in seventh place until he stopped for new tyres, then spun off on lap 18, damaging the base of the engine on a kerb. There was only a slight improvement at Jarama on 4 June in the Gran Premio de España, but there had been a dramatic technical development in grand prix design that set all the teams back.

Lotus had produced a new car, the Type 79, which broke new ground with the exploitation of the aerodynamics of the underside of the car; by using a venturi effect and sliding side skirts there was a remarkable increase in road-holding and cornering speeds aided by the 'ground effect' that the new system created. The Lotus 79 had won the Belgian race and now dominated the Spanish event, finishing first and second. Watson had run third for a while, but then fell back and finished fifth after he had problems selecting gears. Lauda, who had risen to fourth place, dropped out on lap 57 when his engine burst.

The exploitation of 'ground effect' had been studied carefully by Gordon Murray for some time, and in the spring of 1978 he devised an even more radical approach. A BT46 was fitted with radiators on top of the engine, while at the rear of the car was a large fan driven from the lower shaft of the gearbox. This fan, which was carefully ducted, drew air up from the underside of the car and through the radiators; it had a dual effect, for as well as cooling it also created a vacuum under the car as the underside was sealed by flexible skirts that rubbed on the road. The vacuum held the car down to the road and gave the same effect as had been achieved with the Lotus

1978: A thoughtful Carlo Chiti at the Monaco Grand Prix. (LAT)

79. The car was tested in great secrecy at Balocco, then at Brands Hatch. The system worked well, but the original plastic fans disintegrated so were replaced by glass fibre; these too broke up, but cast magnesium stood up to the task. The system was not wholly original – something of the kind had been used on the Chaparral, an American sports racing car, but it was a radical breakthrough in grand prix racing.

Two fan-modified BT46s arrived at Anderstorp for the Sveriges Grand Prix on 17 June. As Bernie Ecclestone expected, there was an outcry, and the organisers of the Swedish race received five official protests from other teams, who contended that the system was in violation of the CSI rules governing the construction of grand prix cars. The protests were dismissed and the cars raced. According to Carlo Chiti, Bernie Ecclestone was concerned that if the fan car raced it should not win on its first outing, realising that the rival teams would shout 'Cheat'; appreciating that this could prejudice his position as the chairman of the Formula One Constructors' Association, he wanted victory to wait until the rivals had accepted the revolutionary principle. In practice Watson and Lauda were just behind Andretti's Lotus 79; then in the race Lauda followed Andretti until the Lotus engine broke a piston on lap 46. After that Lauda went into the lead and carried on to win, despite Ecclestone's wishes. Watson spun on the first lap, then retired later with throttles jammed by the dirt thrown up in the spin.

The result gave great satisfaction to the Brabham team and to Alfa Romeo, but the row about the legality of the cars continued. The Swedish club referred the matter to the CSI, which was embarrassed as Murray had told its representatives about the system in secrecy at the Spanish race and had received tacit approval. The matter was resolved on 23 June when the CSI's special commission met and decided that the Swedish result should stand but the fan system would be outlawed immediately,

17 June 1978: The controversial 'ground effect' fan on the Brabham BT46B, photographed at the Swedish GP at Anderstorp. It seems that the outlet temperature is being measured. (LAT)

changing the regulations accordingly.

When the teams assembled at the Paul Ricard circuit for the Grand Prix de France two weeks later, the two BT46s had been put back to the earlier specification but were going well. Watson made the fastest time in practice, being timed on the straight at 177.7mph (286kmh). In the race Andretti led from the start followed by Watson and Lauda, but on lap nine Lauda's race was over. As Jenks said in *Motor Sport*, 'A look in the left-hand air inlet box was sufficient; there were bits of valves, guides and other nastiness to show that the Alfa Romeo engine had destroyed itself.' Watson's car was slightly off colour and he fell back to fourth place, but stayed there until the end.

In the British Grand Prix at Brands Hatch on 16 July it seemed that the BT46 Brabham was going to gain a second victory. The two Lotus 79s retired in the early laps, leaving Lauda in the lead on lap 33, followed by Reutemann's Ferrari and Watson, but the Ferrari closed on the leading BT46 and, as they lapped a tail-ender,

Reutemann slipped by into the lead. Although Lauda tried hard he could not regain the lead and finished second, 1.3 seconds behind, while Watson took third place.

At the Grösser Preis von Deutschland, held at Hockenheim, Lauda's car was losing water as it stood on the starting grid and the engine expired after 11 laps, but Watson had a pit stop in the early laps, then carried on to finish seventh. For the Austrian race Murray moved the radiators to the side pods and both drivers complained that the handling was affected. The race was run in the wet, but the cars started on slick tyres and it was stopped after seven laps with several minor accidents. Both Brabhams survived for the second race, but Watson stalled on the grid, so made a delayed start. Lauda held third place until he spun and hit the barriers; he struggled back to the pit but the car was too badly damaged to continue. Watson meanwhile was working his way up the field and finished seventh.

In the Grote Prijs van Nederland at

17 June 1978: Mario Andretti (Lotus 79) has a slight advantage over Lauda (BT46B) at Anderstorp, while John Watson (BT46B) tries to find a way through behind Lauda. (LAT)

Zandvoort, the two Lotus 79s dominated the race and were uncatchable, but Lauda and Watson shook off the rest of the field and followed home in third and fourth places. Lauda hung on to Peterson in the second Lotus, but before he could attempt to pass he had to ease off as there was a severe vibration at the rear of his car.

The Gran Premio d'Italia at Monza on 10 September was expected to be a fierce race, but was likely to confirm Andretti as World Champion. The Brabhams had problems in practice; in the first session Lauda burst an engine and Watson ran over a kerb, damaging the base of his engine. In the second session Lauda managed to break another engine, which had been fitted with a modified SPICA injection system giving a better

distribution of fuel. The huge crowd were delighted that Villeneuve's Ferrari was on the front of the grid beside Andretti's Lotus, while Lauda was on the second row.

The starter mis-timed the start and switched on the green light while the cars at the rear of the grid were still rolling in from the warming-up lap, so when the field reached the chicane installed before the Curva Granda it was tightly bunched and there was a big collision. Nine cars were wrecked and Peterson was pulled out of his burning Lotus with burns and severely injured legs. There was a long delay while the track was cleared, then when the cars set off again on a warming-up lap there was another accident and further delay. The crowd was restless and jeering, and many

drivers wanted to call off the race, but after a 2½-hour delay the 19 surviving cars were lined up on the grid for a race reduced to 40 laps. This time the starter held them too long before the green light was shown. Villeneuve left the line, followed by Andretti, while the rest waited for the light.

In the opening laps Lauda held fourth place behind Jabouille's turbocharged Renault, but went up to third when the Renault expired. Watson made a slow first lap, but then worked his way up through the field until he was fifth behind Reutemann's Ferrari. It was announced that Villeneuve and Andretti had been penalised a minute for jumping the start, so Lauda led, albeit third. Reutemann tried to challenge for the lead but the Ferrari's Michelin tyres were deteriorating and he fell back and was passed by Watson. The race ran its course with Andretti and Villeneuve still in

17 June 1978: Lauda wins the Sveriges GP with the BT46B. (LAT)

front on the road but behind the Brabhams on time. In the gathering dusk the Brabhams came home first and second, but the crowd was silent knowing that Peterson was badly injured and that the Ferraris had been deprived of a possible victory. The knowledge that Alfa Romeo engines had won was no compensation. It had been a sad and disappointing victory for Brabham and for Alfa Romeo, but even muted celebrations were curtailed when the news was received that Peterson had died of his injuries.

It was a dispirited Formula 1 circus that went across the Atlantic for the final two rounds of the World Championship. Andretti was already Champion, his only possible rival for the title having been Peterson. In the United States and Canadian Grands Prix the Brabhams had no success. In the American race at Watkins

Glen both Lauda and Watson retired with engine failure. The death of Peterson had created a vacancy among the top drivers; it had been arranged that he would drive for McLaren in 1979, and with his death there was a place in that team to be filled. John Watson was offered the drive and it was agreed that he would leave the Brabham team on amicable terms after the Canadian race. Ecclestone had already signed a contract with Lauda for 1979, but Watson's departure left him looking for a new driver. For the Canadian race he offered a drive to the young Brazilian Nelson Piquet, who had been outstanding in Formula 3 and had made a good impression with some Formula 1 drives in a privately entered McLaren in 1978. Piquet went well in practice and finished the race in 11th place, but

Watson went off the road when he tangled with Andretti's Lotus, while Lauda clipped a kerb and damaged his steering.

In the 1978 Championship Lauda had been placed fourth with 44 points and Watson was sixth with 25 points. In the Constructors' Championship the Brabham-Alfa Romeos were third behind Lotus and Ferrari. When he departed, Watson had a light-hearted bet with Ecclestone that he would be placed higher in the 1979 Championship than Ecclestone's two drivers.

Although it was now common knowledge that Alfa Romeo was developing a grand prix car, it was agreed that the company would continue to supply engines to the Brabham team for the 1979 season. In the middle of the 1978 season Gordon

Murray had emphasised to Carlo Chiti and his technicians that if he was to design a car that could take the full advantage of 'ground effect' he needed a vee-configuration engine – the existing flat-12 could not be designed into a car with effective 'ground effect' aerodynamics. Murray's observations were noted, and Chiti and his team set to work with a will. By the late autumn of 1978, after three month's work, a new engine appeared. The design was the Tipo 1260, a V-12 with dimensions of 78.5mm x 51.5mm, giving a capacity of 2991cc. Its title was derived from the number of cylinders and the 60 degree included angle of the cylinder blocks. It used the cylinder heads and other components from the flat-12 and, to Murray's frustration, it was no lighter, weighing 375lb (170kg). As a compensation, however, it was powerful – with Lucas injection it

developed 525bhp at 12,300rpm. To house the new engine Murray designed a new car, the BT48, which had an aluminium and carbon fibre monocoque with the engine as a stressed member. The suspension coil-spring/damper units were mounted inboard and aerodynamic side pods were intended to generate sufficient downforce to render a rear wing superfluous.

The season began early on 21 January in Buenos Aires, and it was evident immediately that all was not well with the Brabham team. Snow had prevented a test session for the BT48 at Paul Ricard, so it went to South America untested. There was only one BT48 for Lauda; Piquet had to make do with a BT46. Practice was spent sorting out innumerable problems with the BT48, and Lauda took over the BT46 so he could qualify for the race. The aerodynamic side pods were causing the BT48 to lift and Lauda

found that it was almost uncontrollable at speed, so the team made up a makeshift rear wing for the race.

In the race there was a multiple crash at the first corner. Piquet was involved and suffered a broken bone in his foot, while the BT46 was wrecked. The race was restarted and Lauda limped round at the back with the BT48, retiring after eight laps without fuel pressure. As the BT46 was beyond repair, a new BT48 was flown out to Brazil for the next Championship race at Sao Paulo on 4 February. Lauda worked very hard and managed to qualify halfway up the field, but in the race he was out after three laps with a broken gear linkage. Piquet eliminated himself after six laps when he found he could not press the brake pedal hard enough with his damaged foot and ran into the back of Regazzoni's Williams.

There was an improvement at the South African Grand Prix on 3 March. Lauda tried very hard in practice and was fourth on the grid. The race began in the rain and Piquet started on dry tyres but stayed in front of Lauda, who had begun on wets. Lauda caught Piquet after a tyre change and they finished sixth and seventh. If hopes had been raised by this result, they were dashed again at Long Beach in the United States Grand Prix West. Both BT48s qualified in the middle of the field but on the first lap of the race Tambay's McLaren collided with Lauda and he was eliminated. Piquet kept running but could only finish eighth.

The teams then had a quick dash back across the Atlantic for the Race of Champions at Brands Hatch the following weekend; this should have been run in March but was postponed as the circuit was snowbound. Piquet had an excellent drive, coming through to take second place behind Villeneuve's Ferrari. Lauda had led the race in the early laps but then stopped to change blistered tyres and could only finish fifth, a lap behind the winner.

Relations were now becoming strained between Brabham and Alfa Romeo, the

1979: The Tipo 1260 V-12 engine developed for Brabham and for Alfa Romeo's return with the Tipo 177.

23 April 1979: Lauda, before the BT48 was eliminated from the GP de España with a water leak. (LAT)

Brabham team complaining that the performance of individual engines varied to a considerable degree, with a possible difference of 600rpm in the peak revs of different engines. Lauda was also becoming dispirited, and there were already clandestine discussions about a drive with McLaren.

The dismal progress continued. In Spain Piquet lasted 16 laps before his fuel injection system broke, and Lauda worked his way up to third place but on lap 63 his engine lost all its water. Two weeks later at Zolder at least the team was consistent – both cars went out of the race on lap 23 with burst engines. There was a slight improvement at Monaco. By an enormous effort Lauda qualified fourth fastest, and in the race he held third place until lap 23, although he was holding up the following cars. Then Pironi tried to push his Tyrrell past the Brabham at the Mirabeau corner, the cars collided and that was the end of

Lauda's race. Piquet ran at the back of the field and was placed eighth, but was not running at the end as a halfshaft had broken with eight laps to go.

In the Grand Prix de France, run on the Dijon-Prenois circuit, Piquet was third fastest in practice and ran in fifth place for half the race, despite a very erratic-handling car. He was out of the race when he spun off on lap 53, and Lauda had already eliminated himself by a spin earlier in the race. Relations were worsening between Brabham and Alfa Romeo, and the performance in the British Grand Prix at Silverstone did not help. Piquet spun off on the first lap and Lauda retired after 13 laps with braking difficulties.

It was the same sorry story in the Grösser Preis von Deutschland, when both cars

went out with engine failure. By now Piquet was showing that he was just as quick as Lauda and in most races was setting a faster practice time. Soon after the German race Bernie Ecclestone met Ettore Massacesi, the Alfa Romeo president, at Malpensa airport outside Milan. In a stormy discussion Ecclestone realised that Alfa Romeo had serious intentions of racing again and knew that he would then be a 'poor relation' when the engines were handed out. Massacesi said that the problems lay with the design and preparation of the Brabhams, so Ecclestone offered to abandon the deal immediately, knowing that this would not suit Massacesi, who wanted a strong Alfa Romeo representation at the Gran Premio d'Italia in September. A truce was called, but it was agreed that the engine deal would finish at the end of the season.

At the Österreichring both cars went out with engine and oiling problems, but at Zandvoort Piquet managed to take fourth place by virtue of still being there as other cars fell out. Lauda was so disenchanted that he pulled out after four laps, excusing himself with a slight wrist injury.

In the Gran Premio d'Italia at Monza on 9 September, Piquet tried to pass Regazzoni's Williams at the Curva Granda on the first lap and spun into the guard rail. The engine and gearbox were torn off but he escaped unhurt. Lauda had a quiet race, keeping going against expectations and finishing fourth. It had been agreed that Brabham would be released from the agreement after the Monza race and could go to the North American Championship rounds at the end of the season with Cosworth engines, but the team had one last commitment with the Alfa Romeo engine.

A non-Championship race, the Gran Premio Dino Ferrari, had been arranged on the Imola circuit, the purpose of which was to enable the circuit to qualify as a Championship venue in 1980 for the Gran Premio d'Italia, or for the Gran Premio di San Marino, which would give Italy an additional Championship round. An abbreviated field turned up but it included the two Ferraris driven by Scheckter and Villeneuve; the former had just clinched the 1979 title at Monza. Lauda was there with a BT48 and he held on to the two Ferraris in the opening laps, then passed Scheckter. He was following Villeneuve and passed him five laps later, taking the lead. In an attempt to regain the lead Villeneuve's Ferrari hit the back of the Brabham, which survived unscathed, though the Ferrari's nose cone was broken and Villeneuve had to stop for a replacement. This left Lauda with a comfortable lead and he went on to win. It was a wholly unexpected victory that must have left both Brabham and Alfa Romeo pondering on how different their joint fortunes might have been.

In four frustrating seasons there had only been three wins, and two of these had been controversial or hollow. The results had done little for the Alfa Romeo name, but the experience had enabled Chiti and his technicians at Autodelta to realise how hard it was to find success in grand prix racing. For John Watson there must have been a wry smile; although he had not had a good season with McLaren, he had won his bet with Ecclestone and had finished in the World Championship ahead of Lauda and Piquet.

Chapter 21

Final failure

WHEN THE BRABHAM TEAM began to use the 115-12 engine in 1976, Carlo Chiti looked at the way the team worked and, more important, how the cars were constructed. It occurred to him that Brabham was doing little that Autodelta could not do, and there was little magic in a Formula 1 chassis that was not already in the T33 and its developments. Autodelta was already making the most difficult bit, the engine, and was on its way to making the gearbox as well. The facilities were available at Settimo Milanese to make a complete grand prix car, which could then be a pure Alfa Romeo, and, most important, if it succeeded none of the glory would be shared. Chiti put his case to the Alfa Romeo board, who agreed, despite the financial problems of the company, that he could begin work on a Formula 1 design. As a preliminary Pirelli was approached as a source of tyres and sponsorship. Pirelli had been out of grand prix racing for many years and were keen to return; Goodyear had been enjoying a monopoly, but this was now being broken by Michelin, and the prestige of success as well as the technical advances that could be gained were attractive.

Chiti and his team designed a conventional monocoque chassis and fitted it with a current 115-12 engine. Called the Tipo 177, it was a rather chunky car and was ready for preliminary testing in the early summer of 1978. Vittorio Brambilla was engaged for the task; he was a tough driver who had been driving for the March team and had gained a single World Championship win in the 1975 Austrian race. He also had a reputation as a driver who collided too often with his rivals during a race.

In August 1978 the 177 was taken to the Paul Ricard circuit in Provence so that Niki Lauda could try it. All the testing by Brambilla had been done on Pirelli tyres, but for the Lauda drive the car was fitted with Goodyears, as to drive on Pirellis, even in a private test, would be in contravention of Lauda's contract with Goodyear. It seems that no attempt was made to set up the 177 on the Goodyears, and after a short drive Lauda pronounced that Autodelta was wasting its time. It was suggested that Lauda was not being wholly fair to the car; he and Ecclestone knew that if the venture forged ahead it would prejudice the Brabham team's engine supply, and at that time there were still hopes that the Brabham-Alfa partnership would come good. In *Motor Sport* Denis Jenkinson commented, 'Without being too specific, Lauda and Ecclestone let it be known that they considered the Alfa-Alfa to be a complete waste of time and suggested it would probably be abandoned. The European press took this up and without an official word from Alfa Romeo everyone was accepting the project was still-born.' This made Lauda and Ecclestone very unpopular with Italian enthusiasts, and some of the lack of enthusiasm for the Brabham win in the tragic Monza race could be attributed to this. Ettore Massacesi was furious when he saw the press reports, and it was announced that testing would continue in the hope of entering a car in the 1979 Gran Premio de Argentina.

Brambilla had been involved in the 1978 Monza accident; although in no way responsible for it, he received serious head injuries when he was stuck by a flying wheel, so was unable to continue with the testing. Another driver, Bruno Giacomelli, was signed up; he had driven for McLaren in some World Championship events and had been the 1978 Formula 2 champion with a March. He was known to the British mechanics as 'Jack O'Malley', and this was inscribed on the side of his car! The testing continued, some of it being done at Brands Hatch, and by the spring of 1979 it was decided that the 177 was ready to race.

It was entered for the Grand Prix de Belgique at Zolder on 13 May, so an Alfa Romeo returned to grand prix racing after an interval of 28 years. The driver was Giacomelli and the car was developed to a state-of-the-art machine with in-board suspension units, sliding aerodynamic side pods with sliding skirts, and flush-fitting side radiators. The car was attended by ten mechanics, led by Chiti and Marelli, and was running on Goodyear tyres, as Pirelli had developed cold feet about a return to racing. Fittingly it was painted red and there was a lack of sponsorship signwriting, apart from the usual trade suppliers.

Giacomelli went fast enough in practice

to be on the same row of the grid as Lauda's Brabham, albeit in 14th place, but unfortunately the race début only lasted for 22 laps, as the 177 was then eliminated in a slight collision with de Angelis's Shadow.

The Autodelta team were playing themselves in gradually, and the next race was the Grand Prix de France at Dijon-Prenois on 1 July. Giacomelli qualified in 17th place on the grid and had a quiet race, stopping to change tyres and for the gearbox to be examined, finishing in 17th place. There was now a lull until the Gran Premio d'Italia at Monza on 9 September. There had been a lot of activity at Autodelta and a new car appeared, the Tipo 179, which had the Tipo 1260 V-12 engine. The shape of the car had been devised by Robert Choulet, of the Parisian aerodynamic consultancy SERA. It had lateral radiators and inboard suspension, and the driver sat well forward. The new car was driven by Giacomelli, and Brambilla, who was fully recovered, had the earlier 177. Both cars were now sponsored by Scaini Batteries. In the race Giacomelli was going well enough to keep company with Lauda's Brabham in the early stages, and when Lauda pulled away Giacomelli kept up his pace and was able to pass Jarier's Tyrrell and Andretti's Lotus. He caught Lauda again but before he could pass he spun off at the Ascari chicane and damaged the rear suspension. Brambilla kept going in the 177 and finished in 12th and last place, a lap behind the winner.

A second 179 was completed in time for the Canadian Grand Prix on 30 September, but Autodelta was annoyed to find that the organisers had not guaranteed entries for the two 179s and they were expected to qualify with a number of also-ran private entrants. The team objected strongly and the organisers retaliated by excluding both cars from the first day of practice. After more altercations, it was agreed that one car should have a guaranteed entry and the other should qualify. Autodelta found this unacceptable and it was decided that one car should run, driven by Brambilla, and Giacomelli would stand down. Brambilla ran well in mid-field during the race but was stopped with a fuel-metering problem on lap 52. At the United States Grand Prix both cars were expected to qualify and this time the team accepted the position; Giacomelli qualified and Brambilla just missed it, but it made little difference as Giacomelli spun off on the first lap of the race.

13 May 1979: At the GP de Belgique at Zolder Alfa Romeo returns to grand prix racing after 28 years. Bruno Giacomelli (Tipo 177) leads de Angelis (Shadow) and Piquet (Brabham). (LAT)

Serious business was effected by Autodelta during the winter of 1979/80. A major sponsorship deal was completed with Marlboro, the American tobacco company that was already sponsoring the McLaren team, so the cars were painted in the Marlboro livery; as a link with tradition, the quadrifolio was placed on the side of the cockpit. The sponsorship was taken with some reluctance by the Alfa Romeo management, but there was considerable opposition to a racing programme from the factory trade unions, who felt that the money could be better spent on higher pay or better workers' facilities. The knowledge that Marlboro was paying most of the bills appeased the workers somewhat.

The 179s were revised with outboard rear brakes, and the rear suspension was modified to keep the uprights out of the airflow. The sidepods were altered to improve the aerodynamics and the monocoque was strengthened. Carbon fibre body panels were fitted and overall the cars were 60lb (27kg) lighter. Giacomelli was retained and was joined by the French driver Patrick Depailler, who had previously driven for the Tyrrell and Ligier teams, winning at Monaco in 1978 and Jarama in 1979. Brambilla was kept in the team to do the test driving at Balocco.

In the first Championship race of the season in Buenos Aires, both 179s scraped in on the back of the grid, but in the race Giacomelli ran steadily and finished fifth while Depailler's engine burst seven laps before the end. In Brazil the result was disappointing: Giacomelli was 11th and once again Depailler dropped out, this time with an electrical fault. In South Africa there was a glimpse of hope as Depailler qualified on the fourth row of the grid ahead of the Ferraris, but in the race his fuel injection played up and the car misfired. He was in and out of the pits continually and finished last, 23 laps behind the winner, Giacomelli went out with a failed engine.

When the circus went to California for the United States Grand Prix West, there was a remarkable improvement. Depailler was third fastest in practice, while Giacomelli was in sixth place on the grid. In the race Depailler ran in a steady second place until lap 18, when he was passed by Jones's Williams, but held on to third until lap 41, when he had a lurid spin after the suspension broke. Giacomelli also spun, causing a multiple accident early in the race, then carried on until he had a collision with Jones when being lapped.

9 September 1979: Vittorio Brambilla in the 177 on his way to 12th place in the GP d'Italia at Monza. More sponsorship is evident. (LAT)

Unfortunately the Californian pace had been misleading. When the cars appeared at Zolder for the Grand Prix de Belgique both were well back on the grid, and in the race Giacomelli was nudged into the pit wall at the start and retired soon after with damaged suspension, while Depailler lasted in mid-field until lap 39 when the exhaust pipes broke off. For Zolder a fourth car had been built and all four were in the paddock; the new car, used only for practice, had a lightened 1260 engine.

The gloom continued at Monaco, where Giacomelli was pushed off by Daly's Tyrrell at Ste Devote on the first lap. Depailler drove a fierce race battling for fourth place, but it ended with a burst engine on lap 51. After Monaco the Autodelta team had a long break; they should have been racing in Spain at Jarama on 1 June, but the politics of motor racing intervened and there were doubts about the validity of the Spanish race as a World Championship round, so in company with Ferrari and Renault the two 179s stayed away. The lay-off did little for the reliability of the cars, and in the Grand Prix de France at Paul Ricard, Depailler went out with a seized shock absorber and Giacomelli stopped when he felt the handling change and suspected a suspension breakage. For the British Grand Prix at Brands Hatch the cars appeared with carbon fibre panels in the monocoque, larger oil coolers, lower engine mountings and modifications to the rear suspension, but it did not help – Depailler went out with a burst engine and Giacomelli had his usual accident.

The team were determined to put on a better show for the Grand Prix von Deutschland at Hockenheim, so a car was taken to the circuit ten days before the race for testing. On Wednesday 1 August Depailler took out one of the earlier cars and went off the track on the very fast eastern curve. He hit the Armco barrier at high speed and was killed instantly; although it was never confirmed, it was suspected that a broken skirt was the reason for the crash. Depailler was 35 years old and a gutsy driver who had tried very hard for the Autodelta team during the short time he drove for it and had been respected for his efforts, particularly as he had been battling with ill-health while he recovered from injuries sustained in a hang-gliding accident during his early races in 1980. Chiti wanted to withdraw Giacomelli from the German race, but left the decision to the driver, who chose to drive. Giacomelli must have

13 July 1980: Patrick Depailler's last race, the British GP at Brands Hatch – the engine will expire after 27 laps. The Tipo 179 now has Marlboro sponsorship. (Guy Griffiths)

realised that the demoralised team needed a boost and did his best. He drove an excellent race, battling hard and at the end finishing fifth, ahead of Villeneuve's Ferrari. At the Österreichring Giacomelli had another brave drive, holding fourth place until he stopped for new tyres. Then, in his excitement to get back into the fray, he left the pits with a wheel not properly fastened, it fell off and that was the end of his race.

Until Depailler's death the Italian press had been agitating for the Autodelta team to run three cars and give Brambilla the third seat. For the Grote Prijs van Nederland at Zandvoort 'The Gorilla' was given his chance. Three cars were taken to the race, all having the tidied-up and lighter engines. Giacomelli did his stuff once again, battling his way up to third place. As he challenged Laffite's Ligier for second place, he tried to outbrake the French driver but ran over a kerb and damaged the underskirts; he was slowed by the damage and eventually retired. By then Brambilla had already spun off and stopped.

As the 1979 Dino Ferrari race had qualified the Imola track as a venue for a World Championship round, the Gran Premio d'Italia was moved there from Monza. Ill-fate struck the Autodelta team again on home ground. A helicopter bringing some of the team from their hotel in Bologna crashed when landing at the circuit on the first morning of practice and several of the mechanics were taken to hospital. Meanwhile Brambilla and Chiti had escaped unhurt when their car crashed into a lorry on the way to the course. In practice, Giacomelli tried very hard and was fourth fastest, timed through a speed trap near the pits at 132mph (214kmh), quicker than the Cosworth-powered cars. He only lasted for five laps in the race; he was following Villeneuve's Ferrari in fourth place when a rear tyre of the Ferrari burst, the 179 ran over pieces of tread, which damaged the rear suspension, and Giacomelli had to stop. Brambilla had already gone a lap earlier when he spun into the barriers.

Autodelta had only five days to pack the cars and equipment for the final two races of the season in North America. Perhaps realising that Brambilla was a liability, his place was given to Andrea de Cesaris, a young Italian driver who had been gaining some impressive results in Formula 2 during the 1980 season. In the Canadian race at Montreal, Giacomelli made a mistake on lap seven and damaged the skirt so had to retire; at the same time de Cesaris's gearbox broke.

Giacomelli must have realised that his credibility in the team was in question so he made handsome amends in the last race of the season, the United States Grand Prix at Watkins Glen. He set the fastest time in practice and some of the older hands in the team must have felt that there were touches of the glory days of the 158 again. In the race Giacomelli took every advantage of his grid position and made a superb start taking the lead; despite everything that the leading grand prix aces following him could do, he was too quick to catch and for 32 laps he led the race. Then a cruel misfortune intervened and his engine died when an ignition coil failed and he coasted to a halt. De Cesaris had retired after three laps when he rammed the back of Daly's Tyrrell. After the race there were some bitter exchanges between Autodelta and Magneti Marelli, who had supplied the offending coil.

The team had little to show for the season and had suffered an enormous setback with the death of Depailler, but Giacomelli's drive at Watkins Glen had shown that the 179 was as good as the opposition and had probably saved the day for Autodelta. Until then the results had been so meagre that there was a strong possibility that Ettore Massacesi would decide to cut the company's losses and end the grand prix programme. There was a move to ban sliding skirts; the grand prix teams were divided on this, but Massacesi felt a strong moral responsibility for Depailler's death and insisted that Alfa

Romeo were among those who supported a ban. The ban was enforced, much to Chiti's disgust, as he felt that Autodelta was mastering this technical problem and would be able to benefit from it in 1981.

There was also another bone of contention in grand prix circles. The grand prix formula provided for supercharged 1500cc engines to compete with the unsupercharged 3-litres. For ten years this provision was ignored, but in 1977 Renault had produced a turbocharged 1500. At first it was slow and uncompetitive, but by 1979 it was winning races, and success was followed by a clamour for a ban. The protesters lost and by the end of 1980 Ferrari had produced a turbo 1500 and so had Chiti. His version, the Tipo 182T, was a 90-degree V-8 with dimensions of 74mm x 43.5mm and a capacity of 1496cc. It had an alloy block and heads, four camshafts, and a SPICA fuel injection pump driven by a jack shaft in the vee, which also drove the water and oil pumps. The four exhaust pipes fed a KKK turbocharger. This engine developed 550bhp at 11600rpm and was displayed to the press and sponsors behind the pit at Imola. For reasons that have never been explained, but probably connected with the problems of keeping it cool, this 1500 turbo unit sat on the shelf at Settimo Milanese for another two seasons.

It was decided that the main barrier between Alfa Romeo and grand prix triumph was the lack of a top driver, so Chiti was told to get one for the 1981 season. He secured Mario Andretti, who had been World Champion in 1978 with a Lotus, but in the next two seasons had seen little success. This was partly because Lotus had lost its way, but also because Andretti himself had become a bit dispirited driving a poor car. Chiti was quoted subsequently by Oscar Orefici in *Carlo Chiti; Sinfonia Ruggente*, 'He was a driver who was on the decline but I only realised this when he began to work for us', though this was a judgement with hindsight and may well

1981: Mario Andretti. (LAT)

with Michelin. New cars were in hand, but as an interim measure the existing 179s were modified with slots in the side pods to encourage a curtain of air at the lower edge of the pods, which was intended to keep the flow of air running under the car and not leaking out of the sides. The cars were now called 179Cs.

The first race of the season was in California, at Long Beach. Andretti went well in practice and also during the race; he never challenged for the lead, but finished fourth. Giacomelli retired at half distance after a minor collision had hurt his hand. The South American races had been moved in the calendar and were now an immediate prelude to the European season. The Brazilian race came first at Rio di Janeiro on 29 March, and it was not a happy race for Alfa Romeo as Andretti was eliminated by a first-lap accident and Giacomelli went out at half distance with ignition failure. It was not much better in Argentina. In practice both cars had handling problems and a lack of revs attributed to faulty coils. Andretti tried a modified 1979 chassis with different weight distribution and modified side pods, called a 179D. In the race both cars sounded rough and finished eighth and tenth.

The European season began at Imola with the Gran Premio de San Marino and neither car made any impact on the results, though Giacomelli did collide with Cheever's Tyrrell; Andretti dropped out with a failed gearbox. In the Grand Prix de Belgique at Zolder at least both cars finished, but only in ninth and tenth places. Monaco did nothing to lighten the gloom and both cars went out after minor accidents. In Spain they came home eighth and tenth, and in France eighth and 15th. Jenks summed up the position in *Motor Sport* after the French race: 'The Milanese firm seem to have got themselves in a bit of a muddle; the 179 and its derivatives suddenly goes well and nobody seems to know why. Then it goes badly and equally nobody knows why. On balance it goes

have been an attempt to shift the shortcomings of the equipment on to the driver. Andretti was not cheap. Chiti continued, 'For one season only, we guaranteed him a figure above half a billion lire, in the values of that time.' Bruno Giacomelli was kept on the payroll, his place secured by the Watkins Glen drive.

The team went to Paul Ricard for winter testing and the 179s recorded some highly impressive times, but with sliding skirts in

place. These had to be abandoned when the ban was enforced, but the cars were modified to comply with the new regulations, which not only banned sliding skirts but also imposed a minimum ground clearance of 6cm. The Ricard tests were done on Goodyear tyres, but Goodyear announced that it was pulling out of racing and the Alfa Romeos would race on Michelins during 1981. Goodyear later had a change of heart, but by then a contract had been signed badly. If they ever win a race it will be more by luck than judgement.'

Bitterly aware of the predicament, the team continued its sorry season. Both cars retired in the British Grand Prix, and at Hockenheim Andretti managed a ninth place, but in Austria it was all out again. Andretti had a fortunate escape in Holland, suffering a suspension failure as he was running along one of Zandvoort's straights at 150mph (240kmh); the car was completely destroyed, but he escaped unscathed. Giacomelli also had a minor accident. In the Gran Premio d'Italia, now back at Monza, Giacomelli did a bit to redeem the morale and prestige of the team

as, despite a track made slippery with occasional showers, he worked his way up to third place, only to find that the car was jammed in fifth gear. He had a long stop to find the other gears and lost two laps, so finished eighth; Andretti retired with a broken flywheel coupling.

Perhaps the Monza drive gave the team new heart for there was a marked improvement in the final two Championship rounds in North America. The Canadian race was run in appallingly wet conditions and the Michelin tyres had a marked advantage over

the rival Goodyears. With this boost, and probably remembering his drive a year before, Giacomelli stayed on the road and finished fourth, albeit a lap behind the winner. The final race was run in Las Vegas on a circuit laid out in a huge car park behind the famous Caesar's Palace hotel. Here Giacomelli maintained his form and was right up with the leaders from the start; he battled for second place throughout the race and eventually finished third, just pipped for second place by Prost's Renault with the margin of 0.4 second. During the race Andretti had risen as

25 February 1982: de Cesaris and Brambilla with the new Tipo 182 at the Hotel Michelangelo. (LAT)

high as fourth before dropping out with broken suspension.

There was a significant change in the Autodelta management during the season. At the British Grand Prix Gerard Decarouge, the technical director of the Ligier team, had a fierce row with Guy Ligier and walked out. Ligier had been the runner-up in the 1980 Constructors' Championship and Decarouge was generally respected as a designer who knew his business. He approached Chiti at Silverstone and asked if there was a job for him at Autodelta. He was signed up and immediately his knowledge and experience had an effect on the team; he knew more about ground effect and skirts than the Autodelta technicians and the results at Montreal and Las Vegas were probably assisted by his modifications to the side pods and under-car air-flow.

During the autumn of 1981 work was in hand for the design of a new car. It is not clear who had the firmest hand on the tiller, as Decarouge, Chiti and Pierluigi Corbari, the engineer who was Sporting Director of Alfa Romeo, all did their bit, though Chiti was in charge of the overall project. The main feature of the new car, the Tipo 182, was a carbon fibre monocoque tub that was made in England by Advanced Composite Components Ltd of Derby; Roger Slomans, the firm's proprietor, did much of the design work. The underside of the tub was moulded into a venturi form. Decarouge and Corbari were responsible for the gearbox, which had the gear change on top, out of the slipstream. The 1260 engine was still used, but the piping and pumps were moved to make the bottom of the engine narrower. In its final form the 1260 developed 548bhp. The suspension of the 182 followed the same arrangements as the earlier cars. The new car was revealed to the press at a reception at the Hotel Michelangelo in Milan on 25 February, but it was a matter of open discussion that it was an interim car while the turbocharged 1500 was awaited.

By the time the press were looking at the 182, the 1982 season was under way. Mario Andretti had departed, probably with relief, but Giacomelli stayed on and was joined by Andrea de Cesaris, who, since his two Alfa Romeo drives in 1980, had been with the McLaren team and had gained an unfortunate reputation for having accidents, often involving other people. Fortunately for Autodelta, unlike Andretti he would not cost a fortune to hire as he was personally sponsored by Marlboro, who may have influenced the decision to sign him up.

The first race of the 1982 season was at Kyalami. The 182s were not ready so the team took the 179s and maintained the expected 1981 form by finishing 11th and 13th. The 182s were ready for the Brazilian race on 21 March, but the team might as well have kept the 179s; de Cesaris went out when his undertray fell off, and Giacomelli's engine failed. The teams stayed on the far side of the Atlantic and went to Long Beach for the United States Grand Prix West on 4 April. De Cesaris went splendidly in practice and, to the bewilderment of the rival teams, set the fastest practice lap, while Giacomelli was fifth fastest. When de Cesaris came into the pits after setting the fastest lap, he and the Autodelta mechanics were crying with emotion – at last success seemed to be at hand.

At the start of the race de Cesaris went into the lead ahead of Arnoux's Renault and Lauda's McLaren, with Giacomelli in fourth place. Giacomelli tried to get past Lauda on lap six, Lauda missed a gear change, Giacomelli shot past and ran into the back of Arnoux, eliminating the Renault and the 182. Lauda then stalked de Cesaris and went past him on lap 15, but the 182 held on to second place until lap 34, when it seems the rear suspension broke and hit one of the walls lining the circuit, knocking off the right-hand-side suspension.

The performance in California must have convinced the Autodelta team that success was within their grasp, possibly at the next race, the Gran Premio di San Marino,

particularly as the field was reduced by the withdrawal of several teams over a dispute with the FIA about the minimum weight of the cars. The hopes were, however, dashed as de Cesaris went out of the race after three laps with fuel feed problems and Giacomelli's engine expired after 25 laps. Reporting the race, Jenks said, 'When you see an Alfa Romeo engineer making notes on a technical sheet about a specific car and there is no engine or chassis number on the sheet, you begin to wonder if the Autodelta racing department works to any sort of system. Their results would indicate that there isn't a system.' Just before the Imola race Autodelta had fitted the turbo 1500 engine into a 179 chassis and tested the car at Monza driven by Giorgio Francia, but the test was inconclusive as an oil pipe broke, the car caught fire and was burned out.

The lack of success and the absence of a system were probably manifestations of a deepening managerial malaise that was coming to a head in the summer of 1982. Chiti and Decarouge did not get on, and Chiti suspected that Decarouge had ambitions to oust him. His suspicions were heightened when he was 'kicked upstairs' by Massacesi and made Chairman of Autodelta, his place as Director General being taken by Mario Felici. Decarouge himself also had problems; Massacesi said that he was spending too much money, to which the Frenchman riposted that he did not have sufficient funds to do a proper job. Chiti had some sympathy for Decarouge's position over funding; he says Massacesi was trying to pay for the whole Formula 1 operation out of the 4 billion lire sponsorship from Marlboro. Massacesi had his own difficulties: he was being leaned upon heavily by IRI, Alfa Romeo was making losses, the Alfasud was not the commercial success that had been hoped for, and the failures in

4 April 1982: A brief moment of hope – de Cesaris (Tipo 182) takes the lead from Lauda (McLaren MP4B) at the start of the US GP West at Long Beach. (LAT)

grand prix racing were not only very costly but were doing nothing for the image of the company.

Failures with tantalising glimpses of hope continued. A new, narrower 182 appeared at Zolder for the Grand Prix de Belgique, but was not raced. The meeting was marred by the death of Gilles Villeneuve in a practice accident. In the race Giacomelli went out in a start-line accident but de Cesaris held second place until the gear linkage broke on lap 35. It was a lot better at Monaco, where Giacomelli made third fastest practice lap; the cars were weighed during practice and de Cesaris's 182 scaled at 593.8kg, well above the minimum 575kg. Giacomelli held third place for five laps until a driveshaft broke, and de Cesaris was holding fourth place until his engine lost its edge when he missed a gear change and over-revved. He held his place but could not chase those in front; with ten laps to go it began to rain and the track became an ice-rink. On the last lap, as the cars in front spun off, de Cesaris was in second place, but almost within sight of the flag he ran out of fuel, so second place was lost; however, he was placed third as he had started the final lap and the car behind was a lap in arrears.

The North American races had now moved to the middle of the season. The United States Grand Prix was in Detroit and de Cesaris was second fastest in practice, but it availed him little as he stopped on the third lap of the race with a broken driveshaft. Giacomelli fought for third place for a while, then he hit a wall. The circus then moved on to Montreal where there was a start-line accident in which Riccardo Paletti, driving for the small Osella team, was killed. In the restarted race, Giacomelli was punted out on lap two by Nigel Mansell's Lotus, but de Cesaris kept going and was running in fourth place when he ran out of fuel on the last lap, so was placed sixth.

Back in Europe the team's Fiat 190F26 transporter trundled round from circuit to circuit but there was little to cheer. Their problems were intensified on 26 June when a freak storm damaged the roof and flooded the workshops at Settimo Milanese. Giacomelli finished 11th at Zandvoort and seventh at Brands Hatch, de Cesaris retiring in both races. Giacomelli managed ninth place in the Grand Prix de France, while de Cesaris went out after a slight accident. It was a bit better in the Grösser Preis von Deutschland at Hockenheim where Giacomelli was fifth, albeit a lap behind, while de Cesaris had a bumping match with Watson's McLaren and retired with a leaking oil cooler. The team hit a nadir at the Österreichring when both cars were eliminated at the start when they collided with each other.

It was marginally better in the revived Grösser Preis der Schweiz run on the French Dijon-Prenois circuit, where de Cesaris was 10th and Giacomelli 12th. During practice for the Gran Premio d'Italia at Monza on 12 September, the turbocharged 182T appeared; de Cesaris tried it but it was not race-fit and was slower than the 182, something that baffled the Autodelta team as it had been quicker when tested at Balocco. In the early laps of the race, de Cesaris and Giacomelli held fifth and sixth places but de Cesaris then lost two laps while a duff ignition coil was changed, and Giacomelli stopped when a side pod came loose.

It had been essential to achieve a good result at Monza, so the fate of the team seemed certain, especially as in the last race of the season at Las Vegas the best the two drivers could do was ninth and 10th places. In the Constructors' Championship the team had achieved a meagre total of 7 points and stood in 10th place. Massacesi was under great pressure from IRI to cut the losses and close down the whole venture, but he was reluctant to do this as he felt the damage to Alfa Romeo prestige would be too great. Then a proposal of salvation came from a surprising quarter. The Marlboro sponsorship came from the cigarette firm,

Philip Morris, and the executive responsible for the management of the sponsorship was Nicolo di San Germano, who suggested that the whole Formula 1 enterprise should be handed over to a Formula 3 team, Euroracing.

Euroracing was based at Limbiate, on the outskirts of Milan, and was run by Giampaolo Pavanello, at first using Marches with Alfa Romeo engines, then team-built Euros. The team had secured the 1981 and 1982 European Formula 3 Championships. San Germano argued that a small team freed from the bureaucracy of the giant Alfa Romeo empire would be able to concentrate wholly on racing and success would follow. The Italian press welcomed the proposal and parallels were drawn with the status of Scuderia Ferrari 50 years earlier. Sadly the idea was doomed from the start. There was a huge gulf between Formula 3 and Formula 1, and Euroracing was no different from the handful of small teams scratching around at the tail-end of grand prix racing; the scheme was merely a reversion to the Ecclestone Brabham days without the massive experience of Formula 1 already possessed by that team. No one had the courage to say that the problem was, as Denis Jenkinson had spotted, the lack of systems, something that had bedevilled the efforts of Autodelta since the first grand prix attempts with the T33 engine.

Massacesi embraced San Germano's suggestions with enthusiasm. It meant that Marlboro would be paying all the bills, though it is not clear if the development and construction costs of the cars and engines were still being borne by Autodelta's budget. Massacesi told Chiti that he must co-operate enthusiastically with Euroracing – it would only be for one season and the grand prix venture would then be brought back in-house – but the main link-man between Euroracing and Autodelta would be Gerard Decarouge.

The change of management brought an end to Bruno Giacomelli's contract and he was told that his services were no longer needed. His place was taken by Mauro Baldi, who had already been a member of the Euroracing Formula 3 team and was 1981 European Formula 3 Champion. Andrea de Cesaris, who was still on the Marlboro payroll, was retained. Three new cars were built to take the turbo engine, the monocoque tubs, made by Advanced Chassis Components, being similar in most respects to the 1982 examples, but the undersides were modified to comply with the new flat-bottom rule. The engines were similar to those that had been tried at Monza the previous September, but Sylo turbochargers were now used.

The first race of the 1983 season was in Brazil. Chiti went to the race and Decarouge was assigned to the Euroracing team as manager. Sadly the changes made little difference, and the form of the 1982 season was maintained. The new rules provided for cars to have spot-checks to ensure that they complied with the weight regulations; cars were stopped during practice and weighed in the pits. De Cesaris ignored a signal to stop for weighing, so he and the car were excluded from the meeting. Baldi started the race but after 26 laps collided with Warwick's Toleman and retired with damaged suspension.

The teams then moved on to the United Grand Prix West at Long Beach and Jenks, who reported the race for *Motor Sport*, summed up the sad story succinctly: 'There were two turbocharged V8 Alfa Romeos in the race, but you would hardly have noticed it unless you were an Alfa enthusiast and then you would have seen Baldi's car crunched up against a concrete wall, and de Cesaris's car retired in the pits with a broken gearbox which the Alfa team described as "electrical trouble".'

The first European race of the season was the Grand Prix de France, which was being run on the Paul Ricard circuit in April in the hope of getting a larger crowd. Great was the joy when de Cesaris set the fastest time in the first practice session, but the joy turned to bitter recrimination when the time was disallowed after it was found that he had been running with empty fire extinguishers and had gained a considerable weight advantage. In the race, with filled extinguishers, de Cesaris lost four laps with gear linkage bothers and Baldi had another accident. When Ettore Massacesi heard about the fire extinguisher incident he was very angry, accusing Gerard Decarouge of damaging the good name of Alfa Romeo; Decarouge was dismissed, and there were dark mutterings that he had been unfairly treated and had been 'set up'. Chiti was unhappy about it and said that the person responsible for the incident was Pavanello, who should have paid for the mistake.

Decarouge was replaced as the Euroracing manager by Luigi Marmiroli from Autodelta, and the new management was in charge for the Gran Premio de San Marino on 1 May. In this race de Cesaris was up to fifth place when his engine gave out and Baldi also stopped with engine problems. The small Osella team turned up with a new car fitted with a V-12 Tipo 1260 engine and had several spare 1260 engines in their transporter, but the car, driven by Piercarlo Ghinzani, was too slow to qualify.

At Monaco two weeks later there was a slight improvement when, against all expectations, Baldi managed to finish the race in fifth place, albeit two laps behind and only achieving this position by keeping going as others fell out, including de Cesaris, whose gearbox failed in the early laps. Ghinzani's Osella failed to qualify.

Alfa Romeo's efforts were on their usual see-saw. At Spa, where the Belgian race had been brought back to a shortened form of the classic circuit, de Cesaris was third fastest in practice and led the race until half distance. It had become the fashion to start cars with half-filled tanks and make a refuelling stop at the halfway mark, but the Alfa Romeo lost its lead through poor pitwork when filling up. Six laps later de Cesaris was out with a burst engine, while Baldi stopped after only four laps with a broken throttle linkage.

When the teams crossed the Atlantic for the two North American races, the Euroracing team returned to the usual form. De Cesaris held third place in the Detroit race until his engine cried enough, while Baldi finished the race in 12th and last place, four laps behind. At Montreal Baldi finished again but once more in 11th and last place, while de Cesaris went out with a burst engine. The engines had been fitted with modified cylinder heads and were being run at lower boost pressures in an attempt to make the cars more reliable; previously the pressure had been 2.2 bar. However, the speed was also reduced and they were back among the tail-enders. Ghinzani had retired the Osella in Detroit and had not qualified in Canada.

There was a five-week pause between the Montreal race and the British Grand Prix at Silverstone, and during this time two smaller carbon fibre monocoques were constructed with reduced capacity tankage, which committed the team to refuelling stops. Both cars finished the race, in seventh and eighth places; de Cesaris had been running in fifth place but lost ground following bad pitwork.

When the teams arrived at Hockenheim for the Grösser Preis von Deutschland there were strong rumours circulating that Alfa Romeo would be withdrawing from grand prix racing at the end of the season. Perhaps this was a spur to the team, for de Cesaris put in a good performance; at two-thirds distance he was running fifth, then as the cars in front of him had troubles in the closing laps he moved up, and when Piquet's Brabham caught fire with three laps to go the Alfa Romeo took second place and finished in that position. Baldi dropped out, as did Ghinzani, while a second Osella driven by Corrado Fabi failed to qualify, but it was the best result of the season so far.

The see-saw tipped again when the Euroracing team arrived at the Österreichring, and both cars retired, de Cesaris with electrical bothers and Baldi with engine failure. The two Osellas trailed round at the back of the field and finished 10th and 11th. Baldi produced some crumbs of comfort when he took fifth place at Zandvoort by keeping going as others dropped out, among them de Cesaris, whose turbo burst; one Osella failed to qualify and the other blew up its engine. It was even worse at Monza where de Cesaris spun off after two laps and Baldi's turbo disintegrated three laps later.

Several World Championship rounds were cancelled, so to keep the sponsors happy an extra race was included in the calendar, the European Grand Prix at Brands Hatch on 25 September. A pneumatically adjustable waste gate or blow-off valve was fitted to the turbochargers for this race. In practice de Cesaris had a substantial accident that wrote off the car, but he

was unhurt. In the race he ran well and finished fourth, once again profiting from the troubles of those in front of him.

The last race of the season was in South Africa, and here the team received further encouragement as de Cesaris kept well up with the pace and was able to take second place, although he offered little challenge to the winning car, Patrese's Brabham. Baldi had a bad day and spun off early in the race.

The 1983 season had done little for the reputation of Alfa Romeo, and it is possible that Marlboro was also disillusioned by the results, for the outcome was a change of sponsor during the winter. The new backer was the Italian fashion and clothing firm of Benetton, starting a sponsorship career in Formula 1 that would lead to the 1995

6 October 1985: At the European GP at Brands Hatch Ricardo Patrese is the last driver to finish a grand prix in an Alfa Romeo, though the 184T is only in ninth place. (LAT)

Constructors' Championship. The bright red and white Marlboro colours were replaced by a green scheme, reminiscent of the colours of the British teams before the national colours were abandoned in favour of commercial livery. The change of sponsor also resulted in a change of drivers. Benetton wanted its own men, so de Cesaris, with his Marlboro connections, was out, as was Baldi. In came Riccardo Patrese from the Brabham team, a driver with an erratic record, some spectacular failures and near misses accompanied by impressive wins at Monaco and Kyalami. Patrese was joined by the American Eddie Cheever, who had done the rounds of the teams since entering Formula 1 in 1978 and came from

6 May 1984: Eddie Cheever (Tipo 184T) in the 'United Colors of Benetton' will run out of fuel within two laps of the end of the GP di San Marino. (LAT)

the Renault team, where he had picked up several second and third places during 1983.

Supported by the new funds from Benetton, and working at Euroracing, Marmiroli designed a new carbon fibre monocoque tub that was slimmer than the previous cars; the suspension remained unchanged, though there were detailed changes to provide for the needs of Goodyear tyres, as the team had changed their allegiance from Michelin. Autodelta did more work on the engines, which were now reported to be developing 670bhp at 11800rpm, an impressive figure but still inadequate compared with the 850bhp of the M12/13 BMW, which was then the current benchmark of Formula 1 power.

All the Formula 1 teams went to Rio de Janeiro on 16 January for testing prior to the first championship round in Brazil on 25 March. The new 184s were quick on the straights but there were still the recurrent turbo failures. In the Brazilian race Cheever drove steadily to finish fourth, a lap behind the winner, but Patrese fell out with a broken gearbox, a malady that also eliminated Ghinzani's Osella, which was now using a Tipo 183 turbo engine.

In the South African race two weeks later, the fortunes were reversed. It was Patrese who took fourth by keeping going and Cheever who fell out, this time with a radiator leak. Ghinzani's Osella was destroyed when it caught fire after he went off the road in practice. The team settled down to

a familiar and depressing pattern of failure for the following races, both cars retiring at Zolder, Imola and Dijon, while at Monaco it was worse as Cheever could not even qualify. The woes continued in the Canadian, United States and British races, though in the American race at Dallas Ghinzani's Osella managed to save a small piece of Alfa Romeo honour by taking fifth place. The Formula 1 regulations had been changed at the start of the season and fuel tankage was restricted to 220 litres with a ban on refuelling stops, so in several races the Alfa Romeos dropped out during the closing laps with empty tanks, though not running in competitive places.

The misery at the circuits was matched by that at Milan. Chiti had told Massacesi that it was a mistake to let Marmiroli design and build the new chassis at Euroracing, and commented that it was merely a

19 October 1985: The nadir – both 184Ts are eliminated from the South African GP at Kylami after Cheever collides with Patrese on the first corner of the first lap. (LAT)

revamp of the 1983 design. As a result, Massacesi criticised Pavanello and his management of the team, while Pavanello and Chiti fell out. Massacesi told Chiti that he must take no part in the Formula 1 project and should only concern himself as Chairman of Autodelta and in the activities of that company. Chiti was replaced within the Euroracing team by Giovanni Tonti, who had built up a considerable reputation developing turbo Lancias in endurance sports car racing.

Perhaps it was Tonti's influence, but there was a slight improvement at Monza. The race was bitterly fought and many of the prominent runners dropped out. Cheever, driving with restraint to conserve fuel, worked his way up and was in third place five laps before the end when the fuel ran out. Patrese, who may have used less throttle, kept going and inherited third

3 November 1985: The final curtain – Cheever in the 184T during the Australian GP at Adelaide, the last appearance of an Alfa Romeo in a grand prix. He retired after five laps, while Patrese lasted until lap 42. (LAT)

place, although a lap behind the winner at the end. Ghinzani should have been fourth but he too ran out of fuel, and the second Osella, driven by the Austrian driver Jo Gartner, came home fifth. There seemed to be a slight improvement in reliability as well as a drop in fuel consumption, and in the two final races of the season, the European Grand Prix on a new short circuit built at the Nürburgring and the Portuguese race at Estoril, Patrese was sixth and eighth respectively.

The in-fighting at Milan reached a climax in the early autumn. Tonti wanted to replace the Alfa Romeo turbos with German KKKs, and when these were delivered Chiti told Massacesi that the team had been

'ripped off' with the excessive price. Relations between the warring parties had reached a point where there was no hope of any reconciliation, and in November Chiti resigned. With his departure went the last vestiges of Autodelta's autonomy, and immediately it was incorporated into Alfa Romeo to be managed directly from Arese.

During the 1984 grand prix season the Toleman, built by a small British team, had impressed observers with its handling. Its driver was a newcomer, Ayrton Senna, so the handling of the car may have been flattered by the driver's ability, but John Gentry, the Toleman designer, was retained to design a new Alfa Romeo chassis for the 1985 season. A new monocoque tub was prepared with revised suspension, and the finished car became the Tipo 185T. Unfortunately Gentry was only engaged to design the chassis and was not retained for the subsequent development work, so he joined Renault, leaving Tonti and his team to carry out the equally demanding task of making the car race-worthy. More work had also been done on the 182T, which now became the Tipo 815-84T and was reported to develop 720bhp at 11000rpm.

When the cars went to the first round of the 1985 Championship in Brazil on 7 April, the practice times showed that no progress had been made during the winter. On a 3.1-mile (5km) circuit, Patrese was 4 seconds slower than the fastest car, Alboreto's Ferrari, and in the race both cars failed to finish. A sorry pattern was established and it was not until the fifth Championship round in Canada that the team had its first finish, with Patrese in 10th place. In the next race, the United States Grand Prix at Detroit, Cheever achieved the best placing of the season when he came ninth, a placing equalled by Patrese at Silverstone.

The statistics of the 1985 season tell it all. In 32 starts the team recorded 24 retirements. So desperate had the team become that by mid-season, after the British Grand Prix, the 185Ts were discarded and the 184Ts were brought out again in the hope that the earlier cars might get better results. Towards the end of the season there were strong rumours that Alfa Romeo would be withdrawing from Formula 1 and this was confirmed in December. It is not known if Benetton precipitated the decision, but that company's sponsorship was given to the struggling Toleman team during the season, and at the end of the season the Toleman team was bought by Benetton and renamed, so it seems likely that Euroracing would have needed a new sponsor if racing had continued.

For Alfa Romeo the decision cannot have been hard. There had been no victories during the six seasons that the Autodelta/Euroracing team had been competing. There had been some glimmers of hope of success, but at the end the Formula 1 venture had done nothing for the name of Alfa Romeo and had destroyed any lingering aura that was left from the days of the 158. When the exhaust of Patrese's Tipo 184T broke on lap 42 of the Australian Grand Prix in Adelaide on 3 November 1985 a story ended – it was the last Alfa Romeo to race in a grand prix, and in the light of subsequent events it seems unlikely that an Alfa Romeo will ever appear again on a grand prix grid.

Epilogue

WHILE THE EURORACING TEAM had been achieving so little in 1985, the small Osella team had been racing and gaining results that were no worse. Piero Ghinzani was joined by the German driver Christian Danner, but they had a miserable season; the engines lacked sufficient power and the best placing was ninth by Ghinzani at Estoril. For 1986 Osella continued to have a supply of 815-84T V8 turbo engines from Settimo Milanese.

Since Tonti had joined Autodelta in mid-1984 he had been busy working on a new engine design with the intention of having it ready if the Euroracing Formula 1 project continued into 1986. He produced a twin-cam turbo four-cylinder engine, having much in common with the BMW used successfully by Brabham between 1982 and 1984. This was the Tipo 415-85T with dimensions of 92mm x 56.4mm and a capacity of 1498cc; fitted with the KKK turbo that had upset Chiti, it was reputed to develop 820bhp at 10,500rpm on 3.8 bar boost.

At first Benetton seemed interested, but went to BMW instead. Ligier showed great interest in the 415-85T and designed and built a car, the JS29, for the engine, which was fitted with Garrett twin-turbos and developed 900bhp at 10,500rpm with a 4-bar boost. The prototype was tested at Imola early in 1987 by René Arnoux, who complained that there was an inadequate response when the throttle was opened; this was cured by fitting smaller turbos, but then the power was reduced. Relations broke down in March 1987 when Arnoux criticised the engine during an interview on Italian television; this was regarded as damaging to the reputation and image of Alfa Romeo and the following day the company announced that it had withdrawn from the agreement with Ligier. The four-cylinder turbo engine was not seen again.

November 1985: The rejected Tipo 415-85T engine.

In November 1986, in pursuit of a policy of rationalising the Italian motor industry, IRI agreed that Fiat should take over the control and management of Alfa Romeo, which then became a Fiat subsidiary; the take-over took effect on 1 January 1987. Osella had struggled through 1986, still using the obsolete turbo V-8; the team had hoped to buy engines from Motori

Moderni, a company established by Chiti when he left Autodelta, but did not have sufficient funds to buy the engines so Alfa Romeo agreed to supply the V-8 for the rest of the season. Osella's efforts were sadly inadequate and the best result was Ghinzani's 11th place at the Österreichring. At the end of the season the remaining V-8 engines were sold to Osella at a bargain price, and the team began to modify the engines with ideas of their own, new cam boxes being cast with 'Osella' replacing 'Alfa Romeo'. The modifications did little to help a lost cause and the only result in 1987 was a 12th place at Imola. For 1988 the team was down to one car and managed a ninth

place at Monaco, but at the end of the season the modified turbo V-8 engines were abandoned and replaced by Cosworths for 1989, so the last Alfa Romeo engines faded away ignominiously from the grand prix world.

The departure of the Osella-modified engines should have been a sad end to a heroic story, but there was one final ironic twist in the tale. It had always been an ambition of Enzo Ferrari to win the Indianapolis 500 with one of his cars. In the early 1980s, when he was having a dispute with the Formula One Constructors' Association, Ferrari resolved to withdraw from grand prix racing and

devote his efforts to North American CART events and Indianapolis. A turbocharged 2.65-litre V-8 was designed for this purpose, but the dispute was settled and Ferrari was persuaded by John Barnard, the British designer who had left McLaren to join Ferrari in 1986, that the project should be allowed to die. The engine was put on one side at Maranello and forgotten.

In 1969 Fiat had bought from Ferrari 40 per cent of the shareholding in the company, with an option to buy the 49 per cent held by Enzo Ferrari after his death. Ferrari died on 14 August 1988, and two days after his death Fiat announced that it would exercise the option to buy the outstanding shares. The Fiat executives did an audit of the assets at Maranello and came upon the V-8 turbo engine. It was

25 May 1986: Christian Danner takes his Osella, fitted with an 815-84T V-8 engine, round La Source hairpin during the Grand Prix de Belgique at Spa-Francorchamps. He retired after two laps. (LAT)

30 May 1990: Roberto Guerrero in the March 89CE with the Alfa Romeo-labelled Ferrari engine. He was placed 23rd in the Indianapolis 500. (Indianapolis Hall of Fame Museum)

decreed that the engine would be used for its original purpose, but it would not be raced as a Ferrari. With the insensitivity for tradition that seems to emerge when one motor manufacturer takes over another, it would be called an Alfa Romeo.

March, which at that time was the most successful constructor of racing chassis for the American market, was commissioned to build a car to house the engine. The result was the March 89CE-Alfa Romeo. It was first raced in the US in 1989. Patrick Racing, at that time the most successful team in United States racing, was engaged to race the car in 1990. It ran at Indianapolis, driven by Al Unser Sr and Roberto Guerrero, but with no great success; during the season Unser crashed at Michigan and was badly hurt. In 1991 the March chassis was replaced by a Lola T91, and the car was driven by Danny Sullivan, but still gained no successes. It was not an Alfa Romeo product, but is mentioned here to complete the story.

With the March 89CE and the Lola T91, the wheel had almost come the full circle. If the story had ended in 1951 it would have been one of triumph and high endeavour. The events of the 1970s and 1980s were not worthy of the great traditions that had gone before, but nothing in those dismal, later years can dim the glory of the golden age of the red cars bearing the quadrifolio and the heroic men who drove them.

Appendix 1

The drivers

THE FOLLOWING ARE BRIEF biographies of drivers who won three or more major races for Alfa Romeo.

ANTONIO ASCARI (1888–1925)

Ascari was born the son of a blacksmith at Bonferraro di Sorga, near Mantua, on 15 September 1888, and in his youth worked on the racing cycles of Giuseppe and Arturo Nuvolari, the father and uncle of Tazio. The family moved to Milan in the early 1900s and Antonio became an agricultural engineer. Pursuing an interest in cars. he acquired the agency for Alfa Romeo in Milan, opening a showroom at 4 Via Castelvetro immediately after the end of the First World War. He bought a 1914 Grand Prix Fiat and won his first event with it, the 1919 Parma–Poggio de Berceto hill climb. A month later he took the Fiat to Sicily and fought for the lead in the Targa Florio, his first race, until he went off the road. His ability was recognised at Portello and he drove Alfa Corse-entered cars in several events in 1920, 1921 and 1922 with minor success, though there was a setback when he was hurt in a crash during the 1922 Mugello race.

Ascari should have won the 1923 Targa Florio but broke down in sight of the finish. He repaired the car, then carried two helpers across the line apparently to win the race, but was told to reverse back to the place of the breakdown and do the distance again without the helpers. While this was happening Sivocci swept by to win the race.

Ascari won his first race in 1923, the Circuito di Cremona with an RL Targa. He was frustrated again in the 1924 Targa Florio when he again broke down in sight of the finish and had to push the car across the line, losing his lead.

When the new P2 appeared, Ascari was the first driver to race it, repeating his win at Cremona. He had more frustration in the GP de l'ACF at Lyon when his P2 broke down while in the lead with only 30 miles (45km) to go. In the Gran Premio d'Italia at Monza he dominated the race, leading from start to finish. In 1925 he had an equal mastery in the Grand Prix de Belgique at Spa, but when leading the GP de l'ACF, run in the wet at Montlhéry on 26 July 1925, he spun off the road and received fatal injuries when the P2 overturned.

Antonio Ascari was the first Alfa Corse driver of world class stature and was regarded by many as the leading driver of his generation. His son Alberto was World Champion in 1952 and 1953, driving a Ferrari, but was himself killed in a testing accident at Monza in 1955.

GASTONE BRILLI PERRI (1893–1930)

Brilli Perri was born in Florence on 24 March 1893, a member of an aristocratic Florentine family, and assumed the title of Count Brilli Perri, though he was not entitled to it. He began racing motor cycles in 1914, and after the First World War started competing with cars. His first important race was the 1920 Circuito di Mugello in

which he came fifth driving a 1914 GP Nazzaro. During 1921 and 1922 he raced a 1914 GP Fiat, coming second at Mugello, and also drove a works Steyr in the Targa Florio. Successes came in 1923, when he set fastest time at the Pistoia and Parma–Poggio hill climbs with a Fiat and Diatto, then won the Mugello race with a Steyr.

His ability was recognised at Portello and he joined the P2 team in 1925. He retired at Spa and was withdrawn at Montlhéry

Gastone Brilli Perri. (Guy Griffiths Collection)

after Ascari's death, but gained an impressive win in the Gran Premio d'Italia at Monza. He also won the Coppa della Perugina with a 3-litre Ballot.

When Alfa Corse withdrew from grand prix racing Brilli Perri was one of the apparent 'purchasers' of a P2, and with it he was second in the Rome race in 1926; driving the Ballot he won the Circuito del Savio. By 1928 he was racing a T35C Bugatti, but drove a 1500-6C Alfa Romeo at Montenero and was also a member of the Materassi Talbot team. After Materassi's death at Monza, Brilli Perri became the principal driver for Scuderia Materassi in 1929, driving a 1500cc GP Talbot and winning at Tripoli and Mugello.

Alfa Corse was now racing again and he joined the team, coming third in the Targa Florio with a 1500-6C. Reunited with a P2, he won his heat in the Gran Premio di Monza, then finished the 1929 season with wins on a P2 at Cremona and on the Bardo circuit in Tunisia. Brilli Perri had arranged to drive again for Alfa Corse in 1930, but was killed in a practice accident driving a Materassi Talbot at Tripoli on 22 March 1930. At the time of his death he had matured into a driver who was capable of matching such aces as Varzi and Nuvolari, and his results at the end of the 1929 season showed that he had the ability to move into the top echelon of drivers.

ANTONIO BRIVIO (1905–94)
The Marchese Antonio Brivio was born on 27 December 1905 at Vercelli, north-west of Milan, where his family were the local aristocratic landowners. After some minor local events, he began racing a French Derby voiturette in 1927. He carried on with the Derby in 1928 and also joined Scuderia Materassi driving one of the 1500cc GP Talbots. His first placing with an Alfa Romeo was at Alessandria in 1930 when he finished fifth in a 1500-6C; he also took fourth place with a Materassi Talbot at Pescara. His first outright win came at the Biella hill climb with a 1750-6C in 1931,

Antonio Brivio. (Guy Griffiths Collection)

and at the end of the season he became an active member of Scuderia Ferrari, although certainly one of the paying customers. Driving for the Scuderia in 1932 Brivio picked up several places in grand prix events, won the Spa 24-hour sports car race and was second in the Mille Miglia. He showed his ability by winning the 1933 Targa Florio with a Monza, and went on to finish first in the Swedish GP the same year.

Ettore Bugatti recognised Brivio's ability and in 1934 he left the Scuderia and joined the Bugatti team, but had little success apart from a second place at Spa, as the T59 he drove was completely outclassed by the German teams. In 1935 he went back to Scuderia Ferrari and won the Targa Florio again, driving a P3, and won at Cosenza, also with a P3. During the season he picked up several places in more important races, but like his Scuderia team-mates he could do little against the German teams. He received an invitation to drive for Auto-Union in 1936, an indication of his ability,

but stayed with the Scuderia and gained a major success winning the Mille Miglia with a 2900-A; driving a 12C-36 he was third in the Grösser Preis von Deutschland at the Nürburgring, and second at Pescara with an 8C-35. His last Alfa Romeo victory was in the Gran Premio del Valentino in 1937 driving a 12C-36.

Brivio retired from the sport at the end of the 1937 season, when Scuderia Ferrari was absorbed into Alfa Corse. During the Second World War he lived in South America and in 1952 made a brief comeback winning his class with a Ferrari in the Mille Miglia. For many years he was a familiar figure at World Championship events as a representative of the FIA, and may be regarded as the father of the World Championship, as he made the initial proposal to the FIA in 1949. He died at Milan in 1994.

Brivio was a good second- or third-string driver who could be quick on his day, but lacked the brilliance to go to the top in grands prix; he could, however, be relied on to bring a car home and his sports car results show his qualities.

GIUSEPPE CAMPARI (1892–1933)
Campari was born at Lodi, 20 miles (35km) south-east of Milan, on 8 June 1892. He started work as an apprentice with the infant ALFA company and soon became a test driver. His first competition drive was with a 40-60 at the 1913 Parma–Poggio di Berceto hill climb, when he was second in his class. In 1914 he drove in his first race, the combined Giro di Sicilia/Targa Florio, coming fourth with a 40-60. It seems that Campari remained at Portello during the 1914–18 War and resumed his competition career when hostilities ended. He had the distinction of being the first driver to win a race with an Alfa Romeo when he took first place in the 1920 Circuito di Mugello with a 40-60, repeating this success in 1921.

When Jano's P2 appeared, it was Campari who gained its first victory in the 1924 GP de l'ACF at Lyon, and he remained a member of the P2 team until the withdrawal from racing at the end of the 1925 season. During the next two seasons, when the P2s were allegedly in private ownership, Campari was very active, he won with a P2 at Pescara in 1927 and 1928 and also gained several successes with Portello-prepared 1500-6Cs in sports car races including the Targa Abruzzo. He was Italian Champion in 1928, and in 1929 he won the Mille Miglia with the first of the new 6C-1750s.

When Scuderia Ferrari was formed in November 1929, Campari was engaged as the team's professional driver and for the next two seasons both the Scuderia and Alfa Corse were his entrants. The 8C Monza was introduced in 1931 and, sharing a car with Nuvolari, Campari gained the car's first victory in the Gran Premio d'Italia; he also won at Pescara with the twin-engined Tipo A, and finished the season as Italian Champion. The 1932 season was not a happy one for Campari; despite his opposition Caracciola had joined the Alfa Corse team and Campari found himself regarded as the third-string driver; he was even being supplanted by Borzacchini, who had come from Maserati. At the end of the season Alfa Corse withdrew from racing, leaving the task to Scuderia Ferrari. Campari, smarting from his diminished status, joined Maserati.

With Maserati he gained his final victory in the GP de l'ACF at Montlhéry, but during the month after that race he found that he was being joined in the Maserati team by Nuvolari and Borzacchini, who had fallen out with Enzo Ferrari. Campari went back to Ferrari and drove the P3s for the rest of the season. He was driving a P3 in the Gran Premio di Monza on 10 September when he went off the track on the opening lap of the race; being killed instantly when the car overturned. Borzacchini was killed in the same accident, and Czaikowski was also killed later in the day.

Apart from his motor racing ability,

Campari had a fine operatic voice, and while critics considered that he was not in the top flight, he made some professional appearances. He had intended the Monza race to be his last, and hoped to make a living in opera. Campari, his ample girth showing evidence of his love of good living, had been the bedrock of Alfa Romeo racing success for nearly 20 years. A talented and versatile driver, he was universally loved by his team-mates and deeply mourned.

RUDOLF CARACCIOLA (1901–59)

Caracciola was born at Remagen-am-Rhine on 30 January 1901, the son of a hotelier. He was apprenticed to the Fafnir company and drove a Fafnir in his first race at Avus in 1922, finishing fourth, then won his first race at Russelheim a month later. He then joined Mercedes, initially as a salesman, but was later loaned a car and gained 13 victories in 1923 and 25 in 1924. His first major

Rudolf Caracciola. (Guy Griffiths Collection)

win was the 1926 Grösser Preis von Deutschland at Avus, and he repeated this win in 1927 at the Nürburgring. Driving SS and SSK sports cars, Caracciola won the 1929 Ulster TT and the 1931 Mille Miglia, sharing the distinction, with Stirling Moss, of being the only non-Italians to win the race. In 1931 he won the Grösser Preis again and also succeeded at Avus and in the Eifelrennen with a Mercedes SSKL.

At the end of 1931 Mercedes withdrew from racing so Caracciola joined Alfa Corse. At first, largely at Campari's insistence, his Monza was painted white to differentiate him from the Italian members of the team, but after a win in the Eifelrennen he became a fully acknowledged team member and with the new P3 won the Grösser Preis at the Nürburgring and the Gran Premio di Monza; with the P3 he was also European Mountain Champion.

The withdrawal of Alfa Corse at the end of 1932 left Caracciola without a drive, so he formed Scuderia CC with Louis Chiron, driving a pair of Monzas. A serious crash in practice at Monaco left him with a shattered femur and he was unable to race for a year. When he recovered he joined Mercedes-Benz, which had returned to racing in 1934 and, with the Auto-Union team, dominated grand prix racing until the beginning of the Second World War in 1939. Caracciola was the recognised leader of the Mercedes team and won 18 grands prix as well as gaining many places; he was the European Champion in 1935, 1937 and 1938.

He became a Swiss national and spent the War years there. In 1946 he went to race at Indianapolis and crashed in practice, suffering severe head injuries. When Mercedes returned to sports car racing with the 300SL in 1952, Caracciola joined the team and, after taking fourth place in the Mille Miglia, he crashed in practice at Berne, fracturing his femur again; after that he retired from the sport. His health failed and he died at Monchenberg on 28 September 1959.

Regarded by many as the greatest driver

of the 1930s, his results showed that he was arguably the equal of Nuvolari; when he raced for Alfa Corse in 1932 he was just reaching full maturity as a driver and his best years came later with Mercedes-Benz.

LOUIS CHIRON (1899–1979)

Born in Monaco on 3 August 1899, Chiron served in the French Army as a staff car driver during the First World War. His father was maitre d'hotel at the Hotel de Paris and the debonair Chiron worked as a dance partner in the hotel in the early 1920s. A rich American woman sponsored him in minor events in 1925 with a Brescia Bugatti, and in 1926 he was sponsored by the Swiss, Alfred Hoffman, heir to the Hoffman-La Roche pharmaceutical empire, who bought him a T35C Bugatti. Chiron repaid this sponsorship by running away with Hoffman's wife, Alice

His first important win was in the 1926 Grand Prix du Comminges. He joined the Bugatti works team in 1927 and found his form the following year with wins at Rome, Reims and San Sebastian, culminating with victory in the Grand Prix d'Europe at Monza. In 1929 came another win at San Sebastian and at the Nürburgring, where the Grösser Preis was for sports cars. Still with Bugatti, Chiron won the Grand Prix d'Europe at Spa in 1930 and, using the new T51 Bugatti, won at Monaco in 1931 and shared victory with Varzi in the GP de l'ACF at Montlhéry.

In 1932 Chiron experienced a lean year as the Bugattis were outclassed by the Monzas and the new P3, but in 1933 he joined with Caracciola to race two Monzas in the Scuderia CC. Caracciola was unable to compete after his Monaco crash, but Chiron carried on until August, when he accepted an invitation to join Scuderia Ferrari. He won his first race at Marseille with a P3, went on to win the Masarykuv Okruh at Brno, and finished the season with victory in the Gran Premio de España.

The arrival of the German teams in 1934 changed everything, but Chiron, driving a P3, scored a famous victory in the GP de l'ACF at Montlhéry and also succeeded at Reims and in Morocco. In 1935 the Scuderia was fighting a losing battle against the Germans, and Chiron's only win was a minor one at Nancy. He crashed his P3 at Berne and was not fit for the latter part of the season, but he scored a valiant second place with the Bimotore at the Avus and was praised for his third place in the Eifelrennen ahead of the majority of the German cars.

At the end of 1935 Chiron parted with Ferrari. He had been unhappy with criticism in the Italian press, the politics of the Abyssinian crisis had made his position uncomfortable, and his personal life had been upset when Alice Hoffman left him to marry Caracciola. He signed with Mercedes, but after several retirements and a crash at the Nürburgring he left the team and went off to drive for Talbot in sports car races.

By the start of the Second World War he had virtually retired form the sport, but he made a successful return in 1946 driving for Talbot and won the GP de l'ACF at Lyon in 1947 and the GP de France at Reims in 1949. He went on to race Maseratis and OSCAs in the early years of the World Championship, and his final race was at Monaco in 1955 when he was sixth driving a Jano-designed Lancia D50. He had shown his versatility by winning the 1954 Monte Carlo Rally.

After his retirement Chiron became a major organiser of the Grand Prix de Monaco; he died on 22 June 1979. He was probably at his peak in the early 1930s and at that time may well have been the fastest driver of all, as he showed at Spa in 1931. Unlike some of his contemporaries he had great sympathy with his car and could nurse home a sick car when others would have broken it.

PHILLIPE ETANCELIN (1896–1981)

Etancelin, always known as 'Phi Phi', was born at Rouen on 28 December 1896. He worked in the family business as a wool merchant and began racing in 1927 with a T35B Bugatti; after some minor events he won his first major race, the GP de la Marne at Reims. In 1929 he had a T35C and won at Reims, Comminges and La Baule; keeping the T35C in 1930, he scored his greatest victory winning the GP de l'ACF at Pau and also the minor race at Grenoble. When the Monza was offered to customers in 1931, Etancelin had the first. Before it was delivered he had a final Bugatti win at St Raphael, but with the Monza, painted blue, he drove mainly in French races and had a run of profitable wins, taking first place at Dieppe, Grenoble and Comminges.

With the appearance of the P3 in 1932 the going was harder for the independents, but Etancelin went to the lesser races and won at Peronne, also picking up several places. In 1933 the Monza campaigned its third season and Etancelin was the winner at Reims and at Peronne; he was leading the GP de l'ACF on the last lap when he had clutch trouble and was passed by Campari within sight of the flag. In 1934 he abandoned Alfa Romeo in grands prix and bought a new 8CM Maserati, which made him a thorn in the side of Scuderia Ferrari, which was now frequenting the lesser events to earn money and avoid the German teams; he picked up several places and beat the P3s at Dieppe. He remained faithful to Alfa Romeo at Le Mans, where he won the 24-hour race driving with Chinetti. In 1935 he raced Maseratis with Trossi's Scuderia Subalpina and also bought a new V-8 Maserati, but it was outclassed, though it gave him one win at Pau early in 1936.

Etancelin had a season away from racing in 1937, but returned in 1938 and 1939 to drive a 4½-litre Lago-Talbot for the French team. The car was outclassed by the Germans, but he picked some places by keeping going. After the Second World War he had the distinction of being the first driver to race an Alfa Romeo when he brought out the elderly Monza for the Bois de Boulogne meeting in September 1945. In 1946 and 1947 he drove a Maserati and

Delage without success, and in 1948 he bought one of the first of the new Lago-Talbots.

For the next four seasons Etancelin was a regular member of the grand prix circus, although over 50 years old he was still capable of offering a serious challenge, and gained a number of places and one win in the 1949 GP de Paris at Montlhéry. His most impressive drive was in the GP d'Italia at Monza in 1949 when he took second place behind Ascari's Ferrari. His last race was at Rouen in 1953, and he died on 13 October 1981.

With his cap turned back-to-front and his wheel-sawing driving style, Etancelin was one of the great characters of grand prix racing for nearly 25 years. A formidable competitor in the early 1930s, as typified by his wheel-to-wheel duel with Nuvolari at Nice in 1933, driving identical Monzas, it was surprising that Scuderia Ferrari did not sign him up. He was certainly as good as Lehoux or Dreyfus, but his somewhat intermittent race appearances seem to indicate that he may have put his business interests before racing and may not have been interested in becoming a full-time professional.

LUIGI FAGIOLI (1898–1952)

Fagioli was born at Osimo, near Ancona, on 9 June 1898, and with his nickname 'The Abruzzi Robber' the motoring press in the 1930s sometimes gave the impression that he was a rough, uncouth hillbilly. Nothing could have been further from the truth – Fagioli was a cultured man, a qualified accountant who had a substantial holding in a family pasta-making business. He began racing in 1925 with an 1100cc Salmson driving in hill climbs, and his first race was the Coppa del Perugina in which he was third. He followed this up a month later by taking second place in the Coppa Acerbo at Pescara. He continued with the Salmson in 1926 and 1927, getting four second places in the latter season, including the cyclecar class of the Targa Florio. In 1928 he moved up a class, buying a 1500cc

Tipo 26 Maserati, and again picked up a number of places, with the consolation of setting fastest time at the Tolentino hill climb. It was much the same story in 1929, but Fagioli was noticed for his performance in Tripoli when, driving the Salmson in the 1100cc class, he battled wheel-to-wheel for the whole race with Biondetti's similar car and was beaten on the line by 0.2 second.

He made few appearances in 1930, but for the Coppa Ciano at Montenero he had a works 2½-litre Tipo 26 Maserati and gained his first victory. The next year he had a full season driving in all the major grands prix, but the Maserati was not fast enough to beat the new Monza and it was not until the Gran Premio di Monza at the end of the season that Fagioli had a win, beating all the recognised aces. In 1932 the Maseratis were quicker with 2.8-litre engines, and Fagioli was up with the front runners all season, but now had to contend with the new P3 so only had one victory at Rome. He would have won the GP d'Italia at Monza but for poor pitwork.

The next stage of Fagioli's career came when Nuvolari left Scuderia Ferrari and joined Maserati in the middle of the 1933 season. Fagioli responded by going to Ferrari to take the vacant seat. Driving a P3 he had immediate success with wins at Pescara, Comminges and in the GP d'Italia on the fateful day when Campari, Borzacchini and Czaikowski were killed. The results he gained with Scuderia Ferrari secured him the 1933 Italian Championship.

During the winter of 1933/34 Fagioli was asked to test the new Mercedes W25. He liked the car so abandoned Ferrari and signed with Mercedes for 1934, achieving wins at Pescara, Monza and San Sebastian. He stayed with Mercedes for 1935 and won at Monaco, Avus and Barcelona. Mercedes had a bad season in 1936 and Fagioli saw little success; his proud temperament made him a difficult team member as he felt his talents were not fully recognised. He stalked away from Mercedes and joined Auto-

Union for 1937, but only drove in three races before being taken ill and retiring from the sport, not racing again before the Second World War.

Fagioli reappeared in 1948, having two insignificant outings with a 4CL Maserati, so it was a matter of great surprise when he was signed up by Alfa Corse to drive in the team of Tipo 158s when Alfa Romeo returned to racing in 1950. Although nearly 52 years old he fully justified the selection and in the 1950 season gained four second places and two third places, coming third in the World Championship. He was retained by the team in 1951 but only drove in one race, the GP de l'ACF at Reims, his last grand prix. At half distance he handed his car over to Fangio who went on to win, so the victory was shared and Fagioli went into the record book as the oldest driver to win a World Championship round.

In 1952 he crashed a GT Lancia Aurelia in practice for a sports car race at Monaco. His injures seemed slight, but he died three weeks later on 20 June. Fagioli's abilities have probably never been fully recognised. In the mid-1930s his results showed that he was right at the top, and he was a model member of the Alfa Corse team in 1950/51.

JUAN MANUEL FANGIO (1911–95)

Considered by many to be, with Nuvolari, the greatest racing driver of all time, Fangio was the son of an Italian father who went to Argentina in his childhood. He was born at Balcarce, about 200 miles (300km) from Buenos Aires, on 24 June 1911. He was apprenticed as a motor mechanic, then started his own garage business. He built a special based on a Ford A with a V-8 engine, which he drove in his first race at Necochea in 1938, finishing seventh. He moved on to a modified Chevrolet and gained his first win in the International Grand Prix of the North, a race over open roads from Buenos Aires to Lima and back, a distance of 5920 miles (9519km), in September 1940. Other successes followed, and when the South American series of races began after the Second World War, Fangio was prominent and came to the notice of the visiting drivers.

With sponsorship from General Peron he went to Europe for the first half of the 1949 season and won five races, three with Maserati and one each with Ferrari and Gordini. When Alfa Corse returned to racing in 1950 with the 158, Fangio was signed up, and had a most successful season with wins at San Remo, Monaco, Spa, Reims, Geneva, Pescara and Silverstone. He was runner-up in the World Championship to Farina. It has been suggested that Fangio was slightly bitter about the result of the Championship, feeling that the team had given him inferior cars and preferred Farina. In 1951 the battle for the Championship was much harder as Ferrari was in the ascendant, but Fangio won at Berne, Reims, Bari and Barcelona and gained several places, finishing the season as World Champion.

When Alfa Romeo withdrew from racing at the end of 1951 Fangio signed with BRM, but the 1952 and 1953 World Championships were run for Formula 2 cars and BRM was left on the sidelines. Fangio raced a Maserati in 1952 and was badly hurt when he crashed at Monza, being out of action for nearly a year. In 1953 he raced for Maserati again and was runner-up in the Championship. With the start of the 2½-litre Formula in 1954, he stayed with Maserati until Mercedes returned to racing with the W196, halfway through the season. His results with both marques gave him the 1954 Championship. The 1955 season was abbreviated after the Le Mans crash, but Fangio won four of the six rounds and was second in another, so the Championship was his again.

As Mercedes had pulled out at the end of 1955 he went to Ferrari in 1956 and raced the Jano-designed D50 Lancia-Ferrari, winning the Championship once more. In 1957 he went back to Maserati and, driving a 250F that was probably inferior to the opposition, he won his fifth World

Championship. After two races in 1958 he retired from the sport, leaving a record that has never been beaten or equalled.

A quiet, modest man, Fangio gained world-wide respect, affection and admiration for his astonishing ability; he had the remarkable combination of Nuvolari's 'tiger' combined with Chiron's sympathy for the car. When he died on 17 July 1995 he was universally mourned.

GIUSEPPE FARINA (1906–66)

Born in Turin on 30 October 1906, Farina was the son of one of the founders of the coachbuilding firm of that name. He qualified as a doctor of engineering before starting his motor racing career. His first event was the Aosta-Grand St Bernard hill climb in 1932, but it was an inauspicious beginning as he crashed his 1500-6C Alfa Romeo and was taken to hospital with slight injuries. After gaining experience in hill climbs and rallies, he began racing with a Monza of the Scuderia Subalpina in 1934. The car was outclassed, but at the end of the season he bought a 1500cc 4CM Maserati, and with this he kept up with the Scuderia Ferrari P3s at Biella, coming third ahead of Brivio. He then took the Maserati to Czechoslovakia and won a major voiturette race on the Brno circuit. In 1935 he remained with Scuderia Subalpina, driving a variety of Maseratis, but in grands prix there were no victories, though he picked up several places.

His driving ability was noted by Enzo Ferrari and he joined the Scuderia in 1936, staying with it in 1937. Once more he picked up a number of places driving an 8C-35 and a 12C-36, but had only one victory, at Naples in 1937. When Scuderia Ferrari was absorbed into Alfa Corse early in 1938 Farina was retained, and during 1938 he concentrated on representing Alfa Romeo in grand prix racing with the 308 and 312, picking up places when the German teams showed uncharacteristic unreliability; he did not drive the 158 in its early races. For the 1939 season he was

recognised as the leading driver of the team, and as well as the 3-litre cars he drove the 158, winning at Livorno and Berne. At the Swiss meeting he drove a 158 in the full grand prix and held the Mercedes for several laps. Farina finished his pre-war career by winning at Tripoli in 1940. He was Italian Champion in 1937, 1938 and 1939.

When racing was resumed in 1946 Farina was in a 158 and won the first major event at Geneva, but later in the season there were tensions between the drivers in the team and he was not selected for 1947. He did not race in that year but came back in 1948 with a Maserati and gained a number of successes, the most important at Monaco. He then joined the new Ferrari team for the latter part of the season and scored a first win for a Formula 1 Ferrari at Garda in 1948. In 1949 he drove a Maserati as an independent and was the only driver to give a challenge to the Ferrari team. When Alfa Corse returned to racing with the 158 in 1950, Farina joined the team and took first place at Silverstone, Berne and Monza, his results making him the first FIA World Champion. He stayed with the team in 1951 and, in a hard season battling with the Ferraris, had only one victory at Spa.

With the withdrawal of Alfa Romeo at the end of 1951 Farina joined Ferrari. The old Formula 1 had been abandoned and the World Championship was being run under Formula 2 rules. He was the second string in the team to Ascari, who was at his peak, and in two seasons Farina won only one grande épreuve at the Nürburgring in 1953. When Ascari joined Lancia in 1954 Farina's prospects looked brighter, but then Mercedes returned to racing and the Ferraris were outclassed. Farina suffered burns halfway through the 1954 season in a sports car race at Monza, and did not return until 1955, but though he picked up some places he could not beat the Mercedes. His last grand prix drive was at Spa in 1955, when he finished third, and apart from two abortive attempts to run at Indianapolis he retired from the sport.

After retiring he ran Jaguar and Alfa Romeo dealerships, and was killed in a road accident at Chambéry, driving a Lotus-Cortina, on 30 June 1966. A tough, courageous driver who was always willing to take on a fight, there was a less happy side to Farina's nature as he had a ruthless streak and was involved in several accidents during his career involving the deaths of other drivers.

TAZIO NUVOLARI (1892–1953)

Regarded by many as the greatest driver of the interwar era, Nuvolari comes high on any enthusiast's list of all-time great drivers. He was born on 16 November 1892 at Casteldario, about 10 miles (15km) from Mantua. His father and uncle were famous racing cyclists, so Nuvolari was brought up in an atmosphere of wheeled competition. He served in the Italian Army during the First World War and began racing motor cycles in 1920. His first car race was the Circuito del Garda on 22 May 1921, when he drove an Ansaldo, but he continued to race motor cycles and his first win with a car was at the Circuito del Golfo del Tiguilio on 11 April 1924, driving a Tipo 18 Bianchi. With Bianchi he was the 1924 500cc motor cycle champion of Italy. In 1925, though he only raced motor cycles that season, he was given a trial by Alfa Corse, which was seeking to fill the vacancy left by Antonio Ascari's death. He drove a P2 at Monza but crashed during the test and was slightly hurt.

It was motor cycles again in 1926, when Nuvolari won the Italian 500cc Championship for the second time, but in 1927 he joined forces with Varzi, forming Scuderia Nuvolari with Type 35 Bugattis, and won at Rome and Garda, also gaining several places. In 1928 there were wins at Tripoli, Pozzo and Alessandria, but the arrangement with Varzi broke down and, after a relatively poor 1929 season with no wins but several places, Nuvolari joined Alfa

Corse and Scuderia Ferrari for the 1930 season. With a 1750-6C he won the Mille Miglia and the Ulster TT and gained several hill climb victories with a P2. He had another good season in 1931 with the advent of the 8C, and there were wins in the Targa Florio, the GP d'Italia and at Montenero. He was coming to the peak of his powers by 1932, driving Monzas and the new P3, and there were wins at Monaco, the Targa Florio, the GP d'Italia, the GP de l'ACF, Montenero and Pescara, these results making him the 1932 Champion of Italy.

Although the 1933 season began well with a Mille Miglia win, relations broke down between Nuvolari and Ferrari as Alfa Romeo withdrew the P3, and the Monza he had to use was obsolescent. However, driving the Monza he gained wins at the Eifelrennen and Nîmes, and also won the Le Mans 24-hour race, sharing an 8C with Sommer. Halfway through the season, Nuvolari left Scuderia Ferrari and joined Maserati, winning at Spa in his first race for his new team and following this with a win at Montenero. He also won the Ulster TT with a K3 MG. In 1934 he fluctuated between Maserati and Bugatti, driving the Type 59, but his season was interrupted by a crash at Alessandria when he fractured his leg, and there were only two minor wins at Modena and Naples at the end of the season.

The quarrel was patched up with Ferrari for the 1935 season, but there was now almost insurmountable opposition from the German teams, he was still driving the obsolete P3, wins came in minor events at Pau, Bergamo, Biella and Turin. Nuvolari drove the Bimotore at Tripoli and Avus but was defeated by tyre failure, though he broke international class records with the car. At the Nürburgring in the 1935 GP von Deutschland Nuvolari had his greatest win of all; driving a P3, he outdrove the German teams and gained a remarkable and wholly unexpected victory. He finished the season with wins at Montenero, Nice and Modena,

the latter being the first success for the new 8C-35.

The 8C-35 was outclassed as soon as it appeared, but in 1936 Nuvolari gained some victories against the German teams by dint of his superb driving; he won at Barcelona, Budapest, Milan and Modena, and had a most profitable trip to the United States, winning the Vanderbilt Cup. The introduction of the 12C-36 did nothing to redress the balance in 1937, and his only win was at Milan. He had talks with Auto-Union about a contract and drove an Auto-Union at Berne; becoming disillusioned with Alfa Romeo, he left Alfa Corse after his 308 caught fire in practice at Pau in April 1938, announcing his retirement.

However, three months later he signed with Auto-Union, and after an uneasy start mastered the new technique needed for a rear-engined car, winning the GP d'Italia and the Donington GP. He only had one win in 1939, at Belgrade in the very last race before the outbreak of the Second World War.

When the War ended Nuvolari began racing again with a 4CL Maserati. However, his health was failing – he was suffering from emphysema – and some of the magic had gone from his driving. He nonetheless won the GP d'Albi in 1946, and in 1947 gained a remarkable second place in the Mille Miglia with an 1100cc Cisitalia. He also won two minor races with a sports Ferrari; the second of these, at Parma on 13 July 1947, was his last racing victory. The next three seasons marked a gradual decline in his powers and his last success was a class win in his final event, the Palermo–Monte Pellegrino hill climb in April 1950, driving an Abarth. His health continued to decline and he died at Mantua on 11 August 1953.

Nuvolari's sheer virtuosity and his ability to win a race when all the odds were stacked against him set him apart from his rivals; at his peak in the mid-1930s he had a quality that no one could match. There was another side, however – he was arrogant and fiercely self-centred, and had little mechanical sympathy with his cars, from which he always expected a performance to match his own. None of this can detract from a man, who probably shares with Fangio the distinction of being the greatest driver to race an Alfa Romeo.

RAYMOND SOMMER (1906–50)

Sommer was born in Paris on 31 August 1906. His family were carpet manufacturers at Sedan, on the edge of the Ardennes, and it was the prosperity of the business that enabled him to start racing. He began in 1930 driving a 4.7-litre Chrysler Imperial – the race seems to have been the GP de Picardie – and he gained his first success in 1931 when he won the unlimited class with the Chrysler in the Spa 24-hour race, but retired at Le Mans. In 1932 he bought a Mille Miglia 8C and gained a major victory at Le Mans, sharing the car with Luigi

Raymond Sommer at Silverstone, two weeks before his death. (Guy Griffiths)

Chinetti; he also bought a Monza, which he campaigned in the latter half of the 1932 season. He picked up several places and finished the season by winning at Miramas, beating Nuvolari's P3, which lost time through poor pitwork. In 1933 he began the season with a new 8CM Maserati, but after a few races he reverted to the Monza, forming a team with another up-and-coming driver, Jean-Pierre Wimille; there were some places but no wins. He gained a second victory at Le Mans, this time sharing an 8C with Nuvolari.

In 1934 Sommer drove an 8CM Maserati, but hardly finished a race, being plagued with mechanical problems, so for the 1935 season he bought a 1932 P3 from Scuderia Ferrari, winning at Comminges and also in the GP de l'UMF at Montlhéry. The elderly P3 was completely outclassed in 1936, and the next year Sommer joined Scuderia Ferrari, driving a 12C-36 and sometimes appearing in an 8C-35 ostensibly as a private entrant. By 1937 the 8C and 12C were as outclassed at the P3 had been the year before, and Sommer had nothing to show for the season. When the Scuderia was taken over by Alfa Corse, Sommer was retained but had no success in 1938; in the two races when he drove a 158 it broke down. During the abbreviated 1939 season Sommer raced a 308 in grands prix as a private entrant, but it was certainly a thinly disguised works entry.

During the Second World War Sommer was in the French Resistance, and at the end of the War he brought out the 308 and picked up some places before abandoning it for a Maserati, with which he scored several wins during the 1946 season, the most memorable at St Cloud when both 158s retired. He had little fortune with a works Maserati in 1947 and spent some time away from the sport with illness, but drove the ill-fated CTA-Arsenal, the French equivalent of the BRM, on its only appearance.

When Ferrari entered grand prix racing in 1948 Sommer was signed up as a works driver and remained for 1949, but halfway through the season he left Ferrari and became a private entrant with a 4½-litre Lago-Talbot, finishing the year with a win at Montlhéry. He had some successful drives for Gordini in Formula 2. Keeping the Talbot in 1950, in another memorable drive he led the 158s at Spa until the Talbot expired. He also won several Formula 2 races with a Ferrari. Sommer's last GP drive was in the BRM on its début at Silverstone, when it broke down on the startline. Two weeks later, on 10 September 1950, he was driving an 1100c Cooper in a minor Formula 2 race at Cadours when he crashed after an apparent mechanical failure and was killed instantly.

Sommer's nickname of 'The Lionheart' summed him up: he was a tremendous fighter, and while all too often his car broke under him, he was usually in the lead or fighting for it. In grand prix racing he was a 'nearly' man, and his results did not do justice to his ability, though his continuous failures seem to show that he expected too much of his cars.

CARLO FELICE TROSSI (1908–49)

Enzo Ferrari said of Trossi, 'He spent the whole of his life … as an amateur.' Count Trossi, a rich aristocrat, was born at Gaglianico, near Biella, in 1908, in the castle owned by his family. He was a rich man, his fortune coming from his estates, the wool industry and the Banco Sella, owned by the family. He started competition motoring in 1928 with a Mercedes in minor events, then had a Bugatti. With his wealth and his interest in motor racing he was a natural sponsor of Scuderia Ferrari, and at the end of 1931 he bought the shares of Alfredo Caniato in the Scuderia and became its president at the beginning of 1932.

Ferrari found that his new president, though an amateur, had a driving ability that approached that of the professionals, and he made his mark immediately by taking second place in the 1932 Mille Miglia with an 8C. During 1932 and 1933 he drove mainly in hill climbs, with several wins, and also had some successes with sports cars, notably in the Targa Abruzzo. In 1934 he was promoted to the full racing team, driving a P3, and showed his maturity by winning at Montreux, Vichy and Biella. As a diversion he built his own grand prix car with an aircraft-type radial engine, but it was a complete failure.

The going was hard for the Scuderia against the German teams in 1935, and Trossi only picked up places in the lesser races. The manner in which the Scuderia was becoming wholly professional did not suit Trossi's lifestyle, and he ceased to drive for it in August 1935, at the end of the season resigning as president. Subsequently Trossi must have sold his shares in the Scuderia to Alfa Romeo to have enabled the company to get an 80 per cent holding in the Scuderia when it was taken over two years later.

In 1936 he formed Scuderia Torino, racing Maseratis, and was highly successful with voiturettes. Later, joining the Maserati works team, he became Italian 1500cc Champion in 1936 and runner-up in 1937. However, ill-health was affecting him and he retired from some races feeling unwell. He stayed with Maserati until 1940, when he joined Alfa Corse for the Tripoli race, finishing third on his first drive with a 158.

During the Second World War Trossi served as a pilot with the Regia Aeronautica and rejoined Alfa Corse to drive the 158s when racing began again in 1946. He won the Circuito di Milano in 1946 and the GP d'Italia in Turin in 1947. By 1948 he was a sick man, but he continued to race and won the GP d'Europe at Berne. His last race was the GP di Monza in September 1948, when he was second, but his health then declined rapidly and he died of lung cancer on 9 May 1949. His death was almost certainly one of the factors that prompted Alfa Romeo to stop racing in the 1949 season.

Trossi's results show that he had as much ability as the best of his contemporaries, but Ferrari's verdict was probably right – he was a natural amateur and was not 'hungry' enough to put the final edge on his driving that would have taken him to the top. Perhaps he should be regarded as the greatest of all the amateur drivers.

ACHILLE VARZI (1904–48)

In the early 1930s, for every enthusiast who regarded Nuvolari as the best driver of all, there was an equal number who proclaimed the same of Varzi. He was born at Galliate, about 25 miles (40km) west of Milan, on 8 August 1904, the son of a prosperous textile manufacturer. He started racing motor cycles in 1923, and in his first season was Italian 350cc Champion riding a Garelli. He went on to ride for Sunbeam and was Italian 500cc Champion in 1926. In that year he bought a T37 Bugatti, and his first major event was the GP di Milano, but he went back to motor cycles in 1927, riding for Moto-Guzzi.

His fiercest rival in motor cycle racing was Nuvolari, who suggested that they should join forces in a team, Scuderia Nuvolari, to race a pair of T35 Bugattis during the 1928 season. The preparation of the cars was supervised by Nuvolari, who always seemed to have the better car, and towards the end of the season, in a decision that caused much ill-feeling between the partners, Varzi terminated the arrangement and bought a P2 from Campari. Sharing the car with Campari, Varzi was second in the GP d'Europe. Varzi had a good year in 1929 as the P2 won at Alessandria, Rome, Montenero and Monza, and he was Champion of Italy. The P2 was bought back by Alfa Corse at the end of the season and rebuilt, so in 1930 Varzi was a works driver with an updated car; he won at Alessandria again, and gained his legendary, and almost incendiary, victory in the Targa Florio. Nuvolari was driving a P2 for Scuderia Ferrari, and by mid-season their duels were becoming bitter, especially as Nuvolari had just beaten him in the Mille Miglia, so Varzi left Alfa Corse and joined Maserati. With a Tipo 26M he won at Pescara, Monza and San Sebastian.

In 1931 Varzi joined Ettore Bugatti and raced a T51, winning at Tunis and Alessandria and sharing the victory with Chiron in the GP de l'ACF at Montlhéry, though he was defeated by the conditions in another legendary Targa Florio drive. Varzi stayed with Bugatti in 1932, but the T51 was outclassed by the P3 and his only win was at Tunis. He continued with Bugatti in 1933, probably hoping that the promised T59 would redress the balance with the P3, but it was with a T51 that he won at Monaco after his heroic duel with Nuvolari. He went on to win the controversial 'lottery' race at Tripoli, and also won at the Avus. When the T59 appeared at the end of the 1933 season it was not competitive, so Varzi left Bugatti and joined Scuderia Ferrari, where a vacancy had been left by Nuvolari's departure to run a Maserati as an independent. He won at Tripoli, just beating the Scuderia new boy Moll by a length, and was also successful in the Targa Florio, at Montenero and Nice; settling the score of 1930, Varzi beat Nuvolari in the Mille Miglia.

Varzi realised that the German teams were unbeatable, so in 1935 he joined Auto-Union and won at Tunis and Pescara. He signed with Auto-Union again in 1936 and won at Tripoli. His personal life began to intrude into his racing when he formed a relationship with Ilse Pietsch, the wife of another Auto-Union driver, who encouraged him into drug addiction. He had a narrow escape when he crashed at Tunis, and after that his driving declined noticeably. Auto-Union did not retain him in 1937, and apart from a voiturette win with a Maserati at San Remo in 1937 and a brief appearance with an 8CTF Maserati at Tripoli in 1938, he disappeared from the racing scene.

During the Second World War he beat his addiction and, fully fit, joined Alfa Corse in 1946 to race the 158. He was right back to his old form, winning at Turin and coming second at Milan after winning his heat. During the winter of 1946/47 he took a 308 to South America and won at Rosario and Interlagos. Back with the 158 in 1947, he won at Bari and took three second places, then in the winter went back to South America and, with a modified 312, won at Interlagos again. His first race with the 158 in 1948 was at Berne, and during practice on 30 June he took out the experimental 158/47. He lost control in the rain, the car hit a kerb and overturned at a low speed. Varzi died almost instantly from head injuries.

During the early 1930s at a time when Nuvolari was still approaching his prime, Varzi was right at the top and was possibly the best driver of that era, though on his day Chiron may have been quicker. Quiet, elegant and introverted, he was the antithesis of Nuvolari, but technically was his equal. Having beaten his drug addiction, his ability was just as evident when he returned to the sport in the immediate post-war seasons.

JEAN-PIERRE WIMILLE (1908–49)

Wimille was regarded by many as a World Champion who never wore the crown. He was born in Paris on 26 February 1908, the son of a journalist, and his entry into racing was sponsored by Mme Mareuse, who raced a touring T40 Bugatti and bought a T37A Bugatti for him. His first important event was the 1930 GP de l'ACF at Pau and he continued with the T37A for the early part of the 1931 season. In May he bought a new T51 in collaboration with Jean Gaupillat, a rich amateur, and they ran in the GP d'Italia at Monza where Wimille's driving made a good impression. The 1932 season saw his first win in the GP d'Oranie with the T51, and in mid-season he bought a Monza and won his first race with it, the GP de Lorraine. He continued with the

Jean-Pierre Wimille. (Guy Griffiths Collection)

Monza in 1933 and picked up some good places but no wins. He joined the Bugatti works team in 1934 and drove the outclassed T59, his only success coming in the last race of the season in the GP d'Algérie. In 1935 he soldiered on with the works T59 but could only gain some places in the lesser events. It was the same dismal tale in 1936, though the T59 had become the T59/50 monoposto, but he did win at Deauville and came a profitable second behind Nuvolari in the Vanderbilt Cup.

In 1937 Bugatti concentrated on sports car racing and Wimille had a successful season, his best result being a victory at Le Mans. Bugatti made a feeble return to grand prix racing in 1938 but gave up halfway through the season, and Wimille was invited to join Alfa Corse; unfortunately the

308 and 312 he raced were little better than the Bugatti. It may have been political policy, as he was not given a chance in the 158, which seemed to have been reserved for Italian drivers, but he had some consolation with another win for Bugatti at Le Mans in 1939.

Wimille enlisted in the L'Armée de l'Air at the start of the Second World War, joined the Resistance after the fall of France, and ended the War as a liaison officer in North Africa. He won the very first post-war race in the Bois de Boulogne in September 1945 with the previously outmoded Bugatti, then in 1946 he had wins in the Bois de Boulogne and at Perpignan with a 308. Alfa Corse recruited him again to drive the 158 and he won his heat at Geneva, was third in the final and was third at Turin.

He found his real form in 1947, when he only had two drives in the 158 but won both, at Berne in the GP der Schweiz and at Spa in the GP de Belgique. It was the same in 1948 – he began the season with a second place at Berne, then had a hat-trick of wins at Reims in the GP de l'ACF, Turin in the GP d'Italia and in the GP di Monza. When not engaged with the 158, Wimille had been racing a Gordini successfully in Formula 2, and he took one of these to South America for the winter series in 1948/49. While practising for the Gran Premio de Gen Peron at Buenos Aires he crashed early in the morning of 28 January 1949 and died of head injuries shortly afterwards.

In the 1947 and 1948 seasons Wimille had shown that he was the finest driver in grand prix racing – a new star. Fangio would soon take his place and openly acknowledged that he had been a pupil of Wimille and had learned much of his craft from him. Wimille had intended to make a career in politics when he retired from motor racing.

Appendix 2

Brief specifications of the principal Alfa Romeo racing cars

40-60 (1913–22)
Engine
110mm x 160mm, 6082cc, four cylinders in line
Pushrod ohv by two camshafts in crankcase
Fixed head, cast-iron block and crankcase
Two valves per cylinder, two updraught carbs
82bhp at 2400rpm

Transmission
Multi-plate clutch; four speeds

Chassis
Channel section
Semi-elliptic springs front and rear
Mechanical drum brakes on rear only
850 x 160 tyres

Weight
2425lb (1100kg)

Dimensions
Wheelbase: 9ft 8in (2950mm)
Track: 4ft 9ins (1450mm)

GRAND PRIX (1914–21)
Engine
100mm x 143mm, 4490cc, four cylinders in line
Two overhead camshafts
Fixed head, cast-iron block, alloy crankcase
Two valves per cylinder, two updraught carbs
88bhp (1914) 102bhp (1921) at 3000rpm

Transmission
Multi-plate clutch; four speeds

Chassis
Channel section
Semi-elliptic springs front and rear
Mechanical drum brakes on rear only
860 x 160 tyres

Weight
2315lb (1050kg)

Dimensions
Wheelbase: 9ft 10in (3000mm)
Track: 4ft 9in (1450mm)

RL TARGA FLORIO (1923–24)
Engine
76mm x 110mm, 2994cc (1923), 80mm x 120mm,
   3620cc (1924), six cylinders in line
Pushrod ohv by camshaft in crankcase
cast-iron detachable head and block, alloy
   crankcase
Two valves per cylinder, two updraught carbs
88bhp at 3600rpm (1923), 125bhp at 3800rpm
   (1924)

Transmission
Multi-plate clutch; four speeds

Chassis
Channel section
Semi-elliptic springs front and rear
Four-wheel mechanical brakes
820 x 120 tyres

Weight
2160lb (980kg)

Dimensions
Wheelbase: 9ft 5ins (2880mm)
Track: 4ft 9½ins (1460mm)

P1 (1923)
Engine
65mm x 100mm, 1990cc, six cylinders in line
Two overhead camshafts
Fixed head, cast-iron block, alloy crankcase, welded
   water jackets
Two valves per cylinder, two updraught carbs
80bhp at 4800rpm

Transmission
Multi-plate clutch; four speeds

Chassis
Channel section
Semi-elliptic springs front and rear
Four-wheel mechanical drum brakes
820 x 120 tyres

Weight
1874lb (850kg)

Dimensions
Wheelbase: 8ft 8ins (2650mm)
Track: front 3ft 11½in (1200mm), rear 4ft 1in
   (1240mm)

P2 (1924–30)
Engine
61mm x 85mm, 1987cc, eight cylinders in line
Two overhead camshafts
Fixed head, cast-iron block, two-piece alloy
   crankcase, welded water jackets
Two valves per cylinder, Roots supercharger
140bhp (1924), 155bhp (1925), 175bhp (1930) at
   5500rpm

Transmission
Multi-plate clutch; four speeds

Chassis
Channel section
Semi-elliptic springs front and rear
Four-wheel mechanical drum brakes
525 x 19 tyres (front), 600 x 19 (rear, 1924),
   29 x 550 (rear, 1930)

Weight
1653lb (750kg) (1924), 1720lb (780kg) (1930)

Dimensions
Wheelbase: 8ft 7½in (2635mm)
Track: front 4ft 3in (1300mm) (1924), rear 3ft
   11½in (1200mm) (1924), front and rear 4ft 6in
   (1380mm) (1930)

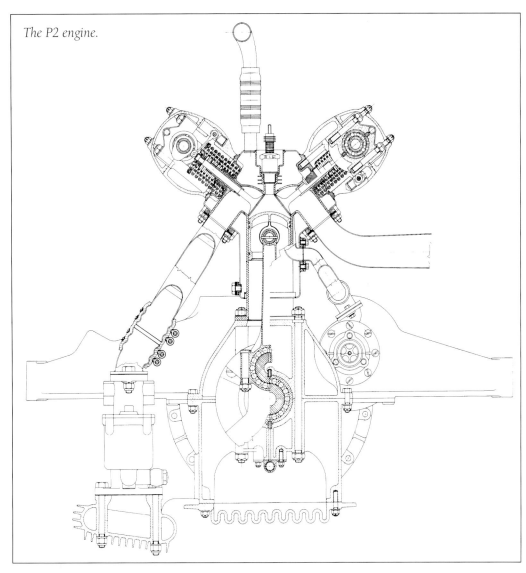

The P2 engine.

Two overhead camshafts
Fixed head, cast-iron block, alloy crankcase
Two valves per cylinder, Roots supercharger
115bhp at 5200rpm (total 230bhp)

Transmission
Two multi-plate clutches
Two three-speed gearboxes with linked change
Two propshafts

Chassis
Channel section
Semi-elliptic springs front and rear
Four-wheel mechanical drum brakes
600 x 18 tyres (front), 600 x 19 (rear)

Weight
2046lb (980kg)

Dimensions
Wheelbase: 9ft 2in (2800mm)
Track: 4ft 6in (1380mm)

MONZA (1931–33)
Engine
65mm x 88mm, 2336cc (1931), 68mm x 88mm,
    2556cc (1933), eight cylinders in line
Two overhead camshafts
Detachable head, block and crankcase in light
    alloy
Two valves per cylinder, Roots supercharger
165bhp at 5400rpm (1931), 180bhp at 6500rpm
    (1933)

Transmission
Multi-plate clutch; four speeds

Chassis
Channel section
Semi-elliptic springs front and rear
Four-wheel mechanical drum brakes
29 x 550 tyres

Weight
2024lb (920kg)

Dimensions
Wheelbase: 8ft 8in (2650mm)
Track: 4ft 6in (1380mm)

P3 (TIPO B) (1932–35)
Engine
65mm x 100mm, 2654cc (1932–3), 68mm x
    100mm, 2905cc (1934–5), 71mm x 100mm,
    3165cc (1935), 78mm x 100mm, 3822cc (1935),
    eight cylinders in line
Two overhead camshafts
Fixed head, alloy block and electron crankcase
Two valves per cylinder, two Roots superchargers

6C-1500 MMS (1928–9)
Engine
62mm x 82mm, 1487cc, six cylinders in line
Two overhead camshafts
Fixed head, cast-iron block, alloy crankcase
Two valves per cylinder, Roots supercharger
84bhp at 5000rpm

Transmission
Multi-plate clutch; four speeds

Chassis
Channel section
Semi-elliptic front and rear
Four-wheel mechanical drum brakes
27 x 475 tyres

Weight
1896lb (860kg) in sports trim

Dimensions
Wheelbase: 9ft 0in (2750mm)
Track: 4ft 6in (1380mm)

6C-1750 SS (1929–30)
Similar to 6C-1500 except:

Engine
65mm x 88mm, 1752cc
95bhp at 5000rpm

Chassis
28 x 525 tyres (1930)

TIPO A (1931)
Engines
Two mounted in parallel, each:
65mm x 88mm, 1752cc, six cylinders in line

215bhp at 5600rpm (1932–33), 255bhp at
5400rpm (1934/5), 330bhp at 5400rpm (1935)

Transmission
Multi-plate steel and dural clutch; four speeds
(1932–4), three speeds (1935)
Two propshafts

Chassis
Box section welded
Semi-elliptic springs front and rear (1932/34),
Dubonnet independent front, reverse quarter
elliptics rear (1935)
Four-wheel mechanical drum brakes (1932–34),
hydraulic actuation (1935)
600 x 19 tyres (1932/34), 650 x 18 front, 650 x 19
rear (1935)

Weight
1543lb (700kg) (1932–34), 1595lb (725kg)
(1935)

Dimensions
Wheelbase: 8ft 8in (2650mm)
Track: front 4ft 6in (1370mm), rear 4ft 3ins
(1300mm)

BIMOTORE (1935)
Engines
Two 2905cc or 3165cc P3 engines, one in front and
one behind the driver
525bhp total (5910cc), 540bhp total (6330cc)

Transmission
Multi-plate steel and dural clutch
Propshaft from rear engine to central gearbox,
attached to rear of front engine; three speeds
Separate propshaft to each rear wheel.

Chassis
Welded box section
Dubonnet independent front, semi-elliptic rear
Four-wheel hydraulic drum brakes
550 x 20 tyres (front), 700 x 20 (rear)

Weight
2266lb (1030kg)

Dimensions
Wheelbase: 9ft 2 ins (2794mm)
Track: 4ft 6in (1380mm)

8C-35 (1935–36)
Engine
78mm x 100mm, 3822cc, eight cylinders in line
Fixed head, alloy block, electron crankcase
Two valves per cylinder, two Roots
superchargers
330bhp at 5400rpm

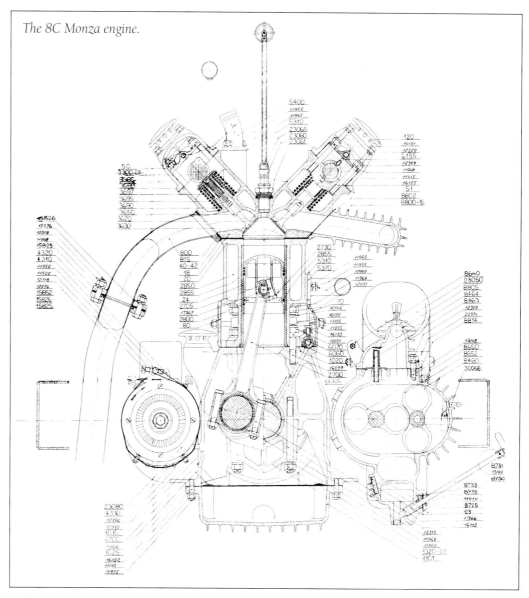

The 8C Monza engine.

Transmission
Multi-plate steel and dural clutch; four-speed gearbox
in unit with rear axle

Chassis
Box section welded
Twin trailing links with coil springs front, swing axles
with transverse leaf spring rear
Four-wheel hydraulic drum brakes
650 x 19 tyres

Weight
1617lb (735kg)

Dimensions
Wheelbase: 9ft 0in (2750mm)
Track: 4ft 5in (1350mm)

12C-36 (1936–37)
Similar to 8C-35 except:

Engine
70mm x 88mm, 4064cc, 12 cylinders in 60-degree
vee
Two overhead camshafts per cylinder block
Fixed head, two alloy blocks, electron
crankcase
Two valves per cylinder, single supercharger
370bhp at 5800rpm

Chassis
650 x 18 tyres (front), 700 x 18, 19 or 20 (rear)

Weight
1804lb (820kg)

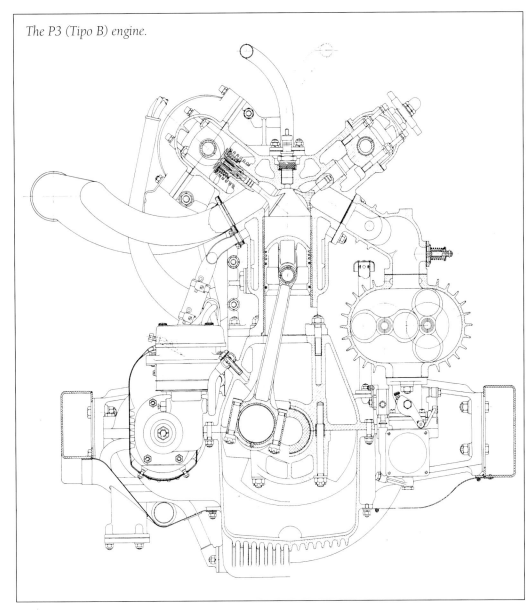

The P3 (Tipo B) engine.

12C-37 (1937)
Similar to 12C-36 except:

Engine
72mm x 92mm, 4495cc
430bhp at 5800rpm

Chassis
525 x 19 tyres (front), 700 x 19 (rear)

Weight
1782lb (810kg)

Dimensions
Wheelbase: 9ft 2in (2800mm)
Track: 4ft 5in (1350mm)

308 (1938/39)
Similar to 8C-35 except:

Engine
69mm x 100mm, 2991cc, eight cylinders in line
Two overhead camshafts
Fixed head, light alloy block, electron crankcase
Two valves per cylinder, two Roots
    superchargers
295bhp at 6000rpm

Chassis
525 x 19 tyres (front), 700 x 19 (rear)

Weight
1914lb (870kg)

Dimensions
Wheelbase: 9ft 0ins (2750mm)
Track 4ft 5 ins (1370mm)

312 (1938)
Similar to 12C-37 except:

Engine
66mm x 73mm, 2995cc, 12 cylinders in
    60-degree vee
350bhp at 6500rpm

Chassis
525 x19 tyres (front), 700 x 19 (rear)

Weight
1936lb (880kg)

Dimensions
Wheelbase: 9ft 0in (2750mm)
Track: front 4ft 5in (1370mm), rear 4ft 8in
    (1430mm)

316 (1938–39)
Similar to 12C-37 except:

Engine
58mm x 70mm, 2958cc, 16 cylinders in
    60-degree vee
Two overhead camshafts per cylinder block
Fixed head, alloy blocks, electron crankcase
Two valves per cylinder, two Roots superchargers
440bhp at 7500rpm

Chassis
550 x 19 tyres (front), 700 x 19 (rear)

Weight
2024lb (920kg)

Dimensions
Wheelbase: 9ft 0ins (2750mm)
Track: front 4ft 5in (1370mm), rear 4ft 8in
    (1430mm)

158 (1938–48)
Engine
58mm x 70mm, 1479cc, eight cylinders in line
Two overhead camshafts
Fixed head, alloy blocks, electron crankcase
Two valves per cylinder, single Roots supercharger
    (1938–46), two-stage Roots superchargers
    (1946–48)
195bhp at 7000rpm (1938), 225bhp at 7500rpm
    (1939), 254bhp at 7500rpm (1946), 275bhp at
    7500rpm (1947), 310bhp at 7500rpm (1948)

Transmission
Multi-plate clutch; four-speed gearbox in unit with rear axle

Chassis
Tubular
Twin trailing arms and transverse leaf front, swing axles with transverse leaf rear
Four-wheel hydraulic drum brakes
600 x 18 tyres (1938), 550 x17 front, 700 x 18 rear (1939–48)

Weight
1364lb (620kg) (1938–40), 1540lb (700kg) (1946–48)

Dimensions
Wheelbase: 8ft 2in (2500mm)
Track: 4ft 1in (1250mm)

159 (1950–51)
Similar to 158 except:

Engine
425bhp at 9300rpm

Chassis
De Dion with transverse leaf rear
550 x 17 or 550 x 18 tyres (front), 700 x 18 or 700 x 19 (rear)

Weight
1562lb (710kg)

177 (1979)
Engine
77mm x 53.6mm, 2995cc, flat-12 cylinders
Two overhead camshafts per bank
Light alloy heads, blocks and crankcase
Four valves per cylinder, fuel injection
520bhp at 12000rpm

Transmission
Two-plate clutch; five or six speeds

Chassis
Alloy monocoque
Double wishbone and in-board coilspring/dampers front, double wishbones with radius arms and inboard coilspring/damper units rear
Hydraulic disc brakes front and rear
9.5/25.0 x 15 tyres (front), 16/28.0 x 13 (rear)

Weight
1290lb (585kg)
This was the minimum permitted weight – the car certainly always exceeded it

Dimensions
Wheelbase: 8ft 11in (2740mm)

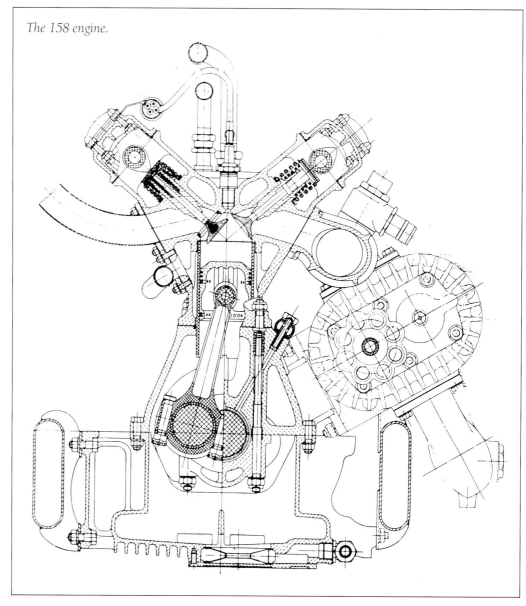

The 158 engine.

Track: 5ft 6in (1700mm) (front), 4ft 11in (1500mm) (rear)

179 (1979–81)
Same as 177 except:

Engine
78.5mm x 51.5mm, 2995cc, 12 cylinders in vee
Twin overhead camshafts per bank
Light alloy heads, blocks and crankcase
Four valves per cylinder, fuel injection
525bhp at 12300rpm

Weight
1340lb (609kg)

182 (1982)
Same as 177 except:

Engine
548bhp at 12300rpm

Chassis
Carbon fibre monocoque

Weight
1179lb (535kg)
Ballast was added to reach minimum weight

The 159 engine with two-stage superchargers.

182T (183T, 184T and 185T) (1982/85)
Similar to 182 except:

Engine
74mm x 43.5mm, 1497cc, eight cylinders in vee
Two overhead camshafts per bank
Light alloy heads, blocks and crankcase
Four valves per cylinder, turbocharger
720bhp at 11000rpm

Appendix 3

Principal victories of Alfa Romeo racing cars

Event	Driver	Car
1920		
Circuito di Mugello	Campari	40-60
1921		
Circuito di Mugello	Campari	40-60
1923		
Targa Florio	Sivocci	RL
Circuito di Cremona	Ascari	RL
1924		
Circuito di Cremona	Ascari	P2
Coppa Acerbo	Ferrari	RL
Grand Prix d'Europe	Campari	P2
Gran Premio d'Italia	Ascari	P2
1925		
Coppa Acerbo	Ginaldi	RL
Grand Prix d'Europe	Ascari	P2
Gran Premio d'Italia	Brilli Perri	P2
1927		
Coppa Acerbo	Campari	P2
1928		
Coppa Acerbo	Campari	P2
1929		
Circuito di Alessandria	Varzi	P2
Premio Reale di Roma	Varzi	P2
Coppa Ciano	Varzi	P2
Gran Premio di Monza	Varzi	P2
Circuito di Cremona	Brilli Perri	P2
Grand Prix de Tunisie	Brilli Perri	P2
1930		
Circuito di Alessandria	Varzi	P2
Targa Florio	Varzi	P2
1931		
Targa Florio	Nuvolari	Monza
Gran Premio d'Italia	Campari/Nuvolari	Monza
Grand Prix de Dieppe	Etancelin	Monza
Coppa Ciano	Nuvolari	Monza
Circuit du Dauphine	Etancelin	Monza
Coppa Acerbo	Campari	A
Grand Prix du Comminges	Etancelin	Monza
1932		
Grand Prix de Monaco	Nuvolari	Monza
Targa Florio	Nuvolari	Monza
Eifelrennen	Caracciola	Monza
Gran Premio d'Italia	Nuvolari	P3
Grand Prix de Picardie	Etancelin	Monza
Grösser Preis von Lemburg	Caracciola	Monza
Grand Prix de Lorraine	Wimille	Monza
Grand Prix de l'ACF	Nuvolari	P3
Grösser Preis von Deutschland	Caracciola	P3
Coppa Ciano	Nuvolari	P3
Coppa Acerbo	Nuvolari	P3
Gran Premio di Monza	Caracciola	P3
Grand Prix de Marseille	Sommer	Monza
1933		
Grand Prix de Tunisie	Nuvolari	Monza
Circuito di Alessandria	Nuvolari	Monza
Grand Prix de Picardie	Etancelin	Monza
Targa Florio	Brivio	Monza
Eifelrennen	Nuvolari	Monza
Grand Prix de Nîmes	Nuvolari	Monza
Grösser Preis von Lemburg	Bjornstad	Monza
Gran Premio de Pena Rhin	Zanelli	Monza
Grand Prix de la Marne	Etancelin	Monza
Mannin Moar	Lewis	Monza
Sveriges Grand Prix	Brivio	Monza
Coppa Acerbo	Fagioli	P3
Grand Prix du Comminges	Fagioli	P3
Grand Prix de Marseille	Chiron	P3
Gran Premio d'Italia	Fagioli	P3
Masarykuv Okruh	Chiron	P3
Gran Premio de España	Chiron	P3
1934		
Grand Prix de Monaco	Moll	P3
Circuito di Alessandria	Varzi	P3
Gran Premio di Tripoli	Varzi	P3
Grand Prix du Maroc	Chiron	P3
Targa Florio	Varzi	P3
Avusrennen	Moll	P3
Mannin Moar	Lewis	P3
Grand Prix de Montreux	Trossi	P3
Gran Premio de Pena Rhin	Varzi	P3
Grand Prix de l'ACF	Chiron	P3
Grand Prix de Vichy	Trossi	P3
Coppa Ciano	Varzi	P3
Grand Prix de Nice	Varzi	P3
Grand Prix du Comminges	Comotti	P3
Circuito di Biella	Trossi	P3
1935		
Grand Prix de Pau	Nuvolari	P3
Targa Florio	Brivio	P3
Coppa Citta di Bergamo	Nuvolari	P3
Grand Prix de l'UMF	Sommer	P3
Circuito di Biella	Nuvolari	P3
Grand Prix de Lorraine	Chiron	P3
Gran Premio del Valentino	Nuvolari	P3
Grand Prix de Dieppe	Dreyfus	P3
Grösser Preis von Deutschland	Nuvolari	P3
Coppa Ciano	Nuvolari	P3
Grand Prix du Comminges	Sommer	P3
Grand Prix de Nice	Nuvolari	P3
Circuito di Modena	Nuvolari	8C-35
Coppa Edda Ciano	Tadini	P3
Donington Grand Prix	Shuttleworth	P3
Coppa della Sila	Brivio	P3
1936		
Gran Premio de Pena Rhin	Nuvolari	8C-35
Gran Premio de Sao Paolo	Pintacuda	2900A
Magyar Nagy Dij	Nuvolari	8C-35
Circuito di Milano	Nuvolari	8C-35
Coppa Ciano	Nuvolari/Pintacuda	8C-35
Coppa Edda Ciano	Tadini	8C-35
Circuito di Modena	Nuvolari	12C-36

Event	Driver	Car	Event	Driver	Car	Event	Driver	Car
Donington Grand Prix	Ruesch/Seaman	8C-35	**1946**			**1950**		
George Vanderbilt Cup	Nuvolari	12C-36	Coupe de la Resistance	Wimille	308	Gran Premio di San Remo	Fangio	158
			Grand Prix du Roussillon	Wimille	308	British Grand Prix	Farina	158
1937			Grand Prix de Bourgogne	Wimille	308	Grand Prix de Monaco	Fangio	158
Gran Premio del Valentino	Brivio	12C-36	Grand Prix des Nations	Farina	158	Grösser Preis der Schweiz	Farina	158
Coppa Principessa di Piemonte	Farina	12C-36	Grand Premio del Valentino	Varzi	158	Grand Prix de Belgique	Fangio	158
			Circuito di Milano	Trossi	158	Grand Prix de l'ACF	Fangio	158
Circuito della Superba	Trossi	12C-36				Gran Premio di Bari	Farina	158
Gran Premio di Rio de Janeiro	Pintacuda	8C-35	**1947**			Grand Prix des Nations	Fangio	158
			Gran Premio de Rosario	Varzi	308	Circuito di Pescara	Fangio	158
Gran Premio di Milano	Nuvolari	12C-36	Grösser Preis der Schweiz	Wimille	158	International Trophy	Farina	158
			Grand Prix de Belgique	Wimille	158	Gran Premio d'Italia	Farina	158
1938			Gran Premio di Bari	Varzi	158			
Gran Premio di Rio de Janeiro	Pintacuda	308	Gran Premio d'Italia	Trossi	158	**1951**		
						Grösser Preis der Schweiz	Fangio	159
Coppa Ciano Junior	Villoresi	158	**1948**			Ulster Trophy	Farina	158
Gran Premio di Milano	Villoresi	158	Gran Premio de Sao Paolo	Wimille	308	Grand Prix de Belgique	Farina	159
			Grösser Preis der Schweiz	Trossi	158	Grand Prix de l'ACF	Fangio/Fagioli	159
1939			Grand Prix de l'ACF	Wimille	158	Gran Premio di Bari	Fangio	159
Coppa Ciano	Farina	158	Gran Premio d'Italia	Wimille	158	Gran Premio de España	Fangio	159
Coppa Acerbo	Biondetti	158	Gran Premio di Monza	Wimille	158			
Prix de Berne	Farina	158						
			1949					
1940			Gran Premio de Argentina	Galvez	308			
Gran Premio di Tripoli	Farina	158						

Bibliography

Altieri, Paolo and Lurani, Giovanni *Alfa Romeo 1910–1982* (Automobilia, 1982)

Bellu, Serge *Blue Blood* (Frederick Warne, 1979)

Birkin, Sir Henry *Full Throttle* (G. T. Foulis & Co, 1933)

Blight, Anthony *The French Sports Car Revolution* (Haynes, 1996)

Boddy, William *Montlhéry* (Cassell, 1961)

Borgeson, Griffith *The Alfa Romeo Tradition* (Automobile Quarterly, 1990)

Bradley, W. F. *Ettore Bugatti* (Motor Racing Publications, 1948)

Targa Florio (G. T. Foulis & Co, 1956)

Caracciola, Rudolf *A Racing Driver's World* (Cassell, 1962)

Carli, Emanuele Alberto *Settant'Anni di Gare Automobilistiche in Italia* (AC d'Italia, Editrice dell Automobile, 1967)

Cherrett, Angela *Alfa Romeo Tipo 6C* (Haynes, 1989)

Alfa Romeo 8C Modello 2300 (Veloce Publishing, 1992)

Cimarosti, Adriano and Zagari, Franco *Monza, Il Gran Premio d' Italia* (Federico Motta Editore, 1989)

Colombo, Gioachino *Origins of the Ferrari Legend* (Haynes, 1987)

Court, William *Power and Glory* Volume 1 (Macdonald, 1966)

Grand Prix Requiem (Patrick Stephens, 1992)

Delsaux, Jean-Paul *Francorchamps 1948–1960* (Author, 1990)

Dreyfus, René (with Beverley Rae Kimes) *My Two Lives* (Aztex Corpn, 1983)

Earl, Cameron C. *Quicksilver* (HMSO, 1996)

Eason-Gibson, John *Motor Racing 1946* (Motor Racing Publications, 1948)

Motor Racing 1947 (Motor Racing Publications, 1949)

Fangio, Juan Manuel *My Twenty Years of Racing* (Temple Press, 1961)

Ferrari, Enzo *The Enzo Ferrari Memoirs* (Hamish Hamilton, 1963)

Fusi, Luigi *Alfa Romeo Tipo A* (Emmeti Grafica, 1982)

Le Alfa di Merosi et di Romeo (Editrice Dimenzione, 1985)

Le Alfa Romeo di Vittorio Jano (Autocritica, 1982)

Tutte le Vetture Alfa Romeo dal 1910 (Emmeti Grafica, 1978)

Green, Evan *Alfa Romeo* (Evan Green Pty, 1976)

Griffiths, Trevor R. *Grand Prix: The Complete Guide* (Blitz Editions, 1997)

Gunston, Bill *World Encyclopaedia of Aero Engines* (Patrick Stephens, 1986)

Henry, Alan *Brabham, The Grand Prix Cars* (Hazelton Publishing, 1989)

Fifty Years of Ferrari (Haynes, 1997)

March, The Grand Prix and Indy Cars (Hazelton Publishing, 1989)

Hibbert, Christopher *Mussolini* (Longman, 1962)

Hodges, David *The Alfa Romeo Type 158/159* (Profile Publications, 1967)

The French Grand Prix (Temple Press, 1967)

The Monaco Grand Prix (Temple Press, 1964)

Huet, Christian *Gordini: Un Sorcier, Une Equipe* (Editions Christian Huet, 1984)

Hull, Peter *The Type RL Alfa Romeos* (Profile Publications, 1966)

Cars in Profile: Alfa Romeo Tipo B (Profile Publications, 1973)

Hull, Peter and Slater, Roy *Alfa Romeo: A History* (Cassell, 1964)

Jane's Encyclopaedia of Aviation (Jane's Publishing, 1980)

Jenkinson, Denis *Directory of Historic Racing Cars* (Aston Publications, 1987)

(Editor) *Fangio* (Michael Joseph, 1973)

Kupelian, Yvette and Sirtaine, Jacques *Soixante Ans de Competition Automobile en Belgique 1896–1956* (Kupelian & De Bock)

Ludvigsen, Karl *The Mercedes-Benz Racing Cars* (Bond/Parkhurst Books, 1971)

Lurani, Giovanni *La Storia de la Mille Miglia* (Istituto Geografico de Agostini, 1979)

Racing Round the World (G. T. Foulis & Co, 1956)

Monza: Official Year Books, 1960–64 (SIAS, 1961–65)

Moore, Simon *The Immortal 2.9* (Parkside Publications, 1986)

Montagna, Paolo *The Legendary Italian Grand Prix* (AC Promotion, Milan, 1989)

Moretti, Valerio *Grand Prix Tripoli* (Automobilia, 1994)

When Nuvolari Raced (Veloce Publishing, 1994)

Nixon, Chris *Racing the Silver Arrows* (Osprey, 1986)

Nye, Doug *History of the Grand Prix Car 1945–65* (Hazelton Publishing, 1993)

History of the Grand Prix Car 1966–91 (Hazelton Publishing, 1992)

Orefici, Oscar *Carlo Chiti: Sinfonia Ruggente* (Edizioni di Autocritica, 1991)

Orsini, Luigi and Zagari, Franco *La Scuderia Ferrari* (Editoriale Olimpia, 1979)

Maserati (Emmeti Grafica, 1980)

Owen, David *Viva! Alfa Romeo* (Haynes, 1976)

Pomeroy, Laurence *The Grand Prix Car*, Volumes 1 & 2 (Temple Press, 1954)

Posthumus, Cyril *The German Grand Prix* (Temple Press, 1966)

Rosemeyer, Elly Beinhorn and Nixon, Chris *Rosemeyer!* (Transport Bookman Publications, 1986)

Setright, Leonard *The Grand Prix Car 1954/66* (George Allen & Unwin, 1968)

Sheldon, Paul and Rabagliati, Duncan *A Record of Grand Prix and Voiturette Racing*, Volumes 1–5, 8–10 (St Leonards Press, 1987–96)

Small, Steve *The Grand Prix Who's Who* (Guinness Publishing, 1996)

Smith, Herschel *A History of Aircraft Piston Engines* (Sunflower University Press, 1980)

Taruffi, Piero *Works Driver* (Temple Press, 1964)

Varisco, Franco *The Genesis of Ferrari* (Hyde Park Group, 1990)

Venables, David *The Racing 1500s* (Transport Bookman Publications, 1984)

Yates, Brock *Enzo Ferrari* (Doubleday 1991)

Newspapers and periodicals

L'Auto
Autocar
Autocourse
Automobilia
Autosport
Classic & Sports Car
Classic Car
La Gazetta dello Sport
L'Auto Italiana
Motor
Motor Racing
Motor Sport
Motori, Aero, Cicli e Sports
Speed
The Times
Vintage Sports Car Club Bulletin

Index

Pavesi: 156
Pedrini: 11
Pena Rhin, Gran Premio de: 79, 89, 104, 113
Penske (car): 215, 216, 218
Perkins, Larry: 215, 216
Peron, Eva Duarte: 161, 172
Peron, General Juan Domingo: 161, 164, 170, 172, 254
Perouse, M: 78
Pescara, Circuito di: 181
Pessatti, Pablo: 161
Peterson, Ronnie: 208–210, 219, 224, 225
Petit, Emil: 65
Petacci, Claretta: 153
Peugeot (car): 12, 25, 30, 40
Philip Morris: 238
Piacenza, Istituto Technico: 8
Pietsch, Ilse: 112, 166, 192, 257
Pietsch, Paul: 75, 112, 148, 192, 193
Pintacuda, Carlo: 49, 100, 104, 107–110, 112, 113, 117, 118, 122–124, 135, 145, 147–150
Piper (aircraft): 218
Piquet, Nelson: 225–228, 239
Pirelli: 17, 53, 186, 189, 221, 229
Pirola, Nino: 128
Pironi, Didier: 227
Pistoiese, Coppa della Collina: 249
Pogliano, Angelo: 14
Pogliano, Zefferino: 14
Polesine, Circuito del: 30
Poland, German invasion of: 149
Pomeroy, Laurence: 39, 40
Poore, Dennis: 164
Porsche (car): 203, 211
Porsche, Ferdinand: 35, 96, 121
Portugal, Gran Premio de: 243
Premio Reale di Roma: 44, 49, 55, 61, 67, 68, 250
Prost, Alain: 235
Pryce, Tom: 218
Putti, Prof: 79, 100

Race of Champions: 213, 216, 226
Ramponi, Giulio: 30, 33, 42, 45, 47, 75, 80, 119
Rangoni, Lothario: 149
"Raph, Georges" (Raphael Bethenod de Las Casas): 106, 164
Reale Automobile-Club d'Italia (RACI): 35, 45, 50, 73, 108, 125, 139, 144
Record of Grand Prix and Voiturette Racing, A: 54
Redlefsen: 212
Rees, Noel: 89
Regazzoni, Gianclaudio (Clay): 215, 216, 226, 228
Regia Aeronautica: 40, 47, 60, 84, 85
Reichschancellor: 74, 77
Renault (car): 7, 224, 232, 233, 235, 242, 244
Resta, Dario: 31
Reutemann, Carlos: 212–216, 219, 223, 224
Rex: 119
Rhineland, German re-occupation of: 120
Ricard, Paul: 210
Ricardo Consulting Engineers: 144
Ricardo, Harry: 144, 146
Ricart-Espana (car): 121
Ricart y Medino, Wifredo Pelayo: 121,

127, 131, 142, 144–146, 149, 151–153, 154
Rimini, Giorgio: 16–18, 27, 28, 43, 56
Rindt, Jochen: 205, 207, 212
Rio di Janiero, Gran Premio de: 117, 123, 135
RIV: 84
Rizzoli Istituto: 79
Rocco, Giovanni: 148
Rodriguez, Pedro: 205
Rohan, Vicomte de: 69
Rolland-Pillain (car): 35
Rome-Berlin Axis (German-Italian Axis): 144, 146
Romeo & C, Ing Nicola SA: 14
Romeo, Nicola: 13, 19, 30, 40, 41, 43, 47
Romeo, Nicola & CSA Italiana: 14, 15, 30, 43, 47, 129
Ronzoni: 10
Rosario City Grand Prix: 161, 165
Rosemeyer, Bernd: 101, 105, 108, 112–114, 117, 123, 125
Roselli, Arnaldo: 97
Rosenberger, Adolf: 50
Rosier, Louis: 179, 181
Rossi di Montelera, Count: 212
Rossi, Severino: 28
Rousillon, Grand Prix du (Perpignan): 156
Royal Air Force: 139, 150–152
Royal Automobile Club (RAC): 170
Rudge (motor cycle): 145
Ruesch, Hans: 118, 164
Rutzler, Hermann: 25

Sailer, Max: 19, 37
Salamano, Carlo: 35
Salmson (car): 65, 253
Samiero, Vasco: 79
Sanesi, Consalvo: 56, 144, 151, 156, 158, 159, 161, 162, 164–167, 170, 175, 183–189, 191, 196
San Germano, Nicolo: 238
San Marino, Gran Premio di: 228, 234, 236, 239, 242, 246
Santoni, Antonio: 10
Satta, Orazio: 154, 156, 157, 166, 170, 172, 188, 191
Savio, Circuito di: 25, 30, 250
Savoia-Marchetti (SIAI Savoia): 85
Scaini (battery): 230
Scat (car): 10, 11
Scheckter, Jody: 216, 218, 222, 228
Schmid, Hans-Gunther: 218
Schweiz, Grosser Preis von: 94, 107, 118, 125, 138, 148, 161, 177, 185, 238, 258
Scuderia Ambrosiana: 166, 170
Scuderia CC: 74, 75, 77, 81, 251, 252
Scuderia Ferrari: 53, 54, 56, 58, 66–68, 72, 74, 75, 77–81, 85, 87, 88–91, 94–101, 103–105, 107, 109–111, 114, 116–119, 121, 123, 124, 131, 134, 145, 170, 174, 203, 238, 250, 251, 253, 255, 256
Scuderia Materassi: 51, 66, 250
Scuderia Nuvolari: 47, 53, 255, 257
Scuderia Nuvolari-Ferrari: 79, 81
Scuderia Serenissima: 203
Scuderia Subalpina: 252
Scuderia Torino: 110, 138, 257
Seaman, Richard (Dick): 110, 119, 123, 124, 126, 136, 147

Segrave, Henry: 31, 32, 34
Senna, Ayrton: 243
SERA: 230
Serafini, Dorio: 174, 183
Serenissima, Societa per Azioni Automobili Turismo Sport: 203
Severi, Francesco: 63, 110, 117, 118, 133, 136, 137, 139–141, 145, 147, 148
Shadow (car): 218
Sheldon, Paul: 54, 72, 75, 183
Shuttleworth, Richard: 105, 107, 109
Siena, Eugenio: 66, 72, 75, 80, 112, 122, 133, 134
Simca-Gordini (car): 164, 165, 167, 169, 170, 172, 256, 258
Sivocci, Ugo: 17–19, 21, 23–27, 31, 59, 201
Slater, Roy: 24
Slomans, Roger: 236
Smith-Winby, John: 7, 8
Snipe, Cyril: 11
Societe Italiana di Credito Provinciale (SICP): 13, 14
Soler-Roig, Alex: 210
Sommer, Raymond: 73, 75, 77–80, 104, 106, 107, 109, 119, 123–125, 133, 134, 138–141, 145, 147, 149, 154, 156, 158, 159, 161, 162, 164, 169, 170, 175, 179, 180, 183, 256
South African Grand Prix: 213, 218, 221, 226, 231, 236, 240, 242
Spa 24-Hour race: 79, 134, 151, 175, 250, 256
Spanish Army Air Force: 121
Spanish Civil War: 113, 117, 120, 121, 138
Speed: 122
Speer, Albert: 152
SPICA (fuel injection): 213, 224, 233
Starace, Achille: 68
Stella, Ugo: 8, 9, 10, 13
Stewart, Jackie: 208
Stewart, Max: 205
Steyr (car): 23–25, 30, 35, 39, 249
Stiles, FW: 51
Stommelen, Rolf: 215
STP: 208
Straight, Whitney: 80, 88, 91, 94
Stuck, Hans: 49, 89–92, 101, 103, 105, 108, 112, 117, 118, 123, 218
Stuck, Hans-Joachim: 218–220
Sudetenland, German occupation of: 141
Sullivan, Danny: 247
Sunbeam (car): 27, 31, 39, 40
Sunbeam (motor cycle): 46, 51
Sunbeam Talbot Darracq: 45
Superba, Circuito della: 123
Supercortemaggiore, Gran Premio: 201
Surcoeuf: 31
Surfers' Paradise: 204
Surtees, John: 207, 216
Susa-Moncenisio hill climb: 62
Svenska Isloppet: 75
Sveriges Grand Prix: 218, 223
Sveriges Sommar Grand Prix: 80, 81, 250
Sylo (turbocharger): 239

Tabacchi: 54
Tadini, Mario: 53, 55, 77, 80, 87, 89, 104, 107, 108, 110, 112, 118, 121, 132, 135

Talbot (car): 45, 47, 48, 50, 66, 250
Talbot-Darracq: 161
Tambay, Patrick: 226
Tarabusi, Augusto: 16, 23, 24
Targa Abruzzo: 97, 251, 257
Targa Florio: 11, 12, 16–18, 24, 30, 45, 49, 54, 58, 68, 77, 88, 98, 150, 185, 209, 211, 249, 250, 253, 255, 257
Targa Florio: 10
Taruffi, Piero: 66, 67, 72, 77, 78, 81, 87, 88, 138, 140, 147, 180, 181, 183, 185, 186, 193, 197
Tasman Series: 203–205
Tauber, Henri: 128, 129
Tavoni, Romolo: 202
Teffe, Manuel de: 117
Temporada Series: 203
Tenni, Omobono: 166
Teretonga International: 204
Testi, Feruccio: 53
Thinwall Special (car): 184–186, 188, 197
Thomas, Rene: 39
Thomson & Taylor: 122
Thorne, Joe: 124
Titan (tractor): 14
Tolentino-Colle de Paterno hill climb: 253
Tomaselli: 9
Tonti, Giovanni: 243–245
Torchy, Paul: 39
Tour of Italy (bicycle): 68
Traianus, Marcus Ulpius, Emperor of Rome: 8
Trevisan, Bruno: 112, 154
Tripoli, Gran Premio di: 45, 47, 52, 77, 87, 97, 99, 103, 112, 122, 133, 145, 150, 187, 250
Trossi, Count Felice: 66, 75, 81, 87, 90, 91, 94, 95, 101, 104, 106, 110, 121–126, 133, 134, 137, 149, 150, 157–159, 161, 162, 164–166, 170, 256
Truman, President Harry S: 172
Tunisie, Grand Prix de: 51, 66, 75, 99, 113, 250
Tyrell (car): 210, 219, 222, 227, 230, 232
Tyrell, Ken: 208

Ugolini, Nello: 90, 99, 100, 106, 112, 117
Ulster Tourist Trophy: 251, 255
Ulster Trophy: 186
Umberto, Crown Prince of Italy: 56, 72, 81–83
UMF, Grand Prix de l': 104, 256
United States Army Air Force: 153
United States Grand Prix: 208, 216, 219, 225, 230, 233–235, 238, 239, 242, 244
United States Grand Prix West: 208, 213, 218, 221, 226, 231, 234, 236, 239
United States 12th Air Force: 153
Unser, Al senior: 247

Valentino, Gran Premio del: 104, 122, 158, 200, 250
Vandervell C A (Tony): 184
Vanwall (car): 184, 208
Varzi, Achille: 46–56, 58–64, 66–68, 71, 72, 75–77, 81, 86–89, 91–95,

97, 99, 100, 107, 108, 112, 116, 118, 121, 126, 133, 157–162, 164–167, 192, 250, 252, 255, 257, 258
Varzi, Norma (Colombo): 166
Verdi, Giuseppe: 11
Versailles, Treaty of: 148
Vichy, Grand Prix de: 91
Vickers Armstrong Wellington (aircraft): 151, 152
Victor Emmanuel lll of Italy, King: 22, 152
Victoria Cross: 150
Villars, Julio: 78
Villeneuve, Gilles: 222, 224, 226, 228, 233, 238
Villoresi, Emilio: 121, 123, 133, 136–141, 145–147, 149
Villoresi, Luigi: 136, 137, 140, 145, 148, 150, 156–158, 161, 164–167, 170, 172, 175, 177, 180, 181, 183–188, 191, 193, 194, 196, 198, 201
Visconti family: 9
Vizcaya, Pierre de: 40
Volpe (car): 169
Volpi, Count Giovanni: 203

Wagner, Louis: 30, 31, 33, 35, 36, 40
Waldthausen, Karl de: 81
Walker, Peter: 189, 191
Walkerley, Rodney: 158
Wanderer (car): 23
Warwick, Derek: 239
Warwick Farm: 204
Watkins Glen 6-Hour race: 210
Watson, John: 215, 216, 218–224, 228, 238
Weber (carburettor): 75, 112, 130
Weber, Eduardo: 25
Weimar Republic: 65
Werheim, Ernesto: 7
Werner, Christian: 30, 37
When Nuvolari Raced: 96
Widengren, Per-Viktor: 75
Wilhelm ll of Germany, Kaiser: 105
Wilhelm, Crown Prince of Germany: 105
Williams (car): 226, 228, 231
"Williams" (William Grover-Williams): 47, 62, 154
Wimille, Jean-Pierre: 61, 69, 81, 84, 95, 104, 105, 108, 116, 118, 119, 133, 136–138, 140, 149, 154, 156–159, 161, 162, 164, 165–167, 170, 172, 256
Winn, Billy: 118
Wolf (car): 216, 218, 222
Works Driver: 78, 197
World Championship of Drivers: 70, 73, 173, 175, 183, 185, 188, 191, 196, 199, 201, 204, 206, 207, 213, 215, 224, 225, 228, 229, 232, 233, 249, 250, 254
World Championship for Manufacturers: 211, 212
World 48-Hour Record: 106
World Land Speed Record: 103

Yates, Brock: 19, 25

Zanelli, Juan: 79
Zborowski, Count Louis: 36, 37
Zehender, Goffredo: 59, 61, 67, 75, 79, 81, 82